Con Yeager Co   for Cures & Casings
Zelienople PA 1606█
    412-452-4120   Ask ✓ W9-CNO-351
        144 McGill Rd

King & I. C. INC.
Raw & Processed Meats
Portersville P.A.
412-368-8721

Pepperoni casing - 1 Doz 612   Code #1788
Capacola casing - 2 Doz #196⁸   Code# 1360
Salami casing   1 Doz 5.88 Code# 14.80

Great Sausage Recipes
and Meat Curing

GREAT SAUSAGE RECIPES

AND

MEAT

CURING

by Rytek Kutas

With sketches by
Christine Engla Eber

Macmillan Publishing Company
New York

Collier Macmillan Publishers
London

Macmillan Publishing Company
866 Third Avenue, New York, N.Y. 10022
Collier Macmillan Canada, Inc.

Library of Congress Cataloging-in-Publication Data
Kutas, Rytek.
    Great sausage recipes and meat curing.
    Reprint. Originally published: Buffalo, N.Y.: Sausage Maker, ©1984.
    Includes glossary, index.
    1. Sausages.   2. Meat, Smoked.   3. Meat, Dried.
I. Title.
TX749.K76   1987   641.6'6   86-31113
ISBN 0-02-566860-9   -

Macmillan books are available at special discounts for bulk purchases for sales promotions, premiums, fund-raising, or educational use. For details, contact:
    Special Sales Director
    Macmillan Publishing Company
    866 Third Avenue
    New York, N.Y. 10022

10 9 8 7 6 5 4 3

Printed in the United States of America

Upon request, the author will send you free information on sausage-making and meat-curing supplies. Write to: The Sausage Maker, Inc., 177 Military Road, Buffalo, NY 14207.

ACKNOWLEDGMENTS

The gratitude that I owe to my parents, Mary and Stanley Kutas, cannot be measured. They played an enormous role in my becoming a sausage maker and subsequently writing this book. The sad note in my life is that these two Polish immigrants did not live to see some of the knowledge they passed on to me being used in the world's finest learning institutions.

Henry Kutiej gave me that extra shove whenever I became discouraged. He was a guiding force in my involvement in sausage making and writing a book on the subject. His comfort and inspiration will be missed.

Clarence (Wayne) Puckett was the first to suggest to me that I become more deeply involved in the art of sausage making and meat curing. I am truly grateful for his support.

I must also acknowledge my gratitude to my teacher John Sommers. It was this Bavarian sausage maker who moulded Henry Kutiej and me into accomplished sausage makers.

I am much obliged to Julius (Bo) Bozinski, a mail-order executive, who recommended to me that I write a book and find a way to market it through the mail.

My feelings of indebtedness go to a great man and a good friend, Craig Claiborne. It was his newspaper article in the *New York Times* in April 1980 that caused my small mail-order company to become solvent and surge forward. No other person gave me better counseling or advice.

I am very grateful to Griffith Laboratories for their advice on spices and technology. They were a source of never-ending assistance whenever I had problems.

Many thanks also go to John Yurkus and Lucille Lapham of the International Natural Sausage Casing Association (INSCA) for their help and encouragement and for the artwork they generously supplied for this book.

Last, but definitely not least, I must thank Peggy Burke and Peter Drumsta for enduring my hieroglyphics and for expertly shaping this book into its final form.

CONTENTS

Preface to the Revised Edition 7
Introduction 9
How It All Began 11

CHAPTER I
Curing Meat 15
Artery Pumping 36
Brining Meat 42
Cures 43
Reusing Brines 45
Spray (or Stitch) Pumping 38

CHAPTER II
Smoking Meat 46
Smoke Generators 52
Smokehouses 64
Smokehouse Controls 66
Smoking Procedures 55

CHAPTER III
Natural Casings 79
Salted Casings 90

CHAPTER IV
Collagen and Synthetic Fibrous Casings 97
Curved Collagen Casings 100
Fibrous Casings 103

CHAPTER V
Selecting and Storing Meat 113
Grinding Meat 145
Meat Combinations 151
Refrigeration 119
Sanitation 120

CHAPTER VI

Permissible Ingredients in Meat Processing 152
Salt 155
Spices 153
Sweeteners 157

CHAPTER VII

Fresh Sausage 170
Diet Sausage 171
Making Patties 175

CHAPTER VIII

Smoked and Cooked Sausages 191
Emulsified Sausage 192

CHAPTER IX

Specialty Loaves and Sausage 258

CHAPTER X

Game Meat 274

CHAPTER XI

Specialty Meat 289

CHAPTER XII

Semi-Dry Cured Sausage 327
Relative Humidity 330
Sodium Acetate 331
Air Drying 333
Dry Curing, Government Specifications 336-340
Sausage Drying Rooms 342
Dry Curing Cooked Sausage 364

CHAPTER XIII

Dry Cured Sausage and Meat 366
Destroying Trichinae 369

CHAPTER XIV

Fish and Seafood 396
Preservation and Smoking 398,417,419,423,428

CHAPTER XV

Wholesome Meat Act 443
Building Specifications 446

CHAPTER XVI

Opening a Sausage Kitchen 453
How I Got Into Sausage Making 458
Kitchen Layout 479

CHAPTER XVII

100-Lb. Meat Combination Formulas 484

Glossary 495
Index 499

PREFACE TO THE REVISED EDITION

As tens of thousands of the original edition of this book were being sold, I started to receive a substantial amount of mail. Because I both wrote and published the original edition, a great many people could correspond with me directly rather than try to contact me through a large publishing company unequipped to forward a lot of mail. Needless to say, I helped everyone I could and established many new bonds of friendship. The majority of inquiries concerned cures, the products needed to produce them and where to purchase these supplies. I contacted two of the mail-order companies in the United States selling related products, but they didn't want the business. Since there really wasn't anywhere to send these people, I decided to open a mail-order business of my own—The Sausage Maker, Inc.

The business grew over the years, and we mailed out hundreds of thousands of catalogs containing a wide array of equipment, supplies and spices. In large, bold print we also offered to help anyone with problems he might encounter while making sausage and smoking and curing meat. Many people wrote in for advice and also asked for additional recipes not found in the book. As newspapers and magazines throughout the country wrote articles recommending the company and praising my book, the number of inquiries increased even more. This wealth of correspondence and the numerous phone calls we were getting showed me that *Great Sausage Recipes* could be made a better book.

This revised edition incorporates my answers to many of my readers' and customers' queries. I have also added more information and suggestions for the person just starting to make sausage or cure meat. Since some of the information included in the first edition was accumulated many years prior to its publication in 1976, this revision has brought the information completely up to date. The technology of sausage making and meat curing, like that of all other sciences, has seen rapid progress in the last fifty years. Some of the processes and products once used are now obsolete and even banned from use. I have included the latest information available, from the meat industry itself, on efficient and safe meat handling.

Since it was first published, *Great Sausage Recipes* has been used as a text in the food science programs of many prestigious universities and colleges, as well as in trade schools and high schools. It also reaches learning institutions in Australia, England and Canada. Here again was another reason to revise the book so that it could become even more than "the most comprehensive sausage manual in the *English* language," an evaluation made by world-famous author and food editor of the *New York Times,* Craig Claiborne.

INTRODUCTION

To many people, making sausage is fun. There are also those who know nothing about it but find the process intriguing. To the more dedicated, it is an art. It means being able to process more than 100 items, including ham, corned beef and smoked fish, as well as dry-cured products, such as hard salami and pepperoni, and lunch meats and meat loaves, which are also considered sausage. Try to visualize removing all of these products from the meat case at your local supermarket and it will surprise you how little will remain.

To get sausage-making and meat-curing experience, the traditional method has been to work for a sausage maker. For the most part, this sausage maker will have acquired his expertise through the years by word of mouth. If you were in his good graces, you might be lucky enough to find out all of his secrets. The unfortunate part of this hand-me-down system is the typical loss of much technical information, which can cause the recipients great frustration and leave them nowhere to turn. Try to get information from another sausage maker and he will try to run you out of the country, be he a professional or Grandpa Brown. I know of no other group of people who guard their secrets so jealously.

While there are some excellent books on various aspects of the subjects of sausage making and meat curing, they are usually highly technical and prohibitively priced. Consequently, they are often never seen in bookstores or libraries. This book was written to fill this void and provide a low-cost, complete introduction to the making of sausage and the curing and smoking of meats.

While I do not consider myself a writer or an author of books, I am a sausage maker with many years of experience and training. In this book, I explain what I have learned—what my eyes have seen and what my hands have done. I also share the valuable information I have obtained from sausage-making and meat-curing seminars held by the industry.

Plans for this book started over twenty-five years ago when I opened my first sausage kitchen in the western part of the United States. Since I am of Polish descent and craved kielbasa, my business featured this particular sausage. Word soon got around and many sausage lovers showed up. I sold some Polish sausage, but most of the people who came by asked for types of sausage that I never knew existed. I soon found out that knowing how to make one kind of sausage does not make one a sausage maker, and I began to custom-make small amounts of sausage for my customers. Needless to say, there were many failures, but it was all good experience.

It is because of these failures that this book was written—to eliminate all of the failures for you. I have filled the book with helpful suggestions and have written it in simple language detailing each step. The book will be useful to the homemaker who wants to make a few pounds of sausage for family use, as well as to the farmer or homesteader who raises his own livestock and wants to know more about making good sausage and dry-curing and smoking meats. It has also been planned to satisfy the many instructors and librarians who have written to me asking for a book of this type and to meet the needs of someone planning to venture into this type of business on a commercial basis.

The over 175 recipes have also been tailored to meet the needs of the reader preparing a small or large batch of sausage. I'm sure that you will find that these recipes are excellent. They have been refined over many years' time as I accumulated them from the ethnic groups that they represent.

How It All Began

Sausage making can be traced to the time of Homer, some 900 years before Christ. In his *Odyssey*, he describes Odysseus as restless, "As when a man beside a great fire has filled a stomach with fat and blood and turns it this way and that, is very eager to get it quickly roasted." Obviously he is referring to some animal casing (stomach) that is used to this day in the making of blood sausage.

Incidentally, that description bears a striking resemblance to the traditional "Black Pudding" eaten in Scotland today. It has also been reported that sausage was made and eaten by the Babylonians some 1500 years before Christ, and also in ancient China. The ancient Greeks had a name for sausage, "oryae." They also had other names for the specific types of sausage they made.

Fifth-century B.C. literature refers to salami, a sausage which is thought to have originated in the destroyed ancient city of Salamis on the East Coast of Cyprus. Sausage had achieved such fame that Epicharmus wrote a play called *Orya - The Sausage.*

The Romans called it "salus," meaning salted or preserved meat; it is from this Latin root that we get the word sausage. The Romans were known to have made fresh sausage of pork, white pine nuts chopped very fine, cumin seed, bay leaves and black pepper. They were very fond of this fresh sausage and it was closely assocated with their festivals.

11

As the Roman Empire crumbled and the Christian era began, Constantine, the "Great Emperor of Rome," banned these wild festivals and sausage along with them. Actually, sausage was not banned because it was bad, but rather because it was too good. The ban riled the Romans and they resorted to bootlegging this meat "delicacy." Speakeasy sausage kitchens prospered during the reigns of several Christian Emperors until strenuous popular protest eventually forced repeal of the ban.

By the Middle Ages, sausage making had become an art practiced commercially in many localities. Many of the early sausage makers became so adept in spicing and processing distinctive types of sausage that their fame quickly spread throughout Europe.

A sausage that originated in Frankfurt, Germany became known as the Frankfurter. Another produced in Bologna, Italy became known as Bologna Sausage. In similar fashion, Genoa salami was named after Genoa, Berliner sausage after Berlin, Braunschwieger after Brunswick, Germany, and Goteberg summer sausage after Goteberg, Sweden.

Because refrigeration was unknown and the canning process not yet developed, the dry type sausages were developed. In the colder regions, the dwellers of these countries made a semi-fresh sausage that could keep well for some time. This is where the "summer sausage" expression comes from. It was made to be eaten in summer.

By the same token, the availability of other ingredients also was a factor in the development of specific kinds of sausage. A plentiful supply of oatmeal was available in Scotland, so a great deal of this was used in making sausage. Cabbage was used in the sausage of Luxemburg, and potatoes with Swedish potato sausage. Almost all primitive people made some sort of sausage. Even our own American Indians combined dried beef with dried berries and shaped it into a cake.

As immigrants traveled to America they brought their knowledge of sausage making and their preferences with them. Sausage making was as much a part of pioneer life as the log cabin. Needless to say, populations grew, cities were formed and sausage kitchens along with them. They duplicated the homemakers' recipes on a commercial basis.

It should be noted, however, that not all the favorite sausages originated in Europe. Philadelphia scrapple originated with the Chester County, Pennsylvania farmers as a home product. Ingenious American sausage makers created new combinations of meats and spices. Old world products were then adapted to new taste preferences. .

Sausage making had taken on more precise and technical dimensions. Fewer people bothered to make sausage as it became readily available.

Fortunately for us, these great sausage recipes did not vanish, as many people for one reason or another still made their own sausage. Even now, if you had the time and could reach all these ethnic groups, there would be someone who would be delighted and proud to pass on a part of their heritage. It is simply a matter of knowing where to look for this information, including the very technical sources as well.

CHAPTER I

Curing Meat

CRITICISM OF NITRITE USE

Some years ago—for those who are not aware—the Massachusetts Institute of Technology (M.I.T.) conducted a scientific study concerning the use of nitrites and nitrates in curing meat.

The scientists who conducted these experiments used rats and were able to induce cancer in these little animals. They fed the rats controlled amounts of nitrites in order to accomplish this. As with most studies of this nature, a lot of good was produced—but also some bad. Unfortunately, the good parts of this study were not given any publicity, even though the good far outweighed the bad. It then has to be considered that all the news media is more interested in sensationalism and scaremongering.

In fact, I personally have been touched a number of times by such distortions. After certain interviews, I would either read or watch and couldn't believe what I was seeing. Articles would get edited and these people would only let you see what they felt was best for them—not you, but them. In fact, a certain food editor interviewed me and printed one of my recipes. She changed the recipe around so badly it no longer resembled the original recipe. This was done to make it easier for her readers to make this sausage at home.

The food faddists and consumer groups, along with TV and the press, always are eager and literally pounce on the bad side of this research, even though 99% of it was good. According to them, everything will produce cancer.

Take the case of drinking beer. Some research was done and traces of nitrosamines (a cancer-producing agent) were found in beer. The media sensationalized these findings for weeks, but never said how good it could be. I've been drinking beer for over 35 years and will continue to do so, as will many other people.

Another victim of bad reporting in the media is the case of monosodium glutamate, better known as "MSG." There are many others as well.

The real truth of the matter is the scientific study done by M.I.T. was poorly done; even worse, the facts were badly distributed to the media. The scientists used rats in their studies, and fed them enough nitrite to equal their eating 400 pounds of bacon per day.

Did any of the press or media report this? You guessed it, the answer is NO. Consider what feeding a rat 400 pounds of candy would do; think about the results for a moment. Or better still, 400 pounds of beer would clearly kill this little animal. I think if a human ate 400 pounds of anything in one day he or she would probably die of a heart attack or probably explode. I would hardly call this good research.

These little animals should have been fed an amount of nitrite equal to 4 or 5 ounces of bacon—an amount a person might eat several times a week. It then becomes clearer as to what the effects on the body might be. There is no question that the reporting on the use of nitrites and nitrates has been badly distorted and overly sensationalized by the above-mentioned groups. They conveniently failed to report the good findings of these reports with the proper use of these products.

More intriguing is the fact that the Sioux Honey Association has taken it upon themselves to issue a notice of warning that infants less than 1 year of age should not be fed honey. The association made this statement because honey contains a higher amount of botulism spores which can sometimes be fatal to an infant.

The association is aware of the fact that our body produces its own nitrites, which are a natural defense against food poisoning. They also are aware of the fact that, in its first year of life, an infant is just starting to develop this defense system. I have to wonder how the food faddists will cope with this fact, since honey is almost a sacred food to them.

There is no question that the reporting on nitrites has been, to say the least, one-sided and sensational. Practically no coverage has been given to more than 95% of the research, which states some of the good things nitrites can accomplish when used properly.

CURING MEAT

Probably the least-understood subject in the world today is the curing of processed meats and sausage. I think it would be safe to say that not one person in 50,000 really knows what is happening when a piece of meat is being cured.

In a national magazine, I actually read some do-it-yourselfer calling a dried-out piece of meat a cured product. Nothing could be further from the truth.

References to the use of nitrate as a cure can be traced back several hundred years. When using nitrite to cure meat, it combines with the pigment of the meat to form a pink color and flavor the meat as well.

Flavor in what way? To give you an example about flavoring the meat, let us consider the leg of a hog, better known as ham to most people. The leg of pork when cooked or roasted is, pure and simple, roast pork. However, when this very same pork is injected or pickled in brine, it now becomes "ham" after being boiled or cooked in a smokehouse.

What a difference in flavor we have between roast pork and boiled or smoked ham! It is the nitrite that has the ability to impart these special flavors. Without its use, there would be no hams, bacons, picnics, or Canadian bacon, and all we would have is pieces of cooked or roast pork. Additionally, nitrites also help to prevent rancidity in the storage of meats.

Most important of all, nitrite protects the meat products from the deadly toxin known as botulism. The botulism poisoning we are talking about is the most deadly form of food poisoning known to man.

Very simply diagnosed, your vision is blurred in less than a day. You have trouble holding up your head, as your neck muscles are not working very well. A little while later, you have difficulty in speaking. All the neck and throat muscles do not function, and you see everything double. This is then followed by the failure of chest and diaphragm muscles, cardiac arrest, and then pulmonary failure.

It's all over in about three days if not detected. This is botulism, or food poisoning: insidious, painful and deadly. Worst of all, botulism can produce its deadly toxin even without a foul odor or other sign of contamination. Botulism spores are the most resistant forms of life known to man.

Cures are critical in the manufacture of smoked and cooked meat to prevent food poisoning. Botulism spores are found in every type of meat or vegetable. They are harmless and cause no problems. Lack of oxygen, low acidity, proper nutrients, moisture, and temperatures in the range of 40 degrees F. to 140 degrees F., however, are where the problems begin.

It becomes obvious that sausage and meat are consistently smoked in these temperature ranges. The sausages are moist, and the smoke or heat eliminates the oxygen creating perfect conditions for food poisoning if you do not use cures.

For home use, however, you should not confuse the cooking of meat in your oven with smoking meat in a smoker. Most ovens will build up a 200 degree F. temperature on the "low" setting, and most people start baking well over that temperature. This high starting temperature prevents botulism spores from surviving. This information is only meant to impress you with the fact that when you smoke meat at a low temperature, the real possibility of food poisoning is present.

Often I've had people tell me that their grandparents didn't use cures when smoking meats, since some people feel cures are not necessary. Would a person so young really know what his grandparents were doing? Probably not.

Or better still, back in the good ol' days, how many people died of natural causes? An excuse a physician would give you when he couldn't diagnose why the person died, no matter how old or young the patient was, was that the cause was "natural." Fortunately for us the physician today can easily diagnose food poisoning problems, and this book was written to help avoid them.

In much simpler terms, how many times have you read about food poisoning around Thanksgiving and other holidays? The well-intentioned cook decides to make the dressing for the turkey the night before. This gives her more time to do many other important things the next day. She stuffs the turkey the night before, and places it in the refrigerator to be cooked the next day.

Unfortunately, she doesn't know she is creating ideal conditions for food poisoning. Obviously, the stuffing that she put into the turkey is somewhere between 40 and 140 degrees F. Because the various parts of dressing have some sort of liquid in them, the moisture is also there. Lastly, she sews up the turkey to create a lack of oxygen in its cavity.

It is that simple to create food poisoning: proper temperatures of 40-140 degrees F., moisture, and lack of oxygen. To be sure, whenever you smoke any kind of product in the low range of 40-140 degrees F., it should be cured. If you can't cure it, don't smoke it. It doesn't matter if it's meat, fish, poultry, cheese, or vegetable; don't take the chance. It's a pretty good bet that anything you will smoke has some moisture in it. You are removing oxygen when smoking the product and the temperatures are ideal.

Do not forget this one cardinal rule: **IF IT CAN'T BE CURED, DON'T SMOKE IT.**

Most nitrite used in curing meat disappears from the product after it has accomplished its curing effects. Within two weeks after curing, the amount of nitrite remaining in a product may be as little as one-fourth the amount initially added to it. Cured meat products typically contain 10-40 parts per million (PPM) at the time of purchase.

Your mouth and your intestines manufacture nitrite, and there is some evidence that our intestines' nitrite prevents us from poisoning ourselves with the very food we eat every day, since there is moisture in the stomach, lack of oxygen, and correct temperatures for food poisoning.

Furthermore, there has been some evidence of crib deaths when the infant was not able to manufacture enough nitrite in its system and, consequently, died of food poisoning.

Even more interesting, just to name a few nitrite-containing vegetables, plain old ordinary beets have been found to contain 2,760 PPM of nitrite; celery, 1,600 to 2,600 PPM; lettuce, 100 to 1,400 PPM; radishes, 2,400 to 3,000 PPM; potatoes, 120 PPM; and zucchini squash, 600 PPM. The source for these nitrites in the vegetables comes from nitrogen fertilizers. It is nitrogen that helps to produce the green color in vegetables and to make them grow faster.

It makes little difference whether you fertilize your vegetable garden out of a bag of chemicals or cow manure. The chemical end result will be the same – nitrogen equals nitrite.

In recent years, a number of books have been written on the subjects of meat curing and sausage making by people with no background or actual experience in this field. It is frightening to read that these people have recommended the use of ascorbic acid purchased at your local drugstore to cure sausage or meat. There is no documented scientific proof that botulism can be prevented by using ascorbic acid to cure meat. **You are risking food poisoning if you are using ascorbic acid to cure meat.**

The use of these nitrites for curing meats has recently come under attack by various groups of people and some government agencies. Unfortunately, there is no other substitute in the world today that can do the job. The next best thing to do is to find out if we can actually do without these chemicals, or simply lower the levels of their use.

At this time, I cannot think of anything more timely to put down on paper than the most recent rule changes proposed by the "Animal and Plant Health Inspection Service." The following paragraphs will give you a better insight on curing meats. These rules are already in effect and have been followed by the large meat processors for the past 20 years. The following was taken from the "Animal and Plant Health Inspection Service (9 CFR parts 318, 381) Nitrates, Nitrites and Salt," U.S. Dept. of Agriculture, Animal and Plant Inspections Service, Washington, D.C.

"STATEMENT OF CONSIDERATIONS" are used in the opening paragraph of this document and in this statement of considerations, unless otherwise noted, the term "nitrate" shall mean sodium nitrate, the term "nitrite" shall mean sodium nitrite, and the term "salt" shall mean sodium chloride (common table salt).

The curing of meat and poultry products is based partly on the art as practiced over thousands of years and partly on sound scientific principles developed during the last 80 years.

Meat was first preserved with salt as the curing agent in the Saline Deserts of "Hither, Asia" and the coastal areas. These desert salts contained nitrates as impurities. Even in Homer's time (900 B.C.) curing meat with salt, followed by smoking, was an established practice. Cato (234-149 B.C.) wrote careful instructions for dry curing hams. It included rubbing with salt, overhauling with salt, rubbing with oil, smoking, and rubbing the ham again with a mixture of oil and vinegar.

However, it was not until Roman times that the reddening effect now attributed to nitrate was mentioned. The Romans had learned from the Greeks the technique of curing pork and fish with salt, and they were probably the first to establish a trade market for cured meats. Meat cured with salt containing nitrate, and even nitrite impurities developed a characteristic cured flavor and color as well as the properties of a preserved product. In time, the cured flavor became highly desirable to many people.

Reference to the use of nitrate itself can be traced back several hundred years. Its use continued after the pasage of the "Federal Meat Inspection Act of 1906."

Chemists and meat scientists of the early 1900's determined that the active agent responsible for the color and flavor changes was nitric oxide, which was formed from nitrate during the curing process. Nitrite in turn is formed from nitrate, but the formulation process is difficult to control.

Therefore, once the mechanism was understood, the department in 1925 formally authorized the direct addition of nitrite, permitting no more than 200 parts per million (PPM) of residual nitrite in a finished product. This limit has been in force and unchanged since then.

In the late 1960s, questions were raised about the use of nitrites in foods and their combination with other compounds in the food or in the body to form nitrosamines. The Federal Food and Drug Administration (FDA), the Department of Health, Education and Welfare, and the Department of Agriculture organized a scientific study group to carefully review information and data concerning this matter. This group has met regularly since its organization in 1970.

In 1970, the House Intergovernmental Relations Subcommittee conducted hearings on the issue of nitrosamine formation and the possible involvement of nitrite in cured foods. The matter was widely discussed by the public and the media, and further studies were carried out by the scientific community. Numerous conferences were held during 1972 to discuss available information on the role of nitrite in curing and preserving, and to determine what new information was needed. Again, further research was scheduled cooperatively among industry, FDA, and the Department.

Early in 1972, the Department was petitioned to ban or greatly reduce the amount of nitrite used in the curing process. The Department denied the petition, indicating additional information was needed on the chemistry associated with nitrosamine formation.

Another factor associated with the problem, and one which would not be ignored, was the recognized role of nitrites in inhibiting the growth of Clostridium Botulinum. These bacteria under favorable conditions can produce the deadly toxin responsible for the food poisoning known as botulism. Information in literature indicated that in the 1920's, scientists were demonstrating the antimicrobial effect of nitrite and further investigation continued through the years. In the early 1970's, concentrated research studies were begun to learn more precisely the antimicrobial role of nitrite in modern forms of meat products.

In a short time, sufficient data was gathered to satisfactorily confirm the inhibitory action of nitrite to the growth of Clostridium Botulinum as well as the levels required to accomplish the desired effect. The studies clearly showed that the amount of nitrite needed to inhibit botulinal toxin formation was dependent upon the quantity of nitrite introduced into the product, rather than the residual level of nitrite in the finished product.

It has been necessary for the Department to act carefully and deliberately in this matter, since it recognizes that, in its desire to reduce levels to eliminate the possibility of nitrosamine formation, the very real public health hazard of botulism cannot be ignored.

Late in 1973, the Secretary of Agriculture appointed an expert panel on nitrites and nitrosamines to advise him on this difficult and controversial subject. The panel consisted of six well-qualified scientists, who represented various disciplines considered important to the evaluation of the problem. The first three meetings were devoted to presentations by scientists to help the panel build the proper foundation for its deliberations. Papers were presented on the occurrence of nitrite and nitrate in various foods, and a detailed report was given on the meat curing process and its chemistry. The panel also heard discussions on the toxicology, chemistry, and microbiology of nitrite, and on the toxicology and chemistry of nitrosamines. In addition, the role of ascorbates (salts of vitamin C) in curing was discussed.

Notice of time and place of each meeting was published in the federal register at least 15 days prior to each meeting. The meetings were open to the public and were attended by a large number of participants from industry, the research community, and the media. All persons in attendance were given an opportunity to ask questions and participate in the deliberations. Copies of all papers presented and the minutes of the meetings were distributed upon request and are now on file with the hearing clerk of the Department and available for inspection during regular business hours.

At its fourth meeting, the panel formulated three recommendations. After review and approval of these recommendations at the fifth panel meeting, a report was made to the secretary. The recommendations of the panel were:

1. That the use of nitrate salts in the curing process be discontinued in all meat and poultry products with two exceptions, dry-cured products and fermented sausage products. These two product categories were to be addressed at a later date when additional data are available.

2. That the level of nitrite salt permitted to be added for curing meats and poultry be limited to 156 parts per million (PPM) in all processed products with the exception of bacon and dry-cured products. Recommendations for these later products was deferred pending availability of further research data.

24

3. The current regulation permitted 200 PPM residual nitrite salt level be reduced in various product categories to reflect what is achievable with current technology. The panel believes that 100 PPM in cooked sausage products, 125 PPM in canned and pickle cure products, and 50 PPM in canned sterile products would be sufficient to maintain product safety. Action on bacon, fermented sausage products and dry-cured products was deferred until additional research data being developed became available.

It was the consensus of this panel that these recommendations are consistent with all safety considerations. Levels of nitrate and nitrite were decreased, thus reducing the consumer's exposure to the potential hazards of nitrosamines, nitrosamides, and related chemicals; at the same time, sufficient levels are maintained to protect the consumer against the very real hazard of botulinal poisoning.

To date, no substitute for nitrite has been discovered. No compound or treatment has been found that will produce the characteristic product that possesses nitrite's antibotulinal properties. Researchers are still trying to find a replacement.

The work of the expert panel is not concluded at this point. The panel will continue to review pertinent research findings developed in current studies on dry-cured products and fermented sausages, and they will determine whether to recommend further changes in permissible levels of nitrate or nitrite. The expert panel will meet again during the comment period on this proposal. The panel's comments on those portions of this proposal which go beyond their present recommendations will become part of the record and will receive consideration.

As recognized by the panel, a special problem exists with bacon. The fact that a nitrosamine is formed during its frying is apparently unique to this product. The levels found have been decreasing steadily and are in the range of 10-20 parts per billion. The meat industry has advanced this reduction through voluntary adjustments in curing procedures.

The Department, however, recognizes that greater efforts need to be directed toward the removal of nitrosamines from bacon. The problem has been discussed with the meat industry and the Food and Drug Administration. The meat processing industry already has begun studies designed to develop a possible solution to the problem and has indicated its interest to commit additional resources to the work. New processing procedures are being explored which are directed toward preventing the formation of nitrosamines in bacon during frying. An assessment of the need of further action will be carried out both during and at termination of a 1-year period. The Department also is considering the establishment of maximum levels of nitrite and minimum levels of ascorbate or erythorbate in the curing of bacon. Data available to the Department indicates that the proposed levels lead to reduced amounts of pre-formed nit-rosamines in bacon.

As a result of the panel's recommendations, the Department proposed that other related matters warrant discussion. Thus far, most of the attention with respect to nitrates and nitrites has been directed toward red meat products.

However, for several years, a considerable number of products have been developed using poultry in lieu of red meat. Such products have the same basic characteristics as the red meat items, and also need protection from botulinal toxin formation. Therefore, the Department believes it necessary to make the same proposal with respect to poultry products as that set forth for meat products.

The Department is aware that some consumers have expressed a desire to purchase products cured solely with salt. This should be considered, and every person should be given an opportunity to comment. Accordingly, the Department is proposing that salt (sodium chloride) be included in the list of approved curing agents. Such use would be for salt-cured products with sufficient brine concentration, or a water level such that Clostridium Botulinum will not grow.

Based upon current information, the Department believes the finished product should have a minimum brine concentration of 10 percent or a maximum water activity of 0.92. This brine concentration can usually be attained by using 7 pounds of salt per 100 lbs. of meat. It is determined in the finished product by analyzing for salt and moisture and dividing the salt content by the moisture content.

Water activity (usually abbreviated Aw) refers to the available water in a product which microorganisms depend on for growth, since their nutrients must be in solution. The Aw for fresh meat is

26

0.99 or above, a compared to an Aw of 1.0 for pure water. This Aw for meat is near the optimum for many varieties of microorganisms, although many can grow with a lower Aw. As the Aw decreases, the conditions favoring microbial growth also decrease. An Aw of 0.92 or lower will provide ample assurance that Clostridium Botulinum will not grow.

An additional consideration of this proposed rule making relates to the use of curing agents in food for babies. The greater toxicity of nitrite to infants in relation to adults has been recognized for several years. For that reason, the addition of nitrite to baby foods has not been practiced for some time, although some products generally marketed as toddler foods do contain some cured products.

Therefore, to clarify this matter, the Department is proposing to deny the use of nitrates or nitrites, or meat ingredients containing nitrates or nitrites, in meat and poultry food products intended for very small children. These usually are marketed as infant (strained) and junior (chopped) foods.

At this point, we have discussed sodium nitrate or nitrite. However, potassium nitrate and nitrite are used on a limited basis. These agents produce the same results as their sodium counterparts. Because the potassium nitrate and potassium nitrite salts are heavier than their sodium counterparts, it is necessary to permit greater amounts of the potassium salts in order to obtain the same amount of nitrate and nitrite. This proposal makes a distinction in quantities permitted on that basis.

In establishing required levels of nitrite to be introduced into the product, the wording of the panel's recommendations implies a concern that the maximum quantities not be exceeded. While this is true, it is not the only point of interest. The secretary cannot ignore the bacteriostatic properties of nitrite and the amount necessary to inhibit the growth of Clostridium Botulinium, since in the absence of nitrites, it appears that certain meat and poultry products could become adulterated.

What those exact levels are will vary, depending on the product and its microflora, method of preparation, packaging and handling practices. Processors need to exercise special care in keeping with good manufacturing practices to assure adequate introduction of nitrite into the product.

This means that careful control will be necessary in cases where pickle is recirculated, cleaned, and reused, so that it will not be diluted. Pickle solution held for several hours also will require special attention by the processor to determine the extent of the nitrite dissipation. Further considerations by the panel or Department or both may be necessary in this connection.

Another consideration with respect to this proposal concerns the level of nitrite introduced into pickle-cured products. For the purpose of determining compliance with the requirements, the quantity of curing agent introduced into the product would be determined on the quantity of curing pickle injected into the product, regardless of the quantity which may drain out.

Because of the necessity to maintain strict control of the quantity of curing agents introduced into the product, it would no longer be permissible to submerge injected product in curing pickle (cover pickle), or to totally pickle cure the product by submerging it in curing pickle. However, processors could use brine solutions provided the finished product is in compliance with the other requirements.

A prohibition on curing by submerging in pickle could affect some small processors of cured products who live in cold regions of this country. The temperature of their facilities is influenced considerably by the outside temperatures. Because the product may freeze and not cure, it has been necessary to employ the use of pickle in the curing process to successfully cure the product. This processing procedure would have to be changed.

This proposal, for purposes of defining permissible levels of residual nitrite, makes a distinction between shelf-stable, canned-cured product and commercially sterile canned-cured product. The shelf-stable product depends upon a mixture of nitrite salt and meat pasteurization to prevent the germination of Clostridium Botulinum spores. Commercially sterile product receives heat treatments sufficient to destroy Clostridium Botulinum spores.

Based on the data and information available to the Department at this time, it is proposed to implement the expert panel's recommendations by limiting the use of sodium and potassium nitrites and nitrates as follows:

A limit would be established of 2183 parts per million (PPM) of sodium nitrate or 2497 PPM of potassium nitrate (3.5 ozs. sodium nitrate or 4.2 ozs. of potassium nitrate per 100 pounds of meat) to be added to dry-cured products; and 1716 PPM of sodium nitrate or 2042 PPM of potassium nitrate (2.75 ozs. sodium nitrate or 3.3 ozs. potassium nitrate per 100 lbs. of meat) to be added to fermented sausages.

A limit would be established of 624 PPM of sodium nitrite or 768 PPM of potassium nitrite (1 oz. sodium nitrite or 1.23 ozs. potassium nitrite per 100 lbs. of meat) to be added in dry-cured products and 156 PPM of sodium nitrite or 192 PPM of potassium nitrite (0.25 oz. sodium nitrite or 0.31 oz. potassium nitrite in 100 lbs. of meat) to be added in fermented sausages.

Whether nitrate, nitrite, or a combination of both are used in dry-cured and fermented-sausage products, the residual nitrite calculated would be limited to 200 PPM; and in canned-cured products, whether perishable, shelf-stable, or sterile, in cooked sausages, and in other cured perishable products (other than bacon), a limit would be established of 156 PPM of sodium nitrite or 192 PPM of potassium nitrite introduced by pumping of solid pieces of meat or otherwise incorporated into comminuted products.

Canned-cured sterile products would be limited to a residual nitrite of 50 PPM calculated as sodium nitrite; all other canned-cured products would be limited to a residual nitrite of 50 PPM calculated as sodium nitrite; all other canned-cured products prepared with curing solutions to 125 PPM; and cooked sausage to 100 PPM. In addition to the above, which are in connection with the expert panel's recommendations, the following also are being proposed by the Department:

·Use of sodium or potassium nitrites and nitrates would not be permitted in meats used in commercial preparation of infant (strained) or junior (chopped) foods.

·The maximum amount of nitrite permitted to be added to bacon would be limited to 125 PPM and a requirement would be established that ascorbate or erythorbate be used at the maximum rate currently permitted by regulation.

·Salt would be permitted as a preservative when added to products in an amount sufficient so that the finished product has a minimum brine concentration of 10 percent or a water activity (Aw) no greater than 0.92.

·The foregoing requirements with respect to nitrates, nitrites, and salt would also apply to poultry and poultry products which are prepared in a manner similar to those prescribed for red meats.

As stated previously, it is recognized that special problems exist with bacon. In this regard, the Department has been assured by the meat industry that it is accelerating studies under way concerning processing procedures which are directed toward preventing nitrosamine formation in fried bacon.

At the same time, the hazard of botulism will have to remain an important consideration throughout. The Department will continue to cooperate with the industry and the FDA in developing this needed information. This work should be substantially completed within one year's time from the date of this publication (on or before Nov. 11, 1976). Both during and at the end of this period, progress on achieving a nitrosamine-free product will be evaluated and a determination as to need for further action will be made. The Department recognizes that 1 year may not be adequate to resolve this matter entirely, but believes that sufficient information can be developed to better define what further steps might be necessary.

Washington, D.C. on October 30, 1975
(The above rule changes are still in use and considered current as of revision of this book.)

In reference to the above rules, I think it would be fair to say that some people may find them confusing. To eliminate some of this confusion, I think that this is the ideal time to discuss the cures and the manufacturers of these products.

The amounts of cure that are proposed in these new rules speak in parts per million (PPM), so it isn't even practical to talk to everyday people in these terms. This information or rule change is directed at the large processors of meats and also the manufacturers of the cures. I think the use of these products, however, should also be made clear to the average person or small processor.

Since the parts per million (PPM) of nitrites vary for the bacon, hams, and such, it is at this point that credit be given to the manufacturers of these cures. Today, there are cures that are available pre-packaged in smaller amounts with the proper amounts of nitrites in them as called for by these new rules. The manufacturers see to it that the correct amounts are added.

You can simply purchase a ham cure, bacon cure, poultry cure, or sausage cure, having the proper amounts of nitrites in them on a per hundred weight basis. In fact, these cures are available today with flavors added to them that will enhance the flavor of the meat that is being cured.

Nitrites and nitrates should both be used with great caution because they are both poisonous. This is the controversial part of these chemicals and the reason for strict limits which have been placed on their use. Obviously, excessive use of these cures could present a health hazard and could also result in nitrite burn of the meat being cured. A green or white discoloration of the meat indicates nitrite burn. These cures should always be used with great caution when being weighed and should also be well-mixed and distributed properly by a responsible person.

When using 1 or 2 teaspoons of cure to make sausage, it is an excellent idea to dissolve the cure in the water you are going to mix with the meat. This method will give you better distribution of the cure.

Sodium nitrate and potassium nitrate are used in a very limited way in modern curing. In a manner of speaking, neither potassium nitrate or sodium nitrate will cure meat or give it that pink color we hear so much about. It must first undergo a change and break down to nitrite, and then sodium or potassium nitrite, which is further reduced to nitric oxide. It is the nitric oxide that really cures the meat.

In either case, there is no real need to use a nitrate compound to cure meat. The short-term schedules for curing meat today simply do not require the need for the nitrate-to-nitrite step. As mentioned earlier, the nitrate compounds are used only in dry-cure products. Potassium nitrate and potassium nitrite will provide the same results as sodium nitrate and sodium nitrite.

Although the quantity of nitrite used is very small, its effect determines whether the meat is properly or improperly cured. If too little nitrite is used, you can have cure development, but the cure color stability is poor.

Griffith Laboratories first used a product developed in Europe, where nitrite was mixed with salt and a larger quantity of the salt-nitrite mix could be used in meat. Mr. C.L. Griffith soon learned that this mechanical mix could lead to serious problems. The blend was not foolproof. In such a mechanical mix a portion of the nitrite might separate from the salt, with the result that one measure might contain

The above is a photograph of 6.1 grams of sodium nitrite, the amount allowed by federal law to cure 100 pounds of meat. The 50-cent coin in the photograph gives an idea of the small amount needed.

more nitrite than another. This variation, even when small, could lead to variations in the finished product.

Mr. Griffith conceived the idea of making an absolutely foolproof cure. He wished to make a fusion of the cure with the salt, much as a metallurgist does when he makes alloys from cooper, nickel and iron. Mr. Griffith realized that in order to make this fusion he could not simply mechanically blend dissimilar chemical ingredients. He decided that he would dissolve the salt, nitrite, and nitrate in water to have a completely clear uniform solution.

This saturated solution was then dried on drum rolls, and in the flash drying on the rolls, the curing ingredients became interwoven within the salt crystal, making any separation impossible. For all practical purposes, an alloy was formed. In developing Prague Powder, proportionate amounts of salt, nitrite and nitrate were used so that when 4 ounces of Prague Powder were added to 100 pounds of meat, the quantity of nitrite imparted in the meat was precisely the legal limit permitted by the Meat Inspection Division of the United States Department of Agriculture.

SALTPETER

What, exactly, is saltpeter? I know of no other product in the world that has been used so widely while being so misunderstood. The people who don't understand saltpeter include people who use it as part of their everyday jobs, farmers and just plain homemakers.

Probably worst of all, it is very difficult to find a definition for this product in your local library. The information just isn't there until you start research at college levels, or until you take a course in sausage making or meat curing.

I can remember — as a boy during World War II — what a big joke saltpeter was. Rumors said that soldiers in our armed forces were being fed saltpeter to suppress their sexual appetites. This was a pretty widely held belief. But the people who spread this rumor just didn't know what they were talking about or what saltpeter really is. All most people really knew was that saltpeter was used to make gun powder. And they knew if it was used to make gun powder, it just couldn't be any good for you.

Clearly and simply stated, saltpeter is a very deadly poison. Its chemical name is potassium nitrate. The use of saltpeter was greatly limited by the U.S. Dept. of Agriculture in 1975. Potassium nitrate is no longer allowed for curing in smoked or cooked meat or sausages. However, it still is allowed very sparingly in making dry-cured sausages such as hard salami, but in greatly reduced amounts.

How can it be, then, that up to 10 sausage-making and meat-curing books have appeared in bookstores across the U.S.A. since 1975, calling for the use of saltpeter in the formulas or recipes?

Again, this goes back to the small amount of information available for people who are researching the subject. Not only is saltpeter misunderstood, few people know how to use it.

To this day, saltpeter is nothing more than a term most people simply associate with curing meat or making sausage. To a hunter or someone familiar with guns, it's gun powder. It should also be noted that sodium nitrate also is in the same class as potassium nitrate, and also is banned.

Cures help develop the deep, dark mahogany color during the smoking process. During smoking, the color of the meat generally can get about twice as dark as without cures. Commercially, the cosmetics of smoked meat are quite important, since the general public associates the dark brown color wih smoked meats — and rightly so.

I think it's also quite important when making a batch of sausage at home. Even though I only smoke sausage for my own consumption, I feel great when I can smoke sausage, meat or poultry to a picture-perfect brown and be able to tell someone, "I did this." It's nicer than any piece of meat you could ever buy. It gives me a real sense of acccomplishment.

NOTE: After cures are used in the making of sausage or curing meats, it is extremely important that the utensils and equipment be washed thoroughly. Nitrites are readily retained by utensils and equipment, and if not properly washed, nitrites can easily be passed on to other products. If you are making fresh sausage like Italian or breakfast, you will get an undesirable curing effect; the consumer can boil, cook or broil the product for hours and it will still have the appearance of raw meat. It is customary to make all fresh sausages first, followed by products that are cured.

ARTERY PUMPING

The artery pumping of pickle into ham is not really new; this method has been around for some time. It is the most efficient method of distributing the curing pickle uniformly and quickly through the meat. The arterial system through which the blood was carried becomes a pipeline for the pickle that cures the ham.

When the carcass is butchered, it is extremely important to find and save the artery and vein. This is usually done before the carcass is being disassembled.

Since every cell of the living animal is fed by blood circulating through the capillary system, what could be more efficient than to use nature's "pipeline" to distribute curing pickle to every cell in the ham! A minimum operation – with minimum time in cure! No part of the ham is missed, not even the bone marrow, as pickle surges through the arteries into the remotest capillaries.

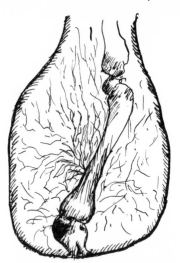

Since every cell of the living animal is fed by blood circulating through the capillary system, what could be more efficient than to use nature's "pipeline" to distribute curing pickle to every cell in the ham! A minimum operation—with minimum time in cure! No part of the ham is missed, not even the bone marrow—as pickle surges through the artery into the remotest capillary.

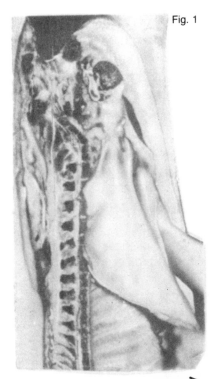

Fig. 1

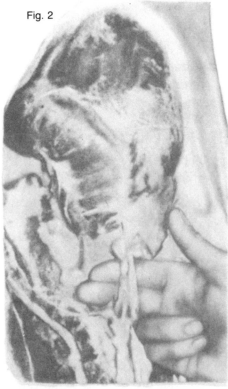

Fig. 2

FINDING & SAVING ARTERY

Cut the artery long—before the "fork" where the branches enter the ham—for quick, easy pumping. If artery has been cut too short, pump each branch separately. If artery cannot be located, it will be necessary to Spray Pump.

It is extremely important that the artery be left long on the ham to simplify insertion of the needle for *Artery Pumping*. Loosen leaf-fat with the fingers, separating it from backbone and ribs as demonstrated in Fig. 1. Remove the leaf-fat, exposing the artery as illustrated in Fig. 2. Leave a covering of fat on the artery to keep it moist and elastic.

(CAUTION: Alongside the artery is the vein—smaller, darker, and brittle rather than elastic. Will not take pickle, but will rupture.)

37

FINDING & SAVING ARTERY

Cut the artery long—before the "fork" where the branches enter the ham—for quick, easy pumping. If the artery has been cut too short, pump each branch separately. If the artery cannot be located, it will be necessary to spray pump.

It is extremely important that the artery be left long on the ham to simplify insertion of the needle for artery pumping. Loosen leaf-fat with the fingers, separating it from the backbone and ribs as demonstrated in Fig. 1. Remove the leaf-fat, exposing the artery as illustrated in Fig. 2. Leave a covering of fat on the artery to keep it moist and elastic.

CAUTION: Alongside the artery is the vein—smaller, darker, and brittle rather than elastic. It will not take the pickle; it will rupture.

SPRAY PUMPING OR STITCH PUMPING

If the artery has been severed and there is no choice but to cure a ham by this method, use the same pickle formula as in artery pumping. With a spray needle, pump 12% of the ham's weight along the bone, around the joints and vertically in the thicker lean portions of the ham or shoulders. (12% allows for loss of about 2% due to seepage.) After spray pumping, cure in cover pickle.

Spray pumping is really quite simple, and almost anyone can do a good job. Various formulas will tell you to use so many gallons of brine solutions, and the amounts can range from 2½ to 100 gallons depending on the size of operation. In either case, the meats are pumped with this brine and then immersed in the left-over solution for further curing.

During immersion, the surface of the meat will be penetrated by the brine to give you a more even cure. The length of time for immersion is a matter of individual preference. Commercially, a ham or other kind of meat is pumped with a gang of needles and is ready for the smoker in 24 hours. For home use, this would not be the case. One needle simply cannot do as good a job as the 20-30 needles that are used commercially in a high-speed operation. You spray-pump the cure to the center of the meat and you immerse for at least 3-4 days, so the surface will be more evenly cured. If you prefer a saltier product, you can let it cure for up to a week or 10 days.

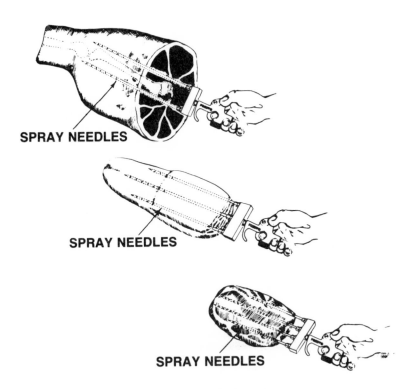

SPRAY NEEDLES

SPRAY NEEDLES

SPRAY NEEDLES

Spray pumping meat with a gang of needles.

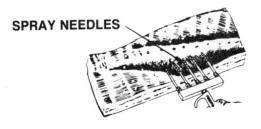

SPRAY NEEDLES

A cut away showing bacon spray pumped with a gang of needles.

MEAT PUMPS FOR ARTERY, SPRAY OR SWITCH PUMPING MEAT

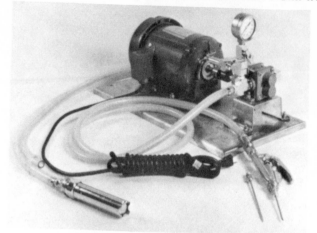

Electric Meat Curing Pump

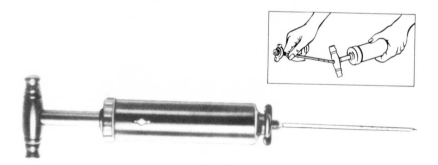

16-oz. Meat Curing Pump

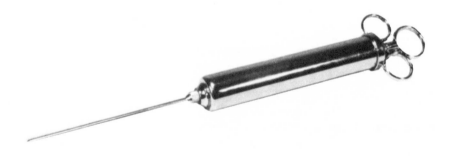

4-oz. Meat Curing Pump

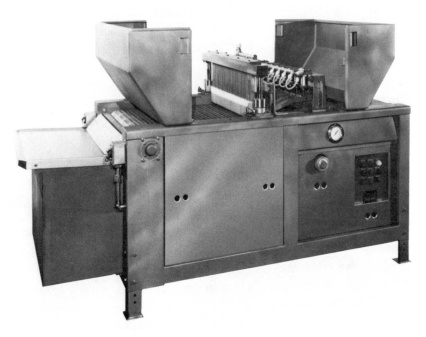

A High-Production Pickle Injector
The above piece of equipment is designed with 240 hypodermic needles for uniform pickle distribution. It can cure the bacon as fast as
you can put it into the machine. Manufactured by Chemetron Process
Equipment.

BRINE SOAKING

For many years the only process for curing meats was brine soaking. The product was placed into a brine solution and held there until there was complete penetration of the meat.

This type of curing is a relatively slow process and has severe limitations in curing large pieces of meat. The meat being cured has to be held in the brine solution for an appropriate length of time. Obviously, the solution's penetration time for small pieces of meat is just a matter of days. On the other hand, curing a large piece of meat can stretch into weeks, and then we have a race against time. We are hoping the meat will cure before it spoils.

You might consider the fact that when you brine-cure a ham, you are using a fresh piece of meat. When placing this fresh meat in the brine, the cure and salt will slowly penetrate the meat. If the ham is larger, it obviously will take longer to penetrate all the way to the center. If the ham is older or you don't know its age, it may be unfit for curing. This is due to the fact that meat starts deteriorating as soon as it's butchered, and only refrigeration or freezing arrests the process.

The center of the ham remains fresh for 2-3 weeks before it is penetrated, and it is not unusual for the ham to spoil from the center. In fact, it is usually the marrow in the bone which will spoil first; the meat then follows.

There is no question that forcing a brine solution directly into the meat clearly has its benefits over brine soaking. It should also be noted that skin and fat are definite barriers to cure penetration.

It is worthwhile to note that brine soaking is still a widely accepted practice today. In most cases it is a simple case of economics and generally is used by very small processors.

CURES

For the sake of a clearer understanding, the phrases "Prague Powder No. 1" and "Prague Powder No. 2" will be used in all the recipes of this book to denote the use of cures. This is being written to avoid a lot of confusion when using the word "cure" and to underscore the idea that cures are primarily used to prevent botulism (food poisoning) as well as to impart flavors and some preservation.

To some people the word "cure" is used when they are only seasoning meat at various temperatures. Other people consider removing moisture from meat as curing it. There is no such thing as curing meat or sausage without actual cures.

Incidentally, fresh sausages are never cured; only products that are smoked and cooked or the dry-cured products must be cured.

PRAGUE POWDER NO. 1   Pink in color

Prague Powder No. 1 is a basic cure that is used to cure all meats that require cooking, smoking, and canning. This would include poultry, fish, hams, bacon, luncheon meats, corned beef, pates, and many other products too numerous to mention. Prague Powder No. 1 is a combination of a small amount of sodium nitrite on a salt carrier. To be more specific, a pound of Prague Powder No. 1 contains 1 ounce of sodium nitrite to each 1 pound of salt. The formulas in this book clearly tell you which cure to use when it is needed.

This is also a good time to mention that it only takes 4 ounces of Prague Powder No. 1 to cure 100 pounds of sausage, 2 ounces for 50 pounds, and only 1 ounce for 25 pounds. When curing 10 pounds of meat, it takes a little less than ½ ounce of Prague Powder No. 1. Put another way, 4 level teaspoons equal about 1 ounce of Prague Powder, or 2 level teaspoons will cure 10 lbs. of sausage.

PRAGUE POWDER NO. 2   white in color

Prague Powder No. 2 is a cure specifically formulated to be used with dry-cured products. These are products that do not require cooking, smoking or refrigeration. Prague Powder No. 2 is also on

43

a salt carrier and contains one ounce of sodium nitrite along with .64 ounces of sodium nitrate to each one pound of salt.

Prague Powder No. 2 can be compared to the time-release capsules used for colds one finds in the local drugstore. The sodium nitrate keeps breaking down into sodium nitrite, then nitric oxide, to cure the meat over extended periods of time. As mentioned earlier, the amount of nitrite remaining in a cured product within 2 weeks after curing may be as little as one-fourth the amount initially added. If we are to dry cure a sausage or meat properly, it simply cannot be done with a cure containing sodium nitrite only. It dissipates too quickly, as some products require curing for up to 6 months.

Specifically, Prague Powder No. 2 should not be used for cooked or smoked bacons. After a great deal of experimentation, it has been found that very small amounts of sodium nitrite (Prague Powder No. 1) are required to cure bacon. A combination of sodium nitrite and sodium nitrate in cured bacon has been found to produce nitrosamines (cancer-producing cells) when fried at high temperatures. This problem exists only with bacon and not with ham, sausage, luncheon meats or any other cured meats.

In the past 4-5 years a great deal of research has been done to find a substance to replace nitrite in processed foods, but to no avail. It will be extremely difficult to find a substance that will do all the work of nitrites—destroy botulism, help prevent rancidity, prolong preservation, give the meat color, and impart all those special flavors to hams, bacons, corned beef, pastrami, and such.

A characteristic of fresh-cured meat is its grey color. After you mix the meat, it only takes a matter of minutes for the meat to start turning grey. It then takes heat in the range of 130-140 degrees F. in order to attain the pink color which is so closely associated with cured meats.

It is important to remember that curing meats is not a cure-all for preventing various problems like spoilage. Too many people are under the impression that a cured and smoked product requires little or no refrigeration. It is only the dry-cure meats that do not require refrigeration.

But even these products are almost always found in a refrigerated meat case when being purchased. Obviously, you minimize such things as unwanted mold and extend the life of the product dramatically.

CURING FRESH MEAT

Over a period of time, a number of people have either cured or asked about curing fresh meat products like breakfast sausage or other fresh sausage. It simply is not necessary to cure them, as these products usually are fried, broiled, baked or boiled. The rapid high temperature the product is brought to eliminates the chance of food poisoning. The balance of the fresh meat is usually frozen or used up. It is usually at the prolonged low temperature of 40-140 degrees F. that botulism can start, along with moisture and lack of oxygen. It is not necessary to cure fresh sausage or meat.

REUSING BRINES

Reusing brines is a tempting but bad practice. To begin with, the cures purchased for commercial use are so inexpensive that there is no reason to save the used brine; it is always discarded after each individual use. Also, this brine solution has been absorbed into the meats being cured. Clearly, this weakens this brine, and it no longer has the strength you need to cure other meat.

Lastly, the juices of the meat itself dilute the brine, and then it becomes contaminated with bacteria. Bacteria is a fact of life and simply unavoidable. Reusing a brine could easily spoil a fresh batch of meat.

CHAPTER II

Smoking Meat

SMOKING MEAT

How do we know that meat is smoked? One way is the very distinctive color that is going to show up to let you know that the meat is smoked.

The color that develops in smoked meat or sausage is the result of the carbon compounds combining with the meat pigments. Additionally, the cures that we use when smoking give the meat a red color; during the drying process, these cures help to bring out the color even more. Part of the color you find is from drying the surface of the meat and part is from the carbon compounds in the smoke itself.

On the other hand, it is possible to get some less desirable colors from the tar compounds in the smoke when using the wrong type of wood for smoking. These tar compounds can give your meat a black, sooty appearance and impart a bitter flavor to the meat.

An important reason for smoking meats is to produce flavor. To get mellow flavors, one has to avoid the use of woods containing tar compounds. The very hard woods contain aromatic compounds which give flavor to the meats. Among the hardwoods the best for smoking probably is hickory. A good combination of hardwoods, however, also can give you good results. Even though fruitwoods are popularly used in the smoking of sausage and meats, one has to be very careful, as they contain excessive amounts of tar compounds. Fruitwoods seldom are used for smoking meats by sausage makers. Yet the German Westphalian ham is smoked in juniper wood or juniper berries, which produce a distinctive flavor. The finished product resembles a large piece of anthracite coal.

So what else goes on in a smokehouse? One of the more important things that happen to smoked meat is the preserved quality it develops and the coagulation of the surface meat. Smoke emits a number of acids which will cling to the meat and form an outside layer of skin. The acid itself performs an important role in preserving these meats, particularly preventing the growth of surface mold and bacterial compounds.

An example of coagulation, or forming of the outside skin, is a skinless frankfurter. The normal process is to stuff a synthetic casing that is not edible with emulsified meat. It is then linked into 5 or 6 inch lengths and placed into the smokehouse. The acids in the smoke will penetrate the casing during this cycle, and coagulate the surface protein of the frankfurther and form the skin.

The next process, of course, is to remove the product from the smokehouse and cool it. The frankfurthers are then put through a stripping machine that removes the plastic casing. Now you have a skinless frankfurther that is held together as if it were stuffed into a natural casing, but in reality it is in its own coagulated skin, developed by the acids in the smoke.

This book mentions a number of times that all air pockets should be pricked if they appear on stuffed sausages. Obviously, pricking the casing will cause no harm because of coagulation during the smoking cycle.

Another interesting thing about coagulation is the smoking of hams, picnics, and any other meats which are stuffed into a stockinette for smoking. The stockinette bag usually is put on very tightly, and the meat is placed in the smokehouse. After the entire cycle of smoking is completed, the meat is cooled off for the appropriate time called for in the formula.

Then it is time to remove the stockinette bag. But if you haven't noticed, the stockinette bag coagulated with the meat and has become one piece. It is literally impossible to remove the stockinette without ripping off chunks of meat. This, however, can be avoided by dipping the stockinette into vinegar or liquid smoke, as both contain acids that will prevent the stockinette from sticking.

So now we know what goes on in a smokehouse. The sausage or meat is smoked to attain a distinctive color, give the meat flavor, and also to give it some preserved qualities.

Last of all, during all of these stages, the meat is being slowly cooked. Depending on the product, its size and the flavor desired, the process can take from 3-4 hours to 3-4 days. It would be fair to say a small-diameter sausage from 32-42mm can be smoked and flavored in a few hours at 160 degrees F. The penetration required is not very deep. When we smoke salami, bologna, etc., however, the penetration takes proportionately longer. Obviously, a ham can take up to several days.

A 20-Lb. Capacity Electric Smoker For Home Use
The above is a smokehouse patterned after a 300-lb. capacity professional smoker. It was designed with controls to maintain heat. Manufactured by The Sausage Maker, Inc.

A 100-Lb. Capacity Electric Smokehouse

The above smoker is totally insulated with thermal insulation capable of withstanding 1000° F. temperature. This means it can be used on the outside in cool weather without fear of losing internal temperatures. Comes complete with controls. Manufactured by Marstan Industries.

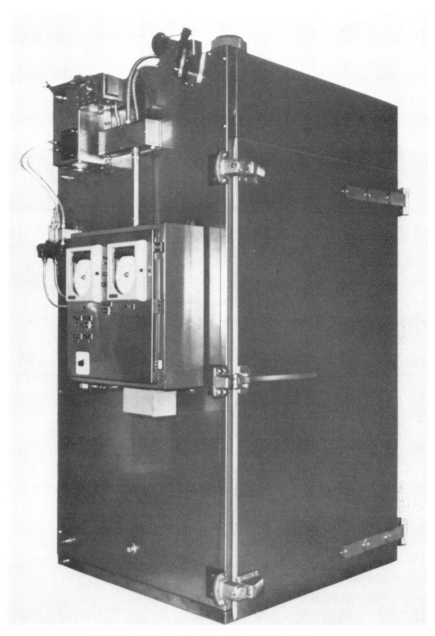

300-Lb. Capacity Gas-Fired Smokehouse
The above smoker is all stainless steel construction. It is equipped
to have an oscillating air flow that prevents hot or cold spots experienced in other types of smokehouses. It is also available in 500- or
1000-lb. capacities. Manufactured by Enviro-Pak.

SMOKE GENERATORS

Not too many years ago, a smokehouse simply consisted of a large house. The smokehouse always had pits in which the fire was started using hardwood, and the fires were watched carefully until they consisted of hot coals. It was then that the sawdust or wood (presoaked in water overnight) was thrown on these hot coals to create a larger volume of smoke or smudge. Since the smokehouses were rather large, more than one fire sometimes was needed to distribute uniform heat and smoke.

As the years went on and smoked meats and sausages became more popular, new ways had to be devised to better control the smoking and the cooking of these meats, and to produce larger volumes as well. Controls were devised using natural gas to heat the smokers, using the same gas to smudge the sawdust or wood as well. The process no longer required throwing sawdust on the hot coals, which in turn eliminated the ashes from getting all over the meats. Smoke generators were developed and fired up on the outside of the buildings, filtering the smoke through water and carrying it into the smoker through a large diameter pipe or ductwork. Also, the shrinkage that took place in the process was reduced or sometimes eliminated.

There is a lot to say about the benefits of a smoke generator, and the first benefit is in cold smoking. There are many products that are dry cured and held without refrigeration. These products can become moldly unless they are treated in some way. It is quite difficult to make smoke without heat, and this is where a smoke generator is at its best.

A smoke generator will pump a significant amount of smoke into a smoker which not only will flavor the meat, but coat the meat with some of the acids that prevent bacteria growth. There are many books on the market today that tell you a product should be cold smoked. Unfortunately, the people who wrote these books didn't have any idea how to produce cold smoke without heat. Very simply, the answer is a smoke generator, and it can be used to smoke such products as meat, fish and cheese.

Personally, I find that the primary benefit of a smoke generator is the fact that you need not spend time tending a smokehouse.

Depending on the size of the smoke generator, it can produce smoke for 5-10 hours at a time. The container is filled and the damp sawdust is fed either automatically or by gravity. Long periods of smoking often are required for large hams, etc. It is a real pleasure to be able to go to sleep at night knowing this machine will still be doing its work when you get there in the morning.

Last, but also very important, is the fan that blows the smoke in, helping to distribute the heat in a smokehouse more evenly. This produces a more evenly cooked product. Even heating sometimes is a problem in a smoker, as temperatures can vary in the top or the bottom.

DAMP VERSUS DRY SAWDUST

When using any kind of sawdust or wood to smoke meat, it is a good idea to make sure it is damp. There are some good reasons for this. First of all, when you use damp sawdust, it won't burn up or catch fire. It also imparts a very gentle flavor during the smoking process. If you smoke meat with dry sawdust, you will find it has a more prounounced smoke flavor. It is customary to only dampen the sawdust, not soak it in water. You'll also find that damp sawdust will burn for a much longer period than dry sawdust. Personally, I don't like meat smoked with a dry sawdust.

Automatic Feed Smoke Generators

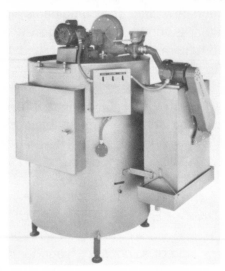

A large Tipper smoke generator. This smoke generator can produce enough smoke to supply a 6-cage smokehouse, or will smoke over 2000 pounds of sausage at one time. Manufactured by Chemtron Mepaco.

The above smoke generator is equipped with a 2 cubic foot sawdust hopper. This will give you 10-15 hours of smoke production. It is also equipped with a 12-hour auto timer shut-down control. Manufactured by Enviro-Pak.

SMOKING PROCEDURES

First, the dampers are allowed to be wide open, allowing the moisture to escape in the drying process. Unless the meat or sausage is dry, it is almost impossible to do a good job of smoking. These products must be dry to the touch before they start to take on any color at all.

In this first stage, the sausage can even be dried and partially cooked into a nice brown color, and then the smudge or smoke applied. As for the drying of this meat or sausage, there really is no specific time required. Even though the formulas specify time periods, you can simply look in on the product from time to time until you have achieved desired dryness or color.

In all the formulas, with the temperature instructions, there usually are directions as to the positions of the dampers: ¼ open, ½ open or closed. These positions are used once the product is completely dry. The smoky color of the sausage actually starts in the drying stage and then the smoke is applied. If you wish, you may add paprika to the sausage formula; this will help give the sausage a deeper brown color.

The amount is optional: 4-8 ounces to 100 pounds of meat. Great caution should be taken not to speed up the drying process in the smokehouse. The drying process has to be done slowly and it requires some degree of patience.

If you increase the temperature of the smoker, trying to speed up the drying process, two things will happen. First, the heat will cause the sausage to perspire, and condensation takes place. This keeps the outside of the sausage constantly wet and will not allow the meat to take on any color. Secondly, the cooking process will be starting too quickly, emitting grease through the casing before the casing can dry out. This will cause the product to look as if it isn't smoked, and will make it look very greasy no matter how lean a meat was used to make it. The casing can also become tough due to excessive heat.

There is no doubt that the meat will have a smoked flavor if it is kept in the smoker for the specified times, but nothing can be done to give it any color. The outside of the meat or sausage must be dry to the touch of your fingers; this means no grease as well, or it will be impossible to give the product a smoked color.

One of my favorite tricks has been to keep the smokehouse door cracked open. Allowing it to remain open permits the moisture to escape more readily, which in turn helps to dry the product faster. At this time, let me point out that a smokehouse should not be stuffed with 400 pounds of meat when it is designed to handle 250 pounds. To begin with, the formulas all tell you to space the meat properly; this means that the meats should not be touching each other. If they are, they will not be smoked at the points of contact. The smoke flavor will be there, but white spots will appear at the points of contact since the smoke couldn't get to these points. Again, this will give the product a less appealing look.

Also, if the meat or sausage is packed too tightly into the smokehouse, the circulation of the warm air will be very poor. This in turn will not allow the moisture to escape. It will take 2-3 times as long to dry the product and just as long to smoke and cook it. As you can see, the reason behind proper spacing is to help dry the product and insure even smoking.

SMOKEHOUSE STICKS. Usually come in 42-48" lengths. Available in aluminum, stainless steel rod, hard woods and U shaped stainless steel.

COOKING CABINET

Smoking to some degree is a relatively quick process, and the diameter of the sausage or product is the most important factor. Obviously, a sausage having a 1½" diameter can be smoked in a few hours; however, a ham is much thicker and it takes several days for the smoke to penetrate. In either case, the final process of cooking can be done in steam cookers.

Sausage smoked and cooked right in the smokehouse is fine for a small operation, since it takes from 8-10 hours to complete the entire process. In a larger operation, however, when a steam cooker is available, you usually can produce three times as much product in this same period of time. While it takes 3 hours to smoke the product and an additional 5-6 hours to cook it, the steam cabinet will cook the product in a matter of minutes.

In the earlier years, before the steam cabinet, the cooking of sausage was done in large cooking tanks to finish off the process. For home use, you can smoke a product in your smoker and finish the job on your kitchen stove by cooking it. Or you can just leave it in the smoker to get the job done.

Remember, temperatures are the same when you cook in water or in a smoker. The steam cooker process is different and shorter, and the manufacturer of the cabinet usually includes operating instructions for the various types of meats that would be cooked in that manner.

Electric Vat Cooker
The above cooker is completely portable and of stainless steel construction. This piece of equipment is ideal in a small sausage kitchen to cook by-products for making sausage, as well as cooking the sausage itself. Manufactured by Zubek Co.

INTERNAL TEMPERATURES

The internal temperatures that have to be attained in sausage making are of extreme importance. Great care has to be taken, as it can mean the success or failure of the finished product. For the most part, 152 degrees F. is the figure one usually sees in most of the sausage recipes and meat formulas. There are some exceptions when making a sausage with meat other than pork, but when in doubt, you are always safe at 152 degrees F. internally, no matter what meat you are processing.

By the same token, it is of equal importance that the heat of the smoker itself does not exceed the specified temperatures. When in doubt, do not exceed 160 degrees F.

Smoking any kind of meat at 160 degrees F. until the internal temperature reaches 152 degrees F. is indeed a slow process and can take many hours. Commercially, meat is smoked to a nice dark color at the specified temperatures, then placed into a cooker or steam cabinet until the internal temperature reaches 152 degrees F.

It is very easy to tell if the product has been overcooked. When cooking any kind of luncheon meat like bologna, etc., the fibrous casing will become full of liquid. The same applies to sausage or wieners. A sure sign of overcooking sausage in a smokehouse is a shriveled sausage and grease all over the floor (or too much grease in the cooking utensil). Temperatures must be followed precisely.

However, it should be noted that fat in a product like sausage or cured meat does serve a useful purpose. In fact, it does help bind the sausages and lunchmeats or salamis. Fat or lard, when warm, is usually in liquid form. When cooled, it becomes rigid and solid. When sausage or lunchmeat is cooled properly (usually overnight), the fat along with the meat and other products become nice and firm or solid, and cuts or slices neatly.

You can rest assured that when you see fat dripping from a salami or sausage in the smoker, you are overcooking the product. There is no question about this fact. When the product is finished, cooled and sliced, it will usually crumble as the binding power of the fat has been lost.

I think it should be noted that the above is not necessarily true

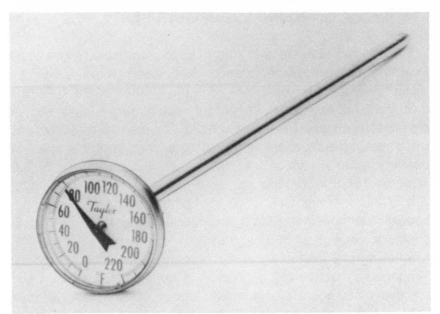

The above baby dial thermometer has a range of 0° - 220°. It is only 6 inches long but an absolute must in sausage making and smoking meat. It is not designed for use in a kitchen oven or other high temperature compartments.

Notice the thermometer is placed in the top, rather than the bottom, of the sausage. This prevents grease from dripping on the floor of the smokehouse.

60

when smoking fish or poultry since these products can be smoked and cooked in the 200 degree F. range. At this high temperature, the use of cures is unnecessary.

I think it's also worthy to note that fat is desired by many people in their sausage. In fact, there are a number of formulas that call for more fat than average, and in some cases you just can't get away from it. A cooked capicola is one such product, or a smoked pork butt. These meats are usually cured and smoked in one piece and it is difficult to know how much fat is in these products. The Italian sopressata and some dry-cured salamis are some examples of formulas that can call for larger amounts of fat and are even desired. There are many people who like fat and who, right or wrong, don't worry about cholesterol. I am one such person. As a child growing up in the 1930's, we used the leftover bacon fat to make our popcorn. Further still, we would render some salted pork fat with finely chopped onions. We would then let it sit overnight and simply use it in place of butter, which very few people could afford in those days. I must confess that from time to time I make popcorn with bacon fat. In addition, I will still render the pork fat as mentioned above and enjoy every moment of eating this way.

SHOWERING WITH COLD WATER

For the most part, sausages, cooked salami, wieners, bologna and the like are showered with cold water after removal from the smokehouse. The reason is that it will prevent the sausage and larger luncheon meats from shriveling up. This happens very rapidly, so the product should be put under the cold shower quickly. Remove from the smoker and place under the shower, as quickly as that. Needless to say, a shriveled-up sausage is less appealing to the eye than a fully packed, firm sausage. If the sausage should become shriveled, you may put it into hot water and cook it to bring back its firmness. Then shower with cold water.

BLOOMING

After the sausage or product is cooled with cold water, it is allowed to remain at room temperature for drying. If you prefer to have sausage with darker brown colors, simply let the sausage hang at room temperature. The longer the product is allowed to hang at room temperature, the darker its color it will become. This is called "blooming" the product.

LIQUID SMOKE

In addition to speeding up the process of cooking sausage and various meat products, another use also has been found for the cooker cabinet. Today a great many sausages need only be flavored with smoke. The steam cabinets of today can be purchased with atomizers (spray nozzles) already installed. The liquid smoke is simply sprayed on the small-diameter products, and the entire process of cooking and smoking is over in a matter of minutes.

A great many processors simply add a certain amount of liquid smoke to the product when it is being mixed or pumped with pickle. A great many people use this processing today for a variety of reasons.

To begin with, the air pollution control boards prefer this process, as it does away with polluting the air. That is not to say that you may not have a conventional smokehouse. Rather, for the larger processors, liquid smoke does away with smoke generators and the storage of sawdust and leads to what seems to be a cleaner and less costly operation.

It is doubtful that there are large sausage manufacturers and meat processors who use the old-fashioned method of smoking meats today. I would venture to say there is very little sausage in a supermarket meat case today that is not flavored with liquid smoke. If you do not have a favorite sausage kitchen where you can buy your smoked meats, chances are the smoked products you are buying have been smoked with liquid smoke.

As for the liquid smoke itself, it is made by burning green hickory wood; the smoke is then condensed into a liquid. This is then processed with the undesirable particles filtered out. The liquid can be used by adding it directly to the meat, spraying the product before cooking, atomizing in a smokehouse, and even introducing this liquid onto a hot plate, where it will vaporize into the smoke itself.

An important advantage gained from using liquid smoke is the

A Gravity-Fed Liquid Smoke Atomizer

This is a 2-h.p. model and is ideal for smoking 300-500 lbs. of sausage.
Manufactured by Koch Mfg.

fact that it does enhance the peelability of a skinless frankfurter when using synthetic casings. Application of the smoke solution to the surface of the frankfurter during the heating or cooking process helps to coagulate the meat protein to form a smooth skin texture. Also, when used on the product internally or externally, this same liquid smoke minimizes microorganism growth. Finally, the desired level of smoke flavor is controlled through standardization for the consumer's satisfaction.

Various products require substantial smoke flavor; others require an almost imperceptible level, just enough to bring out the seasonings and natural flavors of the particular products being processed. Commercially you generally can do the job with liquid smoke as well as with wood smoke itself. You can achieve the same flavor, color, and preservation qualities.

Natural liquid smoke flavors should be used according to the flavor desired, and test lots should be run accordingly. To obtain good distribution in fine or coarse chopped sausage, dilute the liquid smoke with the water you are going to use to mix with the meat. The recommended usage level for 100 lbs. of meat is four ounces of liquid smoke. For a small batch of five pounds of meat, add one teaspoon.

Liquid smoke also is used when brining products for smoking like hams, bacon and picnics. Add one ounce per gallon of brine and pump the product to 12 percent of its weight.

For home use, liquid smoke also can be used by adding four teaspoons per one gallon of water.

The above information regarding the use of liquid smoke is based on the usage of "Griffith's Royal Smoke." Various manufacturers of this product supply information for its use, and it can be purchased in powdered form or in a concentrated oil.

SMOKEHOUSES

Building your own smoker is quite simple, and in most cases cheaper than trying to buy one. Other than a commercial smoker, there aren't any smokers on the market today that can truly smoke 25 lbs. of meat or sausage at one time. If there were, I'm sure they would cost in excess of $100.

If you are a do-it-yourselfer, you can build a smoker for under $10 that will handle as much as 50 lbs. of deer salami or sausage and 3 or 4 hams at one time. In many cases, the material needed is just lying all around. With little time and work, you can build a very good smoker that will serve all your needs.

BUILDING A SMOKER

I always have favored an old freezer for my smokehouse for a number of good reasons. First, you have a smoker that is about 80% built, and all you have to do is add a little to it. There may be just a few shelves to remove. In addition, it already is insulated and prevents you or anyone else from burning themselves when you have the smoker operational. In effect, we are talking about building a sort of oven. There are only four simple steps to building your own smoker at home:

Incidentally, the amount of heat that is used in a smokehouse of this type isn't enough to cause the rubber gasket or plastic to melt. I have used mine many times with temperatures in the 200 degrees F. range.

DRAFT

Including a draft at the bottom part of a smokehouse not only will serve you well; it is critical. It matters little where you put it, so long as it is included in the design.

During the process of drying sausage or meat in a smokehouse, the proper opening in your damper in relation to the draft opening will allow the unwanted moisture to escape. In the beginning of this drying cycle, the dampers and draft always are wide open to create a draft, allowing moisture to escape at a much faster rate. Even during the regular smoking cycle there is a definite amount of moisture coming to the surface of the meat. The draft and damper, even though not wide open, still allow moisture to escape during the entire smoking cycle.

From time to time there is an excessive buildup of heat in a smoker that can easily be removed by adjusting the draft and damper, then readjusting them to the original position when you reach the required temperature. A commercial smokehouse today would set off exhaust fans to push out excessive heat or moisture.

There is a variety of smokers on the market for home use, but very few of these have dampers included. It is simple to install one. I have built a small smoker without controls similar to the ones on the market today. By installing a damper and draft, I was able to keep a very reasonable amount of heat in the smoker to cook and smoke the sausage. Completely closed, the smoker built up excessive amounts of heat. By using a hot plate for my source of heat and adjusting the draft and damper, I was able to maintain 160 or 170 degrees F.

CONTROLS

As mentioned earlier, in prehistoric times and in early America, the meat that was smoked had the moisture removed from it. This was fine in the days when people would barter with each other and the weight of, say, a ham didn't matter as it might be traded for several chickens. It was smoked ham and that was all that mattered in a trade.

Today, however, the words "smokehouse shrink" are of great importance and can determine the success or failure of any size sausage kitchen. With the large volume of meat being smoked today, the processors are aware of smokehouse shrink. Since meat no longer is bartered for, but sold in pounds and ounces, it is obvious why it is so important to control smokehouse shrink.

The temperatures to be followed have been designed to cook the meat at a slow and relatively low temperature, in comparison to the way one would normally cook a roast in the oven. Slow cooking and low temperatures prevent smokehouse shrink.

There was a time, however, when I thought I could speed up the cooking process of this meat by simply increasing the temperature and cooking until the internal temperatures were obtained. This I did, but the next day, when I removed the sausage from the cooler and weighed it, I found that I had only 85 pounds of sausage, instead of the 100 pounds I originally made.

Not enough can be said about smokehouse shrink and how important it is. The need for controls in a smoker, whether for home use or a commercial establishment, obviously are necessary.

When a smoker is built with adjustable controls, you can set your temperature to accommodate any type of meat— beef jerky at 80-90 degrees F., smoked sausages from 120-170 degrees F. and semi-dry cured sausages in the 130-145 degree F. range or higher. It is nice to have a thermometer on the surface of the smokehouse with the probe somewhere on the inside to record the temperatures so you can see them on the outside.

In regard to the formulas of this book or any other, the temperatures play an important part in a variety of ways. The dry or semi-dry sausages cannot be made properly unless the smoker temperatures can be controlled. The slow cooking and low temperatures required improve the keeping qualities of these sausages or hams, which in many cases need not be refrigerated.

Lastly, you need a baby dial thermometer to check the internal temperature of the meat or sausage so they don't overcook. There simply is no other way to do this. A professional sausage maker would not be without these tools. For home use, at the very least, a sausage maker should have a baby dial thermometer.

If you are going to make sausage or cure and smoke meat, there is no question: you should own one of these recording devices. It's one sure way to insure a good job.

A simple smokehouse control has a range of 80°-220° F. and usually comes with a thermocouple about 4 feet long.

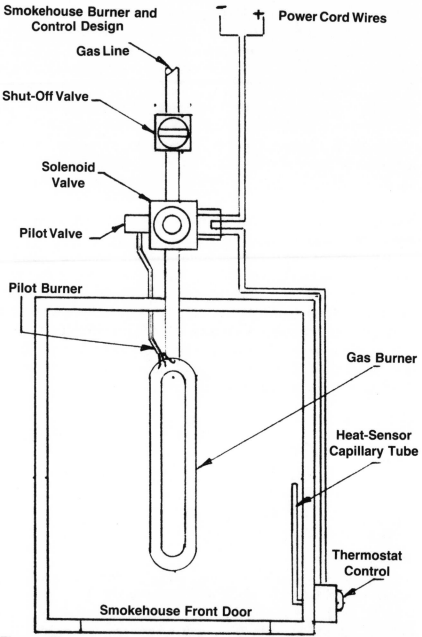

Smokehouse Burner and Control Design

Power Cord Wires

Gas Line

Shut-Off Valve

Solenoid Valve

Pilot Valve

Pilot Burner

Gas Burner

Heat-Sensor Capillary Tube

Thermostat Control

Smokehouse Front Door

The capillary sensor tube usually hangs in the smokehouse about halfway up from the bottom or just below where the meat will hang. Take note that only the burner pilot light and capillary sensor are placed on the interior of the smokehouse. The rest of the apparatus is constructed to be on the outside of the smokehouse.

68

DAMPER

Simply cut out a vent hole on top of the freezer; this allows excess moisture and excess heat that you may not require in your smoker to escape. This hole generally should be about 6" by 6" or 8" by 8". How close you can come to cutting out these dimensions depends on you.

After the vent hole is cut out, you will need a piece of flat metal larger than these dimensions in order to cover it up. This cover is needed to adjust the amount of heat and smoke that you'll want in the smoker. If you want to get fancy, for a few dollars more you can purchase a 6- or 8-inch diameter sheet metal pipe about 3 feet long with a damper and build a smoke stack.

Drill a hole in the side of the smoker that will accommodate a long stem thermometer. This generally is drilled last for a very good reason. After I make my first batch of sausage, I hang the product in my smoker and then I drill my hole for the thermometer. It should be in the center of one side of the smoker and should be drilled just below where the sausage will hang. It is from this point up we will try to regulate the heat in the smoker.

My most recent smoker was made of an old upright freezer using propane gas to heat it. I installed two pilot lights for my heat, but no burners. Also, I used a hot plate to smudge the sawdust, and was able to reach and maintain 200 degrees F. (It is very important that you do not get the idea of doing away with the hot plate and use one of the pilot lights to burn the sawdust. If you do this, you will create dirty black soot that will get all over the meat and walls of the smoker.)

Using this gas smoker, I was able to cook and smoke 50 lbs. of sausage in about 8 hours. Also, I was able to use the smoker seven times to smoke sausage on a 10-gallon container of propane, which is quite cheap. If you are a good do-it-yourselfer or have a good friend who is a plumber, it would be wise to look into building a smoker using natural gas or propane. Almost all commercial smokers use natural gas, as burning gas has a good volume to it which lifts the heat around and through the meat you are smoking. It also helps to lift out the moisture that is drying the product, and the job gets done much faster.

A refrigerator smokehouse using hot coals for the heat supply.

SHEET METAL

Much has been said about electric and gas-fired smokers, but if you live in an area without utilities, you'll have only the fire you build and its hot coals to do the job for you. This heat still can be controlled without problems. Your thermometer and vent are all that are needed to do this.

It's a good idea during the breaking-in period to use your thermometer and start adjusting the vent to give the desired control you'll be needing. All you need is a fire pit in which to build your fire and a trench that will act as a pipe to carry the smoke and heat to the smoker. If you like, you can line the fire pit with brick and use anything available to cover your trench to act as a pipe. It is important to note that YOU MUST BUILD THE FIRE PIT USING THE PREVAILING WINDS. In other words, if the wind blows from the south to the north, your fire pit is south and the smoker is north. The wind will carry the smoke and heat to the smoker for you. You'll need a cover over the top of the fire since this will serve as a draft when partially opened.

Bolt strips of wood ¾" thick and 2"-3" wide on the side of the smoker. You must be careful to place the strips at least 6"-8" below the ceiling. You should allow a space near the ceiling for the moisture to escape while you are smoking meats. It also is a good idea to notch these ¾" by 2." You'll most likely be using round dowels to hang your sausage or meats, so you'll have to be careful so that they don't roll off with your batch of meat into the fire or sawdust. It is an absolute must that you notch these strips.

Also, judge where you want these notches, making sure they are not too close to the back wall of the smokehouse or the door when you close it. Smokestick supports should be spaced 13" apart vertically and notched on 3" centers.

I would advise you not to use old broomstick handles for dowels. These usually have paint on them, which makes them very undesirable for hanging meats.

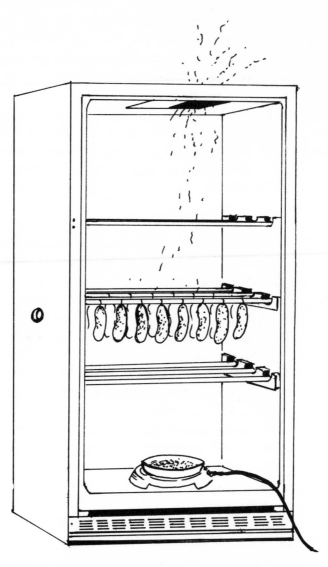

A typical smoker made of an old refrigerator, door is not shown.

HEAT SUPPLY

A hot plate or two is all that is needed to heat up a smoker of this type; it is advisable to use a stainless steel pan or pot for your smudge. Any other type of metal pot or pan will burn up or melt in a short period of time. When placing your hot plate into the smoker, you need not drill any holes for the electric cord. Usually, there is a drain in the old freezer or refrigerator that you can put the cord through. In fact, you can simply place the hot plate into the smoker and let the electric cord drop out through the front door. The door will close without any problems, with no ill effects to the cord.

The only other item required is some sort of cover for the top of the sawdust. This cover will prevent the sawdust from catching fire, as there will be times when some product you are smoking will be dripping grease. It also helps a great deal when you dampen your sawdust overnight. This helps to make a better smudge, stops your sawdust from burning up too fast, and definitely prevents fires.

Now that the smoker is finished, it is imperative that you give it a breaking-in period. Simply fire up the smoker, close the vent and door and let it smoke for about 3-4 hours. You'll no doubt discover that there will be a few spots in the smoker that will leak a little smoke. This is normal, so don't worry about it.

Up to this point we have discussed smokers that use available electricity as well as using old freezers or refrigerators. I think if you look hard at the freezer used to make a smoker, you can now envision that one can be made of almost any type of container you feel will do the job. You may build out of wood, brick or even earth, but be sure that your container is paint free on the inside.

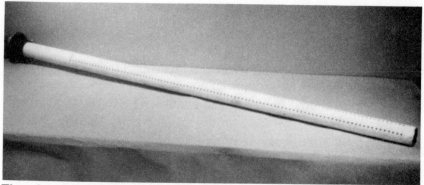

The above is a homemade gas burner made by welding 1 end of a 1½" pipe and drilling 2 rows of holes with about a ⅛" drill bit on ⅜" centers. Oxygen cap on end can be purchased at a plumbing supply house. This pipe was painted white in order to outline the drilled holes to show up better in this photo.

The above is an old bakery oven burner blower gun. The smaller burner in this photo is a simple kitchen stove burner.

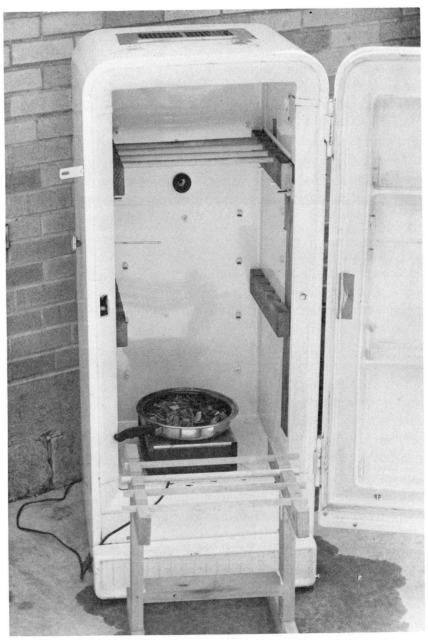

The above is a typical homemade smoker built by Robert Shaw of Huntingdon Valley, PA. Notice the long stem thermometer inside to get a temperature reading. Photo by J.W. Robinson.

BARREL-TYPE SMOKERS

The first smoker I ever saw was the one my father built many years ago; he used a 55-gallon drum. He used apple wood for his fire and for the smudge or smoke. Perhaps it is this type of smoker that will serve your needs if you have no electricity or gas available in your area. In fact, it can be used even if you have utilities available, providing this smoker will suit your needs.

This type is one of the simpler smokers to build at home, yet is very effective. You simply need a 55-gallon steel drum with the top and bottom cut out. You also need a hole at the bottom to be used as a draft. You can hinge the piece already cut out and use it as a little door; about 8" by 8" would be a nice size door. This will give you an entrance to place more sawdust on the hot coals when required, or to be used as an entrance to keep the flame down with a fine spray of water should the coals flare up.

As in the freezer-type smoker, we still require ¾" by 2" strips of wood so that we can hang our dowels. Again, these strips should be placed at least 6" or 8" from the top so that our cover would not touch meat or sausage that is smoking.

You will also need a cover for the top of the barrel. This cover, placed over the top of the barrel, usually has some nail holes punched into it which allow the moisture to escape.

When you have the barrel portion finished you may then build your fire pit. This pit can be built on top of the ground 8 or 9 bricks high; you then place your barrel on top of them. If you wish, you can provide for a door when using these fire bricks. It is much sturdier, however, for your barrel smoker to be sitting on the ground with your fire pit dug right into the ground.

This type of smoker is capable of smoking about 20 lbs. of sausage, but also has one big drawback—your fire is close to the meat. You have to build the smoker to be placed generally over a deep fire pit, so the hot coals will not overcook the bottom part of the product being smoked. With a smoker of this type, it strictly is a hanging-around affair to keep control of the coals and to keep the sawdust from starting aflame.

You might also consider using a 55-gallon drum in the manner we used the freezer; that is, by building the fire pit at one end,

A typical smoker using a 55 gallon drum.

digging a 12-foot trench and placing the drum at the opposite end. As you can see, all it really takes is a little imagination and a few dollars to build a smokehouse.

You'll need a smokestack to let all the moisture out and to be able to regulate the heat. It's also important to build it large enough to let the heat circulate around your product so it can dry, cook and smoke as well. It is not at all necessary that the smoker be insulated. It helps, but is not mandatory. The only other thing needed is a source of heat.

CHAPTER III

Natural Casings

INSCA

The International Natural Sausage Casing Association (INSCA) is an association of natural casing producers. This group was formed to promote the use of natural casings. Its main function is to inform the consumer about sausage that is made with natural casings. INSCA can sometimes provide teaching aids such as wall charts and leaflets for educational purposes. INSCA also encourages the use of their logo, as shown below:

on the packaging of sausage stuffed in natural casings.

INSCA has a total of over 200 members, representing 27 different countries. It should be noted that they don't sell natural casings, only promote their use via TV, radio, magazines and newspapers. They can easily provide the necessary information for purchasing commercial casings in large quantities because they are an association of casing producers.

From time to time I have had occasion to contact INSCA regarding various problems, and they were more than helpful — especially Lucille Lampman, the executive secretary, and John R. Yurkus. It is through their generosity, on behalf of INSCA, that the following pages of drawings and casing sizes were made available.

NATURAL CASINGS

Large Bologna.

BEEF BUNGS

Almost every sausage maker uses Beef Bungs Caps, one of the most popular items in the entire Beef Casing line.

The size of the Caps is determined by inflating the casing with air until it is distended to the same degree that it would be by stuffing. Then the Cap is usually gauged at the curve.

Beef Bungs are used for Capocolla, Veal Sausage, Large Bologna, Lebanon, and Cooked Salami.

Grade	Approx. Diameter	Approx. Capacity Per Piece
Extra Wide Export Caps	5″ & Over	12 lbs./up
Spec. Wide Export Caps	4½—5″	10—12 lbs.
Reg. Export Caps	4 —4½″	8—10 lbs.
Nar. Export Caps	3½—4″	6— 8 lbs.
Domestic Caps	4½″ & Over	9—11 lbs.

BEEF BLADDERS

The largest casings from cattle, beef bladders, are oval, and will stuff from 5 to 14 pounds of sausage. They are used chiefly for Minced Specialty and Mortadella, either in their natural oval form, in square molds for sandwich slices, or in the flat, pear-shaped style.

BEEF BLADDERS

Round and Square Styles

Beef Bladders are used for round Mortadella also round, square, or flat minced specialty.

Grade	Kind	Approx. Diameter	Approx. Capacity Per Piece
Large	Salted	7″ & Over Inflated	11—14 lbs.
Med.	Salted	6″—7″ Inflated	7—11 lbs
Small	Salted	5½″—6″ Inflated	5— 7 lbs.
Small	Dried	8″—10″ Deflated	5— 7 lbs

BEEF MIDDLE

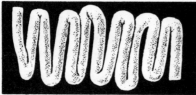

Before Stuffing

Bologna in . . . Sewed Beef Middle

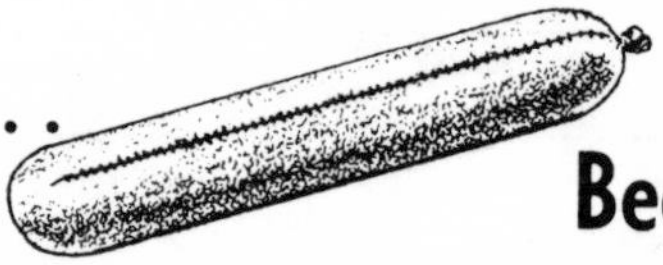

Beef Middles can be used satisfactorily for Leona Style Sausage, all other types of Bologna, Dry and Semi-dry Cervelats, Dry and Cooked Salami, and Veal Sausage.

SEWED BEEF MIDDLES

Kind	Width	Length	Approx. Stuffing Capacity
Single Wall	2½—3″	18—20″	4 —4½ lbs.
Single Wall	3—3½″	18—20″	5¾—6¼ lbs.
Single Wall	3½—4″	18—20″	6¼—6¾ lbs.
Single Wall	4-4½″	18—20″	7 —7½ lbs.

READY-TO-USE BEEF MIDDLES
Sewed Across One End

Width	Length	Approx. Capacity Per Piece
1¾—2″	18—20″	1¾ lbs.
2 —2¼″	18—20″	2¼ lbs.
2¼—2½″	18—20″	2½ lbs.
2½—2¾″	18—20″	2¾ lbs.
2¾—3″	18—20″	3 lbs.

BEEF MIDDLES

Grade	Approx. Diameter	Approx. Capacity Per Set
Extra Wide	2½″ & Over	90—100 lbs.
Spec. Wide	2¼ — 2½	80— 90 lbs.
Medium	2 — 2¼	55— 65 lbs.
Narrow	2 & Down	45— 55 lbs.

Beef Middles are measured in sets of 57 feet each.

BEEF ROUNDS

These casings derive their name from their "ring" or "round" characteristic. There are two general classifications: namely, "Export" Grade and "Domestic" grade. Beef Rounds are usually considered among  the finest on the market because they are liberally measured, accurately calibrated, closely cleaned and fatted, and all scored, tender, and waste material is removed.

Ring Bologna

Beef Rounds are used for Ring Bologna, Ring Liver Sausage, Mettwurst, Polish Sausage, Blood Sausage, Kishka, and Holsteiner.

BEEF ROUNDS

Stuffing capacities indicated are approximate green weights and cannot be guaranteed on account of natural variation of the product.

Beef Rounds are measured into sets of 100 feet each.

Grade	Average Approx. Diameter	Average Approx. Capacity Per Set
Ex. Wide Domestic	44MM & Over	85—95 lbs.
Wide Domestic	40—44MM	75—85 lbs.
Med. Domestic	40MM & Down	60—70 lbs.
Ex. Wide Export	44MM & Over	85—95 lbs.
Wide Export	40—44MM	75—85 lbs.
Spec. Wide Export	37—40MM	70—80 lbs.
Medium Export	35—38MM	65—70 lbs.
Narrow Export	28—35MM	55—65 lbs.

HOG CASINGS

Hog casings for Country Style Sausage, linked Hog Sausage, Large Frankfurts, Kishka, Kielbasa, and Peperoni.

Prepared—Ready-to-Use

Hog Casings are also packed 1 bundle per plastic bag with a specially prepared liquid formula. This solution preserves the casings and keeps them soft and pliable for immediate filling.

This new packaging idea offers labor savings through elimination of usual preparatory work associated with salted product.

HOG CASINGS

Grade	Approx. Diameter	Approx. Capacity Per Bundle	Average Bundles Per Tierce
Narrow	32MM/down	90—100 lbs.	335
Medium	32—35MM	105—115 lbs.	325
English Medium	35—38MM	115—125 lbs.	310
Wide	38—42MM	125—135 lbs.	300
Spec. Wide	42—44MM	130—140 lbs.	290
Extra Wide	44MM/over	135—150 lbs.	260
Medium Shorts	35MM/down	80— 90 lbs.	305
Wide Shorts	35MM/over	95—105 lbs.	285

Hog casings are measured into bundles of 100 yards each. Shorts are 3 to 6 foot lengths.

HOG BUNGS

REGULAR HOG BUNGS . .

Regular Hog Bungs are normally put up as Medium Prime, Large Prime, Export, and Sow selections, each grade denoting a definite size. These are known as "sales grades." The selection is determined by inflating the bung with air, then calibrating it about 22 inches from the large or "crown" end. The various sales grades of Regular Bungs are distinguishable by the natural taper from the "crown" end. They are usually sold and used cut in 34-inch lengths. They are used chiefly for Liver Sausage and Braunschweiger.

REGULAR HOG BUNGS

Grade	Approx. Diameter	Approx. Capacity Per Piece
Sow, 32" cut	2¼"/Over	5½ lbs.
Export, Sow-in. 32" cut	2 1/16"/Over	5 lbs.
Export, Sow-out, 32" cut	2 1/16—2¼"	4½ lbs.
Large Prime, 32" cut	1 15/16—2 1/16"	4 lbs.
Medium Prime, 32" cut	1 13/16—1 15/16"	3½ lbs.
Brok. Shorts (20-34" long)	1 15/16"/Over	3½ lbs.

SEWED HOG BUNGS . . .

Sewed Hog Bungs are produced in double-walled and single-walled varieties. Both varieties are made by sewing two pieces of the smaller sizes of Regular Hog Bungs to obtain a larger, more uniform, finished product. Being "tailor Made," so to speak, Sewed Hog Bungs can be obtained in almost any shape or size. The double-walled type is used almost exclusively for Liver Sausage, Braunschweiger, and Genoa; the single walled for Thuringer and hard Cervelats.

SEWED HOG BUNGS

Used For	Width	Length	Approx. Stfg. Cap.
Viskon Lined Sewed Hog Bungs			
Liver Saus.	3½—3¾"	30—32"	7 — 8 lbs.
Liver Saus.	3 —3½"	30—32"	5¾— 6¾ lbs.
Liver Saus.	2½—3"	30—32"	5¼— 5¾ lbs.
Double Wall—Combined Hog Bung End and Beef Casing Lined			
Liver Saus.	3½–3¾	30–32"	8½-10 lbs.
Liver Saus.	3¼–3½	30–32"	7½-8 lbs.
Liver Saus.	3 –3¼	30–32"	6½-7 lbs.
Liver Saus.	2¾–3	30–32"	5½-6 lbs.
Liver Saus.	2½–2¾	30–32"	5 -5½ lbs.
Double Wall—Hog Bung Ends			
Genoa	3½–3¾"	20"	5 — 5½ lbs.
Genoa	3¾–4"	20"	5½— 6½ lbs.
Single Wall			
Thuringer	3½—4"	30—32"	7½— 8½ lbs
Thuringer	3 —3½"	30—32"	6 – 7 lbs
Thuringer	2½--3"	30—32"	5 — 6 lbs.

Before Stuffing

After Stuffing:
Liver Sausage
and Italian
Salami.

HOG MIDDLE
(CURLY)

While Hog Middles are not so well known as other casings, they are used in large quantities in many territories. They are put up as:

Hog Middles with Caps Off

Hog Middles Caps

The Hog Middle is the same item that is known as "Chitterlings."

CAREFUL PROCESSING FOR HIGH QUALITY

Hog Middles—Caps Off—are not put up to definite specifications as are other casing items, but selected on the basis of saving only the choice, medium-sized pieces. Each piece is cut in about seven-foot lengths and is called a "set."

Hog Middles are easily recognizable by their curly appearance, which also distinguishes the products for which they are used. These are: Certain types of Italian Salami, such as Frisses; Liver Sausage; and Braunschweiger.

HOG STOMACHS

Hog Stomachs are put up in 2 sizes—medium which will stuff approximately 5 lbs. of formula and large which will stuff approximately 7 lbs.

The principal use of this item is for Headcheese, Souse, and Blood Sausage

After Stuffing

86

SHEEP CASINGS

Sheep casings, as the name implies, come from lambs and sheep. They are used principally for pork sausage and frankfurts.

Sheep Casings . . .

are strong . . . yet extremely tender eating. Promptness of handling, modern machinery, thorough cleaning, all combine to produce casings that are strong, clear, free of weak spots, holes, and other imperfections.

Sheep Casings are . . .

of a good, white color. This permits proper smoking or coloring of the frankfurts and gives the desired finish to the pork sausage.

Before Stuffing

After Stuffing:
Fresh Pork Sausage
(front) and Frankfurts.

Prepared—Ready-to-Use

Sheep casings are also usually packaged in a specially prepared liquid solution, 1 or 2 hanks per plastic bag. The solution acts as a preservative, also keeps the casings soft and pliable for immediate filling.

This modern packaging method offers labor savings through elimination of the customary preparation work involved with salted stock.

SHEEP CASINGS

Grade	Approx. Diameter	Approx. Capacity Per Hank
Narrow	16—18 MM	33—36 lbs.
Str. Medium	18—20 MM	38—41 lbs.
Med. Wide	20—22 MM	47—52 lbs.
Str. Wide	22—24 MM	55—60 lbs.
Spec. Wide	24—26 MM	60—64 lbs.
Extra Wide	26/over MM	64—70 lbs.
Shorts—3 to 6-foot lengths		
Str. Medium	18—20 MM	34—36 lbs.
Med. Wide	20—22 MM	40—45 lbs.
Str. Wide	22—24 MM	45—50 lbs.
Spec. Wide	24—Up	50—54 lbs.
Sprinklers (Pork Sausage Only)		
Wide	22/over MM	53—57 lbs.
Medium	18—22 MM	40—45 lbs.

Sheep Casings are measured into hanks of 100 yards each

NATURAL CASINGS

Surprising as it may seem, there aren't many books today that deal with the subject of casings for the making of sausage. The only way to obtain information is from the people who sell these products, and that mostly is word-of-mouth.

In light of the incredible amounts of sausage that are made in this country alone, one would think there would be a wealth of information dealing with this particular subject. Instead, there virtually is no information available anywhere. In the next few pages, you will be surprised to learn about the many types of natural casings that are available today. It truly is an industry in itself.

A casing is calibrated by inflating it with air until it is distended to the same dimension that it would be by stuffing it with meat. The larger casings used for bologna or salami usually are measured in inches or millimeters. For the most part, all casings today are measured using the metric system.

Anyone thinking about opening a sausage kitchen would do well to start out by using natural casings. There are a number of good reasons for this. To begin with, natural casings are readily available in every section of the United States. In addition, these casings are available in small quantities, more commonly known as hanks or bundles. These hanks of casings can usually be relied on to make a specific amount of sausage.

For instance, the 32-35mm up to 40-42mm sizes in the hog casings can be used to make from 100-125 lbs. of sausage per hank. However, when using 22-24mm to 24-26mm lamb casings you will find that 1 hank only will give you about 50-60 lbs. of sausage. Generally speaking, the small-size casing only allows you to stuff half the amount of meat into a bundle of casings and will cost you twice as much when you purchase it. Since lamb is not the primary meat one sees in a meat counter today, it is understandable that these casings will cost considerably more.

More and more sausage makers are using the 32-35mm hog casings to make a breakfast sausage, as you can actually stuff twice the amount of meat into one hank of these casings. Theoretically speaking, you are getting twice as much for your money.

Another advantage gained by using natural casings is that they can be linked with relative ease. With little practice or effort you can make sausage to specific orders (4-5 links to the pound). For home use, the natural salted casings just can't be beat. The casings are sold in bundles that make up to 120 lbs. of meat, but it isn't likely that many people would make this amount of sausage at one time. This being the case, the unused portion of the natural casings are then repacked in table salt and can be kept for an indefinite period of time under refrigeration. Never use iodized salt.

However, these casings are not without their drawbacks. To the novice unraveling these casings, they have a tendency to tangle and become knotted. With patience you can overcome this problem with relative ease. Natural casings usually are packed in salt. This being the case, the individual casing has to be flushed out with water and rinsed on the outside as well. Sausage kitchens no longer use this type of casing as it is time-consuming and costly, but the salted casings are still best for home use.

For the commercial sausage kitchen, preflushed natural casings are available. They come packed in sealed plastic bags filled with solution. The solution helps to keep the casing soft, pliable and ready for immediate filling. In addition to being ready for immediate use, they very seldom knot up as they are removed from the container one at a time.

For stuffing sausage in a commercial sausage kitchen, this particular type of casing is cheaper by far to use than salted casings. The reasons are especially obvious when the preflushed bundles cost only pennies more. The preflushed casings have a shorter shelf life—about 30-40 days under refrigeration—so this type of casing is not very good for home use unless you plan to make a large amount of sausage and use them up. But, this is a great casing for a commercial sausage kitchen, which usually makes sausages by the hundreds and thousands of pounds.

On the other hand, a natural casing is great for making dry or semi-dry salami or sausages. When the natural casings are stuffed with meat they will shrink equally with the meat while in the drying stage.

This cannot be said for synthetic casings. The meat packed into a synthetic casing would dry, but the casing would not. You then would have a shriveled-up looking sausage, not very appetizing.

By the same token, there are synthetic casings available today that will shrink away proportionately with the meat while in the drying stage.

Unless you own a large commercial sausage kitchen, this type of casing is prohibitive from an economic standpoint. The manufacturers of these casings require that large amounts be purchased at one time, and the minimums usually run in the hundreds of dollars.

SALTED CASINGS

Salted casings come to us from all over the world: Australia, New Zealand, Argentina, etc. The main reason for this is the fact that natural casings produced in the United States are used up by the meat packers themselves. There just aren't enough to go around, so the rest of the natural casings are imported.

Salted casings have a very long shelf life when stored properly. To give you some idea, these casings come to us in the cargo hulls of ocean-going vessels and are not refrigerated. The vessels sometimes take two months to arrive in our ports. The very same casings are immediately refrigerated as soon as they arrive.

It boils down to this: an unrefrigerated casing has a life expectancy of around six months. Put in a refrigerator, this very same casing packed liberally in salt has an indefinite shelf life. In other words, it will last until it is used up. Store casings at 40-45 degrees F.

Unrefrigerated, these salted casings quickly begin to give off a strong odor even though they themselves are not spoiled. Put them back under refrigeration and this odor for the most part disappears.

TOUGH CASINGS

Occasionally, some people do have problems with tough natural casings. By their very nature, natural casings can sometimes be tough. Salt itself can help toughen the casings, so they do take some abuse.

For home use, I have found that rinsing and flushing a casing and then refrigerating overnight will help. This seems to remove more salt from the casing itself, which in turn helps to tenderize it. It you don't mind a little extra work, you can flush the casings again before their use; this may also help. It is quite difficult to pinpoint why natural casing are sometimes tough. Even the food the animal ate could have a bearing on this problem.

It is equally important not to put stuffed sausage in a hot smokehouse. The gradual raising of the temperature will prevent toughening of the sausage. Too much heat is almost a guarantee that the casings will be tough.

When placing a casing on a stuffing horn, it should always go on loosely. If you have difficulty placing the casing on the nozzle, it is an indication that the nozzle is too large. The casings must go on very loosely. Forcing a casing on an oversized nozzle will almost always result in breakage and/or the casing not coming off the nozzle properly. A good rule of thumb is that a ½" nozzle is to be used with casings in the range of 22-28mm, and ¾" nozzle should be used for the 30-36mm range, and a 1" nozzle should be used for casings over 38mm.

Improper stuffing of the sausage itself can also make a person believe the casing is tough when in fact it is not. Sausage should always be stuffed as firmly as possible, rather than loosely.

Finally, never put a sausage into boiling water. Instead, start cooking in cold water, bringing the temperature up gradually. Bring to a boil and then simmer until cooked.

AN ASSORTMENT OF CASINGS. The small hank of casings are lamb casings. The large bundle is a hank of hog casings. Compare the fine strands of the lamb as opposite the hog casings. The bundle of casings in the plastic bag is of the preflushed variety. These casings come packed in a solution and have a shelf life of 30 to 40 days. Unless you plan to make at least 100 pounds of sausage, these casings are not practical for home use. Salted casings can be kept for years packed in salt, under refrigeration.

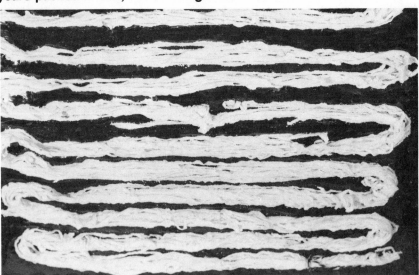

The first step in unraveling casings is to have the whole bundle stretched out on a long table. All casings come tied on one end with cotton twine. In using a long table, the casings are unraveled easier one at a time, and there is less chance for knotting.

FLUSHING SALTED CASINGS

In making sausage while using a natural salted casing, flushing the casings usually is the first step. To save aggravation, a bundle of casings should be unraveled on as long a table as possible. Since a single strand of the casing can be as long as 12 feet, the table or platform to be used should be at least 7-8 feet long. The casings can be unraveled much easier and there will be less knotting up.

After all the casings are unraveled and set in little stacks, the sink should be partially filled with water. In addition, a suitable container (about 2 qts.) to hold 1 bundle of casings should also be half-filled with water.

The casings are then flushed one at a time. The casing is opened at one end and placed under the faucet in the sink. A suitable amount of water is allowed to enter into the opening and is then flushed out the other end. (The length of the casing depends on the amount of water allowed to enter.)

The flushed casing then is placed into the container, allowing one end of the casing to hang out over the side of the container. When the casings all are flushed, put them in the cooler until they are ready for use. If possible, use a container that has a cover with it. The container should be filled the rest of the way with cold water, and the cover then placed over the top. This prevents the casings from drying out.

When you actually use the casing, it is good practice to place more water into it before placing it on the stuffer horn. The casing should be allowed to come off the stuffer horn as easily as it went on.

Be very liberal with the water when using natural casings. If you are not, you will find that the casing will stick to the stuffer horn and you will wind up breaking more casings than not. In addition, you will have an excessive amount of air pockets in the sausage. Many times these cannot be avoided, so be sure you pin prick as many of these air pockets as you can. Otherwise, they will fill up with grease during the smoking or cooking process.

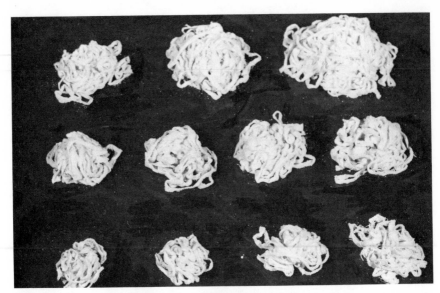

Casings in small stacks after being unraveled.

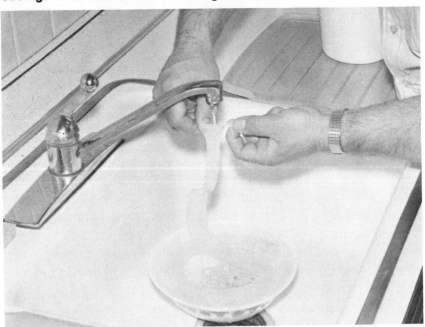

When flushing casings, the outside should also be washed. This usually takes care of itself by partially filling a container or sink with water. As you are filling the casing with water, the other part is dropped into a container and washes by itself as the water is being flushed through the inside.

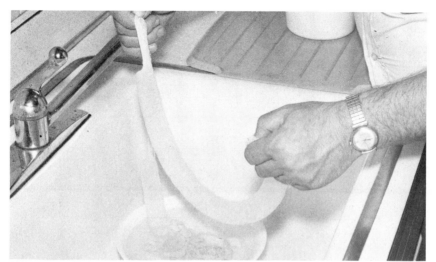

When flushing a salted casing, allow for 12 to 18 inches of water to enter the casing before flushing from one end to the other.

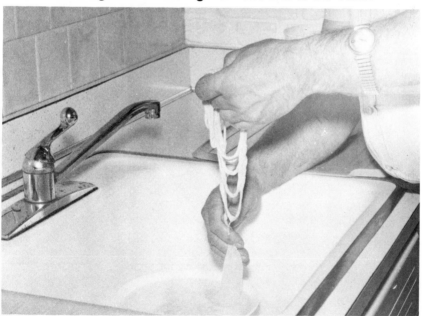

After filling the casing with water, be sure all water and air is removed otherwise the casing will float in the container and become knotted with the other casings. Flushed casings are placed into a container one on top of the other to prevent knotting. After casings are flushed and placed into the container, fill with a very slow stream of water. A quick fill of water will cause the flushed casings to tangle and become knotted.

The proper way for casings to look after being placed into a container.

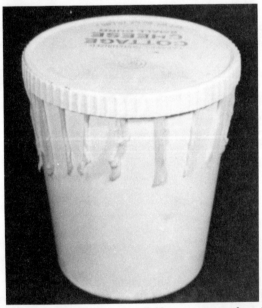

A container with a cover should be used if you are going to store casings overnight. Storing casings overnight before use tends to make the casings more tender.

CHAPTER IV
Collagen and Synthetic Fibrous Casings

COLLAGEN CASINGS

What is a collagen casing? There are a few people using them today, but not many people know what they really are. A great many people actually call a collagen casing a "synthetic casing." It is not; a collagen casing is exactly what the name implies–collagen–and it is edible.

These casings are made from the hides of cattle. Once the flesh and fat are removed from the inside, the hair is then removed from the outside. The hide is then split in half by a special machine. The hair side is used for leather, and the flesh side or corium layer is used in the manufacture of collagen casings. This raw material is ground and swelled in an acid, then sieved and filtered and extruded into casings. Following this simple explanation of collagen casings, I would like to explain the reasons for their use today.

Before collagen casings came into being, the sausage makers were confronted with several major problems. In servicing the hotels, restaurants, and various institutional areas (schools, hospitals, prisons, etc.) it was found that their products were not readily acceptable, since portion control plays such a big part in today's world. The meat processors could supply any size hamburger, steak, or other meats as well.

It was just natural then, that sausage would have to come under portion control as well. Because natural casings are erratic in size, it was difficult, if not impossible, to give any kind of portion control, especially when using an automatic sausage linking machine. This machine can give you correct length of the sausage but never the correct weight.

When natural casings are purchased in bundles (or hanks) they clearly specify the size you are buying. For Italian sausage you would get 32-35mm; for Polish sausage you get 38-42mm. Notice that you are getting four different sizes when you get 38-42mm. Notice that you are getting four different sizes when you order one hank. The lamb casings used for breakfast sausage also come in several different sizes per bundle.

In either case, the natural casing of animals differ in size and cannot be controlled. This, of course, is hardly noticeable to the housewife. With an institution or restaurant it's a different story. A housewife simply buys by the pound; a restauranteur wants to know how many to a pound. The restauranteur will feed a certain amount of people by the pound. They require that each person has the same amount as the other when they order the same type of dinner plate.

No matter what the product, each plate has a certain number of ounces of meat on it; the owner then can easily figure out his profit. In addition, the dinner plates go out in an equal size. The patty-making machines today can give you any size that you require in a hamburger or breakfast patty: 2 to the pound, 3-4 and even 9-10 to the pound. You may get as little as you want or as much as you like to the pound.

The collagen casing today gives the restauants and institutions the control they want. A hospital knows that to prepare eight breakfasts, it takes 1 pound of breakfast sausage to do the job. Most breakfasts are served with two breakfast sausages, and the sausages generally are made 16 to the pound. In addition, they can better control how much product they are ordering. Getting to the larger-type sausages (i.e. Polish sausage or knockwurst), portion control becomes even more critical.

The uniformity of the collagen casings certainly is a major factor for consideration by anyone making large amounts of sausage. This uniformity has allowed the sausage makers to be able to sell their products anywhere and enable them to secure more business.

Because of the uniformity of the collagen casings today, the result is superior machinability. Practically all the linking machines on the market today can use collagen casings. The ability to produce uniform links at high speed obviously results in an increased flow of product, larger volumes, and less time. Naturally, this decreases the cost of production with great consistency. The sizes available

Collagen casings.
99

today range from 14mm-45mm.

The versatility of these casings makes them usable to any smoking process. In many instances, the smoking cycles may be shortened because of the rapid uptake of the smoke color. This in turn leads to less smokehouse shrink, thereby increasing the profit picture. Collagen casings are taken right from the box to the stuffer horn without additional washing or handling. They already are clean and sanitary and available for any type sausage you may want to process.

Collagen casings, since their inception, have only been used by the commercial sausage kitchens and are only available in 16- or 20-foot lengths. After stuffing a casing full of meat, it's like having a 16- or 20-foot iron pipe on your table full of meat. It has always taken the use of an automatic linking machine to form the link and tie it off with string. Straight collagen casings cannot be linked manually by twisting, as they simply will not hold the link; they always unravel. By the same token, these casings can be tied off in links manually if you don't mind the extra work involved by doing the tying.

CURVED COLLAGEN CASINGS

As with all technology, advances always are being made, and collagen casings are no exception. They are now available with a natural curve extruded into these 16- and 20-foot casings. As the meat is stuffed into these casings, they immediately are curved and ready to be placed on a smokehouse stick. In addition, they can even be linked into 6"-7" links without unraveling. Obviously, these casings now are practical for the smaller sausage kitchens or home use.

For years many sausage makers as well as the do-it-yourselfers have been looking for casings that already have a brown color to them. I was one of these people when I first got into sausage making on a professional basis. I felt we could do away with smoking completely or get a much better job done in less time.

Unfortunately, at the time, collagen casings still were not developed. However, a breakthrough has been made, and collagen casings now are available with a dark brown color. You now can bypass the smokehouse if you like.

100

By the same token, if you still prefer to use the smokehouse, as I do, you will be amazed at the deep mahogany colors that can be attained. Best of all, these colors do not fade away and hold up for longer periods of time. This makes the products more saleable as well. Collagen casings in the range of 30mm and over should only be used for smoked or dry-cured sausage. They are not desirable for stuffing fresh sausage.

It is important to note that collagen casings require refrigeration, just as natural casings do. These casings need only be kept at 50 degrees F. or lower, but without it they will become brittle. If for some reason the casings do become brittle, simply dip in water and use. DO NOT SOAK.

All collagen casings are imported, and are not manufactured in the U.S.A. as of this writing.

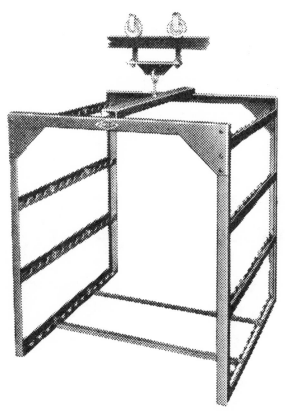

A smokehouse cage. Generally used with an overhead rail, can also be used for sausage or meats.

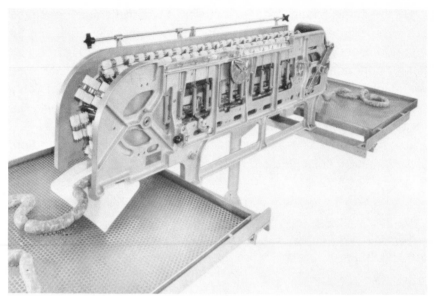

FAMCO sausage linker. This linking machine is used for linking break-fast sausage links. It also has the feature of cutting the sausage in pairs or single links as it discharges the sausage. Manufactured by FAMCO, Inc.

TY-LINKER actually uses a twine to tie off each sausage after it is linked. The linker is adjustable to the length of sausage to be linked. Can be used with either natural or collagen casings in the 40-42 MM range. Manufactured by Linker Machines, Inc.

SYNTHETIC AND FIBROUS CASINGS

There are literally billions of pounds of sausage made each year in the United States alone. There just isn't enough livestock in the entire world from which we can derive enough casings with which to make all these luncheon meats and sausages.

So as you can see, the synthetic casings are actually a blessing. The fact of the matter is that we practically never see any natural casing on sausage or luncheon meats any more. I would estimate that 80% of all the sausage sold at your favorite market today is stuffed into collagen casings, and all the luncheon meat and bologna are stuffed into synthetic casings.

Probably the most popular casings used today are the plastic casings. They even come in an array of colors: usually red for bologna, white for liverwurst and clear-colored for custom smoking (i.e. deer salami, cooked salami, etc.).

There are synthetic casings on the market today that can be used for hard salami, semi-dry sausage, and thuringers. These casings usually are lined on the inside with a coat of protein, which causes the synthetic casing to shrink along with the meat as it is drying out. As with collagen casings, the synthetic casings are uniform and a boon to the sausage industry when it comes to portion control. In addition, when you start to compare the prices of beef bungs or middles against the synthetic casings, it is hard to say no to the use of synthetic casings. The synthetic casing is easier to store, need not be refrigerated and does not have to be cleaned.

Fibrous casings generally are used in making dry and semi-dry sausages. As mentioned earlier, when the insides are coated with protein, this casing has the ability to shrink with the meat when being dried. The fibrous casings have the fibers running through them lengthwise which gives them added strength. You can stuff a salami or sausage much tighter without breaking the casing, thus eliminating most of the air pockets. Truly, without collagen or synthetic casings, you would not see the delicatessen counters as they are known today. There would be a limited supply of sausage, luncheon meats or hot dogs. There is a definite use for the collagen and synthetic casing.

Most manufacturers have synthetic casings available that

are already pin-pricked. A sausage, luncheon meat or salami will smoke just as brown in a synthetic casing as it will in a natural casing. The synthetic casings are porous enough to absorb the smoke. When buying synthetic casings, always make it a point to find out how long they should be soaked in water, as the various manufacturers specify different time periods.

Some sausage makers soak fibrous casings in vinegar or liquid smoke before stuffing. This has a two-fold purpose: The first is to prevent surface mold; the other is to prevent the casing from sticking to the meat after it is smoked (coagulation). I am sure that at one time or another you have tried to peel the casing off a piece of sliced meat. To your dismay, part of the meat peeled off along with the casing. This can be frustrating.

If you do make a salami or some other luncheon meat and encounter this problem, there is a way around it. Before slicing, soak the whole chunk of salami in water for several minutes. The water will soak through and separate the casing from the meat. You can then slice the salami and peel off the casing as usual.

A casing perforator is used to pierce air pockets in large or small sausages.

Fibrous casings before customizing. These casings are available in any length and can be purchased with one end tied.

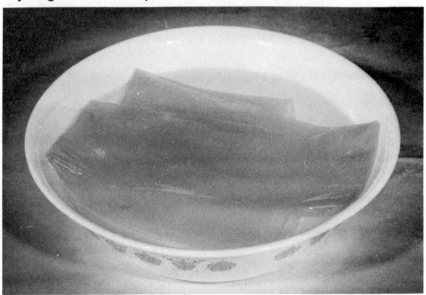

Synthetic fibrous casings must be soaked in water before using. Soaking allows the casing to become flexible and easier to work with. A dry casing can break during stuffing as it is sometimes brittle; a soaked casing will give to some degree. The manufacturers of these casings will specify the time periods required for soaking.

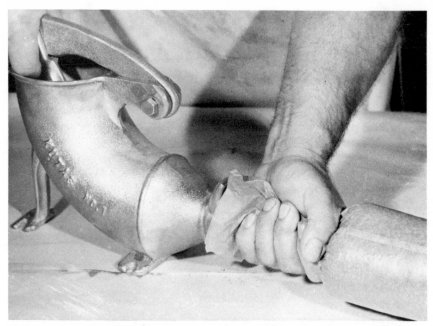

The large synthetic casings are stuffed a section at a time. Note the hand holds the casing firmly while wrapped around the nozzle of the stuffer with great pressure being applied. The meat is packed very hard into the casing to eliminate air pockets.

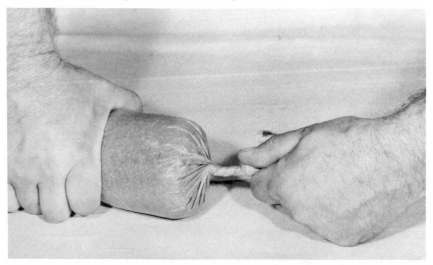

After the casing is stuffed, it is a good idea to grab hold of the untied end with one hand and the entire salami with the other hand. The untied end is held firm while the salami is being twisted to a point that it becomes firmer still.

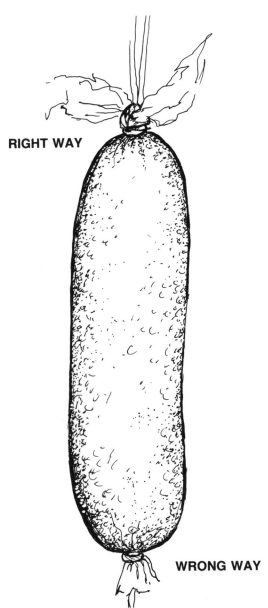

RIGHT WAY

WRONG WAY

When making the large type bologna or salamis it is imperative that great care is taken in the tying of the twine properly. Take note that the top of the salami is spread out like a butterfly and the twine is tied in a criss-cross manner. This is the proper way to tie these sausages and both ends should be tied in this manner. If the sausage has a knot as shown in the bottom part of this drawing, the meat as it warms, will cause the knot to slip off causing loss of the meat.

107

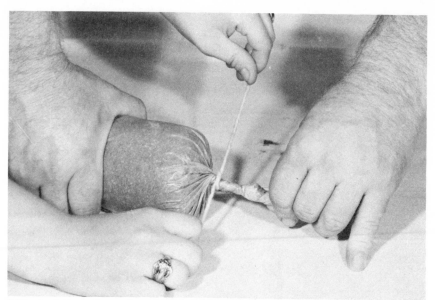

After twisting the salami, it usually requires two people to finish this operation; one to hold the salami while it is firm, and the other person to tie it.

Unless a machine is used to tie each end of a salami, not enough can be said about this particular operation. Both ends must be tied in the manner shown or the meat will slip out of the casings during the smoking and cooking periods. There is no other way to tie a salami.

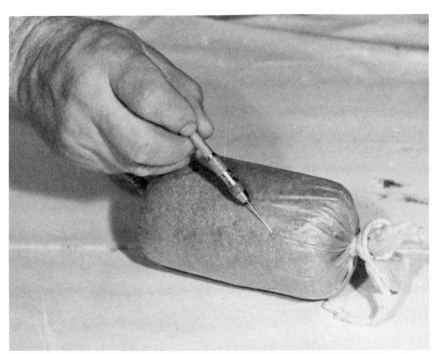

Even though a casing may be packed firmly and tied properly, there always seems to be a few air pockets to be punctured. It's a good idea to puncture as many of these air pockets as possible to avoid the fat from forming in these pockets during smoking and cooking.

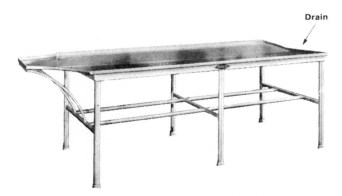

Drain

SAUSAGE STUFFING TABLE

Available in lengths of 6' to 12' and up to 4' in width. Note that the top of the table has a turned up rim and beveled to the center. This prevents the sausage from sliding off the table and excess water to drain off into one end of the operation.

Below are a couple of manual hog ring pliers. If you've ever made any appreciable amount of salami, tying the ends with string, you'll appreciate the value of these pliers. I've had my hands bleed more than once when using string to tie salami.

MANUAL-LOAD
Hog Ring Pliers

Spring-Loaded
Hog Ring Pliers

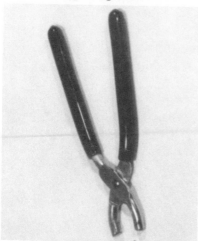

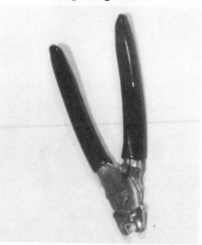

These pliers are a fine tool to use for closing both ends of a salami. It requires one person to hold the salami and the other to load the pliers and clip each end shut.

The above pliers are a better quality since they are a spring-loaded, factory-built tool. The hog ring is held in place by the spring and doesn't fall out. The salami casing is twisted shut, pliers picked up and the end is closed, making this a one-person operation.

Hog rings come in different sizes.

Clark clips come in one size and can be made to fit any casing up to 8 inches in diameter.

Salami closed with hog ring.　　Salami closed with clark clip.

The clark clips are only used to seal the bottoms of the casings. The tops are usually tied with butcher twine or hog rings. You can seal all casings from beef stick to bologna.

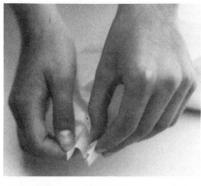 

First, casing is folded and trimmed to fit into clip. Place cas- ing into clip and squeeze tightly with pliers.

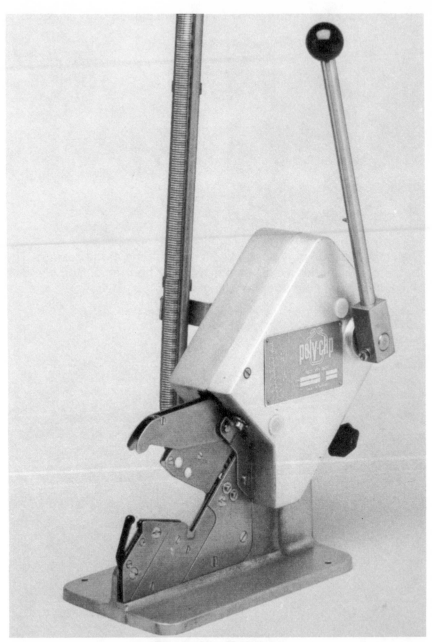

Single Clip Machine
This machine is designed to close salamis and bolognas. It can be used with natural or artificial casings. It is especially useful in smaller and medium-size plants as they don't require compressed air for operation. Manufactured by T.W. Kutter, Inc.

112

CHAPTER V

Selecting and Storing Meat

SELECTING MEAT AND STORAGE

The first and biggest secret to making a good sausage is the use of good grades of meat. It stands to reason that if you purchased a roast in the supermarket you would pick out the best you could find. A roast full of fat and gristle would not be very desirable; it would not be tasty and would cook away. It is foolish to see people make sausage with lots of leftover trimmings that contain mostly fat. This indeed makes bad sausage.

Sausage made with excessive fat and gristle will taste bad and cook away. A small amount of fat is desirable in a good roast as well as in good sausage. This helps to make it tender and juicy; no fat, on the other hand, will make the meat dry and also bad-tasting.

used in making sausage. They generally are very good grades of meat and are recommended for making good sausage.

These meats already contain a certain amount of fat. The ratio of fat and meat called for in these recipes generally runs about 25% fat and 75% meat. This is a good rule to keep in mind. Once in a while, a pork butt will have an excess amount of fat which can be trimmed off and thrown away. If you have the butcher grind your meat for you, always have him trim out the gristle, sinew, blood clots and excess fat, for they serve no useful purpose.

It is desirable to purchase the meat the same day you are going to make the sausage. If this isn't possible, try not to store the meat in your refrigerator for more than a couple of days, especially if it is already ground. Otherwise the meat will start turning a black or dark grey color. Pork against pork, or pork against any other meat, will start to turn black. This isn't very appealing to the eye, even though your meat isn't spoiled.

A regular meat cooler used by your butcher holds temperatures of around 32 degrees F. Your home refrigerator is usually kept around 40 degrees F. because of the vegetables and various items that would freeze at 32 degrees F. Do not store the meat too long before use.

When you make sausage, either fresh or smoked, always treat it as fresh meat. It is a good idea to set aside the amount of sausage that you will use in the next couple of days and freeze the rest.

Freezing helps to retard spoilage and seals in the flavor of the spices. It is highly recommended not to make any more sausage than you can use in a period of 4-6 weeks. After this period of time it has been found that the sausage will lose all its flavor. A sausage made using garlic as one of the ingredients will lose its flavor in a period of 6 weeks while stored in the freezer.

I have mentioned that freezing retards spoilage. You can actually spoil a product in your home freezer if it is kept there long enough. Your home freezer is usually kept about 0 degrees F., where a commercial freezer is kept at around minus 25 degrees F. or colder. At this temperature you can stop spoilage in a commercial freezer. As you can see, there are some important differences in comparing our home freezers and refrigerators against the ones used in commercial operations.

An important note should be made here about smoked sausage as well as smoked meat. Because meat or sausage is smoked, many people tend to think that this meat should last a lot longer. This is not true. The amount of extra time a smoked product will last is not even worth mentioning.

There is very little difference between smoked products and fresh meat products. Both should be treated as fresh meat. As you read the formulas for smoked sausage and meats, you will find that there are no great amounts of time involved in smoking a sausage. In fact, you might be surprised at the short amount of time that is required to smoke a sausage.

A plastic cutting board. Hardwood boards or tables are no longer acceptable for cutting meats as they help to breed bacteria. Plastic boards can be easily washed in a sink. Knife marks are scraped off with a dough scraper.

115

Pork Butts

The pork butt is the most widely-used meat in making sausage. For the most part, a regular pork butt is the type most generally available in the local super market. There is such a thing as fancy pork, but it is only available in markets that specialize in meat.

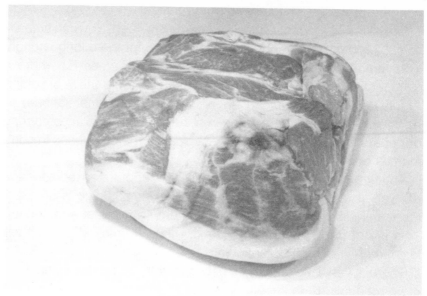

Regular Pork Butt

Fancy Pork Butt

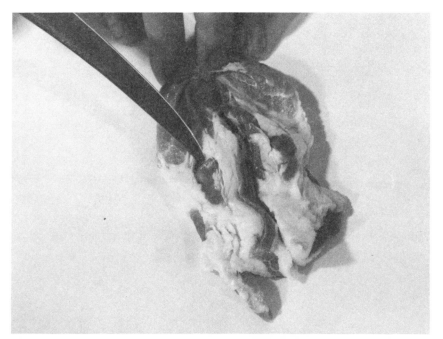

When boning a pork butt, try to be on the lookout for the gland, as shown above at the end of the boning knife. These glands are bitter, and should be removed when possible.

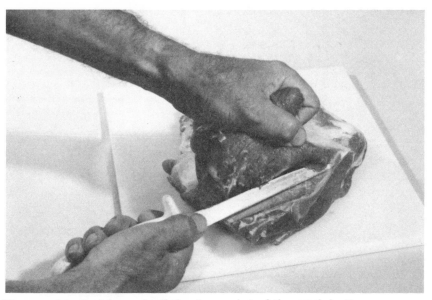

The meat is first boned off the top point of the pork butt.

The knife is then placed on the pork butt just behind the bone on top.

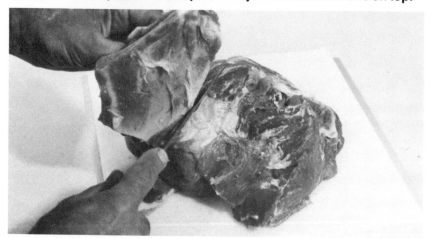

Meat is removed off the entire blade bone.

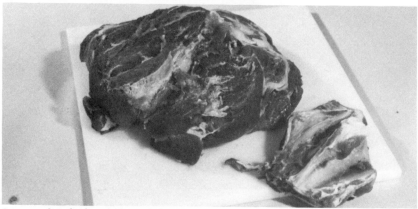

A completely boned pork butt.

REFRIGERATION
(ICE & ICE WATER)

Since this book generally has been written to supply information for sausage making and curing meats in the home, I feel that more detailed information should be given in reference to refrigeration, ice and ice water.

From the time an animal is slaughtered, you generally can assume that mother nature starts to take over; that is, the meat will start to deteriorate. By the use of refrigeration, ice or ice water, we can slow down this process, until the meat is processed or used up. For the most part, it is best to store the meats at between 34-38 degrees F., prior to processing. Just about all the formulas in this book specify that the temperature of the meat should be between 34-38 degrees F. during processing.

Naturally, if the meat is stored at these temperatures, part of the problem is eliminated. The ideal place to process meat or sausage is in a regular walk-in cooler since everything is cool and under refrigeration. Most of us, however, do not own our own coolers, so the next best thing to do is keep everything cool.

Knee operated lavatory

Foot pedal operated lavatory

SANITATION

The whole process of making sausage and curing meats depends a great deal on sanitation. Bacteria and molds are the result of very poor sanitation habits that literally destroy cured meat. These microorganisms are all around us and cannot be destroyed completely. Very good sanitation habits can prevent the growth and spread of bacteria.

Unknown to most people is the fact that a healthy butchered animal is generally sterile and fairly free of bacteria. It is at that time of processing, when the meat is exposed, that problems can begin. It is imperative that meat either be processed or placed under refrigeration as soon as possible.

Processing a recently-killed animal is especially important and critical when making dry-cured salami. It is only the bacteriological microorganisms of the animal itself that are required to give this type of salami the proper flavor or tang. Other unwanted organisms eliminate the consistent flavor of these types of sausages. Fresh meat is ideal for unwanted bacteriological growth that can cause rapid spoilage. Even though the butchered animal is virtually free of bacteria, these organisms can be transferred from the hide of the animal, the surfaces the meat comes in contact with, and even the hands and tools of the workers themselves.

Hair nets or hats should always be worn to reduce the chance of these problems. This would include covering a beard as well. One simple hair contains millions of unwanted bacteriological organisms. If you ever see green spots the size of quarters or half dollars in cured meat, someone did not properly wash their hands after leaving a washroom. It is that simple to contaminate meat. Not enough can be said about a good sanitation program.

Sanitation always should be kept at the highest possible level when making sausage. Always wash your equipment before using it. In using hot water to wash the equipment, be sure you let the equipment cool off before you start making sausage. Equipment not properly cooled will raise the temperature of the meat, and also make the sausage look greasy, no matter how lean a meat you are using. This is called smearing.

It is desirable to make sausage in the cooler hours of the day, either early morning or late evening. Avoid the heat of the day unless you are making sausage under refrigerated conditions. Try not to make sausage in temperatures above 70 degrees F. Always line up in advance all the spices, equipment, casing and whatever other items that will be needed to make sausage. Bring the meat out last, grind it, mix it, stuff it and then put it back in the refrigerator (unless you are going to smoke it).

Ice generally is used in the large sausage kitchen to keep the meat cool when chopping it in the large meat choppers. The RPM's of the cutting blades are so great that the meat temperatures start to rise and ice has to be introduced into the meat chopper to maintain 36-40 degrees F. temperatures.

As a point of interest, it takes about 3-4 minutes to mix the spices and chop 200 pounds of meat to the consistency of breakfast sausage. When you are using a hand meat grinder or a small electric grinder, you are generating heat as well. Since ice will not grind very well, simply make ice water using the ice itself to keep the temperatures of the meat at 34-38 degrees F. or whatever the formula calls for. After the meats are ground and mixed, it is best to keep them in the cooler until they are actually ready to use.

Maintaining the specific temperatures of 34-38 degrees F. also is very important when it comes to curing meats. When you allow the temperature to fall below 34 degrees F., the curing process itself stops. It is absolutely essential that the temperature is maintained above 34 degrees F. On the other hand, the temperature should not exceed 38-40 degrees F. This will cause the meat to start spoiling before it can be cured. It is just as important to maintain the temperature above 34 degrees F. as it is to keep it below 38-40 degrees F. If you maintain the temperature and follow the instructions as outlined in the formulas, you should never spoil any meat.

A separate refrigrator generally is needed if you are going to cure meat at home. The temperature required to prevent meat from spoiling is lower than the temperature needed to keep vegetables and fruit.

STUFFING SAUSAGE

After the meat is ground, the next step usually is the addition of the remaining ingredients that are to be mixed thoroughly with the meat. It is after this that some problems can be created unnecessarily.

Beginning with fresh sausage, it is inevitably stuffed into a casing after mixing. I don't know a single sausage maker who would make it any other way. The meat is ground, mixed, stuffed and placed in the cooler, all in quick order. Or it can be frozen if not intended for immediate use. However, when we get to smoked or cooked sausage, a good number of people have the idea that it is best to season the meat overnight. This procedure usually has been passed on from generation to generation with many family recipes.

Allowing the meat to season overnight causes the meat to set up and absorb all the liquid that you added to the mixture. The meat really does absorb the water, and then sets up like a slab of cement. Needless to say, it becomes exceedingly difficult to remove from the container, and equally difficult to pack into a sausage stuffer. The salt that is mixed with the meat is most definitely used as a binding agent in making sausage, in addition to flavoring the meat. This is not common knowledge; however, besides the salt and spices, the non-fat dry milk or soy protein concentrate will cause the meat to set up even more.

Remember, the longer you take to stuff the meat into a casing, the more problems you'll experience. It is best to get it into a casing right away.

When I first opened "The Hickory Shop" in Las Vegas, I, too, seasoned the meat overnight before stuffing. As our business grew we made more sausage and wound up mixing meat and stuffing sausage all day long. We could no longer allow the meat to season in the mixing tubs overnight because we just didn't have the room. We soon found that it made little difference whether the meat seasoned in the casing or a plastic tub; there was no difference in flavor whatsoever. Needless to say, we were pleasantly surprised. We figured that the key to the whole thing was the mixing of all the spices and ingredients properly.

We found that stuffing the sausage was most definitely faster and easier. At that point in time we had a sausage stuffer that held 20 lbs. of meat with a hand crank that would press the meat down and into the casing. It was far easier to stuff pliable, freshly-mixed meat into a casing than chunks of meat that had been allowed to set up all night.

Another thing we enjoyed was that the mess was over with in one day, so we had more time to do other things. If there was ever any one thing I disliked about sausage making, it's clean-up time. On top of this, we made better use of our smoker by using it every second day, rather than every day. We completely utilized its 300-lbs. capacity rather than smoking 100-150 lbs. a day.

When the Hickory Shop first opened, the meat was mixed by hand. We would add the ingredients and water as well. We really never measured the water, because we were more interested in mixing the meat to the right consistency. After mixing we took a handful of meat and made a fist. When the meat would squirt out between my fingers, it was at the right consistency for stuffing. It was no problem to stuff 100 lbs. of sausage in 10-15 minutes.

It was never this easy when the meat was allowed to season overnight as it came out of the containers in chunks. Then we had to be sure and pack it really well into the stuffer to eliminate all the air pockets. The litte extra water we added to the meat had no bearing on the good-quality sausage we always produced. It simply doesn't take much water to get the proper consistency of meat, especially a fresh sausage as opposed to a product you will smoke and cook.

Another important factor we discovered was that the temperature of the meat rose substantially during the sausage-making process. When you grind meat, the grinder itself produces heat. The ingredients we added were usually stored at room temperature, with the exception of the ice water (ice water was used to try and keep the temperature down).

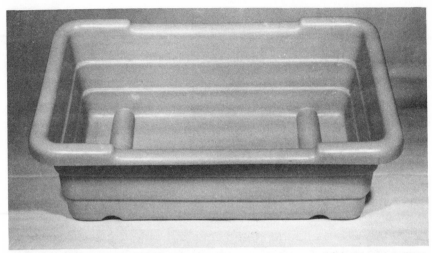

A 50 pound capacity mixing tub.

When making sausage, all spices should be premixed before starting. Above shows 4 bags of premixed spices to be mixed with 25 pounds of meat per bag. Bags contain all spices, soy protein concentrate and cure.

A bag of premixed spices can be placed into a container and mixed with water very well. This is preferred and will give you better distribution rather than trying to mix the spices dry with the meat.

Premixed spices simply poured over the top of the meat in a mixing tub.

25 pounds of meat in a 50 pound mixing tub. Note the adequate room in tub to prevent meat from falling out on the floor or table while mixing.

Placing meat into a sausage stuffer.

126

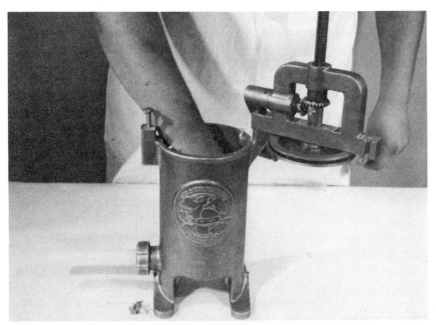

Meat should be well packed into the stuffer using the fist to pack it down. This helps to eliminate air pockets and stop back pressure from building up.

A generous amount of water should be introduced into the casing before placing it on the stuffer nozzle.

Before putting casings on the nozzle be sure you slop plenty of water all over the nozzle. This lubricates the nozzle and will allow the casing to go on easier.

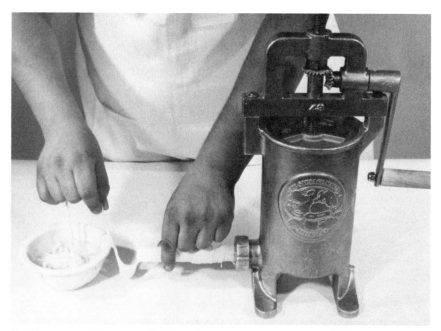

Putting a casing over the nozzle.

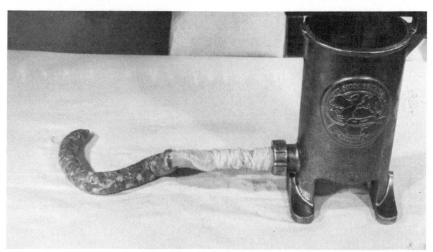

When using a long casing for stuffing, air pockets tend to form in the casing on the nozzle before you are half through or sooner. A lack of water will cause this.

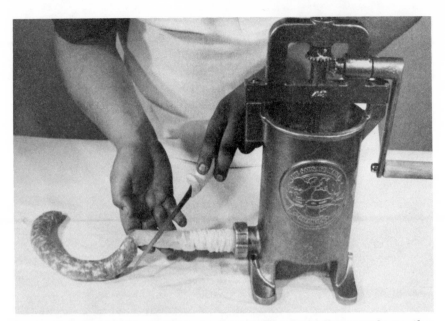

To elmininate the air pockets in the casing, hold the nozzle on the bottom and tap the air bubble with the backside of a boning knife. A needle can also be used to puncture the air bubble.

Note that the casings are at the back end of the nozzle after stuffing an amount of sausage. During the course of stuffing sausage, always try to keep the casing to the front of the nozzle where the meat comes out. This will eliminate air pockets and breakage of the casings.

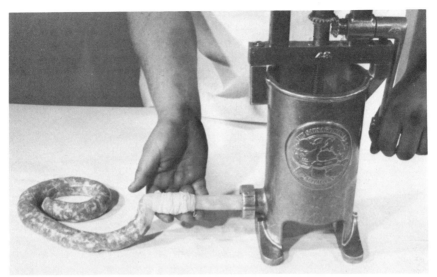

Note the proper positioning of the casing on the nozzle. It should be noted that the casings will come off easier when being stuffed with meat.

When linking sausage, it is best to have all the meat stuffed into the casings.

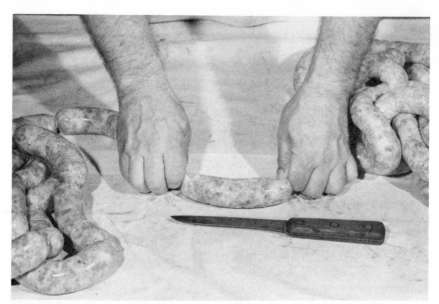

To make a consistent size of link sausage, it is a good idea to make marks on your table for the actual size you require. In the above photo the blade of the boning knife is used to measure each link.

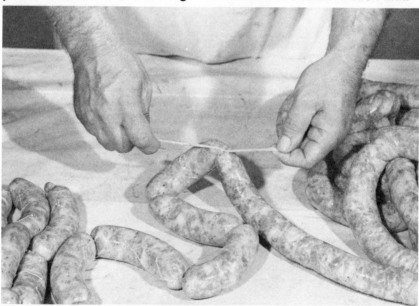

The sausage in the above photograph is linked about 4 to the pound. Note that one long casing has been linked and is being tied together with one that is unlinked. It is best to link in this manner and have one very long continuous linked sausage.

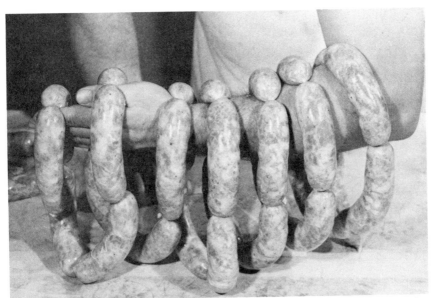

Sausage linked 4 to a pound, picked up by fours and placed over the arm, the proper way to pick up sausage. Take note that the sausage is touching the table; this prevents unwinding of the links. Sausage is never hung on a smokestick in anything but even numbers (2's, 4's, 6's) or the links will unwind.

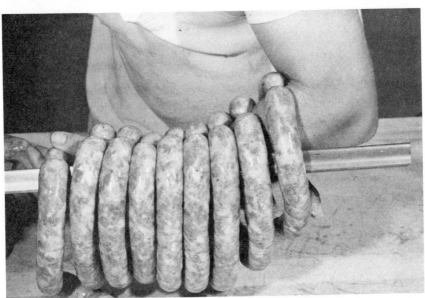

The proper way to place sausage on a smokestick. Note the stick is being placed to the side and under the arm.

133

When removing the sausage from the arm to the stick, it is advisable to let one end of the stick rest on a table or counter top. There are few people who can remove the sausage and hold a full smokestick of sausage with one hand. One end of the stick in the above photograph is resting on a counter top.

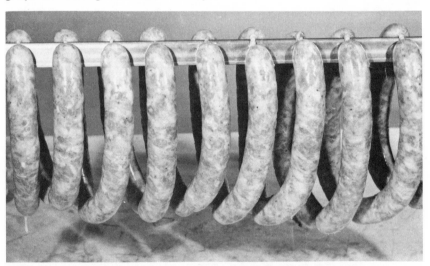

After being placed on a smokestick, the sausage should be properly spaced for smoking. Pieces of sausage touching each other will not acquire the smokey color at the points of contact.

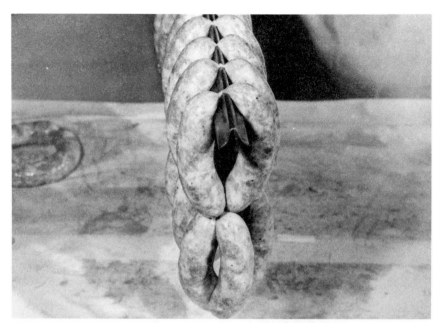

When placing linked sausage on a smokestick, the sausage on each end may be twisted in the above manner to prevent unwinding of the links.

When making round links the sausage is cut in longer pieces when coming off the nozzle. Be sure you have a few inches of casing on each end for easy tying. Needless to say, a bundle of casings will not go as far when making round links as a good deal of the casing is used for tying knots.

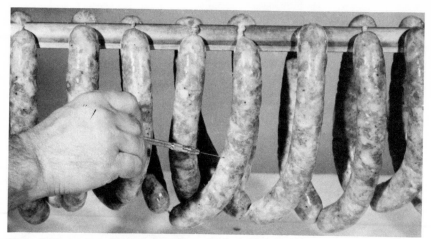

Air bubbles may also be eliminated with a simple household needle.

As a point of interest this photograph was made of a piston (plunger) with meat around it. This is a picture of a plunger after stuffing sausage and is a common occurence in the largest sausage kitchens with the most expensive sausage stuffers. Some seepage must be allowed in order to keep back pressure from building up. Great emphasis is placed on packing meat into a sausage stuffer, but there are always air pockets that cannot be completely removed, which cause back pressure to build up.

Don't be afraid to prick out the air pockets, because they will seal themselves and help keep the juices in the sausages during the cooking or smoking processes. The pin-pricking applies to all casings, natural or synthetic; the size of the sausage or salami makes no difference.

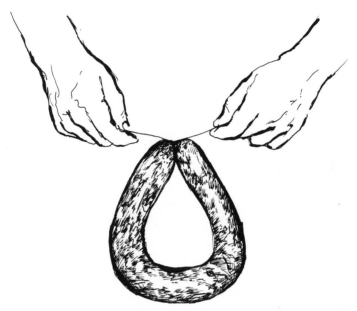

When linking a sausage, this type link must have at least 3 knots tied in it.

Hand-Operated Sausage Stuffers
15-Lb. Sausage Stuffer

The above sausage stuffer is a one-speed stuffer. The piston goes up and down at the same speed. It is similar to the Dick stuffer in all other respects. It is designed for home use or for a sausage kitchen making 500-600 lbs. of sausage per week. Manufactured by The Sausage Maker, Inc.

30-Lb. Sausage Stuffer

The Dick sausage stuffer is manufactured in Germany. It is a two-speed, geared sausage stuffer ideal for a sausage kitchen producing around 1500 pounds of sausage per week. The stuffer is geared for the piston (or sausage press) to come down slowly during stuffing. When it has to be refilled, the handle is changed to another gear and the piston comes up quickly. Available up to 30-lb. capacity.

138

5-Lb. Sausage Stuffer

This 5-lb. capacity sausage stuffer is the smallest one made using gears to do the work. It is ideal for home use. Manufactured by The Sausage Maker, Inc.

3-Lb. Sausage Stuffer

This 3-lb. capacity sausage stuffer is somewhat harder to work with since it is not powered by gears. However, when the correct amount of water is mixed with the meat, then stuffed quickly, it is an excellent machine. Manufactured by The Sausage Maker, Inc.

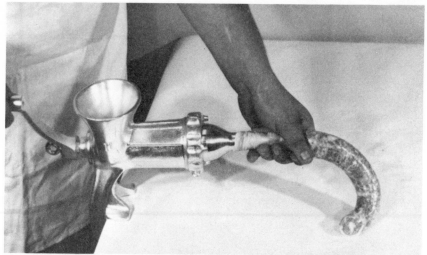

Sausage Stuffer Attachment for Meat Grinder

The above meat grinder and stuffing horn were intended to save money by omitting the purchase of a sausage stuffer. However, this type of apparatus has many drawbacks. The meat must first be ground and spices mixed with it. After this, the meat has to be stuffed through the grinder again to get it into a casing. So, the meat is ground twice. Additionally, you can't properly stuff a large-diameter salami or summer sausage casing. Lastly, it is a very slow process and should only be used if you are going to make just a few pounds of sausage. Recommended only if you have a lot of time.

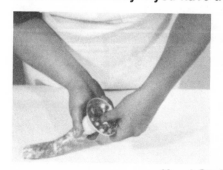 

Hand Stuffing Horn

The array of stuffer tubes shown above are slower yet. However, there are a lot of people who use them and are quite happy with them.

140

The Water-Powered Sausage Stuffer
The Zuber E-Z Pakmobile, a water-powered sausage stuffer, has a 100-lb. capacity and is portable. It is ideal for a small sausage kitchen.

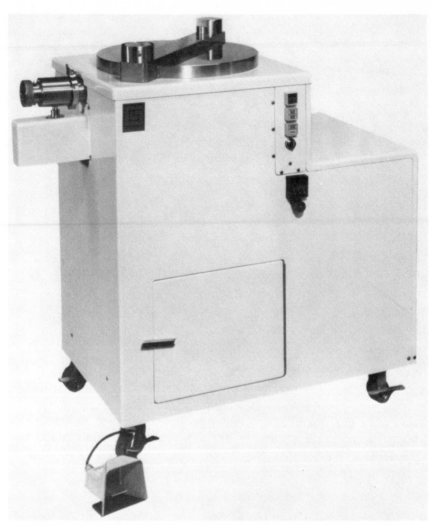

Grant-Letchworth 200-Lb. Capacity Electric Sausage Stuffer
The above is an all-stainless steel sausage stuffer that is controlled
by electric push buttons or a foot switch for a hands-free operation.
Manufactured by Grant-Letchworth.

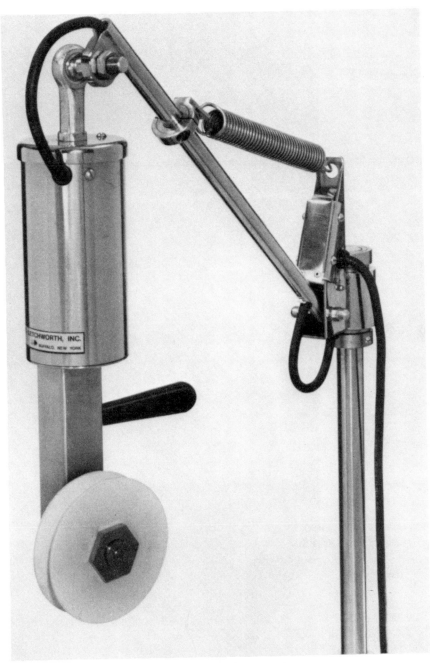

Automatic Casing Applier
The above applies natural casings in half the time it takes to do it by hand. Manufactured by Grant-Letchworth.

50-Lb. Hydraulic Sausage Stuffer
This small unit is completely mobile and of all stainless steel construction. Manufactured by the Smith Equipment Co.

GRINDING MEAT

The various formulas for making sausage in this book actually spell out the size of the chunks of meat that are to be cut up or ground. The size of the meat chunks usually is determined by the ethnic group that a particular sausage represents. For the most part, the recipes in this book are formulated so that they can be made at home using a coarse grind of meat. There are no set rules for the size that meat should be ground to; some people like a fine grind and many people prefer the coarse grind. Some people prefer fat in their sausage and a lot of formulas call for it. Other people do not like fat, but still prefer the coarse grind.

It generally is a good idea to keep all the lean meat separate from the fat meat. You can grind the fat meat very fine and the lean meat coarse. This will give you a lean-looking sausage as the smaller particles of fat will not appear on the surface of the casing, but the sausage will still contain the amount of fat needed to make a good sausage. It is strictly up to individual preference as to the size of meat one wishes to grind, as well as the size of grinding plates one may have on hand at the time.

When making a dry-cured or cooked salami, the grinding of the meat becomes very important. Without the proper handling of the meat, we cannot get the finished product we are seeking.

A number of sausages and luncheon meats have a special appearance that many of us are used to seeing. The mortadella sausage, or luncheon meat, if you wish, would look exactly like bologna if it weren't for the cubes of fat that are mixed with the meat. The same is true for Chinese sausage. It also calls for cubes of fat as part of the formula which gives it a special appearance. Probably more familiar to most people is the cooked or dry-cured salami that shows the distinctive white specks mixed in with the meats.

Special care is required to acquire these distinctive looks in these special products. It is positively not just a case of grinding the meat. The fat products used to give these sausages that special appearance must be very cold and even slightly frozen before they are ground up. The fat usually is ground last and mixed in only after the lean meat and spices already have been mixed. Great care should be taken not to mix the meat too long. The longer the meat

A large meat chopper. This machine can chop 200 pounds of meat to the consistency of a milk shake in about 5 minutes.

An enlarged picture of the cutting blades used in the above meat chopper. These blades are honed once or twice a week and are kept in razor sharp condition.

is mixed, the more heat we generate, and our fat specks start to break down and smearing takes place.

To mix 100 lbs. of meat in a mechanical mixer along with the fat, a period of one or two minutes is adequate. It doesn't take any longer mixing by hand, providing you're not trying to mix 50 or 100 lbs. You are far better off to mix 25 lbs. of meat in a container built to hold 50 lbs. You'll have more room to work and do a much better job.

Mixing the meat by hand also helps to raise the temperature. Then, of course, there is stuffing the meat into a casing, hanging it on a smokestick and simply allowing it to hang at room temperature until it is completely dry. By the time I finish the last stuffer full of meat, the first batch of sausage is already almost dry.

Keep in mind the meat originally came out of a 38-40 degree F. cooler and is almost at room temperature by the time you've finished.

Does it really make any sense at all to place it back in the cooler and lower the temperature back to 38-40 degrees F., then take it out the next day and hold it at room temperature until it's dried properly, allowing the temperature to again rise to 65-70 degrees F.? Not really.

You're better off allowing the sausage to dry completely at room temperature in the first place, then placing it in the smoker.

Practically all the recipes in *Great Sausage Recipes and Meat Curing* tell you to dry the sausage at room temperature before placing it into a preheated smoker. The smoker is preheated so the drying process can be completed at relatively low temperatures — usually in the 120-130 degree F. range.

Only the semi-dry cured or dry-cured sausages are packed into containers since they have to ferment. Needless to say, a pretty good sausage stuffer is required with some sort of crank and press. Air pockets must be removed and more pressure can be applied when stuffing the casings.

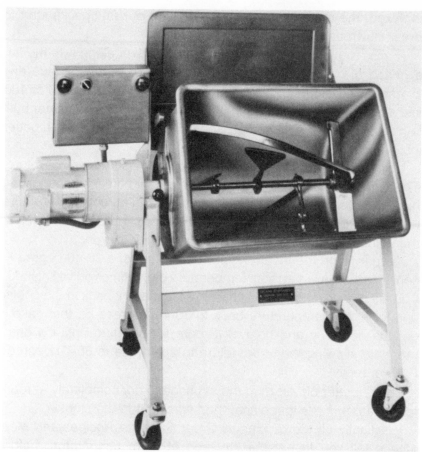

Double-Action Mixer

The above is a double-action mixer that allows a smaller heat buildup in the product being mixed. This machine is capable of blending 150-lbs. of meat with the seasoning in just a few minutes. It is ideal for small sausage kitchens. Manufactured by Leland Co.

FROZEN MEAT

Over the years a lot of inquiries have been addressed to me concerning the use of fresh frozen meat in sausage making. In regard to sausage making, freezing meat has little or no effect on the end product. Freezing is a good way to store meat that is purchased at a good price. It is also handy if you've over-purchased. The meat can be thawed and used when needed. This also includes any kind of game meat.

It is worthy to note that I have thawed meat a number of times only to have found out that I thawed too much. I simply placed it back in the freezer and used it at a later date. I found that I could thaw and re-freeze fresh meat up to three times with no ill effect when making sausage.

It should be pointed out, however, that a residue of blood was left in the container that the meat was thawed in. This is a common occurence when thawing meat and the liquid that comes out of the meat during this period is actually the flavor of the meat that is being lost. It is best to put this liquid back into the meat and mix it if you are going to make sausage. Obviously, if the meat is not going to be used and is re-frozen, some flavor will be lost.

It is desirable to thaw meat at around 35 degrees F. The liquid lost during thawing will be kept to a minimum. If you thaw at room temperature you will find an excessive amount of liquid being leeched from the meat.

In regard to smoked sausage or a cured and smoked piece of meat, it is not a good idea to thaw and re-freeze these products. These types of products can only be frozen once after they're made. Thawing and re-freezing can cause the meat to become mushy. It is best to thaw fresh meat and make a sausage and then use it up rather than making a larger amount and freezing it.

A meat cart loaded with meat boxes. Can be used to store meats or for the curing of sausage meats before stuffing.

All-metal meat storage truck. This truck has a capacity of over 1200 pounds.

MEAT COMBINATIONS

As with the grinding of meat and its size, there also are no set rules as to the type of meat that a person should use in making sausage; that includes the fresh, smoked, dry or semi-dry types. Any combination of meat can be used to make these various sausages. People who have an excess of lamb, rabbit, wild game meat and whatever else there is in the line of meat may use them in making sausage.

Unknown to a lot of people today, a great deal of poultry meat is being used in making the very fine-texture sausages, better known as hot dogs or wieners. Probably the more important thing to remember is the meat and fat ratio required to make these various sausages. In most cases, no matter what type meat is being used, the spices or seasonings that are used give a particular sausage its identity. If one wants to think about it, most luncheon meat and sausage is made of pork; the seasonings and spices are what make them so different from one another.

CHAPTER VI

Ingredients Permissible in Meat Processing

WHOLE SPICES

Whole spices are used in a number of sausages and smoked meat. Besides providing desirable flavors, they also add to the appearance of the product. To name but a few, coarse pepper is used on a pepper loaf or beef; whole pepper in various salamis; bay leaves in pickled pig's feet and pickling spices in corned beef.

GROUND SPICES

Fine ground spices are nearly impossible to purchase in a supermarket or a local restaurant supply house. Most generally, these fine ground spices are used only by sausage makers and are available only from the manufacturers who provide this trade with various products as well as spices.

Fine ground spices have the ability to blend in with the meat so completely they cannot be seen. A case in point is the wiener. The formula calls for approximately nine different spices. Could you imagine a wiener with nine different whole spices in it? Probably more important, the fine ground spices give off more flavor more readily, because grinding breaks down some of the flavor cells of the whole spice and starts the process of releasing the flavor.

GARLIC

From time to time I've had people ask me about the use of fresh garlic cloves versus granulated garlic. There is absolutely no question in my mind: fresh garlic is better. There are several things to consider, however, and the decision is solely up to you.

Commercially, there is no question that granulated garlic is more desirable, for obvious reasons — you don't have to peel it. For home use, I never bother to peel it. I simply weigh what I need, place it in an electric blender with a little water, and liquify it. There is practically no trace of the peelings using this process. There is no question that the aroma of fresh garlic and hickory smoke is unbeatable.

By the same token, in my weaker moments, I frequently use granulated garlic when making fresh Polish sausage. After letting

153

the sausage cool overnight, the liquid of the meat activates the garlic and it is virtually impossible to tell if fresh garlic or dried granulated garlic has been used after cooking. Both are equally good. The only difference between the two is that granulated garlic gives off very little aroma, but the flavor is there.

On the plus side for granulated garlic is the fact that it is always dry and much easier to use. It also stores well, providing it is kept in a container free from air, light and humidity. If these three conditions are not met, the garlic will deteriorate, as it is the most volatile of all spices.

Fresh garlic, which is so good, simply doesn't keep well for any period of time. It always dries out and loses its aroma. I always find myself throwing most of it out. Regarding its use in a sausage formula, the same weight is always used, either fresh or granulated; I find it to be equal in flavor. If a recipe calls for 1 ounce of garlic, you can use either fresh or granulated.

DEHYDRATED CHOPPED ONIONS

We have the same situation with dehydrated onions as we have with garlic. The considerations are the same for commercial or home use. I find it easy to use at home or in sausage making. It is clean and ready to use; simply add a little water to the dehydrated onion and allow it to reconstitute. No question — the dehydrated chopped onions are best for sausage making as they are always in uniform pieces, easy to store and easy to use.

SALT

Salt is one of the most important products in the making of a good sausage as well as in curing meat. In reality, salt has to be considered a spice because it definitely enhances the flavor of meat. It also can serve as a preservative and comes in flake, rock or granulated form.

In order to be sure that you are using a high grade of salt, you can dissolve one or two tablespoons in a glass of water. You have a good grade of salt if the water is clear. If the water is cloudy, you have a low grade of salt that probably contains various heavy metals. Do not use iodized salt for making sausage or curing meats. Canning salt or kosher flake salt is best in making sausage or curing meats since they dissolve more completely.

Purified salt is used by commercial sausage kitchens as a safeguard to be sure they are using a good grade of salt.

It is extremely important that the salt levels, along with the cure, in semi-dry or dry-cured formulas are never changed. These recipes are formulated to give the meat a special flavor and more important, to help destroy trichinosis if it is present in the pork. During the dry cure process, the salt also discourages the growth of unwanted organisms that could alter the tang or flavor of the sausage.

Probably most important of all, salt acts as a binding agent when making dry-cured meat or sausage. For this reason alone it'll probably be a long time before we will be able to see low-salt sausages that are dry cured. Cooked and smoked sausages can be made with less salt because there are a number of products added to it to help bind it after it's processed. These products include corn syrup solids, non-fat dry milk, soy protein concentrate and dextrose. These ingredients combine during the cooking cycle and become one big binding agent which allows the use of less salt.

Salt is also instrumental in modifying some of the protein in processed meat in order to maintain or hold more water. (This does not include dry-cured products.)

As a preservative, it takes extremely high levels of salt, in the 6-8% range, to preserve meat. Normally most sausage is made using 3% or less salt and has to be refrigerated to maintain its freshness. There is very little information regarding the extra-preservative qualities salt would give to a product. This is probably due to the fact that salt can vary a great deal from one product to another.

It is interesting to note that when any kind of meat is mixed with salt and spices, then allowed to season overnight, the end result will be the meat "sets up" or becomes very stiff. This is especially true of dry or semi-dry sausages that have to ferment for a day or so.

It is of extreme importance to note that all the recipes and formulas of this book are based on the usage of granulated salt. This is especially critical in the 10 lb. recipes, since they specify the use of salt in tablespoons. The weight of a tablespoon of granulated salt is greater than a tablespoon of kosher (flaked). The difference between these two salts is great enough to change the end result of the product.

SWEETENERS

Sweetners have a variety of uses in the making of sausage or the curing and smoking of meat. They are available in a wide variety of forms. To name but a few, powdered dextrose can be used as a browning agent in the fresh breakfast or country sausage. When fried, this sausage will have a more even brown color to it.

Powdered dextrose is only 70% as sweet as regular sugar, and also is used in processing dry-cured or semi-dry cured sausages. Powdered dextrose is an ideal nutrient for lactic acid organisms that assist fermentation in these sausages and give us the desired tang or flavor. Dextrose is much heavier than plain sugar and forces itself into the cells of the meat. It is useful to mention here that dextrose also is a useful nutrient for the bacteria which reduce nitrate to nitrite when meats are cured.

Sweeteners also are used to reduce the harshness of salt and to add flavor as well. For example, maple sugar is used in small amounts to produce a bacon with a special flavor and aroma. Carmelized sugar is a sweetener and used primarily to promote browning in cured meats that are smoked or just cooked in a smokehouse.

CORN SYRUP SOLIDS

Corn syrup solids are useful in sausage making, as they have excellent binding qualities when sausage is being cured at lower temperatures. They are especially important in the semi-dry or dry-cured process as they not only add flavor, but help to support the fermentation process. Corn syrup solids help to hold the color of the meat, which is especially important commercially. Fluorescent lights in the meat markets tend to bleach out the meat, but corn syrup solids help to hold the cured color for a longer period of time. There also are a number of artificial sweeteners that are used to provide flavor, but without the accompanying browning, as it is not required at times.

SOY PROTEIN CONCENTRATE OR NON-FAT DRY MILK

A major fallacy is that sausage can contain a lot of cereal. This not only is foolish but not even possible. What you have is a very poor-quality sausage as a result of this condition. A poor-quality sausage, especially when eaten cold or without cooking, has a mushy taste to it and probably contains a good deal of by-products and fat. This gives you that mushy taste that people mistake for cereals.

In fact, the so-called cereals used in making sausage today generally are either non-fat dry milk or soy protein concentrates. If you take a good hard look at these two most widely-used items in making sausage, you will discover that they are really good as ingredients when it comes to making sausage, besides serving a very useful purpose.

Today, most doctors would rather see people use non-fat dry milk rather than whole milk. As for soy protein concentrate, it is just what the name implies. Plus, on a pound-per-pound basis against meat, it contains up to 250% more protein, besides being tasteless. The fact of the matter is the USDA has regulations which permit the use of only 3½% of either of these products at one time per 100 pounds of sausage. These products have a definite, useful purpose in making sausage.

Have you ever wondered why the hamburger you purchase in a restaurant always manages to stay so nice and round and juicy and almost the same size as it was raw? It's not at all like the hamburger we make at home, which has a tendency to crumble and shrink, with the natural juices remaining in the frying pan.

Here is where soy protein concentrates do the job. They help to bind the meat together as well as retain the natural juices of the meat. The job that non-fat dry milk or soy protein concentrates perform in making sausage is very useful indeed. These products are rarely used when making a fresh sausage, because it would give the sausage that bland and greasy look. If this doesn't bother you, however, it's really a good idea to use them. These items are only used in sausage that is going to be smoked and cooked, and the milk or protein has no effect on the appearance of the sausage other than making it look nice and plump.

158

For example, let's make 100 lbs. of sausage to see what effect soy protein concentrates or non-fat dry milk have. In a 100 lb. formula we would use 100 lbs. of meat, about 2-3 lbs. of salt and spices, about 3 lbs. of soy protein concentrate, 1 lb. casings and 10 lbs. water. After the sausage is made we have a net weight of 117 lbs. of sausage.

We now take this 117 lbs. of sausage and smoke it. The sausage is then removed from the smoker, cooled off and weighed, and our end result will be around 105 lbs. What happens here is that during the smoking process the sausage will have shrinkage. The 10 lbs. of water you have used to lubricate the meat for stuffing has left the sausage in this process, but we retained the natural juice of the meat.

If we didn't use non-fat dry milk or soy protein concentrates the end product would be about 85 lbs. of sausage, and it would be quite dry. So the soy protein concentrates or non-fat dry milk help to retain the natural juices of the meat as well as bind it together.

If you are going to use a non-fat dry milk for a binder, your local dairy is usually the only place you can buy it today. The milk has to be a very fine powder and not the granules used for making milk at home. Better still, it should have the consistency of corn starch.

Some people like to use more non-fat dry milk or soy protein concentrate in their formulas. There are limits to observe. If you use more than 5% soy protein concentrate or more than 12% non-fat dry milk, you will alter the taste of the sausage.

PREMIXED SPICES & CURES

As with the casing industry, the spices and cures of today have become an industry in themselves. This may not seem too important to the average person, especially in regard to the premixed spices that these companies supply. Many people feel they can easily premix their own spices for whatever sausage they may wish to make, and rightly so. The formulas in this book allow you to do this.

On the other hand, the cures that one might need using the formulas of this book are not so easily mixed in small quantities and would be more accurately premixed by the manufacturer. The premixed spices and cures have a definite role in making sausage and curing meats. When making larger amounts of sausage, say 500 or 1000 lb. a week, the weighing of the spices can become somewhat of a problem. Not only is this a time-consuming job, but there also is the chance of error by the person weighing the spices, not to mention the large inventories of the various spices that need to be on hand. The 500 or 1000 lbs. of various types of sausage one may produce in any given week is a substantial amount for the small kitchen. On the other hand, a sausage manufacturer making sausage by the tens of thousands of pounds of these same products would really have a problem weighing spices. Naturally, this is where these companies come into the picture.

The manufacturers of premixed seasonings and cures not only have their products to supply, but practically all of them offer you the technological advice that is sometimes required. These companies can offer you a premixed spice or cure of any kind and the formulation for it. In addition, if you have a special formula that you want premixed, they will do that as well and will keep your formula in confidence. You will always have the guarantee from these companies that your private formula will meet all the specifications you require or they will refund your money. This also includes refunding the money that may have been spent on the meat to manufacture the product.

Probably the greatest service that spice companies provide for sausage kitchens and food processors is bacteria-free spices. The average sausage maker, professional or amateur, knows nothing of this and simply never hears about it. A large sausage kitchen or

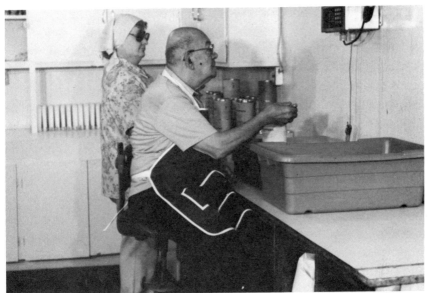

Jo (Janik) Carducci and Uncle Abe weighing and pre-packaging seasoning at The Sausage Maker, Inc.

A Small Ribbon Blender

The above is a ribbon blender used to blend large amounts of spices into sausage seasonings. It is capable of blending 5 cubic feet of product at one time—enough seasoning to make 8,000 lbs. of sausage. Spices packed into 100-lb. or larger containers tend to lump or cake up; hence, a ribbon blender is needed to blend the spices and break up the lumps.

161

food processor, producing thousands of pounds of product, is fully aware of how easily bacteria can spoil a product and reduce its shelf life. Bacteria is a fact of life and usually finds its way into a product by itself, so why shorten the shelf life of the product by not using bacteria-free spices or purified salt?

If you've never given spices very much thought, think about where they come from. They are supplied to us from all over the world, including countries whose health standards are not nearly as rigid as ours. In fact, some of the countries that supply spices have health standards so low, that they are almost nonexistent.

Spices are grown in soil and are not only subject to bacteria but insects as well. These insects cannot always be seen by the human eye. Some spice companies even own their own plantations on a world-wide scale in order to regulate the growth and bring you a fine product.

I think it also should be noted that these premixed seasonings are available today in the form of an oil. In fact, when you are buying these premixed seasonings, almost all of them will come to you on a sugar base, mixed with these oils. The plain old spices, however, still are available to you, if you desire.

The curing of meat and making of sausage can become quite an elaborate process today, and most of these companies can supply you with all the equipment needed to process these products, or the information on where to go and buy it. There is no question that, of all the industries surrounding sausage making and meat curing, the suppliers of premixed spices and cures definitely are the most valuable. As with most suppliers for this business, they also require high minimums to purchase their products.

PERMISSIBLE INGREDIENTS

Self-service meat counters first appeared during the years of the Second World War, as there was a definite manpower shortage. Truly, it was easier to have one person slice and prepack luncheon meats and then place them in a refrigerated counter. Clearly, this was a way of using manpower wisely, rather than to slice various luncheon meats for each customer while sometimes having two or three clerks waiting to use the same slicing machine.

At first, the public rebelled against this new idea of a pre-packaged product, but very soon accepted it—especially when the meat counters no longer contained the big slabs of bacon or luncheon meats to be sliced as each customer desired. Problems began to develop, however, as these pre-packaged sliced meats began to lose their attractive cured color after a day or two. It was very quickly recognized that the deteriorative effects of air and light would have to be overcome.

ERYTHORBATE AND ASCORBATES

For years, the fruit packers have used ascorbic acid and isoascorbic acid as color preservatives. It was felt that these products, which are a part of the vitamin C family, could become very important in achieving more attractive and longer-lasting color in cured and smoked meat.

It was soon found out, however, that because the curing solution contained nitrite, both the nitrite and ascorbic acid were uselessly depleted and nothing was accomplished. In further experimentation, it was then found that using only the salts of these acids was an effective way to prolong the color of cured meats. It is extremely important to note that these salts will not deepen the color of the meat beyond its natural color or prevent spoilage by bacteria.

The use of these products is approved by The Meat Inspection Division of the United States Department of Agriculture. It takes a very small amount of these salts to accelerate the development of color during the curing process and to help immensely in extending the color stability against deterioration from air and light. These products most definitely have to be considered in a commercial sausage kitchen. For use at home, however, there is no benefit to be gained by using these salts. Clearly, they are for commercial use only.

In recent years it was hoped that ascorbates might be the substitute for nitrites in curing meats. A great deal of experimentation was completed in England, using ascorbates to cure meats. Unfortunately, it has been found that by themselves, ascorbates clearly cannot do the same job that nitrites perform. It will be very difficult to find a single product that can perform the four or five steps of nitrites. However, it has been found that using these salts in cured bacon definitely reduces nitrosamine formation during frying. The chemical name of isoascorbic acid has become sodium erythorbate, and sodium ascorbate replaces ascorbic acid. These products are manufactured by Charles Pfizer & Co., Inc., New York, New York.

MONOSODIUM GLUTAMATE (MSG)

Monosodium glutamate, better known as MSG, is another product that has come under close scrutiny over the years. A great deal of bad press has been given to this product by people who know very little or nothing about it. As with nitrites, the benefits this product can provide have been conveniently omitted.

Little do the health-food faddists, organic gardeners or consumer groups know that MSG is simply made of beets or molasses made of beets. In fact, practically all the food we eat already contains glutamate.

For instance, glutamate can be found in all poultry, fish, milk products, red meat and most probably all vegetables. Are we then to give up eating food altogether? I think not. Our body even manufactures glutamate, much the same as it does nitrite.

Previous to its popularity, glutamate was used in the Orient for thousands of years. It has been produced from wheat and corn at one time or another.

To begin with, MSG is made starting with plain old natural food substances. A fermentation process is employed and the end result is a substance looking very much like salt or sugar. It should be noted, however, that MSG is very much different from salt or sugar, which add flavor to food. MSG's role in food is to sort of wake up and enhance the flavor that is already there. I find it difficult to call MSG a chemical, as the above-mentioned groups do. It is clearly a food. For home use, a half-teaspooon per pound of food is adequate. It can be used much the same as salt, before or after cooking.

POTASSIUM CHLORIDE

Potassium chloride is a salt with most of the same properties of sodium chloride (common table salt). The big difference between the two is that sodium gives us the salt taste we know so well. Potassium has a bitter flavor. In addition, potassium chloride is at least 20 times as expensive as sodium chloride.

When a mixture of sodium chloride and a smaller amount of potassium chloride is used, along with various other products that help mask the bitterness of potassium chloride, it is possible to reduce the amount of salt in sausage without altering the flavor.

Even at this time, a number of products are being tested to reduce salt as much as 50% in sausage making. There is no question that over a period of time a product will be found to replace the good taste of salt.

WATER

For the most part, water is simply taken for granted. This should not be the case, because it acts as the carrier for various ingredients, such as brines. In an earlier chapter, impure salt was discussed as a carrier of metals which could interfere with the palatability of meat.

Pure water will have a pronounced effect on these products as well. In a USDA plant, the water is tested from time to time as part of the USDA program.

PHOSPHATES

Disodium phosphate is another ingredient used commercially to decrease the amount of cooked juices escaping from cured hams, picnics, loins, or these very same products when canned. Phosphates have the ability to increase the water-holding capability of muscle protein and that is why they are used. This isn't a product for home use, but is used widely commercially.

To put it in much simpler terms, we often see a cured ham labeled "water added." Does that mean we are getting a ham full of water? Common sense tells us that when we slice this "water added" ham, we most certainly do not have a puddle of water around it or on the table. It simply means that the ingredients like cure, erythorabate and phosphates were dissolved in water and then the ham was pumped its usual 10 or 12 percent of its green weight. There is nothing unusual about this, except when they are smoking and cooking, these hams can lose as much as 15% of the green weight.

In other words, 100 lbs. of hams could easily be reduced to 85 lbs. in a smokehouse. This clearly is too much shrinkage and not acceptable for a number of reasons. If you were smoking 10,000 lbs. of ham, as some of the commercial meat packers do, you would lose about 1500 lbs. of meat in the smokehouse. There are not too many businesses that can stand that kind of a loss.

Even with the use of phosphates, one should expect to have 5% shrinkage, which is more tolerable and doesn't increase the price of the product so dramatically. About all "water added" really means is that someone is trying to sell you a smoked ham of about the same weight as before it was smoked.

I think it is also important to note that government regulations specifically state that products like ham, pork loin or butts shall not contain more moisture in the finished product than the fresh, uncured product.

SECRET RECIPES

There are a great many people and sausage makers who have their own secret recipes for making a specific sausage. Actually, these secrets are not as well-kept as they may think. Over the years, I have had a great many people ask me about a particular sausage that is traditional to some section of this country or to some specific ethnic group. Obviously, I cannot know all the sausage recipes, but there is sometimes a simple way to find out these much-guarded secrets.

To begin with, practically every sausage made has salt and pepper in it. So now you already have the first two ingredients. Take the simple breakfast sausage; it too has salt and pepper, but the sage you add makes it breakfast sausage. Italian sausage also has salt and pepper, but adding fennel seed makes it Italian. Either of these sausages can be made mild, hot, or very hot by simply adding hot cayenne pepper.

There are a great number of people who simply make a sausage with meat, salt and pepper. Smoke or the meat itself can be the primary flavor here. When it's a smoked sausage, Prague Powder No. 1 or some equal product also contributes.

By law, meat processors or sausage makers must put an ingredient label on all the sausage they make, either fresh or smoked. They must state if they are using cures and salt, etc. In some cases they will put on a key spice they use in the sausage.

By the same token, setting aside all salt, pepper, and cures, some people can easily detect the other spices. Let's say you detect sage in a breakfast sausage you would like to duplicate. If you can do this, you may go to any recipe in *Great Sausage Recipes* and locate a formula telling you how much of this spice to use. You will then have an idea of how to make this "secret" breakfast sausage. This is a way to start.

It is not a bad idea to get several people to taste a sausage, then have them write their spice guesses down on pieces of paper and compare notes. With the exception of a few sausages, the most a person would be trying to detect is one or maybe two spices. Obviously, you couldn't do this with wieners or bologna, as they may contain 6, 7 or even 10 different spices, but it can be done with most simple sausages.

CHAPTER VII

Fresh Sausage

DIET SAUSAGE

For home use, a diet sausage is made quite easily, and you'll know the exact contents of the sausage. The formulas and recipes in this book are very clear and products one uses are fully explained.

Probably the easiest sausage of all is a salt-free sausage. You would simply add spices and meat and you have sausage; just omit the salt. The casings are another story. Salted casings should be avoided, as they have an excessive amount of salt even after flushing and soaking. Unsalted casings packed in solution, or collagen casings, would be preferable.

If you like the flavor of smoked sausage, you must use cures to cure the meat. It requires two level teaspoons of Prague Powder No. 1 to cure 10 lbs. of meat. This small amount can be acceptable in some diets. If it is not, you can simply omit the Prague Powder No. 1 and add liquid smoke. You would have a smoke flavor but a fresh sausage, not cured. It could be frozen and cooked as needed.

For people on fat-free diets, all is not lost. As we all know, a certain amount of fat in the sausage does help to bind it and keep it moist as well. You can pretty much create this same condition by using soy protein concentrate and water, thus eliminating the fat. For 10 lbs. of lean meat you would add around 1 pint of water (1 lb.) and 5 ounces of soy protein concentrate. This may be done with either a fresh or smoked sausage.

At one time, the Hickory Shop of Las Vegas, Nevada, of which I was the owner, did supply the Southern Nevada Memorial Hospital and the Sunrise Hospital with salt-free sausage.

FRESH PORK SAUSAGE
(BREAKFAST)

INGREDIENTS FOR 25 LBS.

7 ozs. salt
2 ozs. ground white pepper
½ oz. rubbed sage
¼ oz. ginger
¼ oz. nutmeg
¼ oz. thyme
¼ oz. ground hot red pepper
  (optional)
1½ lbs. ice water

INGREDIENTS FOR 10 LBS.

5 tbsp. salt
1 tbsp. ground white pepper
2 tbsp. rubbed sage
1 tsp. ginger
1 tbsp. nutmeg
1 tbsp. thyme
1 tbsp. ground hot red pepper
(optional)
1 pint ice water

You can make an excellent breakfast sausage using 100% pork butts. This product is of such high quality that it is never seen in a meat market and can only be had by making it yourself. You can also make a breakfast sausage of 50% pork butts and 50% pork trimming and you would still have a sausage of high quality.

All the pork used to manufacture sausage must be chilled from 32-35 degrees F. without fail. Be sure that all the meat is free of blood clots, sinews, bone, skin, glands, etc.

GRINDING & MIXING

Grind all the meat through a ³⁄₁₆" grinder plate and place in mixer. Add all the ingredients and mix well until all the spices are evenly distributed.

STUFFING

Pork sausage may be stuffed into 28-30mm hog casings or 22-24mm lamb casings. Pork sausage also may be stuffed into a cloth bag or a 3½" by 24" fibrous casing.

It is very important that pork sausage not be allowed to remain at room temperature any longer than necessary. Place in cooler as soon as possible. Pork sausage should be allowed to chill and dry in 28-32 degree cooler.

BROWN-AND-SERVE SAUSAGE

When making brown-and-serve sausages, add 1 oz. of prague powder #1 to a 25 lb. formula, or 2 level teaspoons to a 10 lb. formula. Soy protein concentrate should be added—2 cups for each 10 lbs. of meat.

Brown-and-serve sausages are made by stuffing meat into cellophane casings. Sausage is then cooked in a smokehouse without smoke until an internal temperature of 142 degrees F. is attained. Sausage is removed from smoker and showered with cold water. Sausage is then chilled in a cooler until very firm and then cellophane casings are peeled off. This sausage freezes very well.

To prepare sausage, simply brown and serve.

TOMATO SAUSAGE

For added and unusual flavor you may substitute canned tomato juice in place of water.

FRESH POLISH SAUSAGE
(KIELBASA)

INGREDIENTS FOR 25 LBS.
7 ozs. salt
1 oz. sugar
1 oz. fresh garlic
1 oz. coarse black pepper
¼ oz. marjoram
1½ lbs. water
25 lbs. boneless pork butts

INGREDIENTS FOR 10 LBS.
5 tbsp. salt
1 tbsp. sugar
2 large cloves fresh garlic
1 tbsp. coarse black pepper
1 heaping tsp. marjoram
1 lb. ice water (1 pint)
10 lbs. boneless pork butts

GRINDING & MIXING

Grind all the pork butts through a ¼" or ⅜" grinder plate and place in the mixer. Add all the ingredients and mix well, until all the spices are evenly distributed. Deliver to the stuffer using 35-38mm hog casing. Hang on smokesticks spaced properly and let dry in cooler.

NOTE:

Be sure that meat has been chilled between 32-34 degrees F. before starting. All blood clots, bones, cords, etc. must be removed and thrown out. Do not keep sausage at room temperature any longer than necessary.

Making Sausage Patties At Home

Two simple bottle covers can be used to make breakfast patties. The small one here is from a quart pickle bottle and the larger one is from a 1-gallon mayonnaise jar. They can be used to make hamburgers, large Italian sausage patties and others.

Place a piece of patty paper or regular waxed paper on the cap.

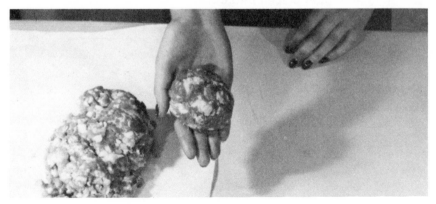

Take amount of meat desired for patty.

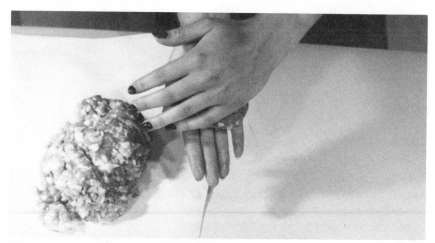

Meat is then rolled into a ball.

Ball of meat is then placed into cap.

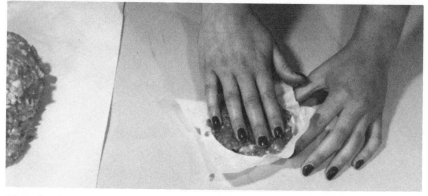

Meat is then pressed into cap, forming the patty shape.

176

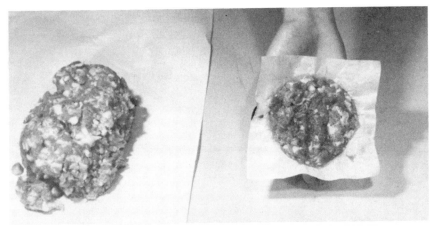

Patty is now formed and ready to be wrapped for the freezer.

The photos above and at right show an adjustable hamburger mold, open and closed.

More on Making Patties At Home

Stuffing a low cost plastic burger or wild game bag with sausage.

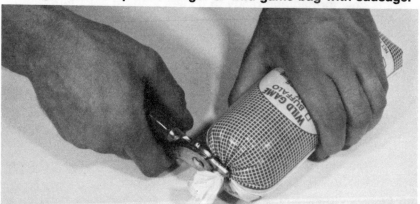

The sausage is then closed and placed into the freezer for 30-45 minutes until partially frozen.

The sausage is removed from the freezer and sliced. Notice the plastic falls off the patties. Wrap and re-freeze.

ONION SAUSAGE

INGREDIENTS FOR 25 LBS.
25 lbs. pork butts
8 ozs. salt
1 oz. powdered dextrose
4 ozs. finely chopped onions
1 oz. coarse black pepper
¼ oz. ground marjoram
1 qt. ice water

INGREDIENTS FOR 10 LBS.
10 lbs. pork butts
3½ ozs. salt
½ oz. powdered dextrose
2 ozs. finely chopped onions
1 tbsp. coarse black pepper
1 tbsp. ground marjoram
1 pt. ice water

Grind pork butts through a ⅜" grinder plate and fat meat through a ⅛" grinder plate. Then add all remaining ingredients, mixing until evenly distributed. Sausage is then stuffed into 35-38mm hog casings and placed into 38-40 degrees F. cooler for 24 hours before using.

CHORIZO

INGREDIENTS FOR 25 LBS.
7 ozs. salt
8 ozs. vinegar
4 ozs. paprika
2½ ozs. hot ground pepper
2 ozs. fresh garlic
1½ ozs. oregano
1½ ozs. black coarse pepper
½ lb. water
25 lbs. boned pork butts

INGREDIENTS FOR 10 LBS.
5 tbsp. salt
about 1 cup vinegar
5 tbsp. paprika
3 tbsp. hot ground pepper
8 large cloves fresh garlic
1 tbsp. oregano
2 tsp. black coarse pepper
1 cup water
10 lbs. boned pork butts

GRINDING & MIXING

Grind all the pork butts through a ¼" grinding plate and place in a mixer. Add all the ingredients and mix well until all the spices are evenly distributed. Chorizo is to be stuffed into a 38-42mm hog casing. Place on smokesticks and let dry in cooler overnight. This particular sausage takes much longer to dry than most others.

While living in Las Vegas for 20 years, I developed a taste for Mexican food. I managed to make a good friend out of Pedro Bossey, who gave me this recipe for chorizo. It is one of my favorites to this day. The history of this recipe concerns Pedro's mother, who emigrated from her native Spain to Mexico City. Pedro emigrated to Las Vegas from there and became an American citizen. After visiting his mother in Mexico City one day, he returned with this chorizo recipe. Thanks, Pete.

COOKED CHORIZO LOAF

A chorizo loaf can be made simply by adding 1 oz. of prague powder #1 to 25 lbs. of meat or one level teaspoon for each 5 lbs. of meat. Also, soy protein concentrate should be added with some water. (14 ozs. of soy protein for 25 lbs. and 3 ozs. to each 5 lbs. of meat.)

Stuff the meat into baking pans and place in an oven or smokehouse at 170 degrees F. until the internal temperature reaches 155 degrees F. You may also stuff this mixture into any size fibrous casing.

FRESH ITALIAN SAUSAGE - SWEET

INGREDIENTS FOR 25 LBS.	INGREDIENTS FOR 10 LBS.
7 ozs. salt	5 tbsp. salt
1½ lbs. ice water	1 lb. ice water (1 pint)
1 oz. cracked fennel seed	3 tsp. fennel seed
1 oz. coarse black pepper	2 tsp. coarse black pepper
1 oz. sugar	1 tbsp. sugar
25 lbs. boned pork butts	10 lbs. boned pork butts

GRINDING & MIXING

Grind all the pork butts through a ¼" or ⅜" plate and place into the mixer. Add all the ingredients and mix well until evenly distributed. Stuff into 32-35mm hog casing.

NOTE:

Be sure that the meat has been chilled between 32-34 degrees F. before starting. All blood clots, cords, bones, etc. must be removed and thrown out. Do not keep sausage at room temperature any longer than necessary.

SMOKING

The smoking of Italian sausage has become more and more popular in recent years. Simply place sausage in preheated smokehouse at 130 degrees F. with dampers wide open until the casings are dry. Gradually increase temperature to 160-165 degrees F.

Applying medium smoke with dampers ¼ open, hold in smokehouse until you obtain internal temperature of 152 degrees F. Remove and shower with cool water quickly so internal temperature is reduced to 110 degrees F. Allow to hang at room temperature until desired bloom is obtained, remove to cooler and hold overnight.

When smoking Italian sausage, add 1 oz. of cure (Prague Powder No. 1) to 25 lb. formula or 2 level teaspoons to a 10 lb. formula. Soy protein concentrate should also be added as called for in any smoked sausage recipe of this book.

182

FRESH ITALIAN SAUSAGE - MILD-HOT

INGREDIENTS FOR 25 LBS.

7 ozs. salt
1½ lbs. ice water
½ oz. cracked fennel seed
1 oz. coarse black pepper
1 oz. sugar
½ oz. crushed hot peppers
¼ oz. caraway seeds
¼ oz. coriander
25 lbs. boneless pork butts

INGREDIENTS FOR 10 LBS.

5 tbsp. salt
1 pint ice water
1 tbsp. cracked fennel seed
2 tsp. coarse black pepper
1 tbsp. sugar
3 tsp. crushed hot peppers
1 tsp. caraway seeds
1 tbsp. coriander
10 lbs. boneless port butts

GRINDING & MIXING

Grind all the pork butts through ¼" or ⅜" grinder plate. Place into the mixer and add all the ingredients. Mix well until all the spices are evenly distributed. Stuff into a 32-35mm hog casing.

NOTE:

Be sure that the meat has been chilled between 32-34 degrees F. before starting. All blood clots, bones, cords, etc. must be removed and thrown out. Do not keep sausage at room temperature any longer than necessary.

ENGLISH BANGERS

INGREDIENTS FOR 10 LBS.
2 tsp. ground white pepper
1 tsp. ground ginger
1 tsp.sage
1 tsp. mace
3 ozs. salt (about 6 tbsp.)
6 ozs. bread crumbs
10 lbs. fat pork butts

PROCESSING PROCEDURE

Meat is chilled to 32-34 degrees F. and ground through ¼" grinding plate. All ingredients are mixed very well with about 2 cups of water. When possible, add cooled pork stock in place of water. Meat is then stuffed into 32-35mm hog casings and whatever sausage not used up is frozen.

English bangers are a very tasty sausage served at breakfast time, much the same as American pork sausage.

The above formula may be used to make all beef breakfast sausage. Use any kind of beef or trimmings, 70% lean and 30% fat.

CABBAGE PORK SAUSAGE

INGREDIENTS FOR 10 LBS.
1 tbsp. ground white pepper
2 tbsp. sage
1 tsp. ground ginger
1 tbsp. ground nutmeg
1 tbsp. thyme
1 tbsp. ground hot red pepper
6 tbsp. salt
1 tbsp. sugar
1 small onion
3½ lbs. cabbage (core removed)
10 lbs. boneless pork butts

A very good pork sausage is made using 100% pork butts, rather on the fat side. Commercial pork sausage usually is made of about 50% meat and 50% fat. The ideal pork sausage is about 30% fat and 70% meat, or a pork butt on the fatty side.

Cabbage is quartered and boiled in water until tender. Cabbage is then removed and allowed to drain and cool. It is then ground through ³⁄₁₆" or ¼" grinder plate along with onions and meat. Add all ingredients and mix very well, stuffing into a 22-24mm sheep casing. Remove to cooler or freeze. This sausage is prepared like regular breakfast sausage.

KOSHER STYLE BEEF SAUSAGE - FRESH

INGREDIENTS FOR 25 LBS.	INGREDIENTS FOR 10 LBS.
1 oz. ground white pepper	1 tbsp. ground white pepper
¼ oz. ground nutmeg	1 tbsp. ground nutmeg
¼ oz. ground ginger	1 tsp. ground ginger
¼ oz. thyme	1 tbsp. thyme
¼ oz. rubbed sage	1 tbsp. rubbed sage
7 ozs. salt	5 tbsp. salt
4 ozs. sugar	3 tbsp. sugar
1½ lbs. ice water	1 pint ice water
25 lbs. chuck	10 lbs. chuck

The meats selected for this sausage should be very high quality and bright in color. Remove all the blood clots, sinews, and gristle. Be sure the meat has been kept at 28-32 degrees F. before grinding.

GRINDING & MIXING

Grind all the meats through a ⅜" to ½" grinder plate. Place into the mixer and add all the ingredients, mix until evenly distributed. (If necessary, you may add ice to keep the meat at 32-34 degrees F.) Remove from mixer and regrind through ⅛" grinder plate. Remove to stuffer packing tightly and use about 22-24mm lamb casings. Remove to cooler after stuffing.

SICILIAN-ITALIAN SAUSAGE
WITH WINE AND CHEESE

INGREDIENTS FOR 25 LBS.
20 lbs. pork butts
5 lbs. lean beef (chuck is okay)
1 oz. powdered dextrose
1 oz. cracked black pepper
8 ozs. salt
1 oz. cracked fennel seed
¼ oz. red crushed peppers
1 qt. wine—chablis
5 ozs. imported Romano Pecorino

INGREDIENTS FOR 10 LBS.
8 lbs. pork butts
2 lbs. lean beef (chuck is okay)
2 tbsp. powdered dextrose
1 tbsp. cracked black pepper
3½ ozs. salt
3 tbsp. cracked fennel seed
2 tbsp. red crushed peppers
1 pint wine—chablis
2 ozs. imported Romano Pecorino

The Romano cheese must be broken or cut up into smaller sized pieces so that it fits into your grinder. Grind cheese through a ⅜" grinder plate at least twice. This breaks it down to a powdery consistency so it can be mixed easily with the meat.

Grind meat through a ⅜" grinder plate and place in a mixing bowl. Add the remaining ingredients and mix thoroughly until evenly distributed. Stuff into 32-35mm hog casing. You may also make this sausage in patties if you like.

This particular sausage tastes best if it is cooked shortly after it is made. It is a good idea to prepare only what you can use up in a couple days. This sausage may be frozen, but the longer it is kept frozen, the more dominant the Romano cheese flavor will become.

Of all the types of Italian sausage made, this is my favorite. It is a sausage usually made during the Christmas and Easter holidays. Many thanks to Leonard Arcadepane of Las Vegas, Nevada who taught me how to make this sausage, and also for his recipe. We spent many Christmas and Easter holidays helping each other make Sicilian and Polish sausages, and then enjoyed the holidays eating these sausages.

HOT WHOLE HOG SAUSAGE

INGREDIENTS FOR 100 LB. BATCHES
4 ozs. ground black pepper

2 ozs. sage

1 oz. ground ginger

1 oz. ground nutmeg

1 oz. thyme

2 lbs. salt

1 oz. ground hot pepper (optional)

TYPE OF HOGS

This type of sausage is made from sows weighing about 300 to 400 lbs. Needless to say, this sausage is made as fast as possible. All spices should be premixed in advance and all utensils should be clean, ready and waiting. If the hog is ground up promptly, and the above instructions are followed, the bacteria count in the sausage will be very low and this in turn will help to extend the flavor of the sausage a great deal. It is worthwhile to note that the carcass of the hog is practically bacteria-free right after the slaughter.

A great many large sausage manufacturers have switched to this method of making pork sausage. Obviously, it saves on the refrigeration expense and gives the product a longer shelf life as well. Ordinarily, the meat has to be refrigerated for a day or so, and when great volumes are involved, this process can save large amounts of money for the processors.

PROCESSING

A hog may be skinned right on the rail and then boned. Cut into strips 3" to 6." After all the meat is boned and the skin removed, quickly inspect all the meat for blood clots and throw them out. The end product should be 60% lean and 40% fat. If the meat is too fat, remove one of the fat backs.

After all the meat is weighed, grind through a ³⁄₁₆" grinder plate and place into the mixer. Add all the ingredients and mix well. Place into the cooler overnight in tubs or pans 5 to 6 inches deep. A

QUICK CHILL IS NECESSARY TO PREVENT SOURING OR GAS-
SING OF THE PRODUCT, SO DO NOT OVERLOAD THE PANS
OR TUBS. After chilling, sausage may be stuffed in cloth bags or
fibrous casings 3½" by 24".

NOTE:

   THIS ENTIRE BATCH OF SAUSAGE SHOULD BE MADE DUR-
ING A PERIOD OF TIME WHEN THE MEAT WILL NOT DROP
BELOW 85 DEGREES F. IF THE MEAT DROPS BELOW THIS
TEMPERATURE THE SPICES DO NOT MIX WELL WITH THE
MEAT AND THE CHANCE OF SOURING IS GREATER.

SWEDISH POTATO SAUSAGE

INGREDIENTS FOR 25 LBS.
1 medium whole fresh onion or
4 ozs. of granulated onions
7 ozs. salt
1 oz. ground white pepper
½ oz. allspice
1 lb. non-fat dry milk
2½ lbs. water
7½ lbs. raw peeled potatoes
  or 2 lbs. potato flour
12½ lbs. pork butts
5 lbs. boneless beef

INGREDIENTS FOR 5 LBS.
1 onion small size, cut up

1 tbsp. salt
1½ tsp. ground black pepper
1 tsp. allspice
1 cup non-fat dry milk
1 cup water
6 potatoes, pared & cut up
  (6 cups)
1½ lbs. lean boneless beef
1 lb. lean boneless pork

GRINDING & MIXING

Grind the meat, potatoes, and onions through a ⅜" grinder plate and place in a mixer. Add all the other ingredients with the water and mix well. After this procedure, regrind through the ⅜" plate again. Stuff into a 35-38mm hog casing.

This sausage is a very perishable product. It keeps best when frozen. This sausage may be served fried, baked or boiled. When kept in a refrigerator, sausage should be placed in container and covered with water.

CHAPTER VIII

Smoked and Cooked Sausage

EMULSIFIED SAUSAGES

Bologna, wieners and products of this type use a very finely textured meat. These types of sausages are made with what is known as emulsified meat. There are a lot of people who would like to make a sausage of this type at home but have had nothing but failure in trying to achieve these results. A simple grinder will not do the job. All you would do is regrind the meat over and over and wind up with a very poor-looking product. It definitely would not appear appetizing. Until just recently, it wasn't possible to do; however, since the introduction of the food processor, it is possible to produce small amounts of these sausages at home.

In using a small food processor at home to make emulsified sausage, there are only one or two rules to follow. Due to the size of these machines, it is always better to buy one that has a direct-drive shaft to turn the cutting knife. The giant meat emulsifiers are made this way. The food processors with belt drives are not quite so durable.

In either case, the meat should be ground first and all the ingredients (except the water) should be mixed very thoroughly until evenly distributed. Then place the meat in the food processor a little at a time, adding a little water as you go along. You should be able to emulsify the meat to such a point that the end result will be pretty close to a store-bought wiener, bratwurst or bologna.

When I first started making sausages in the mid-1960's, we were already being monitored by our local health department for the fat content of the sausage we processed. At random, a health inspector would walk into our little sausage kitchen and help himself to some samples of the various sausages we made.

A week or 10 days later, we would receive a written analysis of the fat content in our sausage from our health department.

Emulsifying Meat at home with a Food Processor
The introduction of food processors in recent years has now made it easier to produce a fine-textured sausage at home. Although not as perfect as a $50,000 meat chopper, it still produces a reasonable facsimile of wieners or bologna at home.

Meat must first be ground using a ¼" grinding plate.

The seasonings are then thoroughly mixed with the meat, omitting water.

The meat is then placed into the food processor, adding ice cold water to help emulsify the meat. Adding water in this step also reduces the strain on the motor of your food processor.

Above photo shows emulsified meat after 3 minutes. Water has been added to reach this stage.

194

Many people would think that a good time to add a lot of undesir-able products to sausage, such as fat, would be when you're emul-sifying it. This situation is only remotely possible today and is only brought up by scaremongers or inexperienced people who are deal-ing with a subject they know little, if anything, about. Sausage makers have been taking a beating for a long time because of these publicity seekers.

A simple-to-operate sample tester that reads out a fat content in seconds. Manufactured by Dickey-John Co.

Today the situation is even more improved. With computer prices coming down so dramatically, practically any decent-sized sausage kitchen can afford a computerized fat analyzer. Since sausage is made in 300-, 500- and even 1000-lb. loads, the meat is checked by the USDA inspector on the spot. If the fat content is too high, the sausage maker is forced to put more lean meat into the batch to bring it up to USDA specifications. If not, it is not allowed to be made into sausage. There is a limit of 30% fat for any and all sausages that can't be exceeded by federal law. All state and local health departments enforce this law. As a sausage-maker and businessman, I always tried to produce a good quality product. It just wasn't worth the trouble of having problems with the health department.

BRATWURST

INGREDIENTS FOR 25 LBS.

1 quart of whole milk, ice cold
9 whole eggs
12 ozs. soy protein concentrate
1 oz. ground white pepper
¼ oz. mace
¼ oz. ginger
¼ oz. nutmeg
7 ozs. salt
5 lbs. boneless veal
12½ lbs. fresh pork shoulders
7½ lbs. lean pork trimmings

INGREDIENTS FOR 10 LBS.

1 pint whole milk, ice cold
3 whole eggs
2 cups soy protein concentrate
1 tbsp. ground white pepper
1 tbsp. mace
1 tsp. ginger
1 tbsp. nutmeg
5 tbsp. salt
2 lbs. boneless veal
5 lbs. fresh pork shoulders
3 lbs. lean pork trimmings

GRINDING & MIXING

Grind all the meat through a ⅜" grinder plate. Place in the mixer adding all the ingredients until evenly distributed. Meat should then be stuffed into a 32-35mm hog casing.

NOTE:

Bratwurst is sold in three different ways: fresh, cooked or smoked. If you wish, bratwurst may be placed into the freezer right after it is made. It can be cooked just before it is used. Or, you may place bratwurst into a cooker at 160 degrees F. and keep it there until an internal temperature of 152 degrees F. is obtained.

If you wish to smoke bratwurst, place in a preheated smokehouse at 130 degrees F. with dampers wide open for about 1 hour or until the casings are dry. After 1 hour, close dampers to ¼ open, gradually increase the temperature to 165 degrees F. and hold it at that level until an internal temperature of 152 degrees F. is obtained. In either case, after smoking or cooking, sausage should be removed and placed under a shower until the internal temperature is reduced to around 110 degrees F.

If you are going to smoke bratwurst, add 4 ozs. of cure (Prague

Powder No. 1) to the 100 lb. formula or 2 level teaspoons to the 10 lb. formula.

The above bratwurst was a sausage made for and served by Alpine Village, Hofbrau and several other restaurants in Las Vegas, Nevada during my ownership of the Hickory Shop Inc. in the mid-60s.

One of the biggest compliments I ever received was from Mrs. Ann Buckingham of Las Vegas. She told me that the bratwurst I made was better than any she ever bought in Germany. Ann was from Hamburg, Germany, became a G.I. war bride, and still lives in the U.S.A. The bratwurst I made for her was coarse-meat variety. Most Americans are not familiar with this bratwurst, as they prefer the emulsified type.

BOCKWURST

INGREDIENTS FOR 25 LBS.
1 quart of whole milk
8 ozs. salt
2 ozs. powdered dextrose
¼ oz. mace
½ oz. ground celery
1 oz. onion powder
1 oz. ground white pepper
1 bunch fresh chopped chives
  or green onions
¼ oz. chopped parsley
¼ oz. grated lemon peel
6 fresh whole eggs
7½ lbs. boneless veal
12½ lbs. lean pork shoulder
5 lbs. regular pork trimmings

INGREDIENTS FOR 10 LBS.
1 pint whole milk
6 tbsp. salt
2 tbsp. powdered dextrose
1 tbsp. mace
1 tbsp. ground celery
4 tbsp. onion powder
1 tbsp. ground white pepper
6 pcs. chives or green onions,
  chopped
6 pcs. chopped parsley
1 piece grated lemon peel
3 fresh whole eggs
3 lbs. boneless veal
5 lbs. lean pork shoulder
2 lbs. pork trimmings

GRINDING

Grind all the meat through a ⅜ grinder plate, adding all the ingredients, and mixing well until all ingredients are evenly distributed.

STUFFING AND COOKING

Bockwurst is to be stuffed into a lamb casing 24-26mm in size and made in links 4-6 inches long; then hung on clean smokesticks. (Do not use a smokestick that can stain the casings, as bockwurst is a white sausage.) Sausage should be placed into the cooker or water and cooked until the internal temperature reaches 152 degrees F. (Be sure the water temperature is not above 165 degrees F.) Place cooked sausage under shower for about 10 minutes to reduce internal temperature to 110 degrees F. and remove to cooler overnight. This sausage also can be frozen and cooked as it is needed.

Bockwurst also is made as a very fine-textured sausage (emulsified) in the Western New York area. It is very popular at Easter time and also goes under the name of "white hot dogs."

198

KNOCKWURST

INGREDIENTS FOR 25 LBS.
2½ lbs. ice water
12 ozs. non-fat dry milk
8 ozs. salt
2 ozs. powdered dextrose
1 oz. Prague Powder No. 1
1 oz. ground white pepper
¼ oz. mace
¼ oz. ground allspice
¼ oz. coriander
1 oz. paprika
¼ oz. garlic powder (optional)
17½ lbs. boneless veal
7½ lbs. lean pork trimmings
  or
17½ lbs. bull or cow meat
7½ lbs. lean pork trimmings

INGREDIENTS FOR 10 LBS.
1 pint ice water
2 cups non-fat dry milk
6 tbsp. salt
4 tbsp. powdered dextrose
2 level tsp. Prague Powder No. 1
5 tbsp. ground white pepper
1 tbsp. mace
½ tsp. ground allspice
1 tsp. coriander
2 tbsp. paprika
1 tsp. garlic powder (optional)
7 lbs. boneless veal
3 lbs. pork trimmings
  or
7 lbs. boneless beef
3 lbs. pork trimmings

GRINDING & STUFFING

Grind all the meat through a ⅛" grinder plate, add all the ingredients and mix well. Sausage should then be stuffed into small or medium beef rounds or 38-42mm hog casings. Sausage should then be placed on smokesticks, properly spaced.

SMOKING

Knockwurst is placed in a smokehouse that is preheated 130-135 degrees F. with dampers wide open. Keep at this temperature for about 1 hour or until the product is fully dry. Smokehouse temperature then should be raised to about 150 degrees F. while applying smoke and held there for 1 hour, or until the desired color is obtained. You may increase smoker temperature to 165 degrees F. and cook until internal temperature reaches 152 degrees F. without smoke, or you may remove to the cooker until the 152 degrees F. is obtained

199

internally. If you are cooking in water, be sure the water temperature is not over 165 degrees F.

NOTE:

Knockwurst usually is not smoked very dark; however, this is optional.

WIENERS
(FRANKFURTERS)

INGREDIENTS FOR 25 LBS.
2½ lbs. ice water
1 oz. Prague Powder No. 1
3 ozs. paprika
2 ozs. ground mustard
½ oz. ground black pepper
½ oz. ground white pepper
½ oz. ground celery seeds
¼ oz. mace
¼ oz. garlic powder
8 ozs. salt
12 ozs. non-fat dry milk or
   soy protein concentrate
2 ozs. powdered dextrose
15 lbs. lean beef (chuck)
10 lbs. lean pork trimmings
   (pork butts)

INGREDIENTS FOR 10 LBS.
1 pint ice water
2 level tsp. Prague Powder No. 1
4 tbsp. paprika
6 tbsp. ground mustard
1 tsp. ground black pepper
1 tsp. ground white pepper
1 tsp. ground celery seeds
1 tbsp. mace
1 tsp. garlic powder
6 tbsp. salt
2 cups non-fat dry milk or
   soy protein concentrate
4 tbsp. powdered dextrose
6 lbs. lean beef (chuck)
4 lbs. lean pork trimmings
   (pork butts)

If you wish, you may use 1 oz. coriander in place of the mace.

Wieners can be made from many different meats, as well as any combination of meats. In some cases, people want to use the leftovers when they butcher their livestock, while others prefer a quality wiener.

GRINDING

For home use, grind all the meat together using a plate with very fine holes. After grinding, mix all the ingredients with water and meat. Mix for 2-3 minutes or until all ingredients are evenly distributed with the meat. After mixing, pack into stuffer using a 24-26mm lamb casing to stuff wieners.

SMOKING AND COOKING

After stuffing, hang wieners on properly spaced smokehouse sticks. Be sure wieners are not touching each other. You may rinse the wieners off with cold water if necessary. Allow wieners to hang at room temperature when using natural casings for stuffing (about 1 hour). When using collagen or synthetic casings, hang at room temperature for about 30 minutes. Wieners should be smoked as follows:

Place into pre-heated smokehouse and dry for approximately 30 minutes. Apply heavy smudge for approximately 1½ hours, gradually raise smokehouse temperature to 165 degrees F. and smoke until internal temperature of 138 degrees F. is obtained. Transfer to steam cabinet cooker and cook at 165 degrees F. for 5-10 minutes, or until an internal temperature of 152-155 degrees F. is obtained. Spot-check various wieners to be sure that these temperatures are obtained.

If you do not have a steam cabinet, you may leave the wieners in the smokehouse at 165 degrees F. until you obtain 152 degrees F. internally.

After smoking or cooking, the wieners should be quickly showered with cool water for about 10 minutes or until the internal temperature is reduced to 100-110 degrees F. After showering with cold water, allow wieners to chill and dry at room temperature or until desired bloom is obtained.

CHILLING

Wieners should be placed in 45-50 degrees F. cooler and chilled until product has reached an internal temperature of 50 degrees F.

TURKEY OR CHICKEN WIENERS

INGREDIENTS FOR 25 LBS.

20 lbs. raw, boneless
  turkey or chicken
3 lbs. chicken or turkey fat
2 lbs. semolina flour
1 oz. prague powder #1
8 ozs. salt
1 oz. ground white pepper
2 lbs. turkey or chicken stock
12 ozs. non-fat dry milk
1 qt. ice water

INGREDIENTS FOR 10 LBS.

8 lbs. raw, boneless
  turkey or chicken
1 lb. chicken or turkey fat
13 ozs. semolina flour
2 level tsp. prague powder #1
3½ ozs. salt
1 tbsp. ground white pepper
13 ozs. turkey or chicken stock
5 ozs. non-fat dry milk
1 pint ice water

All meat and fat must be chilled at 30-32 degrees F. and then ground through a ⅛" grinder plate. Add remaining ingredients, except stock, and mix thoroughly until evenly distributed.

Then place mixture in a food processor a little at a time, adding the stock as you go along. Chop the mixture in the food processor until emulsified, being careful not to overwork. Stuff mixture in 24-26mm sheep casings and let it dry at room temperature for about 30-40 minutes.

Put wieners in a preheated smoker at 120-130 degrees F. with damper and vent wide open. After wieners are dry, close damper and vent and apply smoke for 20-30 minutes. Then increase temperature to 160 degrees F. at a rate of 10 degrees F. every 10 minutes. Continue this process until the internal temperature reaches 152 degress F. Then place the wieners under a cool shower of water until internal temperature is reduced to 85-90 degrees F.

NOTE:
  Boullion cubes may be used to make stock.

VIENNA SAUSAGE

INGREDIENTS FOR 25 LBS.

9 lbs. lean beef
9 lbs. lean veal
7 lbs. lean pork
1 qt. ice water
1 oz. prague powder #1
2 ozs. powdered dextrose
7½ ozs. wheat flour
8 ozs. salt
1 oz. ground nutmeg
¼ oz. ground coriander
¼ oz. ground cardamon
1 tbsp. ground cloves

INGREDIENTS FOR 10 LBS.

4 lbs. lean beef
4 lbs. lean veal
2 lbs. lean pork
1 pint ice water
2 level tsp. prague powder #1
1 oz. powdered dextrose
2¾ ozs. wheat flour
3½ ozs. salt
1 tbsp. ground nutmeg
1 tsp. ground coriander
½ tsp. ground cardamon
½ tsp. ground cloves

Grind the meat through a ⅛" grinder plate. Add the remaining ingredients, except water, mixing thoroughly. Place the meat in a meat processor and emulsify it, adding the water as you go along. Then stuff the mixture into 24-26mm sheep casings. Hang at room temperature for 30-40 minutes or until dry. Place in a preheated smokehouse at 150 degrees F. and hold there for 1 hour. Raise temperature to 165 degrees F., holding until internal temperature reaches 152 degrees F. Vienna sausage is not smoked.

LARGE, LONG AND RING BOLOGNA

INGREDIENTS FOR 25 LBS.
2½ lbs. ice water
1 oz. prague powder #1
1¼ ozs. ground white pepper
1 oz. paprika
¼ oz. nutmeg
¼ oz. allspice
¼ oz. onion powder
8 ozs. salt
12 ozs. non-fat dry milk or
   soy protein concentrate
15 lbs. lean beef (chuck)
10 lbs. pork butts

INGREDIENTS FOR 10 LBS.
1 pint ice water
2 level tsp. prague powder #1
1 tbsp. ground white pepper
2 tbsp. paprika
1 tbsp. nutmeg
1 tsp. allspice
1 tsp. onion powder
8 tbsp. salt
2 cups non-fat dry milk or
   soy protein concentrate
6 lbs. lean beef (chuck)
4 lbs. pork butts

GRINDING

Grind all the meat using a plate with very fine holes. After grinding, mix all the ingredients with water and meat. Mix for 2-3 minutes or until all the ingredients are evenly distributed. If you do not have a mechanical mixer or silent cutter and are mixing by hand, it will take longer than 3 minutes to distribute the ingredients.

STUFFING

Bologna may be stuffed in large cellulose casings, beef bungs or export wide beef rounds for the ring bologna. There are hog casings available that can be used for ring bologna.

SMOKING AND COOKING

After stuffing, hang on properly spaced smokehouse sticks. You may rinse with cold water to remove meat particles. After stuffing, bologna should be kept in a cooler at 40-45 degrees F. until you are ready to smoke. Prior to smoking, bologna should be taken out of the cooler and allowed to hang at room temperature for at least 1 hour before smoking.

Bologna packed in artificial casings should be placed in a pre-heated smokehouse at 130-135 degrees F. for about ½ hour with dampers wide open; then apply heavy smudge for approximately 1½- 3 hours with dampers ¾ closed. Gradually raise the temperature to 165-170 degrees F., cutting off the smudge, and cook until an internal temperature of 155 degrees F. is obtained. If you have a steam cabinet, you may transfer bologna from the smokehouse and cook until an internal temperature of 155 degrees F. is obtained.

When using natural casings, bologna should be placed in a smokehouse at 130-135 degrees F. with dampers wide open for at least 30-45 minutes. Then apply heavy smudge for 2½-3 hours or until the desired color is obtained. Cut smudge, gradually raise the smokehouse temperature to 165 degrees F. and cook until an internal temperature of 135 degrees F. is obtained. Remove from smoker and place in steam cabinet until 155 degrees F. is obtained internally. If you do not have a cooker, leave bologna in the smokehouse at 165-170 degrees F. until 155 degrees F. is obtained internally. Remove from smokehouse and spray with cool water until an internal temperature of 110 degrees F. is obtained.

CHILLING

Bologna should be placed in a cooler at 45 degrees F. until the internal temperature of the product reaches at least 50 degrees F.

SMOKED POLISH SAUSAGE
(KIELBASA)

INGREDIENTS FOR 25 LBS.
2½ lbs. ice water
12 ozs. soy protein concentrate
   or non-fat dry milk
7 ozs. salt
1 oz. sugar
1 oz. prague powder #1
1 oz. black pepper
1 oz. fresh garlic
¼ oz. marjoram
25 lbs. boneless pork butts

INGREDIENTS FOR 10 LBS.
1 lb. ice water (1 pint)
2 cups soy protein concentrate
   or non-fat dry milk
5 tbsp. salt
1 tbsp. sugar
2 level tsp. prague powder #1
1 tbsp. black pepper
2 large cloves fresh garlic
1 heaping tsp. marjoram
10 lbs. boneless pork butts

GRINDING & TRIMMING

Trim off excess fat, remove all blood clots, bone, sinews, cords, etc. and throw out. Grind all the lean meat through a ⅜" grinder plate and all the fat meat through ⅛" plate. Place in mixer, adding all the ingredients and mixing until evenly distributed.

STUFFING

Polish sausage should be stuffed into a larger-size hog casing, preferably 38-42mm. Sausage then is placed on smokehouse sticks and spaced properly. Sausage is permitted to dry. You may dry the sausage as follows:

(1) When stuffing the sausage, it normally is hung on the sausage sticks in the room where you are working. By the time you are finished stuffing the sausage, much of it already is dry. You may put it in a preheated smokehouse at 130 degrees F. with dampers wide open for about 1 hour or until casings are dry and starting to take on a brown color.

(2) Or, you may place sausage in the cooler and leave until the casings are dry.

SMOKING

Sausage is placed in a preheated smokehouse at 130 degrees F. with dampers wide open. Keep this temperature until the casings are dry. Gradually increase temperature of smokehouse to 160-165 degrees F. with dampers ¼ open. Apply heavy smoke and keep in smoker until the internal temperature reaches 152 degrees F.

If you are using a steam cabinet for cooking, remove the sausage from the smoker when it has an internal temperature of 135 degrees F. and cook in the steam cabinet to reach 152 degrees F. internally. Remove from smokehouse and shower with cold tap water until the internal temperature is reduced to 110 degrees F. Allow the sausage to hang at room temperature for about 30 minutes or until the desired bloom is obtained. Place in cooler at 38-40 degrees F. overnight.

BEER SAUSAGE

During the mid-1960's, when I was owner of the Hickory Shop in Las Vegas, the beer sausage made its mark. Probably 80% of the bar owners in Las Vegas were selling this sausage we made. When they placed their initial orders, they were sold a 4-quart electric cooker. To prepare this sausage they would pour in a ½ can of beer and simply let the sausage steam cook in the beer. Hence, the name "beer sausage."

After being cooked, the sausage simply was served on a napkin or a paper plate. Some of the owners provided mustard or crackers and others just the sausage, steam-cooked in beer. This sausage was so popular that it quickly became our number one sausage, and we were producing up to 4000 lbs. a week. Beer sausage literally took Las Vegas by storm; that is, the bar business.

Beer sausage was made simply by using the smoked Polish sausage recipe, but adding hot cayenne pepper. The degree of hotness varied from bar to bar and it was made from mildly hot to very hot. Four ounces of hot cayenne pepper to 100 lbs. of meat will make a hot sausage, and ½ this amount or 2 ounces makes a mild-hot sausage. For a 10 lb. recipe, 1 teaspoon will make a mild-hot sausage. Add two teaspoons and you'll have a pretty hot sausage.

BIERWURST

INGREDIENTS FOR 25 LBS.
15 lbs. lean pork butts
7 lbs. lean beef
3 lbs. fresh bacon
8 ozs. salt
1 oz. prague powder #1
2 ozs. powdered dextrose
1 oz. ground black pepper
½ oz. ground nutmeg
¼ oz. cardamon
¼ oz. fresh garlic
1 oz. whole mustard seeds

INGREDIENTS FOR 10 LBS.
7 lbs. lean pork butts
2 lbs. lean beef
1 lb. fresh bacon
3½ ozs. salt
2 level tsp. prague powder #1
¾ ozs. powdered dextrose
1 tbsp. ground black papper
1 level tsp. ground nutmeg
¼ tsp. cardamon
1 small garlic clove
1 tbsp. whole mustard seeds

Grind the lean pork butts and beef through a 1" grinder plate or cut into 1" cubes. Add the remaining ingredients and mix thoroughly until evenly distributed. Pack the meat into a container not more than 6" high, making sure there are no air pockets. Then place this mixture in a cooler overnight, along with the fresh bacon. The next day, regrind this mixture through a ⅛" grinder plate, and grind the bacon through a ¼" grinder plate.

Combine the mixtures and stuff into a sewed beef casing or small beef bladder. Allow to dry at room temperature for at least one hour. Then place the sausage in a preheated smokehouse at 130 degrees F. with the dampers and drafts wide open. Allow to dry for 45 minutes or until the sausage starts to take on a brown color. At this point, move the draft to ¼ open and increase the temperature to 160-165 degrees F. and begin smoking. Bierwurst is finished when an internal temperature of 152 degrees F. is reached. Place in cooler overnight before using.

SMOKED PORK SAUSAGE
(BREAKFAST)

INGREDIENTS FOR 25 LBS.
1¼ lbs. ice water
1 oz. Prague Powder No. 1
8 ozs. salt
1 oz. ground white pepper
½ oz. rubbed sage
¼ oz. ground ginger
¼ oz. ground nutmeg
¼ oz. thyme
8 ozs. soy protein concentrate
10 lbs. lean pork trimmings
15 lbs. pork butts

INGREDIENTS FOR 10 LBS.
1 pint ice water
2 level tsp. Prague Powder No. 1
6 tbsp. salt
1 tbsp. ground white pepper
2 tbsp. rubbed sage
1 tsp. ground ginger
1 tbsp. ground nutmeg
1 tbsp. thyme
1 cup soy protein concentrate
4 lbs. lean pork trimmings
6 lbs. pork butts

GRINDING & CHOPPING

Be sure that all the pork used has been chilled to about 32-35 degrees F. In addition, pork should be free of blood clots, bones, sinews, etc. Grind all the meats through a ¼" or 3/16" grinder plate. Place in mixer until all ingredients are evenly distributed with spices. Stuff into sheep casings 22-24mm or small hog casings, if available.

SMOKING

Hang on smokesticks, properly spaced, and let dry at room temperature until casings are dry. Remove to a preheated smokehouse at about 120 degrees F. with dampers wide open. Gradually increase temperature to 160 degrees F. and apply a heavy smoke; then reduce the temperature to 150 degrees F. and maintain until an internal temperature of 142 degrees F. is obtained. Remove from smoker, place under cold water shower and reduce internal temperature to 110 degrees F. Let dry at room temperature until desired bloom is obtained. Remove to cooler overnight.

LINGUISA
(LONGANIZA)

INGREDIENTS FOR 25 LBS.
8 ozs. salt
2 ozs. powdered dextrose
1 oz. Prague Powder No. 1
3 ozs. fresh garlic
4 ozs. wine or cider vinegar
4 ozs. paprika
1/4 oz. ground black pepper
1/2 oz. marjoram
2 1/2 lbs. ice water
12 ozs. soy protein concentrate
   or non-fat dry milk
25 lbs. pork butts, certified

INGREDIENTS FOR 10 LBS.
6 tbsp. salt
2 tbsp. powdered dextrose
2 level tsp. Prague Powder No. 1
6-8 large garlic cloves
1 oz. wine or cider vinegar
4 tbsp. paprika
1 tbsp. ground black pepper
1 tbsp. marjoram
1 pint ice water
2 cups soy protein concentrate
   or non-fat dry milk
10 lbs. of pork butts, certified

CHOPPING

Dice or chop all the meat in 1/2" to 3/4" pieces and place in the mixer.

MIXING

After the meat has been placed into the mixer, add all the ingredients except the water and wine or vinegar. Mix until all the ingredients are evenly distributed. Place the meat into curing tubs and let stand in cooler overnight. The next morning place the meat into a mixer and add the water and vinegar (mix the vinegar with the water) and mix very well. Remove to stuffer.

STUFFING

Stuff into 35-38mm hog casings and hang on smoke sticks. Allow the sausage to air dry before placing in the smokehouse. After the sausage is dry, place into cool smokehouse overnight at 100-110 degrees F. The next morning raise the temperature to 130-135 degrees F. and hold this temperature until the sausage firms up.
Remove sausage from smokehouse and allow to hang at room

temperature before placing into 40-45 degree F. cooler overnight.

NOTE:

The USDA regulations class "linguisa" as an uncooked sausage. It is therefore necessary to use certified frozen pork to manufacture this product. The above outlined procedure does not conform to government regulations concerning the destruction of live trichinae.

PRESCRIBED TREATMENT OF PORK PRODUCTS
TO DESTROY TRICHINAE

Required period of freezing at temperature indicated:

Temperature Degrees F.	Group 1 Days	Group 2 Days
5	20	30
-10	10	20
-20	6	12

Group 1 comprises product in separate pieces not exceeding 6 inches in thickness or arranged on separate racks with layers not exceeding 6 inches in depth, or stored in crates or boxes not exceeding 6 inches in depth or stored as solidly frozen blocks not exceeding 6 inches in (depth) thickness.

Group 2 comprises product in pieces, layers, or within containers, the thickness of which exceeds 6 inches but not 27 inches and product in containers including tierces, barrels, kegs and cartons having a thickness not exceeding 27 inches.

The product undergoing such refrigeration or the containers thereof shall be so spaced while in the freezer as will insure free circulation of air between the pieces of meat, layers, blocks, barrels or tierces in order that the temperature of the meat throughout will be promptly reduced to exceed 5 degrees F., -10 degrees F., or -20 degrees F. as the case may be.

MORTADELLA

INGREDIENTS FOR 25 LBS.

8 ozs. salt
1 oz. gelatin
1 oz. Prague Powder No. 1
12 ozs. non-fat dry milk
4 ozs. corn syrup solids
¼ oz. fresh garlic
1 oz. ground black pepper
1 oz. ground mace
¼ oz. coriander
1 tsp. cinnamon
2 ozs. good Italian wine
2½ lbs. ice water
24 lbs. lean pork butts
1 lbs. pork snouts

INGREDIENTS FOR 10 LBS.

6 tbsp. salt
2 tbsp. gelatin
2 level tsp. Prague Powder No. 1
2 cups non-fat dry milk
8 tbsp. corn syrup solids
2 large cloves fresh garlic
1 tbsp. ground black pepper
1 tbsp. ground mace
1 tbsp. coriander
½ tsp. cinnamon
½ oz. good Italian wine
1 pint ice water
9½ lbs. lean pork butts
½ lb. pork snouts

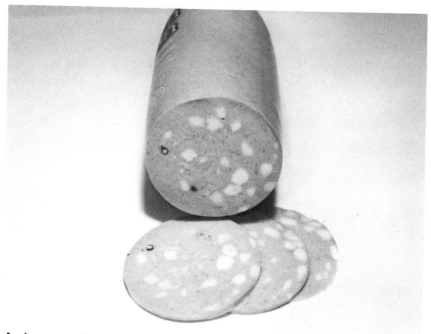

A close-up photo of a mortadella. Notice the fat cubes that make this sausage so distinctive.

GRINDING & COOKING

Grind all the meat through a ½" grinder plate. With the exception of the garlic and pepper, all the spices are boiled in the wine for 15-20 minutes. Place meat in the mixer and add the wine and spices after they have cooled. Dissolve all the gelatin and cure in the water adding it to the meat with the rest of the ingredients. Mix very well until all the ingredients are evenly distributed. Grind all the meat through a ⅛" plate and stuff into pans not over 6" deep; place overnight in 38-40 degrees F. cooler. Stuff into beef bladders or a large cellulose casing.

Place into a smoker preheated to 120 degrees F., gradually increasing the temperature to 170 degrees F. in an 8-hour period. Keep at this temperature until the internal temperature reaches 155 degrees F. If necessary, you may rinse with very hot water to remove the grease before placing under a cool shower. Reduce internal temperature to around 120-125 degrees F. before placing overnight into 40-45 degree F. cooler.

BERLINER SAUSAGE

INGREDIENTS FOR 25 LBS.

1 oz. Prague Powder No. 1
4 ozs. powdered dextrose
12 ozs. soy protein concentrate
  or non-fat dry milk
8 ozs. salt
½ lb. fresh onions
2 tbsp. granulated garlic
1½ ozs. ground white pepper
2 lbs. ice water
15 lbs. lean pork
5 lbs. boneless chuck
5 lbs. boneless veal

INGREDIENTS FOR 10 LBS.

2 level tsp. Prague Powder No. 1
1½ ozs. powdered dextrose
2 cups soy protein concentrate
  or non-fat dry milk
6 tbsp. salt
1 small onion
1 tsp. granulated garlic
1 tbsp. ground white pepper
2 cups ice water
6 lbs. lean pork
2 lbs. boneless chuck
2 lbs. boneless veal

GRINDING & STUFFING

Grind all meat through ³⁄₁₆" or ¼" grinder plate and mix with all ingredients. Stuff meat into 5" fibrous casings and place in cooler for 2 days. Remove meat and keep at room temperature for 3 hours or until internal temperature of product reaches at least 60 degrees F. Remove and put in preheated smokehouse at 120 degrees F. the first hour, and apply smoke while increasing temperature every 30 minutes by 10 degrees until 160 degrees F. is reached. Hold at this temperature until you reach 152 degrees F. and desired color is obtained.

215

KOSHER STYLE SALAMI

INGREDIENTS FOR 25 LBS.
8 ozs. salt
2 ozs. powdered dextrose
1 oz. Prague Power No. 1
2 ozs. ground black pepper
½ oz. paprika
½ oz. ground ginger
½ oz. ground nutmeg
¼ oz. garlic powder
3 ozs. corn syrup solids
25 lbs. lean beef or cow meat

INGREDIENTS FOR 10 LBS.
6 tbsp. salt
4 tbsp. powdered dextrose
2 level tsp. Prague Powder No. 1
2 tbsp. ground black pepper
1 tbsp. paprika
1 tbsp. ground ginger
2 tsp. ground nutmeg
½ tsp. garlic powder
6 tbsp. corn syrup solids
10 lbs. lean beef or cow meat

GRINDING

Grind all the fat meat through a ³⁄₁₆" grinder plate and the lean beef through a 1" plate, or, you may dice into 1" pieces. Place all the meat into the mixer, adding all the ingredients. Mix well and place in 38-40 degrees F. cooler overnight to allow meats to set up. The next day, regrind through ³⁄₁₆" plate.

STUFFING

Be sure you pack the stuffer very tightly with the meat to eliminate all air pockets. Stuff into fibrous casing, 3½" x 24". Hang salami on smokehouse sticks and place into smoker.

SMOKING

Smoker should be preheated to 130 degrees F. and salami should be kept in smoker for at least 1 hour with dampers wide open, no smoke. After this period, allow the dampers to remain about ¼ open and apply heavy smoke, increasing the temperature to 140 degrees F., and maintain for another hour. Raise the temperature to 160 degrees F. for 1 hour and then raise to 170 degrees F., cutting off the smoke.

Keep salami in smoker until the internal temperature reaches 152 degrees F. Remove from smoker and shower with cold tap water until internal temperature is reduced to 110 degrees F. Allow to hang at room temperature until the salami is dry or until desired bloom is obtained. Keep salami out of drafts while drying. Place in cooler overnight before using.

KRAKOWSKA

INGREDIENTS FOR 25 LBS.	INGREDIENTS FOR 10 LBS.
1 lb. ice water	½ pint ice water
8 ozs. salt	6 tbsp. salt
1 oz. Prague Powder No. 1	2 level tsp. Prague Powder No. 1
1 oz. powdered dextrose	2 tbsp. powdered dextrose
1 oz. garlic powder	2 tbsp. garlic powder
1 oz. ground white pepper	3 tsp. ground white pepper
1 tbsp. coriander	1 tsp. coriander
½ oz. ground mustard	2 tbsp. ground mustard
1 tsp. marjoram	½ tsp. marjoram
25 lbs. boneless fresh hams	10 lbs. boneless fresh hams

Krakowska, or KK as it is sometimes called, is made of fresh legs or what is commonly known as fresh hams. The hams are boned and all the lean meat is kept separate. The hams are made as lean as possible and ground through a 1½" grinder plate or cut up into 1-1½" chunks. The trimmings from these hams can be used in this sausage if you can grind them very fine. In most cases, it is best to use the lean meat, as it makes a much nicer sausage. You may add up to 20% of very lean pork butts or pork shanks if available.

MIXING

Place all meats into the mixer and add all the ingredients. Mix well until all the spices are evenly distributed. Remove and place in pans or tubs, packing the meat tightly not over 6" high, and put in cooler overnight. Stuff into fibrous casings 2-3½" in diameter by 24" long.

SMOKING & COOKING

Place in a preheated smokehouse at 130 degrees F. with dampers wide open for 1 hour. Apply a heavy smoke, gradually increasing the smoker temperature to 160-165 degrees F. with dampers ¼ open. Keep sausage in smoker until you reach the desired color or until sausage reaches 152 degrees F. internally. If you are using a steam cabinet, you may remove the krakowska from the smoker when the internal temperature is 130 degrees F. Cook in steam cabinet until internal temperature of 152 degrees F. is obtained.

When sausage is cooked, place under cool water shower until the internal temperature is reduced to 110 degrees F. You may leave at room temperature for 45 minutes or until desired bloom is obtained. Remove to cooler and hold overnight.

BRAUNSCHWEIGER

INGREDIENTS FOR 25 LBS.

1 oz. Prague Powder No. 1
8 ozs. salt
4 ozs. granulated onion
1 tsp. ground allspice
1 oz. ground white pepper
1 oz. powdered dextrose
1 tsp. marjoram
1 tsp. ground nutmeg
1 tsp. ground ginger
1 tsp. ground sage
1 tsp. ground cloves
½ oz. ground mustard
2½ lbs. ice water
11¼ lbs. pork snouts
13¾ lbs. pork livers

INGREDIENTS FOR 10 LBS.

2 level tsp. Prague Powder No. 1
6 tbsp. salt
5 tbsp. granulated onion
¼ tsp. ground allspice
1 tbsp. ground white pepper
2 tbsp. powdered dextrose
¼ tsp. marjoram
½ tsp. ground nutmeg
½ tsp. ground ginger
½ tsp. ground sage
½ tsp. ground cloves
1 tbsp. ground mustard
1 pint ice water
4½ lbs. pork snouts
5½ lbs. pork livers

GRINDING

Grind all meats through ³⁄₁₆" grinder plate. Add all the ingredients to the meat and mix well. After mixing, run through grinder again using ⅛" plate. Stuff immediately into 2¾" to 3" regular or sewed hog bungs.

COOKING AND SMOKING

Have water ready in the cooking tank at 180 degrees F., then carefully place the braunschweiger in the tank. Be sure the braunschweiger is fully submerged. The water temperature should drop to about 160 degrees F. Maintain that temperature until the internal temperature of the braunschweiger reaches 152 degrees F. This should take from 2-2½ hours.

After cooking, braunschweiger should be removed and placed in a container full of ice and water. Add additional ice to chill the braunschweiger as soon as possible. Chilling will take from 1-2 hours. Remove the braunschweiger and hang on smokesticks;

shower with 180 degrees F. water for about 30 seconds to remove all the surface grease from the casing.

Hang at room temperature for ¾-1 hour or until dry. Place in preheated smokehouse at 115-120 degrees F. Hold at this temperature for about 3 hours. Apply a heavy smudge or until the desired color is obtained. Place in 35 degrees F. cooler overnight.

CHINESE-STYLE SAUSAGE

INGREDIENTS FOR 25 LBS.
12 ozs. powdered dextrose
1¼ lbs. soya sauce
1¼ lbs. Chinese white wine
1 oz. Prague Powder No. 1
8 ozs. soy protein concentrate
8 ozs. corn syrup solids
8 ozs. salt
17 lbs. very lean pork
8 lbs. backfat

INGREDIENTS FOR 10 LBS.
about 12 tbsp. powdered dextrose
2 cups soya sauce
2 cups Chinese white wine
2 level tsp. Prague Powder No. 1
1½ cups soy protein concentrate
4 tbsp. corn syrup solids
6 tbsp. salt
6½ lbs. very lean pork
3½ lbs. backfat

GRINDING & COOKING

Cut all the backfat into cubes ¼" to ½"; place these cubes into hot boiling water for a few seconds using a sieve or a screen. This prevents the cubes from sticking together. This is done just before adding the rest of the ingredients. Be sure you allow it to cool properly.

The lean pork also is cut up in cubes ¼" to ½"; mix all ingredients with the pork, except the soy protein concentrate. Let stand for about 5 minutes. Then add backfat and soy protein concentrate and mix well. Let stand another 5 minutes before placing into stuffer. Use a 38-42mm hog casing for stuffing into 5- or 6-inch links. The casings will have to be pin-pricked to insure proper drying. Place in smokehouse without smoke and let dry for 5-6 hours at 120 degrees F. or until desired color is obtained. Remove to cooler overnight.

NOTE:
The USDA regulations class Chinese sausage in the uncooked variety. It therefore is necessary to use certified frozen pork or the following instructions:

PRESCRIBED TREATMENT OF PORK PRODUCTS
TO DESTROY TRICHINAE

Required period of freezing at temperature indicated:

Temperature Degrees F.	Group 1 Days	Group 2 Days
5	20	30
-10	10	20
-20	6	12

Group 1 comprises product in separate pieces not exceeding 6 inches in thickness or arranged on separate racks with layers not exceeding 6 inches in depth, or stored in crates or boxes not exceeding 6 inches in (depth) thickness.

Group 2 comprises product in pieces, layers, or within containers, the thickness of which exceeds 6 inches but not 27 inches and product in containers including tierces, barrels, kegs and cartons having a thickness not exceeding 27 inches.

The product undergoing such refrigeration or the containers thereof shall be so spaced while in the freezer as will insure free circulation of air between the pieces of meat, layers, blocks, barrels or tierces in order that the temperature of the meat throughout will be promptly reduced to exceed 5 degrees F., -10 degrees F., or -20 degrees F. as the case may be.

COOKED SALAMI

INGREDIENTS FOR 25 LBS.
2½ lbs. ice water
8 ozs. salt
3 ozs. corn syrup solids
2 ozs. ground black pepper
1 oz. Prague Powder No. 1
½ oz. whole black pepper
½ oz. cardamon
½ oz. fresh garlic
12 ozs. soy protein concentrate
16 lbs. very lean beef
9 lbs. very lean pork butts

INGREDIENTS FOR 10 LBS.
1 pint ice water
6 tbsp. salt
6 tbsp. corn syrup solids
2 tbsp. ground black pepper
2 level tsp. Prague Powder No. 1
1 tbsp. whole black pepper
2 tbsp. cardamon
4 large cloves fresh garlic
2 cups soy protein concentrate
6½ lbs. very lean beef
3½ lbs. very lean pork butts

GRINDING & STUFFING

Grind all the beef through a ⅛" grinder plate and all the pork through a ³⁄₁₆" grinder plate; add all the ingredients and mix well until evenly distributed. Meat should then be packed into tubs and kept in a cooler overnight at 38-40 degrees F. Remove from cooler and pack into stuffer, eliminating air pockets. Salami is stuffed into 3½" by 24" cellulose casing, or use a fibrous casing.

SMOKING & COOKING

Salami is to be removed and placed in a preheated smokehouse at 130-135 degrees F. for 1 hour. After 1 hour, you may apply a light or medium smoke. Gradually increase smokehouse temperature to 150 degrees F. during the next 30 minutes and hold at this temperature until a desired color is obtained. This will take from 4-5 hours. You may then cut off all the smoke and raise the smoker temperature to 165-170 degrees F. and cook until the internal temperature is 155 degrees F.

Remove salami from smoker and shower with cool water until an internal temperature of 120 degrees F. is obtained. You may allow the salami to hang at room temperature for 30 minutes to 1 hour or until a desired bloom is obtained.

BRAUNSCHWEIGER LIVER SAUSAGE

INGREDIENTS FOR 25 LBS.
12 ozs. non-fat dry milk or
  soy protein concentrate
8 ozs. salt
1 oz. onion powder
1 oz. powdered dextrose
1 oz. Prague Powder No. 1
1 oz. ground white pepper
1 tsp. ground cloves
1 tsp. ground allspice
1 tsp. rubbed sage
1 tsp. ground marjoram
1 tsp. ground nutmeg
1 tsp. ground ginger
12½ lbs. pork liver
12½ lbs. pork snouts

INGREDIENTS FOR 10 LBS.
2 cups non-fat dry milk or
  soy protein concentrate
6 tbsp. salt
2 tbsp. onion powder
2 tbsp. powdered dextrose
2 level tsp. Prague Powder No. 1
1 tbsp. ground white pepper
½ tsp. ground cloves
½ tsp. ground allspice
½ tsp. rubbed sage
½ tsp. ground marjoram
½ tsp. ground nutmeg
½ tsp. ground ginger
5 lbs. pork liver
5 lbs. pork snouts

GRINDING

Be sure all the meat used has been chilled at 32-34 degrees F. All meat is to be ground through a ⅛" grinder plate several times. Place in mixer and add all the ingredients. Stuff into 2¾" to 3" by 30" sewed hog bungs. You may also use a fibrous casing if you wish.

SMOKING & COOKING

After stuffing, place braunschweiger into cooker with water pre-heated to 180 degrees F. Water temperature will drop to 160-165 degrees F. and continue cooking until the internal temperature reaches 152 degrees F. internally. After cooking, place sausage into a container filled with ice and water and allow to cool as rapidly as possible for 1-2 hours.

Remove from water and hang on sticks. You may shower braunschweiger with hot water for about 30 seconds to remove surface grease. Hang at room temperature for about 1 hour or until dry. Remove to preheated smoker at 115-120 degrees F. Apply a heavy smoke at this temperature for approximately 3 hours or until the desired color is obtained. After smoking, you may shower with cool water for about 5 minutes. Let dry and remove to cooler overnight.

METTWURST

INGREDIENTS FOR 25 LBS.
1 oz. Prague Powder No. 1
¼ oz. nutmeg, ground
1 oz. ground white pepper
½ oz. ground celery
½ oz. ground allspice
¼ oz. marjoram
¼ oz. ground caraway seed
¼ oz. ground coriander
2 ozs. powdered dextrose
½ oz. whole mustard seed
  (optional)
8 ozs. salt

INGREDIENTS FOR 10. LBS.
2 level tsp. Prague Powder No. 1
2 tbsp. nutmeg, ground
1 tbsp. ground white pepper
1 tsp. ground celery
1 tbsp. ground allspice
1 tsp. ground marjoram
½ tsp. ground caraway seed
1 tsp. ground coriander
4 tbsp. powdered dextrose
2 tsp. whole mustard seed
  (optional)
6 tbsp. salt

A very good mettwurst is made using 3 kinds of meats: 20% veal, 50% pork butts and 30% beef chuck, or in a 10 lb. recipe, 2 lbs. of veal, 5 lbs. of pork butts, and 3 lbs. of beef chuck.

GRINDING & CHOPPING

Grind all the meats through 1½" grinder plate and place meats in the mixer. Add all the ingredients; mix for 2 minutes or until all the ingredients are evenly distributed. Remove from mixer and re-grind through 3⁄16" plate. Pack meat tightly into curing tubs not over 6" or 8" high. Remove to cooler and cure 24 hours at 40 degrees F.; regrind through 1⁄8" plate mixing whole mustard seed as the meat comes from the grinder.

STUFFING

Stuff into beef rounds that have been washed and cut into pieces 16-18" in length and tied at one end. Tie ends together and hang properly on smokestick. Prick the casings, allowing air that might be trapped into stuffing to escape. Allow to dry at room temperature for about 2-3 hours.

SMOKING

Place in 90-100 degree F. smokehouse with heavy smudge for 8-12 hours. Remove from smokehouse and dip or spray with hot water to plump the casings. Allow to chill down to room temperature (60-65 degrees F.) before placing in the cooler. Allow to hang overnight in the cooler.

NOTE:

The USDA regulations class "mettwurst" as a summer sausage of the uncooked variety. It therefore is necessary to use certified frozen pork to manufacture this product. The outlined above procedure does not conform to government regulations concerning the destruction of live trichinae. Use following instructions:

PRESCRIBED TREATMENT OF PORK PRODUCTS TO DESTROY TRICHINAE

Required period of freezing at temperature indicated:

Temperature Degrees F.	Group 1 Days	Group 2 Days
5	20	30
-10	10	20
-20	6	12

Group 1 comprises product in separate pieces not exceeding 6 inches in thickness or arranged on separate racks with layers not exceeding 6 inches in depth, or stored in crates or boxes not exceeding 6 inches in (depth) thickness.

Group 2 comprises product in pieces, layers, or within containers, the thickness of which exceeds 6 inches but not 27 inches and product in containers including tierces, barrels, kegs and cartons having a thickness not exceeding 27 inches.

The product undergoing such refrigeration or the containers thereof shall be so spaced while in the freezer as will insure free circulation of air between the pieces of meat, layers, blocks, barrels or tierces in order that the temperature of the meat throughout will be promptly reduced to exceed 5 degrees F., -10 degrees F., or -20 degrees F. as the case may be.

FISH SAUSAGE
INGREDIENTS FOR 10 LBS.
1 pt. ice water
1 lb. vegetable shortening
12 ozs. corn starch
4 tbsp. salt
1 tsp. sugar
1 tbsp. ground black pepper
1 tsp. onion powder
1 tsp. garlic powder
1 tsp. ground nutmeg

After the fish are deboned, be sure the flesh is cooled to at least 35 degrees F. before starting. The fish is then ground through a ³⁄₁₆" grinder plate. The salt is then added and mixed thoroughly. This will allow the sausage to bind well. After 10 minutes add the corn starch mixed with the ice water. The spices and shortening are added last, again mixing thoroughly. The mixture is then stuffed into a fibrous casing of your choice (2" or 3½" wide).

The sausage is then cooked in water 200-205 degrees F. until the internal temperature reaches 180 degrees F. The sausage is then promptly cooled in cold water or showered until the internal temperature of 70 degrees F. is obtained. The cooled sausage is then immersed in boiling water for one minute in order to tighten the casing on the product.

Fish sausage is a very perishable product and should be stored at a temperature of at least 35 degrees F. It also keeps well when frozen.

Because this sausage is cooked at such high temperatures, the use of cures is not required. In addition, this sausage may also be made in a loaf for home use and cooked in a loaf pan. If allowed to cool overnight it will slice very nicely as any other lunchmeat.

This loaf may also be flavored with liquid smoke, using 1 teaspoon to each 5 lbs. of meat.

GERMAN BOLOGNA

INGREDIENTS FOR 25 LBS.
18 lbs. lean beef
7 lbs. pork butts
1 oz. ground white pepper
1 oz. ground mustard
½ oz. ground celery
½ oz. ground nutmeg
¼ oz. ground coriander
¼ oz. garlic powder
4 oz. powdered dextrose
12 ozs. soy protein concentrate
2½ lbs. ice water
1 oz. prague powder #1
8 ozs. salt

INGREDIENTS FOR 10 LBS.
7 lbs. lean beef
3 lbs. pork butts
1 tsp. ground white pepper
3 tbsp. ground mustard
1 tbsp. ground celery
1 tsp. level ground nutmeg
1 tsp. ground coriander
1 tsp. garlic powder
1½ oz. powdered dextrose
2 cups soy protein concentrate
1 pint ice water
2 level tsp. prague powder #1
3½ ozs. salt

Chuck meat may be used as lean beef called for in the above formula, along with the pork butts. All meat is ground through a ³⁄₁₆" grinder plate. Ingredients then are mixed and distributed evenly, adding water as you go along. Bologna is usually stuffed into 8" diameter casings; however, for home use you can use 3½", 5", or any size that is handy. Allow bologna to hang at room temperature until casings are dry. Then place in a preheated smokehouse at 165 degrees F. until the internal temperature reaches 150 degrees F. Bologna is removed and quickly cooled with water until internal temperature is reduced to around 90 degrees F. This type of bologna usually isn't smoked and is a coarse-type sausage.

LIVER AND ONION SAUSAGE

INGREDIENTS FOR 25 LBS.
15 lbs. pork liver
*7½ lbs. pork butts
2½ lbs. finely chopped onions
12 ozs. soy protein concentrate
2 ozs. powdered dextrose
1 oz. ground white pepper
¼ oz. ground marjoram
¼ oz. ground cloves
¼ oz. ground ginger
1 oz. prague powder #1
8 ozs. salt
1 qt. ice water

INGREDIENTS FOR 10 LBS.
7 lbs. pork liver
*2¼ lbs. pork butts
12 ozs. finely chopped onions
5 ozs. soy protein concentrate
¾ oz. powdered dextrose
1 tbsp. ground white pepper
1 tsp. ground marjoram
1 tsp. ground cloves
1 tsp. ground ginger
2 level tsp. prague powder #1
3½ ozs. salt
1 pt. ice water

*Whenever possible you may use lean pork snouts in place of pork butts.

Cut pork livers into slices about ½" to ¾" thick. Place liver into boiling water until it is cooked. Then cool liver in cold water and grind through a ⅛" grinder plate. Pork butts (or snouts) are then ground through a ⅜" grinder plate. Remaining ingredients are added and mixed until evenly distributed. Then stuff meat into 40-43mm beef middles.

Place sausage in 160 degrees F. water and cook until an internal temperature of 152 degrees F. is reached. Remove to cooler and allow to set for 24 hours before using.

POLISH HAM SAUSAGE
(Kielbasa Szynkowa)

INGREDIENTS FOR 25 LBS.
25 lbs. very lean pork or ham
8 ozs. salt
1 oz. prague powder #1
2 ozs. powdered dextrose
½ oz. ground black pepper
¼ oz. ground coriander
¼ oz. ground nutmeg
1 qt. ice water

INGREDIENTS FOR 10 LBS.
10 lbs. very lean pork or ham
3½ ozs. salt
2 level tsp. prague powder #1
¾ oz. powdered dextrose
1 tbsp. ground black pepper
1 tbsp. ground coriander
1 tbsp. ground nutmeg
1 pint ice water

Cut lean meat into 1" cubes or grind through a 1" grinder plate. Grind the fat meat through a ⅛" grinder plate. Add the remaining ingredients to the meat and mix thoroughly until evenly distributed. Then stuff the mixture into clear, fibrous 3½" x 24" casings and dry at room temperature for 2 hours (at the same time, the temperature of the meat will be rising slowly). Place the sausage in a smokehouse preheated to 150 degrees F. for 1 hour, applying dense smoke. Then increase the temperature to 165 degrees F. and continue until an internal temperature of 152 degrees F. is reached. Smoke the sausage for 3 more hours, reducing the smokehouse temperature to 150 degrees F. Place in cooler overnight before using.

KIELBASA SERDELOWA
(Serdelki)

INGREDIENTS FOR 25 LBS.
20 lbs. calf meat or veal
5 lbs. fresh bacon
8 ozs. salt
1 oz. prague powder #1
½ oz. ground paprika
1 oz. ground black pepper
1 oz. garlic
12 ozs. non-fat dry milk
2 qts. ice water
2 ozs. powdered dextrose

INGREDIENTS FOR 10 LBS.
8 lbs. calf meat or veal
2 lbs. fresh bacon
3½ ozs. salt
2 level tsp. prague powder #1
1 tbsp. ground paprika
1 tbsp. ground black pepper
1 clove garlic
5 ozs. non-fat dry milk
1½ pints ice water
¾ oz. powdered dextrose

Grind meat through ⅛" or 3/16" grinder plate. Add remaining ingredients and mix well until evenly distributed. Stuff mixture into 24-26mm sheep casings and allow to hang at room temperature until dry. Then place sausage in a smokehouse preheated to 120 degrees F., applying a dense smoke. After one hour, increase the temperature to 165 degrees F. and continue until the internal temperature of the sausage reaches 152 degrees F. Remove sausage from smoker and quickly shower with cold water until the internal temperature is reduced to 90 degrees F. Hang the sausage at room temperature for one more hour before placing in a cooler overnight.

POLISH LEMON SAUSAGE
(Kielbasa Cytrynowa)

INGREDIENTS FOR 25 LBS.

20 lbs. pork butts
5 lbs. lean beef
8 ozs. salt
1 oz. prague powder #1
1 oz. ground black pepper
¼ oz. ground nutmeg
2 ozs. powdered dextrose
¼ oz. very finely chopped
   lemon rind
1 qt. ice water

INGREDIENTS FOR 10 LBS.

8¾ lbs. pork butts
1¼ lbs. lean beef
3½ ozs. salt
2 level tsp. prague powder #1
1 tbsp. ground black pepper
1 tsp. ground nutmeg
1 ozs. powdered dextrose
1 slice very finely chopped
   lemon rind
1 pint ice water

Grind meat through a ⅛" grinder plate. Add remaining ingredients and mix well, adding water as you go along. Then stuff sausage in clear, fibrous 3½" x 24" casings. Place the sausage on smokesticks and hang at room temperature (65-70 degrees F.) for about 2 hours.

Then put sausage into a smokehouse preheated to 150 degrees F. Apply smoke. After one hour, increase the temperature to 160 degrees F. and keep the sausage there until an internal temperature of 152 degrees F. is reached. The sausage will have a nice brown color when completed and the finished weight will be about 95% of the original.

KIELBASA KRAKOWSKA

INGREDIENTS FOR 25 LBS.
12½ lbs. lean fresh ham
7½ lbs. pork butts
5 lbs. veal
8 ozs. salt
1 oz. prague powder #1
1 oz. ground black pepper
½ oz. garlic
¼ oz. cardamon
2 ozs. powdered dextrose
1 qt. ice water

INGREDIENTS FOR 10 LBS.
5 lbs. lean fresh ham
3 lbs. pork butts
2 lbs. veal
3½ ozs. salt
2 level tsp. prague powder #1
1 tbsp. ground black pepper
1 small clove garlic
½ tsp. cardamon
¾ ozs. powdered dextrose
1 pint ice water

Trim fat from meat and grind through a ⅛" grinder plate. Grind lean meat through a ¾" grinder plate. Add the remaining ingredients to the combined meat mixture and mix until evenly distributed. Pack the mixture tightly into containers not more than 6" high, eliminating air pockets. Keep overnight at 38-40 degrees F. Regrind mixture through a ⅜" grinder plate and stuff into 35-38mm hog casings.

Place the sausage on smokesticks and dry at room temperature for about 30-40 minutes. Place sausage in a smokehouse preheated to 130 degrees F. for about 45 minutes with damper and draft wide open. When the sausage starts to take on a brown color, close damper to ¼ open and adjust draft to an almost-closed position. Increase the temperature to 160 degrees F. and maintain until an internal temperature of 152 degrees F. is reached. Remove the sausage from the smoker and quickly shower with cool water until the internal temperature is reduced to 100 degrees F. Place in cooler overnight before using.

RHEINISCHE FLEISCHWURST
(Rhineland Ham Sausage)

INGREDIENTS FOR 25 LBS.
13½ lbs. pork butts
7½ lbs. leg of pork (fresh ham)
4 lbs. smoked bacon
3 ozs. granulated onion
8 ozs. salt
1 oz. prague powder #1
1 oz. ground white pepper
¼ oz. ground cloves
½ oz. ground nutmeg

INGREDIENTS FOR 10 LBS.
5 lbs. pork butts
3 lbs. leg of pork (fresh ham)
2 lbs. smoked bacon
¾ oz. granulated onion
3½ ozs. salt
2 level tsp. prague powder #1
1 tbsp. ground white pepper
1 level tsp. ground cloves
1 tbsp. ground nutmeg

The meat should be chilled to 38-40 degrees F. before starting. Grind the pork legs and butts through a 1" grinder plate. Cut the smoked bacon into ¼"-½" cubes. Mix the meat with the remaining ingredients, blending thoroughly. Then stuff it into beef middles (about 4-4½" in diameter) or use a 5" fibrous casing. After stuffing, let the casings dry and place the sausage in the smoker for further drying at about 120 degrees F. When the casings are dry, increase the temperature to 160-165 degrees F. and keep there until an internal temperature of 152 degrees F. is reached. Then remove from the smoker and shower with cold water until the internal temperature is reduced to 120 degrees F.

A sausage made with a large-size casing (5-8") can easily take up to 10 or 12 hours before you can reach the 152 degrees F. temperature required. To speed this process, you can cook the sausage in water at 160 degrees F. until the 152 degrees F. temperature is reached. In other words—after you have achieved a desirable color in the smoker, the process can be completed by cooking in water.

SULZWURST EINFACH

INGREDIENTS FOR 25 LBS.
12½ lbs. pig skins
6¼ lbs. pig hearts
6¼ lbs. pig meat from head or feet
1 oz. ground white pepper
4 ozs. chopped pimentos
½ oz. ground caraway seeds
1 lb. finely ground raw onions
12 ozs. gelatin

INGREDIENTS FOR 10 LBS.
6 lbs. pig skins
2 lbs. pig hearts
2 lbs. pig meat from head or feet
1 tbsp. ground white pepper
1½ ozs. chopped pimentos
1 tbsp. ground caraway seed
6½ ozs. finely ground raw onions
5 ozs. gelatin

The meat has to be cured in a brine for 3 days using the following ingredients:
2½ gallons ice water
2½ lbs. salt
12 ozs. powdered dextrose
4 ozs. prague powder #1

After curing the meat, place it in a kettle or container and cook for 1½-2 hours. The pork skins should be kept in a cooking net or cooked separately because they are to be ground more finely than the other meat. Cool all the meat and broth, then grind the pork skins through a ⅛" grinder plate. After grinding, mix all the meat with the remaining ingredients, adding 10% of the broth. Allow this mixture to cook until a 160 degrees F. temperature is reached (do not overcook; the binding power of the gelatin will be broken down when you reach 170 degrees F.). Allow to cool, then stuff the mixture into 5" fibrous casings. After the sausage is stuffed, it should be cooled for at least 24 hours before using. You also may use any type of deep cake pan to mold these ingredients.

JAGDWURST
(Hunters Sausage)

INGREDIENTS FOR 25 LBS.
6¼ lbs. lean fresh ham
8¾ lbs. fresh bacon
10 lbs. lean pork butts
8 ozs. salt
1 oz. prague powder #1
2 ozs. powdered dextrose
1 oz. ground white pepper
½ oz. ground coriander
¼ oz. fresh garlic
2 ozs. ground mustard seed
1 oz. ground nutmeg
½ oz. ground ginger

INGREDIENTS FOR 10 LBS.
1½ lbs. lean fresh ham
4 lbs. fresh bacon
4½ lbs. lean pork butts
3½ ozs. salt
2 level tsp. prague powder #1
½ oz. powdered dextrose
1 tbsp. ground white pepper
1 tbsp. ground coriander
1 garlic clove
¾ oz. ground mustard seed
1 tbsp. ground nutmeg
1 tbsp. ground ginger

Trim the fat from the fresh ham and grind with the lean pork butts through a ⅛" grinder plate. Grind fresh bacon and lean ham through a ⅜" grinder plate. Add the remaining ingredients and mix thoroughly until evenly distributed. Stuff the meat into a clear, fibrous 3½" x 24" casing. Allow to dry at room temperature for 30-40 minutes. Then place the sausage in a smoker pre-heated to 130 degrees F. for about 1 hour without smoke. Increase the smokehouse temperature to 165 degrees F. and maintain until the internal temperature of the sausage reaches 150 degrees F.

Do not smoke the sausage for more than 30 minutes during this period.

Jagdwurst is a mild-tasing sausage but somewhat spicy. This is why the smoke is applied for such a short period. The meat, spices, garlic and smoke are being blended into one flavor. Garlic is usually chopped in a blender with a little water to help it along.

TEEWURST
(Teawurst)

Teewurst is a finely ground sausage that easily spreads on a piece of bread when properly made. There are a number of things one must do to develop the special flavor of this sausage. The beef and pork that are used should be from older animals whenever possible. In addition, it is preferable to smoke this sausage with a mixture of oak, beech and juniper berries. The finished product will have a reddish-brown color.

INGREDIENTS FOR 25 LBS.
5 lbs. lean beef
7½ lbs. fresh bacon
12½ lbs. lean pork butts
8 ozs. salt
1 oz. prague powder #1
2 ozs. powdered dextrose
1 oz. ground white pepper
¼ oz. pimentos, chopped
⅛ oz. cardamon
½ oz. good rum
¼ oz. red cayenne pepper

INGREDIENTS FOR 10 LBS.
2½ lbs. lean beef
3 lbs. fresh bacon
5 lbs. lean pork butts
3½ ozs. salt
2 level tsp. prague powder #1
½ oz. powdered dextrose
1 tbsp. ground white pepper
1 tsp. pimentos, chopped
½ tsp. cardamon
¼ oz. good rum
1 level tsp. red cayenne pepper

Grind meat and pimentos through a ⅛" grinder plate. Add remaining ingredients and mix well until evenly distributed. Then regrind meat through a ⅛" grinder plate so you can achieve a finer texture for spreading. Stuff meat into a clear fibrous casing 3½" in diameter. After stuffing, hang the sausage at 68-70 degrees F. for at least 3 hours. Place sausage in a cold smoker with heavy, dense smoke for 2-3 days. You may also smoke it for 8-10 hours at 90-100 degrees F. in dense smoke, but you will get a better flavor if it is smoked for 2-3 days without heat.

Teewurst is a fine quality sausage and does not spoil quickly if kept refrigerated. It is a type of sausage one must acquire a taste for.

IMPORTANT:

Because the above processing procedure does not conform to

the U.S.D.A. regulations concerning the destruction of live trichinae sometimes found in pork, be sure that you are using certified pork, or a pork that has been properly frozen, using the following instructions:

PRESCRIBED TREATMENT OF PORK PRODUCTS
TO DESTROY TRICHINAE

Required period of freezing at temperature indicated:

Temperature Degrees F.	Group 1 Days	Group 2 Days
5	20	30
-10	10	20
-20	6	12

Group 1 comprises product in separate pieces not exceeding 6 inches in thickness or arranged on separate racks with layers not exceeding 6 inches in depth, or stored in crates or boxes not exceeding 6 inches in (depth) thickness.

Group 2 comprises product in pieces, layers, or within containers, the thickness of which exceeds 6 inches but not 27 inches and product in containers including tierces, barrels, kegs and cartons having a thickness not exceeding 27 inches.

The product undergoing such refrigeration or the containers thereof shall be so spaced while in the freezer as will insure free circulation of air between the pieces of meat, layers, blocks, barrels or tierces in order that the temperature of the meat throughout will be promptly reduced to exceed 5 degrees F., -10 degrees F., or -20 degrees F. as the case may be.

WEISSWURST

INGREDIENTS FOR 25 LBS.
12½ lbs. veal
12½ lbs. lean pork butts
8 ozs. non-fat dry milk
8 ozs. salt
8 ozs. soy protein concentrate
¼ oz. onion powder
¼ oz. dry parsley
2 ozs. ground mustard seed
1 oz. ground white pepper
¼ oz. ground celery seeds
¼ oz. mace
2 ozs. powdered dextrose
2 qts. ice water

INGREDIENTS FOR 10 LBS.
5 lbs. veal
5 lbs. lean pork butts
3½ ozs. non-fat dry milk
3½ ozs. salt
3½ ozs. soy protein concentrate
1 teaspoon onion powder
1 teaspoon dry parsley
1 oz. ground mustard seed
1 tbsp. ground white pepper
1 tsp. ground celery seeds
1 tsp. mace
1 oz. powdered dextrose
1 qt. ice water

Grind meat through a ¼" or ⅜" grinder plate. Add all the ingredients except the water and mix thoroughly until evenly distributed. Then place the meat in the food processor, adding the water as you go along. This will help emulsify the meat.

Stuff into a 32-35mm hog casing and make into 5" to 6" links. Place into 160 degrees F. water and cook until an internal temperature of 150 degrees F. is attained. Then shower the sausage with cool water until the internal temperature falls to 75 degrees F. Place in cooler overnight before using.

SMOKED HUNGARIAN PAPRIKA SAUSAGE

INGREDIENTS FOR 25 LBS.
25 lbs. pork butts
8 ozs. salt
2 ozs. powdered dextrose
1 oz. prague powder #1
½ oz. garlic
1 oz. ground black pepper
14 ozs. paprika
1 qt. ice water

INGREDIENTS FOR 10 LBS.
10 lbs. pork butts
3½ ozs. salt
1 oz. powdered dextrose
2 level tsp. prague powder #1
1 large garlic clove
1 tbsp. ground black pepper
1½ ozs. paprika
1 pint ice water

Grind pork butts through a ⅜" grinder plate and the fat meat through a ⅛" grinder plate. Add other ingredients and mix thoroughly until evenly distributed. Then stuff sausage into a 35-38mm hog casing and allow it to dry at room temperature for about 1 hour. Place sausage in a preheated smokehouse at 130 degrees F. with the vents wide open until the sausage starts to take on a brown color. Gradually increase temperature at the rate of 10 degrees F. per hour until 160 degrees F. is attained. Sausage is then smoked at this temperature until an internal temperature of 150 degrees F. is obtained. Remove from smoker and shower with cool water until internal temperature is reduced to 90 degrees F.

The heavy use of paprika in this formula will leave your sausage with a deep reddish-brown color after it is finished.

TURKEY SAUSAGE

INGREDIENTS FOR 25 LBS.
20 lbs. turkey
5 lbs. fat pork butts
8 ozs. salt
1 oz. prague powder #1
2 ozs. powdered dextrose
12 ozs. soy protein concentrate
5 lbs. ice water

INGREDIENTS FOR 10 LBS.
7½ lbs. turkey
2½ lbs. fat pork butts
3½ ozs. salt
2 level tsp. prague powder #1
1 oz. powdered dextrose
5 ozs. soy protein concentrate
2 lbs. ice water

Grind meat through a ³⁄₁₆" or ¼" grinder plate. Add all ingredients except water and mix thoroughly until all the spices are evenly distributed. Then place the meat in a food processor, adding some of the water as you go along to help emulsify the meat.

The mixture is then stuffed into 32-35mm hog casings and linked into 5"-6" pieces. Allow the sausage to dry at room temperature while you preheat the smoker to 130 degrees F. Keep sausage at this temperature for an hour. Increase temperature to 150 degrees F. and hold for one more hour, applying the smoke.

The temperature is then raised to 165 degrees F. and maintained until an internal temperature of 155 degrees F. is reached. Then remove it from the smokehouse and shower it with cool water for 20 minutes. Place sausage in cooler and store overnight before using.

TURKEY OR POULTRY ROLL

Turkey and chicken have distinct flavors and only salt is needed to give additional flavor. The poultry skins are cooked in salted water along with the fat removed from the bird. This broth is then cooled to around 34-36 degrees F.

INGREDIENTS FOR 25 LBS.	INGREDIENTS FOR 10 LBS.
2 lbs. poultry fat	1 lb. poultry fat
15 lbs. poultry meat	7 lbs. poultry meat
4 lbs. broth	1 lb. broth
4 lbs. flour (semolina)	1 lb. flour (semolina)
8 ozs. salt	6 tbsp. salt
1 oz. Prague Powder No. 1	2 level tsp. Prague Powder No. 1

All meats and fat are ground through ⅛" or ³⁄₁₆" grinder plate. Dissolve salt and Prague Powder in broth. Add flour to meat and broth and mix well, stuff into 3½" by 24" clear fibrous casings. Product is placed in a preheated smokehouse at 130 degrees F. and kept there for ½ hour with dampers wide open. A heavy smudge of smoke is then introduced, raising the smokehouse temperature to 150 degrees F. and maintaining for one hour.

Raise smokehouse temperature to 175 degrees F. and hold until internal temperature of product reaches 155 degrees F. Product is then removed and showered with cold water until internal temperature is at 110 degrees F. before placing in cooler overnight. This product is highly perishable but keeps very well when frozen.

Semolina flour is used in making spaghetti. If not available in your area, you may substitute with regular flour.

COOKING MEAT

On the following pages you will find a number of recipes that call for the cooking of various kinds of meat before the sausage-making can actually begin. Some of these products are pork snouts, tongues and skins. In any case, it always is best to cook these meats first, then allow them to cool overnight in a cooler or refrigerator. The meat will set up and will be easier to cut or grind. It is not advisable to grind meat that has not been cooled overnight.

GOOSE LIVER SAUSAGE

INGREDIENTS FOR 25 LBS.
12 lbs. pork liver
*12 lbs. pork butts or pork snouts
1 lb. goose liver
8 ozs. soy protein concentrate
8 ozs. salt
1 oz. prague powder #1
4 ozs. powdered dextrose
1 oz. onion powder
1 oz. ground white pepper
¼ oz. sage
¼ oz. marjoram

INGREDIENTS FOR 10 LBS.
4¾ lbs. pork liver
*4¾ lbs. pork butts or pork snouts
½ lb. goose liver
3½ ozs. soy protein concentrate
3½ ozs. salt
2 level tsp. prague powder #1
1¾ ozs. powdered dextrose
½ oz. onion powder
½ oz. ground white pepper
1 tsp. sage
1 tsp. marjoram

*You should try to use pork snouts from a young hog, as they are very meaty. If not available, use pork butts instead.

The pork livers should be cut into slices about ½" to ¾" thick and placed in cold water for at least 1 hour, then drained. All goose livers should also be washed very well. Then put all the livers in boiling water until they are cooked. Allow livers to cool in cold water, then grind through a ⅛" grinder plate along with the pork snouts.

Remaining ingredients then are added to meat and mixed well until evenly distributed. Stuff mixture into a hog bung or a 3½" x 24" fibrous casing. Place sausage in water at 160 degrees F. and leave it there until an internal temperature of 150 degrees F. is reached. Chill sausage with cold water until the internal temperature drops to around 100-110 degrees F. Place in cooler overnight.

The next day, place the sausage in a preheated smoker at 90 degrees F. and smoke for 3 hours.

SPECIAL NOTE:

The above recipe does call for smoking goose liver. However, I prefer a goose liver that is not smoked.

BOUDIN
(Pronounced Boo-dan)

Boudin is best known in this country by the Cajuns of Louisiana. This is another form of blood sausage originating from France. In general, there are two kinds of boudin and they are very different in composition.

One is boudin blanc, a white sausage usually served during holiday meals. The white color tells us this sausage is made without the use of blood. The more popular boudin is made with blood.

Various stories have circulated over the years concerning the origin of this sausage. One such story says that the French who were driven out of Nova Scotia in 1755 brought boudin with them when they then settled in Louisiana. Over the years boudin sausage has become very popular in some parts of the U.S., especially the south. In either case, there is no question the boudin sausage had its beginnings in France. Practically every area of France has its own boudin sausage, such as boudin auvergne, boudin de Nancy, boudin du Poitou, boudin de Lyar and so on.

The production of this sausage varies very little from one locale to another. The addition of plums, apples, onions, sugar or cinnamon may indicate what area it's from. Like other blood sausages, this sausage is eaten in many ways—as a breakfast sausage or as a main course.

INGREDIENTS FOR 25 LBS.
7 lbs. fat pork meat
9 lbs. raw onions
9 lbs. beef blood
1 oz. prague powder #1

INGREDIENTS FOR 10 LBS.
3 lbs. fat pork meat
3½ lbs. raw onions
3½ lbs. beef blood
2 level tsp. prague powder #1

This boudin sausage recipe calls for six different spices. A number of these spices are in very small amounts. It is best that a mixture of spices and salt be blended for a 100-lb. recipe and then weighed out as needed.

100-LB. INGREDIENT FORMULA

2 lbs. 1 oz. salt
4½ ozs. coarse black pepper
½ oz. ground cloves
½ oz. ground marjoram
½ oz. ground cinnamon
1 oz. ground thyme
40 ozs. total

Ten ounces of the above ingredients is enough to season 25 lbs. of meat. For a 10-lb. recipe, you can use 4 ozs.

The raw onions should be chopped into small pieces and sauteed in lard until they are a golden brown. Allow onions to cool.

Grind pork through a ⅜" grinder plate and place in mixing container. (Be sure all the fat pork has been chilled to at least 38-40 degrees F. before grinding.) Add the cooled onions to the meat mixture along with the other ingredients, including the blood. Mix thoroughly, then stuff into 35-38mm hog casings. Then place sausage in water at 170-180 degrees F. until the internal temperature is at least 160 degrees F. Allow to cool overnight before using.

CAJUN-STYLE BOUDIN

For the most part, the Cajun boudin is the same as any other French blood sausage. As mentioned earlier, there are many variations of this sausage due to geographical considerations and an overabundance of certain ingredients in a particular area.

The Cajun boudin is no different, as rice is abundant in Louisiana and the surrounding area. Rice is the ingredient that makes this boudin so different than the boudin of France.

The recipe also calls for minced parsley and milk (either fresh or evaporated). The milk does tend to shorten the life of this sausage, since milk sours quickly. Freeze sausage that isn't used right away. The following ingredients can be added to a 10-lb. recipe on the preceding page.

5 ozs. seasoning (from previous page)
1 lb. rice (uncooked)
3 tbsp. finely-minced parsley
4 cups milk

Cook rice according to package directions until tender; allow to cool. Add remaining ingredients and mix thoroughly. Then stuff mixture into 40-43mm beef rounds and cook in water at 170-180 degrees F. until the internal temperature is 160 degrees F.

NOTE:

Because the rice will swell, it is recommended that you add 5 ozs. of the ingredients from the previous formula rather than the 4 ozs. called for. The finished product will yield 12-13 lbs. of sausage.

POLSKA KISZKA WATROBIANA
(Polish Blood Sausage with Liver)

INGREDIENTS FOR 25 LBS.	INGREDIENTS FOR 10 LBS.
6½ lbs. liver (pork or beef)	3 lbs. liver (pork or beef)
6½ lbs. fresh bacon	3 lbs. fresh bacon
12 lbs. any combination of	4 lbs. any combination of
pigs feet, snouts or other meat	pigs feet, snouts or other meat
8 ozs. salt	3½ ozs. salt
8 ozs. chopped onions	3½ ozs. chopped onion
¼ oz. marjoram	1 tbsp. marjoram
1 oz. black table pepper	1 tbsp. black table pepper
1 oz. prague powder #1	2 level tsp. prague powder #1
1 qt. blood (beef or pork)	1 pint blood (beef or pork)

All the pork (except the bacon and liver) must be cooked until tender. Allow to cool and remove the bones, if you are using pig's feet. Be sure to save the broth.

Grind the meat through a ⅛" or ³⁄₁₆" grinder plate. Add remaining ingredients (except blood) and mix thoroughly until evenly distributed. Add the blood and mix thoroughly again. Then stuff mixture into 35-38mm hog casings about 15" long, leaving 3-4" of empty casing on each end. Tie sausage into a ring. Place sausage in water at 170 degrees F. until an internal temperature of 160 degrees F. is reached. Then shower sausage with cold water until the internal temperature is reduced to 60-70 degrees F. You may smoke this sausage for about 1 hour after it has dried, if you like.

NOTE:

You can substitute the broth in this recipe for the blood. There are many people who prefer to use the broth as it is less offensive to them than the blood.

FARMER-STYLE LIVER SAUSAGE

INGREDIENTS FOR 25 LBS.

1 oz. Prague Powder No. 1
8 ozs. salt
2 ozs. powdered dextrose
12 ozs. soy protein concentrate
  or non-fat dry milk
4 ozs. onion powder
1 oz. ground white pepper
½ oz. marjoram
1 tsp. ground cloves
1 tsp. ground ginger
8½ lbs. pork livers
8½ lbs. pork snouts
8 lbs. beef tripe

INGREDIENTS FOR 10 LBS.

2 level tsp. Prague Powder No. 1
7 tbsp. salt
4 tbsp. powdered dextrose
2 cups soy protein concentrate
  or non-fat dry milk
5 tbsp. onion powder
1 tbsp. ground white pepper
1 tsp. marjoram
¼ tsp. ground cloves
¼ tsp. ground ginger
3½ lbs. pork livers
3½ lbs. pork snouts
3 lbs. beef tripe

GRINDING

The pork livers have to be scalded in hot water until the thin ends curl up. The pork snouts should be cooked at least 1 hour. If the tripe has not been cooked previously, also cook the tripe for 1 hour. After all the meat has cooled properly, grind it all through a ⅛" grinder plate. You will find that after cooking all the meat there will be shrinkage, so add enough stock to bring the contents back up to green weight. Remove to stuffer and use artificial casings, beef middles, lined sewed hog bungs, or prime hog bungs.

COOKING

Cook in 160-165 degree F. water until the internal temperature of 152 degrees F. is reached. This will require from 1-1½ hours. After cooking, place in ice-filled tub for quick chilling. Keep adding ice to the water if needed. Chill as rapidly as possible, which will require about 45 minutes, and put product in cooler. Product may be wiped with cloth prior to removal to cooler, or sprayed with 180 degree F. hot water. Liver sausage also may be smoked, using smoking instructions for braunschweiger.

RING LIVER PUDDING

INGREDIENTS FOR 25 LBS.

8 ozs. salt
2 ozs. Prague Powder No. 1
1¼ ozs. onion powder
1 oz. ground black pepper
1 tsp. ground marjoram
1 tbsp. ground ginger
1 tbsp. ground cloves
2½ lbs. rye flour
7½ lbs. pork livers
5 lbs. beef tripe
5 lbs. fat pork or jowls
7½ lbs. pork snouts or pork skin
5 lbs. broth

INGREDIENTS FOR 10 LBS.

6 tbsp. salt
4 level tsp. Prague Powder No. 1
½ oz. onion powder
1 tsp. ground black pepper
1 tsp. ground marjoram
1 tsp. ground ginger
1 tsp. ground cloves
1 lb. rye flour
3 lbs. pork livers
2 lbs. beef tripe
2 lbs. fat pork or jowls
3 lbs. pork snouts or pork skins
2 lbs. broth

Add Prague Powder No. 1 and cook all meat until it is well done. Meat is then cooled thoroughly and ground through ⅛" grinder plate. Add all ingredients to meat and mix well, adding broth as you are mixing. Stuff into 40-43mm beef rounds. Place into water and cook until internal temperature is 140 degrees F.

BLOOD SAUSAGE (KISZKA)

INGREDIENTS FOR 25 LBS.
8 ozs. salt
1 oz. onion powder
1 oz. coarse black pepper
½ oz. marjoram
½ oz. ground allspice
1 qt. beef blood
1 oz. Prague Powder No. 1
12½ lbs. pork snouts
5 lbs. pork tongues
2½ lbs. pork skins
5 lbs. buckwheat groats or barley
    (cooked weight)

INGREDIENTS FOR 10 LBS.
6 tbsp. salt
2 tbsp. onion powder
2 tsp. coarse black pepper
1 heaping tsp. marjoram
1 tbsp. allspice
1 lb. beef blood (1 pint)
2 level tsp. Prague Powder No. 1
5 lbs. pork snouts
2 lbs. pork tongues
1 lb. pork skins
2 lbs. buckwheat groats or barley
    (cooked weight)

PROCESSING & GRINDING

All meats must be cooked for at least 2 hours and then cooled. Grind all the meats through a ³⁄₁₆" grinder plate.

Place buckwheat groats or barley in a container and cover with boiling water for at least 2 hours. Be sure you place a cover on the container to prevent too much heat from escaping. (You may cook either of these items until the volume is doubled.) Remove and let cool.

After all the meats and groats have cooled, place in a mixer and add all seasonings, blood, and mix well. Stuff into beef bungs or beef middles. Blood sausage is then cooked in 160 degrees F. water until the internal temperature reaches 152 degrees F. Remove from cooker and shower with cool water until the internal temperature is reduced to 110 degrees F.; place in cooler for at least 24 hours.
NOTE:

Since there always seems to be some breakage in the sausage business, you may add whatever broken sausage you have to the above formula. This blood sausage is spiced quite heavily and will cover up most other spices. You may add up to 4 lbs. of broken sausage to a 25 lb. formula. Be sure you account for the salt already in broken sausage.

253

BLOOD & TONGUE SAUSAGE

INGREDIENTS FOR 25 LBS.
4 fresh onions
1 oz. Prague Powder No. 1
1 oz. ground black pepper
¼ oz. ground marjoram
¼ oz. thyme
¼ oz. mace
¼ oz. ground cloves
8 ozs. salt
9 lbs. pork tongues
9 lbs. pork snouts
3½ lbs. pork skins
3½ lbs. beef blood

INGREDIENTS FOR 10 LBS.
1 medium onion
2 level tsp. Prague Powder No. 1
2 tbsp. ground black pepper
1 tsp. ground marjoram
1 tsp. thyme
1 tbsp. mace
1 tsp. ground cloves
6 tbsp. salt
4 lbs. pork tongues
4 lbs. pork snouts
1 lb. pork skins
1 lb. beef blood (1 pint)

GRINDING & COOKING

Place all pork tongues and snouts into a kettle and cook approximately 2 hours. Let it cool, then grind through a 1" grinder plate. The pork snouts also should be ground through a 1" grinder plate and pork skins should be ground through a ⅛" plate. Pork fat should be diced to ¼" or ¾" cubes and scalded for a few seconds using a sieve or screen.

Place all the meats and ingredients in a mixer and mix well. Stuff by hand into beef bungs and then place in 195-200 degree F. water (but not boiling). Cook approximately 3½ hours. Use a skewer to see if sausage is cooked sufficiently. Remove to container holding ice water, cooling enough that sausage can be handled. Remove to 36-38 degrees F. cooler overnight.

RICE LIVER SAUSAGE
(HUNGARIAN STYLE)

INGREDIENTS FOR 25 LBS.

8 ozs. salt
½ lb. onions
1 oz. ground black pepper
¼ oz. marjoram
½ oz. paprika
2 lbs. rice (uncooked)
12-13 lb. pork heads
6-7 lbs. pork livers
1 oz. Prague Powder No. 1

INGREDIENTS FOR 10 LBS.

6 tbsp. salt
1 large onion
1 tbsp. ground black pepper
1 tsp. marjoram
2 tbsp. paprika
1 lb. rice (uncooked)
5-6 lbs. pork snouts
2½ lbs. pork livers
2 level tsp. Prague Powder No. 1

PROCESSING

Cook all the rice until tender; do not overcook. Cook headmeat until tender and save the broth. Do not boil; simmer only. Onions are to be sliced and fried in lard until they are a golden brown. Liver should be blanched in hot water for about 3 minutes.

GRINDING & COOKING

After all meats have cooled, grind all the headmeat through ⅛" grinder plate and the liver through ¼" plate along with the fried onion. Put all the items in the mixer, adding all the ingredients and the drained rice; then add 10 lbs. of the broth the headmeat was cooked in to bring the finished yield up to 110%. Mix very well until all items are evenly distributed. Stuff into 38-42mm hog casings. Cook sausage in 170 degrees F. preheated water for about 1 hour or until the internal temperature reaches 152 degrees F.

Remove sausage from cooker and place in containers filled with water and ice; reduce internal temperature to 40 degrees F. before placing in cooler overnight.

255

LIVERWURST

INGREDIENTS FOR 25 LBS.

8 ozs. salt
1 oz. onion powder
1 oz. powdered dextrose
1 oz. Prague Powder No. 1
1 oz. ground white pepper
¼ oz. sage
¼ oz. marjoram
¼ oz. nutmeg
¼ oz. ginger
8½ lbs. pork livers
8½ lbs. pork snouts
8 lbs. beef tripe

INGREDIENTS FOR 10 LBS.

6 tbsp. salt
2 tbsp. onion powder
2 tbsp. powdered dextrose
2 level tsp. Prague Powder No. 1
1 tbsp. ground white pepper
1 tsp. sage
1 tsp. marjoram
1 tsp. nutmeg
½ tsp. ginger
3½ lbs. pork livers
3½ lbs. pork snouts
3 lbs. beef tripe

COOKING & GRINDING

Cook pork snouts for approximately 1 hour, let cool and then grind all the meat through a ⅛" grinder plate. (Pork snouts should be weighed before grinding; you may have to add stock to bring snouts back up to green weight.) Add all the ingredients and mix well until all the spices are evenly distributed; regrind again using ⅛" plate. Liverwurst should be stuffed into a beef middle, sewed hog bungs or prime hog bungs.

There also are sewed synthetic casings available. Water should be precooked to 180 degrees F.; liverwurst will then be placed into water and temperature allowed to drop to 160-165 degrees F. Cook until an internal temperature of 150-152 degrees F. is obtained (1-1½ hours). After cooking, remove to a tub filled with ice and water for a quick chill; add sufficient ice to chill as rapidly as possible, which will require at least 45 minutes. Remove from ice water and let dry at room temperature; remove to cooler overnight.

ALTERNATE MEATS

1 cooked hog head
1 cooked hog tongue

1 cooked hog heart
1 cooked hog liver

256

PREPARATION

Cook hog head in kettle until the meat will strip from the bones easily. Cook hearts, tongues and livers until tender. Remove small bones from tongue. Remove all the meat from kettle, being careful to avoid getting any bone mixed with meat. Add 10% stock for each 25 lbs. of meat to bring back to green weight.

CHAPTER IX

Specialty Loaves and Sausage

JELLIED TURKEY LOAF

INGREDIENTS FOR 25 LBS.
25 lbs. cooked turkey
8 ozs. salt
½ oz. onion powder
6 ozs. chopped pimento
12 ozs. gelatin
3 ozs. powdered dextrose
5 qts. broth

INGREDIENTS FOR 10 LBS.
10 lbs. cooked turkey
3½ ozs. salt
1 teaspoon onion powder
2½ ozs. chopped pimento
5 ozs. gelatin
1½ ozs. powdered dextrose
2 qts. broth

Large turkeys are recommended to make this loaf, because the meat comes off the bones much easier if it is cooked. In addition, the ratio of meat to bones is greater.

Turkey meat may be cut into smaller pieces and cooked until it is tender; do not overcook until it falls apart. Then remove the turkey from the broth and allow to cool before boning.

Meat is then ground through a ½" grinder plate and mixed with the other ingredients, except the gelatin and broth. Heat the cooled broth to 160 degrees F., skimming the surface fat before starting. Dissolve gelatin and pour over the meat mixture, mixing thoroughly as you go. Mixture may then be poured into molds or any size fibrous casing. Place in cooler and allow to set overnight before using.

IMPORTANT!

Do not allow the broth to cook beyond 160 degrees F. The gelatin will lose all its binding power at 170 degrees F.

CORNED BEEF HASH

INGREDIENTS FOR 10 LBS.
6 lbs. corned beef
4 lbs. boiled potatoes
3 ozs. onion flakes
1½ ozs. salt
2 level tsp. Prague Powder No. 1

The corned beef is boiled until tender and then cooled off. Grind meat through ³⁄₁₆" or ¼" grinder plate. Peeled potatoes are boiled and cut into ½" cubes. Onion flakes should be soaked until they become tender. All ingredients then are added and gently mixed. This is to avoid mashing the potato cubes. Corned beef may be stuffed into 3½" fibrous casings.

BRAUN LOAF

Braun loaf is a type of sausage usually made by people who raise their own hogs. The meat that is used to make it is available from all the large meat packers. It is sometimes possible to buy this meat in smaller quantities from your local sausage maker when it is not available at your local supermarket or butcher shop.

This sausage or loaf can be made by using any combination of the following meat: pork tongues, pork cheeks, pork snouts and pork hearts. When using hearts, be sure all the arteries and blood clots on the surface are removed. It is also important to note that if you're purchasing pig snouts or cheeks, it is best to buy the meat of a younger animal, as it is usually quite lean. It should also be noted that up to 10% of pork skins may be added to this formula; however, they should be defatted. Pork skins can act as a binding agent when making this loaf.

For each gallon of brine, use 1¼ lbs. of salt and 1½ ozs. of prague powder #1. The meat is immersed in the pickle for at least 7 days at 34-36 degrees F. Then place it in fresh water and simmer until tender.

The pig skins should be cooked separately to prevent overcooking, as this causes them to lose their binding quality. The stock should be put aside for further use after the meat is cooked and allowed to cool. The cooked meat can then be chilled in cool water.

Grind the pork cheeks through a ⅛" grinder plate; the rest of the meat should be cut into 1-1½" pieces. Then weigh all the meat to compare it to the original starting weight. There will be a difference, or shortage, which is then made up by adding the pork skin stock until you reach the original weight. You may add up to 10% more than what you started with.

Then add the following mixture of spices to the stock along with the meat and cook until the water reaches 180 degrees F., stirring the stock as you go along.

5 ozs. ground white pepper
1 oz. ground ginger
½ oz. ground mace
½ oz. ground allspice
1 oz. ground caraway seeds
2 ozs. onion powder

NOTE:

The above spices are enough for 100 lbs. of meat. Add 2½ ozs. of the mixture for 25 lbs. of meat, or 1 ounce for 10 lbs. of meat.

Additional salt or cure are not required since the meat already has been cured and salted.

CHILI CON CARNE

INGREDIENTS FOR 25 LBS.
18½ lbs. lean beef
7½ lbs. beef suet
8 ozs. salt
1 oz. onion powder
½ oz. garlic powder
2 ozs. ground paprika
7½ lbs. wheat flour
1 oz. chili powder
5 lbs. red kidney beans

INGREDIENTS FOR 10 LBS.
8 lbs. lean beef
2 lbs. beef suet
3½ ozs. salt
½ oz. onion powder
1 tsp. garlic powder
¾ ozs. ground paprika
3½ lbs. wheat flour
½ oz. chili powder
2 lbs. red kidney beans

Kidney beans are optional

Grind the beef and suet separately using a ⅜" grinder plate. The suet is melted down, discarding the cracklings. Add the lean beef to the melted suet and cook. You may add water or tomato juice to help the meat cook. Meat should be allowed to brown (or water/juice should come to boiling point, then reduced to simmer).

During the simmering period, add the seasonings (except the beans and flour). After the seasonings are mixed in, add the flour a little at a time, stirring as you go along to prevent bumps.

If you desire kidney beans, they may be added during the last 10 minutes of cooking. Add additional water or tomato juice if the chili is too thick. Pour the chili into molds or fibrous casings and allow to cool. Chili keeps very well when frozen.

HEAD CHEESE

INGREDIENTS FOR 25 LBS.
12 ozs. salt
12 ozs. gelatin, dissolved in
    5 lbs. warm water
1 oz. ground white pepper
¼ oz. ground ginger
¼ oz. allspice
¼ oz. ground caraway seeds
½ oz. onion powder
¼ oz. ground marjoram
¼ oz. ground cloves
12½ lbs. pork tongues
10 lbs. pork snouts
2½ lbs. pork skins

INGREDIENTS FOR 10 LBS.
5 ozs. salt
5 ozs. gelatin, dissolved in
    1 quart warm water
2 tbsp. ground white pepper
1 tsp. ground ginger
½ tsp. allspice
1 tsp. ground caraway seeds
1 tbsp. onion powder
1 tsp. ground marjoram
1 tbsp. ground cloves
5 lbs. pork tongues
4 lbs. pork snouts
1 lb. pork skins

Cure meat for 3-5 days in a brine made with:
2½ gals. water
2½ lbs. salt
12 ozs. cane sugar
4 ozs. Prague Powder No. 1

After curing, place all meat loosely in steam kettle. Cover with sufficient amount of water. Place the pork skins in cooking net. Then cook for approximately 1½-2 hours. After cooking, remove from kettle and let cool. Grind pork skins through ⅛" grinder plate. Grind the remaining meat through a 1½" plate. After grinding, add other ingredients and sufficient amount of cooking stock to arrive at a finished yield of 110-115%.

After the product is thoroughly mixed, stuff by hand into beef bung or hog stomach casings. Place in cooler and chill for 12 hours at 34-36 degrees F. (If forming is done in molds, place molds in ice water for approximately two hours to assist in rapid chilling.) After chilling, remove from molds and place on rack, properly spaced, in 38-40 degree F. cooler. Chill at this temperature.

SOUSE

INGREDIENTS FOR 25 LBS.

2½ lbs. diced red peppers
2½ lbs. diced sweet pickles
12 ozs. gelatin, dissolved in
    5 lbs. warm water
8 ozs. white vinegar
12 ozs. salt
10 ozs. ground white pepper
½ oz. ground mustard
½ oz. ground sage
½ oz. ground cloves
½ oz. onion powder
12½ lbs. pork tongues
10 lbs. pork snouts
2½ lbs. pork skins

INGREDIENTS FOR 10 LBS.

1 lb. diced red peppers
1 lb. diced sweet pickles
5 ozs. gelatin, dissolved in
    1 quart warm water
3 ozs. white vinegar
5 ozs. salt
1 tbsp. ground white pepper
1 tbsp. ground mustard
2 tbsp. ground sage
2 tbsp. ground cloves
1 tbsp. onion powder
5 lbs. pork tongues
4 lbs. pork snouts
1 lb. pork skins

Cure meat 3-5 days in a brine made with the following:
2½ gal. water
2½ lbs. salt
12 ozs. cane sugar
4 ozs. Prague Powder No. 1

After curing, place all meat loosely in steam kettle. Place the pork skins in cooking net; then cover product with water and raise to boiling temperature. Cook for approximately 1½-2 hours. After cooking, remove from kettle and let cool. Grind pork skins through ⅛" grinder plate. Grind the remaining meat through a 1½" plate. After grinding, add other ingredients and sufficient amount of cooking stock to arrive at a finished yield of 110-115%.

After the product is thoroughly mixed, stuff into suitably-sized mold and chill for 12 hours at 34-36 degrees F. Place molds in ice water for approximately two hours to assist in rapid chilling. After chilling, remove from molds and place on rack, properly spaced, in 38-40 degrees F. cooler. Chill at this temperature overnight.

PENNSYLVANIA SCRAPPLE

Pennsylvania scrapple also is known as Philadelphia scrapple to many people. It is truly classed as an original American sausage. It was first developed by the German immigrants who were mistakenly called the Pennsylvania Dutch. The other people of this area had difficulty in pronouncing "Deutsche," so the name of "Pennsylvania Dutch" was given to these German immigrants. Scrapple is a very popular sausage in the Northeastern USA and served for breakfast like corned beef hash, bacon or sausage. A very good scrapple is made of the by-products of beef, pork or both.

INGREDIENTS FOR 10 LBS.
5 lbs. pork meat (ears, snouts, jowls, etc.)
5 lbs. beef cheeks or hearts
1½ lbs. stock from cooked meat
2 lbs. white corn meal
1 tbsp. onion chips
2 tbsp. salt
1 tbsp. ground white pepper
1 tsp. ground celery seeds
1 tbsp. sage
1 tsp. ground marjoram
2 level tsp. Prague Powder No. 1

All meat is placed into a container with the salt and Prague Powder No. 1. Meat is cooked slowly until tender; do not boil. Meat then is removed, allowed to cool off, and ground through a ⅜" grinder plate.

The meat stock then is brought up to boiling, adding all the ingredients except the corn meal. After all ingredients are mixed, add the corn meal slowly to avoid lumps. All ingredients are mixed very well and meat then is added. Scrapple may be stuffed into any size fibrous casings or simply formed in a meat loaf pan. Allow to cool off for 24 hours before using.

ALL-MEAT POLISH SAUSAGE
IN VINEGAR PICKLE

For pickling in vinegar, the all-meat sausage is best. This popular bar sausage must be smoked, cooked and dried before pickling. Corn syrup solids are used in this formula rather than soy protein concentrate. Meat should be pork butts 80% lean, 20% fat.

INGREDIENTS FOR 25 LBS.	INGREDIENTS FOR 10 LBS.
2 lbs. water	1 pint water
8 ozs. corn syrup solids	3 ozs. corn syrup solids
8 ozs. salt	6 tbsp. salt
2 ozs. powdered dextrose	1 tbsp. powdered dextrose
2 tbsp. ground marjoram	1 tsp. ground marjoram
1 oz. Prague Powder No. 1	2 level tsp. Prague Powder No. 1
1 oz. garlic cloves	2 large garlic cloves
1 oz. ground black pepper	1 tbsp. ground black pepper

Above sausage is processed exactly like smoked Polish sausage. After sausage has been smoked, cooked and cooled down, it is placed into a large container and covered with white vinegar.

Let it stand all night to allow various solubles to be released. This step is quite important; if it is skipped the vinegar in the jars will become cloudy, and sediment will settle in the bottom of the jar. The sausage is removed after overnight immersion and placed into jars. Jars are then filled to capacity with white vinegar, making sure there are no air pockets between the sausages. You may add pickling spices to each jar for cosmetic purposes.

It is best to start this process with white vinegar. Finished product holds up very well under refrigatation.

VINEGAR-PICKLED
PORK HOCKS or PIG'S FEET

BRINE FORMULA
1 gallon water
12 ozs. salt
4 ozs. Prague Powder No. 1

CURING AND COOKING

The above formula is enough for 15 lbs. of pork hocks or pig's feet. Meat is placed into container with brine mixture; bring temperature up to 210 degrees F. Heat is shut off and meat allowed to stay in pickle all night. The next morning, bring temperature up to 180 degrees F. and cook until tender. Remove liquid from container and allow cold water to fill up container and overflow. Allow water to keep running into container to cool product down; this also helps to bring unwanted fat particles to the surface.

Feet can be made boneless or semi-boneless, depending on the individual. Feet are soaked in white vinegar overnight. Remove from vinegar and rinse with cold water until all surface fat is removed. If not properly washed, the vinegar will become cloudy. Pig's feet may be packed in jars filled to capacity with white vinegar. You may decorate with whole bay leaves or red peppers.

ALTERNATE METHODS

Pig's feet also are prepared by cooking in water until tender, or until meat is coming off the bones. Pickling spices are added while cooking. About ½ to ¾ of the broth is poured off and then allowed to cool off. After cooking the broth is then tossed or scrambled and served in that manner, like jello.

Another method is to cook until meat separates from bones, adding bay leaves rather than pickling spices. After completely cooked bones are removed, broth and meat are allowed to cool and set up like jello. It is served with a little splash of white vinegar. This is a traditional Polish dish.

OLD FASHIONED LOAF

INGREDIENTS FOR 25 LBS.

4 lbs. ice water
12 ozs. non-fat dry milk
8 ozs. salt
8 ozs. corn syrup solids
¼ oz. coriander
1 oz. onion powder
1 oz. ground celery
1 oz. ground white pepper
1 oz. Prague Powder No. 1
18 lbs. pork butts
7 lbs. beef chuck
8 ozs. soy protein concentrate

INGREDIENTS FOR 10 LBS.

1 quart ice water
2 cups non-fat dry milk
6 tbsp. salt
8 tbsp. corn syrup solids
1 tbsp. coriander
4 tbsp. onion powder
3 tsp. ground celery
1 tbsp. ground white pepper
2 level tsp. Prague Powder No. 1
7 lbs. pork butts
3 lbs. beef chuck
1 cup soy protein concentrate

GRINDING & MIXING

Grind all the lean pork through a ³⁄₁₆" grinder plate into the mixer and add ¾ of all the ingredients except ice water, soy protein concentrate and non-fat dry milk. Mix well. Grind all of the beef plates through ³⁄₁₆" grinder plate, adding the balance of the ingredients. After mixing stuff into pans, bake in a smokehouse for about 8 hours at 170 degrees F. or until the internal temperature reaches 152 degrees F. Remove and let cool overnight under refrigeration before slicing.

NOTE:
For pepper loaf, you may sprinkle coarse black pepper on top of the loaves before cooking.

PICKLE & PIMENTO LOAF

INGREDIENTS FOR 25 LBS.

18 lbs. lean beef
7 lbs. lean pork
5 lbs. ice water
8 ozs. corn syrup solids
1¼ lbs. non-fat dry milk
2 lbs. chopped sweet pickle
2 lbs. chopped pimentos
1 tbsp. ginger
½ oz. onion powder
1 tbsp. mace
1 oz. Prague Powder No. 1
8 ozs. salt
8 ozs. soy protein concentrate

INGREDIENTS FOR 10 LBS.

7 lbs. lean beef
3 lbs. lean pork
2 lbs. ice water
3½ ozs. corn syrup solids
3 ozs. soy protein concentrate
12 ozs. chopped sweet pickle
12 ozs. chopped pimentos
1 tsp. ginger
1 tsp. onion powder
½ tsp. mace
2 tsp. Prague Powder No. 1
6 tbsp. salt
8 ozs. non-fat dry milk

This type of loaf traditionally is a fine-textured luncheon meat (emulsified) and is cooked in pans submerged in water. For home use, this product may be stuffed into 6" fibrous casings.

All meats can be ground with a ¼" grinder plate, then mixed with all ingredients, adding the water last. Stuff into casings or pans and cook in 160 degree F. water until internal temperature reaches 152 degrees F. Place in cold water until internal temperature is reduced to 70-75 degrees F.

VEAL LOAF

This same recipe may be used to make veal loaf. Simply replace the pork with veal and follow the same directions, omitting pickles and pimentos.

HONEY LOAF

INGREDIENTS FOR 25 LBS.
25 lbs. pork butts
2½ lbs. ice cold water
8 ozs. salt
8 ozs. corn syrup solids
1¼ lbs. honey
1 oz. onion powder
1 oz. ground white pepper
½ oz. ground celery
1 oz. Prague Powder No. 1

INGREDIENTS FOR 10 LBS.
10 lbs. pork butts
1 lb. ice cold water
4 ozs. salt
3½ ozs. corn syrup solids
8 ozs. honey
4 tsp. onion powder
1 tbsp. ground white pepper
2 tsp. ground celery
2 level tsp. Prague Powder No. 1

GRINDING & MIXING

Grind all lean meat through a coarse plate about ⅜." All fat meat should be ground through a fine plate either ³⁄₁₆" or smaller. All ingredients are to be mixed thoroughly with meat.

Honey loaf usually is placed in a pan and cooked in water at 160 degrees F. until the internal temperature reaches 152 degrees F. It then is removed and chilled in water until the internal temperature reaches 70-75 degrees F. It is placed under refrigeration for 24 hours before using.

Honey loaf may also be stuffed into a fibrous casing about 5-6 inches in diameter when making this sausage at home. The metal submergable pans are quite expensive and only used in commercial operations.

LEBERKASE

INGREDIENTS FOR 25 LBS.
12 ozs. soy protein concentrate
2½ lbs. ice water
12 ozs. onions
8 ozs. salt
1 oz. powdered dextrose
1 oz. Prague Powder No. 1
½ oz. marjoram
¼ oz. ginger
½ oz. ground mustard
½ oz. nutmeg
1 oz. ground black pepper
8½ lbs. boneless beef, cow or
    bullmeat
8½ lbs. regular pork trimmings
7½ lbs. lean pork shoulder or butts
½ lb. pork liver

INGREDIENTS FOR 10 LBS.
2 cups soy protein concentrate
1 pint ice water
1 large onion
6 tbsp. salt
1 tbsp. powdered dextrose
2 level tsp. Prague Powder No. 1
1 tbsp. marjoram
1 tsp. ginger
1 tbsp. ground mustard
2 tbsp. nutmeg
2 tbsp. ground black pepper
3½ lbs. boneless beef, cow or
    bullmeat
3½ lbs. regular pork trimmings
2¾ lbs. lean pork shoulder or butts
¼ lb. pork liver

GRINDING

Grind all beef, cow, or bullmeat through a ¼" grinder plate. Pork liver should be scalded and ground through a ¼" plate. Then place in mixer and add the cure with soy protein concentrate and ice water. The remainder of the meats should be ground through a ⅜" plate, and placed into the mixer.

Mix well until all the ingredients are evenly distributed. Remove and place all the meat into tubs not over 6" high and place in 38-40 degree F. cooler for at least 1 hour. Remove from cooler and pack into stuffer tightly to prevent air pockets. Leberkase should be stuffed into 3½" by 24" fibrous casings.

COOKING

Preheat water to 180 degrees F.; the temperature will drop to around 160 degrees F. when all the meat is placed into cooker. Cook at 160-170 degrees F. until internal temperature of 152 degrees F. is obtained. Remove and shower with cold water until the internal temperature is reduced to 120 degrees F. Place in cooler overnight. Leberkase may also be packed into baking pans and cooked in an oven using the following temperatures:

120 degrees for 30 minutes

150 degrees for 30 minutes

180 degrees for 30 minutes

180-200 degrees for 3½ hours or until an internal temperature of 152 degrees F. is obtained. Remove and let cool overnight.

NOTE:

This formula may also be used for "Dutchloaf" by simply omitting the pork liver and grinding all the meat through a ¼" grinder plate.

The above leberkase was a sausage made for and served by the Alpine Village in Las Vegas during the mid 1960s during the time I was owner of the Hickory Shop and Hickory Sausage Inc.

CHAPTER X

Game Meat

VENISON OR BEEF JERKY

Beef jerky is one of the most sought after—and probably the easiest to use—of all the recipes in this book. A dried meat closely associated with the early American pioneers, this recipe has been handed down to us in a very simple formula.

It is well-known that this product was usually dry-salted and hung out in some manner to dry. The process reduced the weight of the meat by as much as 80-85%. Obviously, it was lighter to transport, took up less room on these long journeys and required no refrigeration.

During the course of these journeys, many stops were made for a number of reasons, preferably near a stream. The meat could then be placed in a running stream to remove most of the salt. At the same time, this meat was being reconsistuted by absorbing water from the stream. The meat now was more palatable and could be used to make stew or other dishes. The smaller pieces of this salted and dried meat, however, became a sort of snack, eaten at random without removing the salt.

Beef jerky is closely associated with the early American cowboys or miners. In either case, beef jerky still is made the old-fashioned way by either dry salting or brining in a very hard salted water. Then it is simply hung up or laid out to dry; however, a jerky using this type of of formula is not very palatable, and there now are a variety of recipes that make this a very tasty snack.

I think the following recipe will be extremely pleasing to your taste buds.

3 lbs. of lean beef or venison
1 tbsp. salt
1 level tsp. Prague Powder No. 1
1 tsp. onion powder
1 tsp. garlic powder
1 tsp. ground black pepper
¼ cup soy sauce
⅓ cup Worcestershire sauce

PREPARATION

Beef jerky also can be made from a variety of game meats like moose, elk or antelope. You never should use pork, as it sometimes may contain the trichinae parasite. By the same token, if pork were treated to destroy trichinae, by freezing in the prescribed USDA manner stated in the chapter "Destroying Trichinae," you may even use pork to make jerky.

The meat is made as lean as possible by removing all fat, sinew and gristle. Too much fat in the jerky can cause rancid meat. The meat then is cut into strips about ¼" to ½" thick and ½" to ¾" in width. The ingredients then are all mixed and poured over the meat. Meat then should be mixed gently to distribute the sauce more evenly. Let meat marinate in refrigerator for 24 hours. Meat should be overhauled once or twice during this 24-hour period.

DRYING

Jerky may be dried in a variety of ways, depending on your locality. If you live in a dry desert country, you can usually dry the jerky in about seven days or less during summer months in a garage. If you own a fruit dehydrator I am sure that the instructions that came with it can be applied to drying jerky. You can also dry jerky in a kitchen stove – gas or electric. Meat is placed on oven grids, properly spaced apart, and the heat from the pilot light is sufficient to dry jerky in 3-4 days. Attics also are a great place to dry jerky, as that is usually a very dry part of the house no matter how humid the area is. Jerky then is packed in glass containers with metal tops that have holes punched in them to prevent mold.

NOTE:

If you plan to make about 9 lbs. of jerky, the ingredient formulas can simply be tripled. This is a large amount of jerky and would not fit into your kitchen oven at one time. Assuming you would use the attic, or garage in the desert climate, you can easily make a container to hold 9 lbs.

Simply make a rectangular box using 2" by 4" lumber. Dimensions are 2 feet by 4 feet. On the bottom part, nail on a ¼ mesh galvanized screen. Then over the top of this you nail a regular fly screen. After placing jerky into this container, the top is covered with cheese cloth or plain bed sheet. The fly screen keeps insects out of the bottom, and the cloth keeps them out on top. The meat has excellent air circulation.

Preparing Beef Jerky

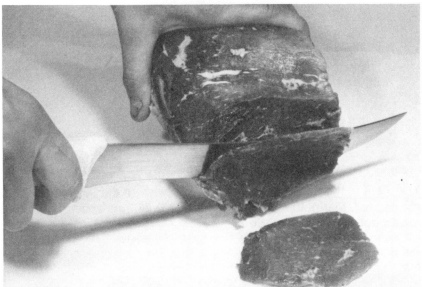

The meat above has been partially frozen for easier slicing. The meat should be sliced in pieces ¼"-½" in thickness, making sure all the fat has been trimmed.

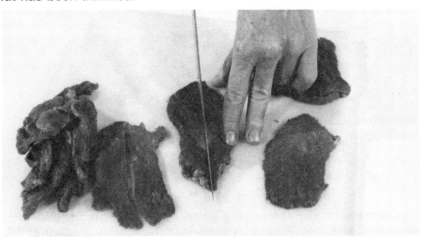

The next step is to cut the sliced meat into strips ¾" to 1" thick.

277

The meat is then placed into a container with all the ingredients and mixed well. Marinate in the refrigerator for 24 hours, overhauling at least once during this period.

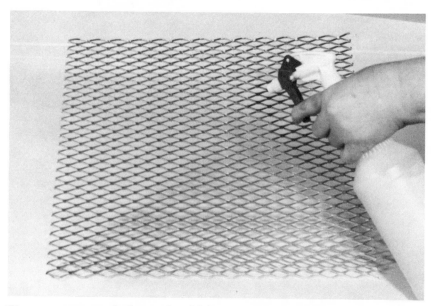

The screens or shelves should be sprayed with some sort of anti-sticking agent like Peeleze. Otherwise, the meat will stick to the shelves after it dries.

The beef jerky is then placed on the shelves, properly spaced, and dried in the smoker at 90°-100° F.

The jerky above has a moisture loss of 70-80%.

SMOKED VENISON POLISH SAUSAGE

INGREDIENTS FOR 25 LBS.

2½ lbs. water
12 ozs. soy protein concentrate
7 ozs. salt
1 oz. powdered dextrose
1 oz. Prague Powder No. 1
1 oz. fine black pepper
1 oz. fresh garlic
¼ oz. marjoram
20 lbs. lean elk or venison
5 lbs. regular pork trimmings

INGREDIENTS FOR 10 LBS.

2 lbs. water (1 quart)
2 cups soy protein concentrate
6 tbsp. salt
2 tbsp. powdered dextrose
2 level tsp. Prague Powder No. 1
1 tbsp. ground black pepper
2 large cloves of fresh garlic
1 heaping tsp. marjoram
8 lbs. lean elk or venison
2 lbs. regular pork trimmings

GRINDING

Chill all meat and grind through ¼" or ³⁄₁₆" grinder plate. Be sure all the blood clots, bones and sinews have been removed. Place all meat into mixer, adding all the ingredients. Mix well until all the ingredients are evenly distributed. Remove, place in stuffer and use 35-38mm hog casings for stuffing.

SMOKING

Let sausage dry at room temperature for about 45 minutes after stuffing. Remove to smokehouse preheated at 120 degrees F. and leave dampers wide open. Sausage will dry more for about 45 minutes. After this period, gradually adjust smoker to 160-170 degrees F. with dampers open. Allow product to smoke until the internal temperature reaches 152 degrees F.

VENISON THURINGER

INGREDIENTS FOR 25 LBS.
11 ozs. salt
1 oz. Prague Powder No. 1
4 ozs. powdered dextrose
1 oz. ground black pepper
¼ oz. ground ginger
4 ozs. corn syrup solids
17½ lbs. lean elk or venison
7½ lbs. fat beef trimmings
14 ozs. Fermento

INGREDIENTS FOR 10 LBS.
8 tbsp. salt
2 level tsp. Prague Powder No. 1
8 tbsp. powdered dextrose
1 tbsp. ground black pepper
1 tsp. ground ginger
6 tbsp. corn syrup solids
7 lbs. lean elk or venison
3 lbs. fat beef trimmings
6 ozs. Fermento

GRINDING

Grind all the meat through ¼" or ³⁄₁₆" grinder plate. Place in mixer with all the ingredients and mix until the ingredients are evenly distributed. After mixing, place all the meat into the curing pans, not over 6 inches high, and pack tightly. Be sure all the air pockets are removed. Let the meat cure in the cooler at 38-40 degrees F. for 3-4 days; the thuringer is properly cured when it has a nice red color. After curing, regrind all the meat through a ⅛" plate.

STUFFING

Pack meat tightly into stuffer to prevent air pockets. Stuff the meat into 2¾" diameter by 30" sewed single-wall beef middles; or, you may use the 3½" by 24" fibrous casings.

SMOKING AND COOKING

To produce a thuringer that has a consistent sour flavor, it is of the utmost importance that the correct curing and smoking temperatures are followed very closely. Close attention also should be given to the weather conditions, which will govern the variations in curing and hanging time.

After stuffing, hang the thuringer on the smokehouse sticks and space properly. Allow the thuringer to hang at room temperature for at least 10-12 hours or until the product is completely dry. If the weather is cool, increase the hanging time of the thuringer to 24 hours; that is, if the temperature is lower than 65 degrees F.

Then place the thuringer into a 100 degree F. smokehouse, apply a heavy smudge and smoke at this temperature for 8-10 hours. Keep the temperature between 100-110 degrees F. during this period. Then raise the smokehouse temperature to 145 degrees F. and heat at this temperature until an internal temperature of 138 degrees F. is obtained. Place in 45 degree F. cooler and chill for at least 24 hours before using.

NOTE:

During the time the thuringer is being smoked, it is extremely important that you not exceed the maximum of 100 degrees F.

SMOKED VENISON COUNTRY SAUSAGE

INGREDIENTS FOR 25 LBS.
20 lbs. venison
5 lbs. fat pork butts
1 qt. ice water
8 ozs. salt
1 oz. ground white pepper
8 ozs. corn syrup solids
1 oz. onion powder
1 tbsp. ground nutmeg
1 oz. Prague Powder No. 1
12 ozs. soy protein concentrate

INGREDIENTS FOR 10 LBS.
6 lbs. venison
4 lbs. fat pork butts
1 lb. water
6 tbsp. salt
1 tbsp. ground white pepper
3 ozs. corn syrup solids
4 tsp. onion powder
1 tsp. ground nutmeg
2 level tsp. Prague Powder No. 1
2 cups soy protein concentrate

GRINDING & MIXING

Grind all meat through a ¼" grinder plate and mix all ingredients well. Stuff into 32-35mm hog casings and link into 6" links.

SMOKING AND HEATING

Remove to preheated smokehouse at 120 degrees F., with dampers wide open for about 1 hour or until sausage is dry. Then apply heavy smoke, gradually increasing temperature of smokehouse to 160 degrees F. Damper is to be about ¼ open while the smokehouse heat is increased at the rate of 10 degrees F. every 30 minutes. Hold until internal temperature reaches 152 degrees F. Remove from smoker and shower with cool water until internal temperature reaches 110 degrees F. Remove and place in cooler for 24 hours before using.

SMOKED VENISON BREAKFAST SAUSAGE

INGREDIENTS FOR 25 LBS.

2½ lbs. water
8 ozs. salt
1 oz. ground white pepper
¼ oz. ground ginger
¼ oz. ground nutmeg
1 oz. powdered dextrose
¼ oz. sage
1 oz. Prague Powder No. 1
20 lbs. lean elk or venison
5 lbs. pork or beef fat

INGREDIENTS FOR 10 LBS.

1 pint water
6 tbsp. salt
1 tsp. ground white pepper
1 tsp. ground ginger
1 tbsp. ground nutmeg
2 tbsp. powdered dextrose
1 tbsp. sage
2 level tsp. Prague Powder No. 1
8 lbs. lean elk or venison
2 lbs. pork or beef fat

NOTE:
When freezing, it is better to omit sage from this sausage, as it makes the meat bitter when stored for long periods of time.

GRINDING

Be sure that all the trimmings are free of all blood clots, bone and skin, and that all meat has been chilled. Grind all meat through a ³⁄₁₆" grinder plate into mixer. Add all the ingredients and mix well, until all the ingredients have been evenly distributed, and then stuff into a 24-26mm lamb casing.

SMOKING

After stuffing, hang all the sausage on the smoke sticks and space properly. Allow the sausage to hang at room temperature for about 2 hours, then place in 110 degree F. smokehouse and immediately apply a heavy smudge. Gradually raise the temperature to 160 degrees F. and hold until 152 degrees F. is reached internally.

If you are using beef instead of pork, you may remove the sausage from the smoker when you have reached 142 degrees F. internally. (After smoking, shower with cold tap water until the internal temperature is reduced to 110 degrees F. Allow sausage to hang for 30 minutes until thoroughly dried, or until a desired bloom is obtained. Remove to cooler for 24 hours.)

SMOKED VENISON SUMMER SAUSAGE

INGREDIENTS FOR 25 LBS.
1 oz. ground black pepper
8 ozs. salt
2 ozs. powdered dextrose
1 oz. Prague Powder No. 1
¼ oz. ground coriander
¼ oz. ground ginger
¼ oz. ground mustard
¼ oz. garlic powder (optional)
3 ozs. corn syrup solids
20 lbs. lean elk meat or venison
5 lbs. regular pork trimmings
14 ozs. Fermento

INGREDIENTS FOR 10 LBS.
1 tbsp. ground black pepper
6 tbsp. salt
4 tbsp. powdered dextrose
2 level tsp. Prague Powder No. 1
1 tbsp. ground coriander
1 tsp. ground ginger
1 tsp. ground mustard
1 tsp. garlic powder (optional)
6 tbsp. corn syrup solids
8 lbs. lean elk meat or venison
2 lbs. regular pork trimmings
6 ozs. Fermento

GRINDING

Be sure all meat has been chilled. Grind all meat through a ³⁄₁₆"
grinder plate. The pork fat or trimmings should be ground through
a 1" plate or cut up in 1" cubes. Place all ground meat and fat
trimmings into mixer and add all the ingredients. Mix well to distribute
all the spices evenly. After mixing, pack into curing tubs and hold
in the cooler for 2 days. Then regrind meat through a ³⁄₁₆" grinder
plate.

STUFFING

Pack meat tightly into stuffer to omit air pockets. Summer sausage
should be stuffed into 2½"-2¾" by 24" beef middles. If not available
you may use fibrous casings 3½" by 24."

SMOKING & COOKING

After stuffing, hang on smokesticks and dry at room temperature
for 4-5 hours. Place in smokehouse preheated to 120-130 degrees
F. Apply a heavy smudge and smoke at this temperature for 3-4
hours or until the desired color is obtained.

Raise the temperature to 165 degrees F. and cook until the internal temperature reaches 145 degrees F. After cooking, shower with cold water until the internal temperature is at least 120 degrees F. After shower, allow to hang at room temperature for 1-2 hours until the desired bloom is obtained. Keep out of drafts. Place in 45 degrees F. cooler for at least 24 hours.

VENISON SALAMI

INGREDIENTS FOR 25 LBS.	INGREDIENTS FOR 10 LBS.
2½ lbs. ice water	1 pint ice water
8 ozs. salt	6 tbsp. salt
1 oz. Prague Powder No. 1	2 level tsp. Prague Powder No. 1
12 ozs. soy protein concentrate	2 cups soy protein concentrate
1 oz. ground white pepper	1 tbsp. ground white pepper
½ oz. nutmeg	2 tbsp. nutmeg
1 oz. fresh garlic	2 large cloves fresh garlic
(optional)	(optional)
3 ozs. corn syrup solids	6 tbsp. corn syrup solids
1 oz. powdered dextrose	2 tbsp. powdered dextrose
20 lbs. lean elk or venison	8 lbs. lean elk or venison
5 lbs. pork fat (preferably back fat)	2 lbs. pork fat (preferably back fat)

GRINDING & MIXING

Be sure that all meats and trimmings are well-chilled before grinding. Grind venison or elk meat through a ³⁄₁₆" grinder plate and cut all the pork fat into 1" squares. Place all the meat into a mixer or tub, adding all the ice water and all other ingredients. Mix until all the ingredients are evenly distributed, then place into a 38-40 degree F. cooler for 24 hours. The next day, remove from cooler and regrind all the meat through a ³⁄₁₆" plate.

STUFFING

Venison salami should be stuffed into beef middles or a fibrous casing. When stuffing, be sure to stuff the meat tightly into the casing to eliminate all air pockets. If there are any air pockets on the surface, you may puncture them with a needle or any other sharp instrument. Place on the smokehouse sticks and space properly.

SMOKING

Place salami in the smokehouse with the drafts wide open. Hold at 130 degrees F. for about 30 minutes or until the surface of the salami is dry. Partially close the dampers and raise the temperature to 150 degrees F., applying the smoke at the same time. After one hour, bring temperature to 165 degrees F. and hold until the internal temperature reaches 152 degrees F.

Remove from the smoker and place under shower until you bring down the internal temperature of the salami to about 120 degrees F.

NOTE:

Since pork fat is being used with this salami, it is essential that an internal temperature of at least 138 degrees F. is reached in order to destroy the trichinae sometimes found in pork.

CHAPTER XI

Specialty Meat

CURING HAM

There is literally no end to the number of formulas available for the curing and smoking of ready-to-eat hams. The number could easily reach a thousand if one took the time to research this information.

The various ethnic groups, the farmers, the thousands of meat-locker plants and many others all could give you different formulas, which most likely would lead you to a lot of confusion. The basic curing and cooking of hams, however, is generally the same.

The types of wood or other materials one would smoke with are what make a difference. The various spices, flavors or sweetners—such as honey, carmel, or maple sugar—also add to these distinctive flavors.

Salt is added to give the meat some flavor, and sugar is added to reduce the harshness of the salt. The sugar also gives the ham additional flavor and can contribute to its browning colors. The length of time a person wants to cure a ham can vary from 2 days to several weeks. The longer the ham is kept in the brine, the saltier the product will be. Spray pumping by far is preferred over brining a ham; brining a ham can take up to several weeks for the cure and flavor to penetrate the interior of the ham.

In this period of time, the bone marrow of the ham could easily spoil, especially if you are curing a ham purchased at your local meat market and you have no idea when the animal was butchered. These long brining periods also can leach the protein out of the ham and cause it to be mushy around the bone after it is smoked and cooled down. There is absolutely no question that spray pumping (stitch pumping) is by far the better process. Prague Powder No. 1 cures the ham so fast that it can be placed into the smokehouse the next day.

Obviously, when a ham is spray-pumped, the cures and other ingredients go to work immediately, as opposed to the slow process of penetration when brining a ham. For home use, some brining always is required, because a single needle pumping a ham will not do a complete job. The commercial processors pump their hams with gangs of needles that cover the whole ham at once, including the surface parts. Two-three days of brining is adequate for the surface of the ham to be cured.

It is very worthwhile to note that hams in the weight range of 12-14 lbs. will generally be more tender. When buying a fresh ham (leg of pork) at your local butcher shop or market, you'll rarely see this size ham in the counter, as they are usually used up by the big meat processors.

As mentioned earlier, the choice for making up a brine (as well as smoking the products) is generally up to the individual. If you know the meat was recently butchered, you may brine your hams without too much worry.

If you are going to use a stockinette to smoke your hams, be sure you soak the stockinette in vinegar or liquid smoke. The stockinette will be easier to remove after the ham is smoked and cooled.

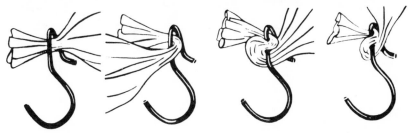

The above photograph shows the proper way to use a stockinette hook when smoking poultry or hams. The stockinette can be washed and reused.

Properly spaced hams.

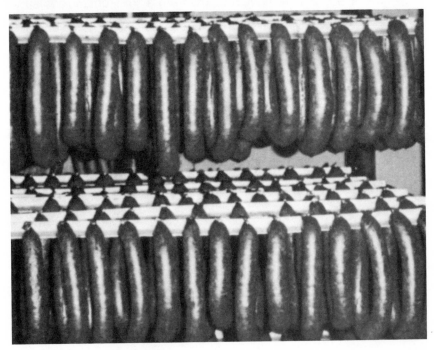

Properly spaced sausage.

SALOMETER

(Brine tester)

A brine tester is an instrument that has been used for many years. At one time it was very important—you couldn't cure meat without it. However, curing meat has come a long way and there is very little use for it when following the meat-curing recipes in this book.

The amount of salt that is required to cure a piece of meat is clearly spelled out. If the salt content is too high, it is possible to lower the amount by weight. However, there are a lot of recipes in the world that do specify the use of a brine tester.

In order to use a brine tester properly, a container should be filled with water at least half or three-quarters the length of the brine tester itself. When the brine tester is placed into the water you will get a reading of 0 degrees and it will sink to the bottom.

It is only after you add salt to the water, mixing thoroughly to dissolve it, that the brine tester will start to float and you will get a reading. When you reach 50% on the scale of the brine tester, it means the water is half-saturated with salt. 100% on the scale means the water is completely saturated with salt. Any more salt added from this point on will be useless.

It is important to note that it takes a considerable amount of salt to make a brine tester float.

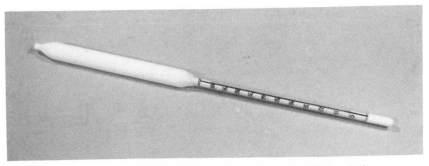

A salometer — for measuring the saturation of salt in a brine.

Using A Brine Tester

The formulas in "Great Sausage Recipes and Meat Curing" spell out the exact amount of salt that is required to cure any given piece of meat. However, there are a lot of people who have their own formulas that came to them one way or another. Lack of a scale is another reason for using a brine tester. A brine tester is used by adding salt to the water until it starts to float. It will take a considerable amount of salt to do this.

The brine testers above have been placed into a 2½-gallon bucket of tap water. Without salt, it reads 0% on the scale. It will not float and sinks to the bottom (right). To the left, it shows a reading of 50%. It took about 4-5 lbs. of salt to saturate the water to this point.

The brine tester above has risen as far as it can go, or 100%. The water is now completely saturated with salt. Adding additional salt at this point is useless; the water can hold no more salt.

CONTAINERS FOR CURING MEAT

Restaurants in your area can be a good source of containers for curing meat. A great many products today are packed in 5-gallon plastic buckets. Among these are peanut oil, mayonnaise and pickles, to name but a few. For the most part, the restaurant owners throw these containers into the trash after they are empty. If you can't get them free, you'll probably pay a dollar or two at the most for one. The good thing about these containers is the fact that they are made of food grade plastic. There are many grades of plastic that can give off toxic materials and are not suitable for curing meat.

When curing a ham you can make about 2½ gallons of brine. (half of a 5-gallon container). When the ham is put into the container, it will displace the brine and the container almost will be filled when the ham is submerged.

BOILED HAM

The boiled ham is the most popular type of ham sold in this country—and probably the entire world. It seems as if all the European countries export a boiled ham to the USA in one form or another. Boiled hams can be purchased packed in cans, fibrous casings, or stockinettes.

The curing process itself is no different from a smoked ham. The major difference is that hams are boiled in water and not smoked, but you may add liquid smoke to the brine if you prefer a smoked flavor. The Western New York area is as famous for its "water-boiled ham" as is Virginia for "Smithfield ham," but on a smaller scale. It is unique and delicious to say the least, and not produced in other parts of the USA.

Only hams in the 12-14 lb. range are used. This in itself will give you a tender ham. The ham is tumbled in a machine that resembles a clothes dryer, but obviously larger. This tenderizes the ham even more. The ham is cured, packed into a stockinette and cooked.

Availability? Only around the Easter and Christmas holidays and mostly by reservation, with 3-4 weeks advance notice. It is that unique. Obviously, this would be rather difficult to produce, but a reasonably good job can be done at home using a 12-14 lb. ham and omitting the tumbling.

The canned-boiled hams we see cannot be duplicated at home, as it takes special equipment to press and form. A boiled ham, however, can be made at home rather easily by boning and stuffing the meat into a fibrous casing. The ham can be cured, cut into smaller chunks, dusted with plain gelatin, then stuffed into 6" or 8" diameter casings. The gelatin will help to bind the meat together so that the ham doesn't fall apart when cooled.

NOTE:

You might consider cutting off the greater part of the shank if you boil the ham in a stockinette, as it will fit a lot better into the cooking container. You might also consider cooking the ham in a smokehouse when using a fibrous casing—without smoke. As you can see, there are various ways to prepare a boiled ham. It simply depends on the individual and the equipment available.

Following this formula is enough for about 25 lbs. of ham:

2 gals. of ice water 38-40 degrees F.
1 lb. 12 ozs. granulated salt
5 ozs. granulated sugar
5 ozs. Prague Powder #1

All ingredients are dissolved in cold water 38-40 degrees F. Be-sure the ham is chilled to the same temperature. Weigh the amount of pickle you will be using to pump the ham to 10% of its weight. Pump the brine into the ham and place into leftover brine to cure for 5 days. Remove from brine, rinse off and cook in 160-165 degrees F. water until the internal temperature reaches 152 degrees F. (these same temperatures apply if cooking in a smokehouse). Ham is removed and placed into cold water for an hour or two until the internal temperature is reduced. Remove carefully to cooler and slice next day.
NOTE: This formula for a boiled ham is quite simple and even difficult for some people to believe. Keep in mind that pork is a highly flavorable meat and the cure helps to impart special flavors. With the salt and sugar added we have a total of 4 items going for us. You may substitute the sugar with same weight of honey if you desire.

SMOKED HAMS

INGREDIENTS FOR 100 LBS.
5½ gallons ice water
  38-40 degrees F.
4 lbs. salt
1½ lbs. powdered dextrose
1½ lbs. Prague Powder No. 1

INGREDIENTS FOR 25 LBS.
5 quarts ice water
  38-40 degrees F.
1 lb. salt
5 ozs. powdered dextrose
5 ozs. Prague Powder No. 1

DRY-CURE METHOD
ARTERY PUMPING

All ingredients are thoroughly dissolved in cold water (40 degrees F.). Hams must have an internal temperature of 38-40 degrees F. before pumping. Weigh the amount of pickle that you will be using to artery pump the ham at 10% of the weight of the ham.

After the ham is pumped, rub in 2-3 lbs. of the above dry mixture for each 50 lbs. of ham. Be sure that you have mixed and distributed the salt, sugar and cure. The cure can cause burn spots on the meat if not evenly distributed. Avoid stacking the hams over 4 high, as this will cause excessive weight on the bottom hams, which in turn will squeeze out the natural juices and the pickle. Hams should be cured at 38-40 degrees F. for 5-7 days. Remove from the cooler and wash the surface salt off the hams with a stiff brush. DO NOT SOAK. Place in stockinettes and remove to smokehouse.

STITCH-PUMPING METHOD

Ham is pumped 10% by weight as above in dry-cure method. Ham should be pumped in the shank and around all the bones in the ham, using the same ingredients as above. Hams then are placed in a container and the cover pickle added. This pickle is the same as was used to pump the ham.

Be sure the hams are submerged beneath the pickle. Remove and place in cooler at 38-40 degrees F. for 5-7 days. Place in stockinettes and put in smokehouse.

PICNICS AND SHOULDERS

Pork butts and pork shoulders are, for the most part, cured exactly as a ham. However, there is one important variation. The picnics and shoulders should be pumped to 15% of their green weight, rather than the 10% for a ham. The reason for this is that during the cure period these two cuts of meat lose from 3-4% more pickle than does the ham. Otherwise, the same formula as processing ham applies to these 2 cuts of meat.

SMOKING

The hams are removed to a smokehouse preheated to 120 degrees F. With drafts wide open, hold for 12 hours. Increase the temperature to 140 degrees F., introducing the smoke, and hold for 8 hours with draft ½ open. Close the drafts, increase the temperature to 165 degrees F. and hold until the internal temperature of the ham is 142 degrees F. For a fully cooked ham, hold until the internal temperature reaches 152-155 degrees F.

The above photo shows a short-shank ham. The shank or hock, as it is known, is also smoked and used as a ham hock with beans, etc. Removing this shank is an especially good idea if you want to cook the ham in water after it's smoked. It is obvious that you can get by with a lot smaller cooking utensil to cook the ham in.

298

ITALIAN-STYLE HAM

In order to make a good Italian-style ham, the ham should be in the 12-14 lbs. range. The ham has to be pumped to 10% of its weight with a curing brine made of the following ingredients:

1 gal. water—38-40 degrees F.
4 ozs. prague powder #1
1¼ lbs. salt
4 ozs. powdered dextrose

After pumping the ham, prepare a dry rub cure according to the following formula:

1 oz. prague powder #1
1 oz. powdered dextrose
½ oz. ground chili powder
½ oz. garlic powder
1 lb. salt

The above mixture is enough for 50 lbs. of ham. Rub the hams well with the above mixture and place in a container to cure. The ham is held for 10 days at 35-40 degrees F. and flattened during this period. Place a clean hardwood board on top of the ham with 15-20 lbs. of weight on top of it.

Then remove the ham and allow it to soak for at least one hour in cool water; then drip-dry for another hour. Afterward, dip the ham in the following prepared mixture:

½ gallon dark molasses
½ gallon water
1 oz. garlic powder

After the hams are dipped, allow them to dry at room temperature for at least 2½ hours before placing in a stockinette bag. Place in a smokehouse preheated to 140 degrees F. and hold for one hour. Increase smokehouse temperature to 160 degrees F. and hold ham there until an internal temperature of 145 degrees F. is reached.

Then reduce the smokehouse temperature to 120 degrees F. and smoke the ham for 12 hours in dense smoke. Ham should then be allowed to cool at room temperature for about 2-3 hours before it is placed in a cooler overnight.

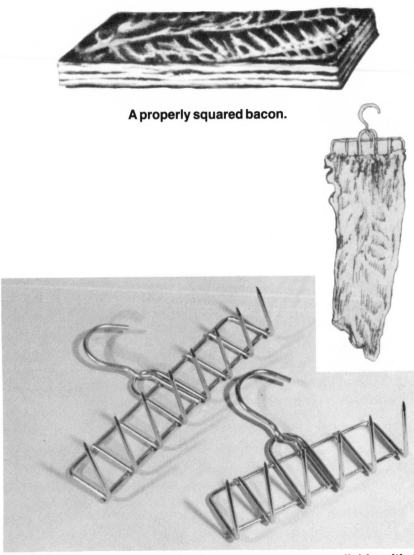

A properly squared bacon.

The above drawings show that bacon hangers are available with 6 prongs for smaller or regular bacon, or 8 prongs for larger bacon.

HONEY-CURED BACON

1 lb. salt
2 ozs. Prague Powder No. 1
1 pint of honey

The above formula will cure about one slab of bacon. The Prague Powder No. 1 and the salt are mixed and then thoroughly rubbed into the bacon. After rubbing, the honey is poured on the bacon and distributed evenly. The bacon is wrapped in a good plastic-lined (freezer wrap) butcher paper and placed in a 38 degree F. cooler for about 6 days.

The bacon then is removed from the cooler and *washed very well*. Excess honey and cure are washed off with luke warm water. Let bacon dry at room temperature for about 30 minutes, then re-move to smokehouse preheated to 135 degrees F. Hold in smokehouse until bacon is dry, with dampers wide open. Dampers then are closed to ¼ open, applying smoke, and held until internal temperature of bacon reaches 127-128 degrees F.

Reduce temperature of smoker to 120 degrees F. and hold until desired color is obtained. Remove and place in cooler overnight before slicing. Be sure that you are using hickory to get the desired flavor of this bacon.

This recipe for honey-cured, hickory-smoked bacon is my favorite when it comes to bacon. Not only is it an excellent bacon, but it is extremely easy to make. The instructions are just too simple to believe. It is slightly messy to prepare, but the end result only can be accomplished at home and cannot be purchased in a meat market.

Preparing A Honey-Cured Bacon At Home

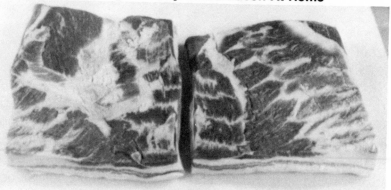

The bacon is skinned and cut in half for easy handling.

The bacon is then rubbed very well with a mixture of cure and salt.

The bacon is then generously covered with honey, placed into waiting freezer wrap and removed to the cooler for 4-5 days.

After 5 days, the bacon is washed by hand to remove excess salt, cure and honey.

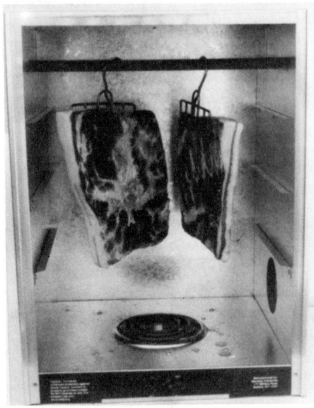

The bacon is then allowed to dry at room temperature, then placed in the smoker. Follow the directions on page 301.

SPRAY INJECTION-CURED BACON

INGREDIENTS FOR 100 LBS.

5 gallons ice water
  38-40 degrees F.
2 lbs. powdered dextrose
1 lb. Prague Powder No. 1
4 lbs. salt

INGREDIENTS FOR 25 LBS.

5 quarts ice water
  38-40 degrees F.
7 ozs. powdered dextrose
3 ozs. Prague Powder No.1
1 lb. salt

PROCESSING

Bellies should be chilled to 38-40 degrees F. before pumping. Dissolve all the ingredients thoroughly in the water. Use this brine to pump 8% of the green weight of the bellies. Bellies then are placed into a container, skin side down, one on top of the other. Be sure container has a drain in the bottom to allow excess curing solution to drain out. Cover with wax paper and remove to 38-40 degree F. cooler for 4-5 days before smoking.

SMOKING

Bellies are removed from cooler and washed with a hot-water shower using a fiber brush. DO NOT SOAK. Remove to a smokehouse preheated to 135 degrees F. Have dampers wide open and start smoking. After the surface of the bacon has become partially dry, close the dampers to ¼ open and hold at 135 degrees until 127-128 degrees F. is obtained internally. Reduce smokehouse temperature and hold bacon until desired color is obtained. Remove to cooler and hold overnight before slicing.

NOTE:
You may lower the salt content of the above formula if a less salty bacon is desired.

SCHINKENSPECK
(Ham-Bacon)

INGREDIENTS FOR 25 LBS.
5 gallons ice water
1 lb. salt
1 lb. prague powder #1
5 ozs. powdered dextrose
5 ozs. ground white pepper
3 ozs. ground juniper berries

INGREDIENTS FOR 10 LBS.
2½ gallons ice water
8 ozs. salt
8 ozs. prague powder #1
2½ ozs. powdered dextrose
2½ ozs. ground white pepper
1½ ozs. ground juniper berries

Ham-bacon is rarely seen in the United States, but is readily available in many European meat markets. My first encounter with this delicious bacon with in England while serving in the armed forces.

Schinkenspeck

I ate a good deal of this bacon while in England and never did figure out what I was eating. I only knew it was much better than the American-style bacon we were served in the G.I. mess halls. We ate breakfast every chance we got in English restaurants. I would have to classify the American bacon we are so used to as a poor man's bacon. In Europe, however, even a poor man eats

305

ham-bacon. No question—this is the king of bacons and is far superior to our American bacon. From time to time I've been able to purchase ham-bacon in the Province of Ontario in Canada, which is only a mile or two away from my present home in Buffalo, N.Y.

As an extra fancy bacon, the Schinkenspeck requires a little extra work to produce. When finished, it will have the appearance of a rolled roast. A fresh bellie (fresh bacon) and a lean leg of pork (fresh ham) are required. Notice in the photograph that the outside of this Schinkenspeck is a bellie and the center is a lean (ham) leg of pork. Both these meats are placed into a brine made by mixing the above ingredients. Remove to cooler for 5—6 days at 40° F. After curing, this meat is allowed to drip dry before rolling into a roast.

The bacon is gently powdered with gelatin, the lean meat (ham) is placed inside it, and then the bacon is rolled around it and tied.

It is not a bad idea to smoke this ham-bacon by placing it into a small stockinette bag. When this is done, place into the smokehouse at 135° F. until an internal temperature of 127°—128° F. is reached. Smoke the bacon very lightly towards the end of the cycle. The smoke should be almost imperceptible.

DRY BOX BACON CURE

INGREDIENTS FOR 100 LBS.
2½ lbs. salt
1¼ lbs. powdered dextrose
11 ozs. Prague Powder No. 1

INGREDIENTS FOR 25 LBS.
10 ozs. salt
5 ozs. powdered dextrose
2 ozs. Prague Powder No. 1

PROCESSING

All the ingredients are to be mixed very well until they are all evenly distributed. The bellies should be refrigerated at 38-40 degrees F. before use and trimmed nicely (squared off). Each belly then is thoroughly rubbed and placed into the box, meat side up. Pack the bellies tightly one on top of the other after they are rubbed and be sure that all the air pockets are omitted.

After 2 days, the bellies should be covered in their own natural brine. If not, make a pickle brine using 1¼ lbs. of the above formula to 1 gallon of water.

Bellies should be cured on the basis of 1 lb. per day (10 lb. belly–10 days). Be sure you do not leave in cure more than 13 days, 3 days past the 10-day limit.

Remove from the curing box and wash the bacon, removing the surface salt. DO NOT SOAK; place in the smokehouse, preheated at 135 degrees F. with dampers wide open. Hold at this temperature until the surface of the bacon is dry. Close dampers to ¼ open, apply smoke, and hold this temperature until an internal temperature of 127-128 degrees F. is obtained. Reduce smokehouse temperature to 120 degrees F. and hold until desired color is obtained. Remove to 36-38 degree F. cooler overnight before slicing.

CANADIAN-STYLE BACON

<table>
<tr><td>**INGREDIENTS FOR 100 LBS.**</td><td>**INGREDIENTS FOR 25 LBS.**</td></tr>
<tr><td>5 gallons ice water
  38-40 degrees F.</td><td>5 quarts ice water
  38-40 degrees F.</td></tr>
<tr><td>1½ lbs. powdered dextrose</td><td>6 ozs. powdered dextrose</td></tr>
<tr><td>8 ozs. Prague Powder No. 1</td><td>2 ozs. Prague Powder No. 1</td></tr>
<tr><td>2 lbs. salt</td><td>8 ozs. salt</td></tr>
</table>

MEAT

Pork loins—be sure meat is chilled to 38-40 degrees F.; the average weight is 12-14 lbs. Remove all the bones, being very careful not to damage any of the meat. Trim down all the fat until you reach the lean meat.

PROCESSING

Dissolve all the ingredients in 5 gallons of cold water. If needed, you may add ice to bring down the temperature of the water. After the brine is made, the loins should be spray pumped to 10% of their green weight. Loins then are placed into the leftover brine and placed in cooler for 4-6 days at 38-40 degrees F. Remove from the cooler and wash under a shower of hot water. Let drain and stuff very tightly into a synthetic casing. You may pin-prick all the air pockets to let entrapped air escape.

SMOKING

Place into preheated smokehouse at 130 degrees F. with dampers wide open; hold for 4 hours without smoke. Gradually increase temperature to 150 degrees F. and close damper to ¼ open; hold for 3 hours, introducing the smoke. Increase temperature to 160 degrees F. and hold until the internal temperature reaches 142 degrees F. Remove from the smoker and cool with cold tap water until the internal temperature is reduced to 110 degrees F. Let hang at room temperature until casings are dry. Remove to cooler over-night before using.

NOTE:

If you are using small loins, you may rub both pieces of the loin on the lean sides with a fine-granulated gelatin. This will help to bind the two pieces that are stuffed into the casing after they are cooled off.

PEA MEAL BACON

Pea meal bacon is another form of Canadian bacon, except that it is cured but not smoked. This bacon is found widely in the Canadian meat markets, especially in the province of Ontario. The pork loins are cured the same way as Canadian bacon. After curing, the loins are dried somewhat and coated generously with yellow corn meal. They are then sliced and fried. If you wish, you may coat both sides of sliced bacon before frying.

Canadian bacon

Peal meal bacon

BEEF BACON

INGREDIENTS FOR 100 LBS.
5 gallons ice water
   38-40 degrees F.
4 lbs. salt
1½ lbs. powdered dextrose
1 lb. Prague Powder No. 1

INGREDIENTS FOR 25 LBS.
5 quarts ice water
   38-40 degrees F.
1 lb. salt
5 ozs. powdered dextrose
3 ozs. Prague Powder No. 1

MEAT

Beef plates

PROCESSING

Beef plates are cured in the brine made from the above formula. Plates are cured for 7-8 days and overhauled on the fourth day. After the plates are cured, they then are washed with hot water, and all the loose surface fat is removed. Bacon is then hung-properly spaced.

SMOKING

Bacon is removed to a smokehouse preheated to 135 degrees F., with the drafts wide open until the surface of the product is dry. Dampers are closed to ¼ open starting the smoke; hold until the desired color is obtained. The drafts are closed and smoke shut off; temperature is raised to 160 degrees F. and bacon is held until an internal temperature of 135 degrees F. is obtained. Shut off heat and let remain in smokehouse for at least 1 hour. Remove to cooler overnight before slicing.

BEEF BACON
(DRY CURE METHOD)

Beef bacon generally is cured the same way that pork bacon is. The only difference is the beef bacon is cured for 6-7 days rather than on the basis of 1 lb. per day.

PASTRAMI

INGREDIENTS FOR 100 LBS.
5 gallons ice cold water
  38-40 degrees F.
1¼ lbs. Prague Powder No. 1
½ oz. garlic juice
2 lbs. salt
1½ lbs. powdered dextrose

INGREDIENTS FOR 25 LBS.
5 quarts ice cold water
  38-40 degrees F.
5 ozs. Prague Powder No.1
1 tbsp. garlic juice
8 ozs. salt
5 ozs. powdered dextrose

MEAT

Use a very good grade of beef plates or well-trimmed briskets.

PUMPING & CURING

Pump the plates or briskets to 15% of their weight. Meat should be placed into curing box or vat and kept submerged while curing in cooler for 3-5 days at 40 degrees F.

SPICING & SMOKING

Remove the cured pastrami pieces from the box or vat and rub all sides with a combination of coarse black pepper and coriander; or you may use coarsely chopped pickling spices. You also may sprinkle the meat with paprika to give it an attractive appearance.

Place in smokehouse preheated at 130 degrees F. with dampers wide open. Hold at this temperature for about 1 hour or until the surface of the meat is dry. Close dampers to ¼ open and apply a light smoke for about 2 hours. Gradually increase the smokehouse temperature to 200-220 degrees F. and hold until an internal temperature of 175-180 degrees F. is obtained internally. Meat then is removed from the smokehouse and allowed to cool at room temperature for 1-2 hours before removing to cooler overnight.

KOSHER STYLE CORNED BEEF BRISKETS

INGREDIENTS FOR 100 LBS.
(for pump and cover pickle)
5 gallons ice water
  38-40 degrees F.
2 lbs. salt
1 lb. Prague Powder No. 1
1 lb. powdered dextrose

INGREDIENTS FOR 25 LBS.
(for pump and cover pickle)
5 quarts ice water
  38-40 degrees F.
8 ozs. salt
3 ozs. Prague Powder No. 1
3 ozs. powdered dextrose

PROCESSING

The briskets are to be spray-pumped to about 12-15% of their green weight. After pumping, the briskets are packed in a vat, flesh side up, and sprinkled with whole pickling spice. The next layer then is packed flesh side down, continuing to pack, flesh to flesh, with the spices in between, until the vat is full. Add enough of the brine until the vat is full. Place cover on top and be sure all the meat is covered with the brine.

CURING

Allow briskets to cure in a 38-40 degree F. cooler for 3-4 days. Brisket then is ready to use.

NOTE:
If you wish, you may use beef rounds if briskets are not available.

Curing Corned Beef At Home

Nothing is better and easier to cure than a corned beef. Almost anyone can do it as it takes a minimum of time and equipment.

Briskets are best for making corned beef, but you can also use beef rounds. The meat is cut into smaller pieces to fit into the container.

The meat is then placed into a container of prepared brine and placed into a cooler for 4-5 days. I always add a handful or so of a good grade of pickling spices. This really gives it a special flavor.

313

SMOKED BACK RIBS

Back ribs, or more correctly pork loin ribs, are the end result after the loin is removed and usually turned into Canadian or pea meal bacon. The rib end of this pork loin usually is cut off. Only the center ribs and loin end are used as back ribs.

During the separation of the loin from the ribs (or boning, if you will) a substantial amount of meat deliberately is left on these ribs. The following formula is enough for about 25 lbs. of back ribs:

2½ gallons cold water

1 lb. salt

8 ozs. powdered dextrose

4 ozs. Prague Powder No. 1

The ingredients are all mixed with the water until completely dissolved. Place back ribs into brine and remove to refrigerator for 2 days. Remove from cooler, hang on hooks, and allow to drip-dry at room temperature for about 1 hour. Place in a preheated smokehouse at 120 degrees F. with dampers wide open to allow further drying. When ribs are dry to the touch, increase smokehouse temperature to 160 degrees F. Apply heavy smoke and hold for 3-4 hours until ribs are a golden brown. Remove and let cool at room temperature for 1 hour before placing into cooler overnight.

The above is the formula used to smoke back ribs for Caesar's Palace Hotel in Las Vegas, Nevada in the mid-60's, when I was an owner of The Hickory Shop Sausage Kitchen. This was truly a gourmet dish, and in those days, sold for $18.50 per person.

CURED AND SMOKED BEEF TONGUES

INGREDIENTS FOR 10 LBS.

2½ gallons water

1 lb. salt

8 ozs. Prague Powder No. 1

Beef tongues are to be washed very cleanly, free of slime. Tongue is then pumped with brine up to about 5% of its weight. It is then placed into pickle to cure for about 8 days. When curing more than one tongue, you must overhaul tongues at the end of the 4th day.

Tongues then are removed, washed clean and placed into a stockinette. Keep tongues at room temperature for about 4 hours while smokehouse is preheating to 140 degrees F. Meat is placed in smokehouse with dampers wide open to allow drying of the tongues. Raise temperature to 180 degrees F. and hold 4-5 hours. Remove to room temperature until internal temperature is reduced to 110 degrees F. Place in cooler overnight before using.

PEPPERED BEEF ROUNDS

INGREDIENTS FOR 10 LBS.
2½ galllons ice water
8 ozs. Prague Powder No. 1
1 lb. salt
2 lbs. powdered dextrose

Use pieces of top or bottom rounds, about 4-5" thick. Meat is pumped with brine 10% of the weight of the meat. The meat then is generously rubbed with the cracked black pepper and laid down in aging container very tightly, with a weighted wooden cover to press meat down. Add just enough brine to cover the meat and let it age for 7 days at 38-40 degrees F.

Meat is removed and placed into a stockinette. Meat also can be laid flat if smokehouse screen is available. The smokehouse should be preheated to 130 degrees F. with dampers wide open, until the surface of the meat is dry. Temperature then is raised to 155 degrees F. with damper about ¼ open. Meat is smoked at this temperature for 4 hours. Smoke then is shut off and temperature raised to 210 degrees F. until the internal temperature of the meat is 165 degrees F. Meat is then placed in cooler for 24 hours before slicing.

SLONINA PAPRYKOWANA
(Polish-Style Paprika Salt Pork)

4 ozs. prague powder #1
2½ lbs. salt
Paprika

A bacon (with the skin removed) is cut in half, lengthwise. Using the above mixture, rub the bacon pieces well. Then lay the bacon in a bed of salt; each piece thereafter should also be covered with salt. Then place the bacon in a cooler for 6-7 days. After this, re-rub the bacon and place in the salt again as done previously.

After 1 more week, remove the bacon from the cooler and wash thoroughly with luke-warm water. Then cut the bacon into pieces 10-12" long and dry for 2-3 hours. Rub the bacon with a good grade of paprika, allowing as much to adhere as possible. You may dredge the bacon in the paprika and tap it, allowing the excess paprika to fall off.

Then place the bacon in a smokehouse at 70-75 degrees F. and smoke for 24 hours until it has a brick-red color. Remove and store in cooler.
NOTE:
This bacon should be treated as raw meat.

SALT PORK

The above process may be followed for salt pork, omitting the paprika and the smoking step. In addition, backfat is very popular in the U.S. when making salt pork. Salt pork can simply be stored in the salt and cure mixture until ready to use after the 2-week period of curing is over.

317

CAPICOLA - FULLY COOKED

INGREDIENTS FOR 100 LBS.
5 gallons ice water
  38-40 degrees F.
1½ lbs. powdered dextrose
8 ozs. Prague Powder No. 1
2 lbs. salt

INGREDIENTS FOR 25 LBS.
5 quarts ice water
  38-40 degrees F.
6 ozs. powdered dextrose
2 ozs. Prague Powder No. 1
8 ozs. salt

MEAT

Lean boneless pork butts, ranging from 3-4 lbs. Be sure butts are chilled to 38-40 degrees F. before using.

PROCESSING

Dissolve all the ingredients in 5 gallons of water at 38-40 degrees F.; if needed, add ice to bring water temperature down. Mix all the ingredients well until they are all dissolved in the water. After brine is made, all the pork butts should be pumped with a spray pump to 10% of the green weight. (A 4 lb. pork butt should be pumped with 6-7 ozs. of brine.) Pump brine on all sides of the butt.

Pork butts should then be placed into the brine and left for 3 days at 38-40 degree F. cooler. After 3 days, remove butts from brine and spray-wash with cool water and let drain. Butts are then rubbed with Spanish paprika and ground red pepper. Amount of pepper to be rubbed is of individual preference. Butts then are stuffed into beef bungs or synthetic casings. After stuffing, the casings must be pin-pricked to allow entrapped air to escape. Hang properly spaced on smoke sticks.

SMOKING

Remove butts to smokehouse preheated to 130 degrees F. with the dampers wide open for 3 hours. Increase the temperature to 150 degrees F. and hold for 2 hours with dampers ¼ open, applying a light smoke. Raise temperature to 160-165 degrees F. and hold until an internal temperature of 152 degrees F. is obtained. Remove from smokehouse, dipping butts into hot boiling water momentarily to shrink the casing. Let hang at room temperature until 110 degrees F. is obtained internally. Remove to 45 degree F. cooler overnight.

SMOKED BONELESS BUTTS

A smoked boneless butt generally is processed the same way as the capicola. The same cure mix may be used, and curing time in cooler is 3-6 days. Omit paprika and red pepper rub. Stockinettes are to be used instead of casings, and a heavier smoke is appied.

DRIED BEEF

INGREDIENTS FOR 10 LBS.
2½ gallons ice water
8 ozs. Prague Powder No. 1
1 lb. salt
8 ozs. powdered dextrose

PROCESSING PROCEDURE

Use a beef round that is completely free of fat. The meat and brine both should be chilled around 38 degrees F. Pump the beef very carefully with the brine, not exceeding 8% of the weight of the meat. Be careful not to overpump one area so as to breathe air pockets in the meat.

The meat then is placed in the curing pickle for 10 days. After curing, the meat is removed and allowed to soak in the tap water for several hours, changing the water every hour.

Meat is removed, allowed to drain and placed in stockinette. Hang meat in a smokehouse preheated to 100 degrees F. for 12 hours to dry. Drafts should be wide open. Temperature then is raised to 115 degrees F. and held for 24 more hours with draft ½ open. Temperature then is increased to about 125 degrees F. for 12 hours with smoke. Temperature is then reduced to 115 degrees F. Shut off smoke and hold until meat shrinks to about 35% of its original weight. Dried beef is sliced paper thin.

DRIED BEEF

For good dried beef you must select a firm piece of meat, properly trimmed. Remove all fat and sinew. When curing more than one piece, the meat generally should be trimmed to equal sizes.

5 GALLON FORMULA
5 gals. water
I lb. prague powder #1
1½ lbs. salt
I lb. cane sugar

Add ingredients to the water and mix thoroughly. Be sure the water is at 38-40 degrees F. Then pump the beef with this brine using no more than 8% of the meat's weight. Care should be taken not to pump too much brine into the meat, because it can cause air pockets. Pump the brine into the center of the beef, pulling the needle out as you are pumping the brine. Then place meat in the remaining brine for 12-14 days.

After the meat is cured, let it soak in water for about 1 hour. The water should be changed once or twice during this period. Then let the meat drip dry and place it in a stockinette bag. The following drying and smoking schedule is recommended:

HOURS	TEMPERATURE	
10 at	100-110 degrees F.	No smoke
12 at	100-110 degrees F.	With smoke
6 at	120 degrees F.	No smoke
7 at	130 degrees F.	No smoke

It is important that the above temperatures are adhered to, especially during the first 22 hours. It is during this time that drying too fast can form a crust on the surface of the meat, which won't allow the remaining moisture to escape.

After 35 hours at the above temperatures reduce the smokehouse temperature to 115 degrees F. Keep the meat there for about 4 days without smoke. The product will shrink about 35-40% but will still have about 50% of its original moisture. The meat should then be allowed to cool gradually in the smoker without heat or at room temperature for about 5-6 hours. Then place in cooler.

CURING & SMOKING POULTRY

As with other meats, poultry must first be cured before smoking. You should, however, be acquainted with this meat before you get started.

Unnoticed by many people is the fact that almost all the poultry that is shipped into a butcher shop these days is packed in ice. The top of every case is generously packed with crushed ice. This is done to prolong its relatively short shelf life—about 7-10 days. Since most butcher coolers are held at 38-40 degrees F., the shelf life of poultry is dramatically shortened.

From the day the poultry is butchered until it reaches the super-market, it can be 2-3 days in transit, packed in ice at about 32 degrees F. Any temperatures higher than that causes the poultry to spoil. Three to four days on the road and a week in someone's refrigerator, and the poultry is spoiled. The shelf life for fresh beef, pork or veal is at least twice as long—and at higher temperatures.

In other words, poultry should either be cooked up in a day or two or frozen. I think it becomes quite clear why we only see frozen turkeys in the butcher shop, and this really makes it hard to tell how old the poultry is. In other words, it's pretty risky business to get a store-bought turkey for curing and smoking.

If you don't know for sure how fresh your poultry is, you are risking spoilage. That can be pretty hard to take after purchasing an 18-20 lb. turkey. By the same token, you can spray-pump the cure into the turkey or poultry right to the meat and let it brine soak for only a couple of days instead of the usual 4-5 days. This puts the odds in your favor. If you raise and butcher your own turkeys or poultry, you'll probably never have these problems.

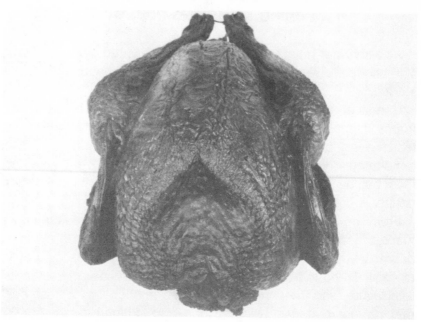

Notice how the above smoked turkey holds its shape after hanging in a smoker for a number of hours. The stockinette bag was used to give the turkey this nice shape.

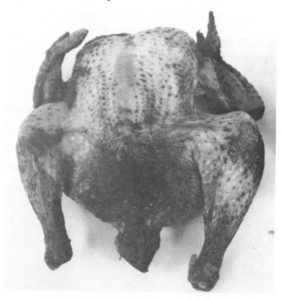

The chicken above was smoked without the use of a stockinette bag. It looks like it is ready to fly. Stockinette bags do enhance the appearance of smoked poultry.

SMOKED TURKEY

INGREDIENTS
5 gallons water
1½ lbs. powdered dextrose
2 lbs. salt
1 lb. Prague Powder No. 1

A maple-flavored sugar may be used in place of the powdered dextrose called for in the above formula to give the bird an unusual flavor. This formula can be used for all poultry.

COVER PICKLE METHOD
Dissolve all the ingredients in water chilled to 38-40 degrees F. Be sure that you have washed the cavity of the turkey very well and that the temperature of the turkey is 38-40 degrees F. before placing into the brine. Turkey should be submerged in brine for at least 4 days at 38-40 degrees F. A larger turkey will take about 5 days to cure.

SPRAY-PUMP METHOD
Dissolve all the ingredients in water chilled to 38-40 degrees F. Pump the turkey with curing solution using 10 percent of the weight of the turkey (20 lb. turkey — pump with 2 lbs. of brine). After pumping, place the turkey in ice-cold water for at least 3 hours. Remove the turkey from the ice-cold water and place in cover pickle at 38-40 degrees F. Remove to cooler at 38-40 degrees F. and allow to cure for 48 hours.

SMOKING
After turkey is cured, wash very well with cold water and place into a preheated smoker at 130 degrees F. Smoke at this temperature for at least 1 hour with damper wide open. Close damper to ¼ open and apply smoke for 5 hours at 130 degrees F.; raise temperature to 140 degrees F. and hold for 4 hours.

Finally, raise temperature to 165 degrees F. and hold until an internal temperature of 152 degrees F. is obtained. Use a dial meat thermometer, inserting the stem close to the ball-and-socket joint of the thigh, as this seems to be the last place the meat becomes thoroughly cooked. Remove from smoker and let the meat temperature drop to about 100 degrees F. before placing into the cooler.

SMOKED TURKEY IS A PERISHABLE PROUCT AND SHOULD BE KEPT UNDER REFRIGERATION AT ALL TIMES.

NOTE:
Sodium nitrite in the curing solution will cause the meat of the turkey to turn pink when it is smoked. If this color is objectionable, you may omit this cure from the formula.

If you decide not to use cure in your brine, it is imperative that you preheat your smoker to at least 180 degrees F. and allow the turkey to dry for at least one hour. The temperature should then be raised to 200 degrees F. and cooked until the internal temperature is at least 170 degrees F. Needless to say, we are now baking or cooking the turkey at more or less normal high temperatures, which eliminates the possibility of food poisoning without the use of cures.

Be sure you insert the thermometer in the thickest parts of the breast, as close to the center as possible. The turkey leg, in the thickest part, is also a good place to check as well.

Personally, I always have preferred to use cures when smoking poultry, for a number of reasons. First of all, I find that cures definitely enhance the flavor of the turkey or chicken. I tried it both ways, but, when cured, the flavor is by far superior.

Secondly, smoking cured poultry at low temperatures allows you to do a much better job of smoking. Using lower temperatures also prevents a great deal of shrinkage, which is very important commercially. The profits are not going up the chimney and the poultry is not dried out as much. I think it is an excellent idea to try both processes to see which one you prefer.

CHAPTER XII

Cured Sausage
Semi-Dry

SEMI-DRY SAUSAGE

Fermentation is the key to making high quality semi-dry sausage with the traditional tangy flavors. These tangy flavors are produced by a specific bacteria that is added to the meat by chance during the handling of the meat, or by deliberately adding a known starter culture as part of the formula. The latter method is more desirable, as we can have controlled fermentation and can produce a consistent product.

Even though semi-dry sausages were being produced for centuries before the coming of Christ, very little was known about what was actually happening inside of these sausages. There was no real control of the fermentation and the flavors varied form batch to batch.

About all that was known for sure was the fact that specific amounts of salt and dextrose were needed to help along fermentation with spices for flavor. Somewhere along the line, however, someone decided to save some meat from the previous batch and then add it to the new batch, etc. This is called "back slopping" and was done to get a more consistent flavor or develop some control each time these sausages were made. It was a start in the right direction, but still not what one could call controlled fermentation.

Back slopping was started after the 1850s when Louis Pasteur concluded his experiments with fermentation. It was then realized that a bacteriological culture was helping to produce these tangy flavors in semi-dry sausages. An accumulation of fermentation products caused these tangy flavors, of which lactic acid is predominant. We began to find out that dextrose is a food for the lactic acid organism to feed on.

For best results, 12 ounces of dextrose per 100 lbs. of meat is required to obtain optimum growth of this lactic acid organism. Dextrose is not intensely sweet and is, therefore, used instead of sugar. It supports the fermentation far better than sugar or other sweeteners.

The amount of salt also is very important in the production of semi-dry sausage. Salt is not only a spice that contributes flavors to semi-dry sausages; it also helps to select the right organisms for fermentation and prevents the growth of undesirable organisms as well.

A humidity indicator (hygrometer)—a must if you are going to dry-cure meat or sausage.

HUMIDITY

It seems strange indeed that maintaining a high relative humidity is an important step in the process of dry-curing a salami or other meat. Most people think it should be the other way around; the lower the humidity, the quicker we can dry cure the product.

The dry curing process requires controlled humidity and temperatures to support the fermentation process. A proper level of humdiity helps to maintain a proper moisture balance that will give us optimum growth of the lactic acid organism, in order to produce the tangy flavor required. On the other hand, too high a humidity can result in the development of undesirable molds. Humidity that is too low can cause dehydration on the surface of the sausage and cause "case hardening."

Put another way, it simply means overdrying the sausage on the exterior too quickly. This overdrying actually forms a hard ring on the outside of the sausage. This condition will not allow the rest of the moisture to escape from the center of the sausage being dry-cured. Once the sausage or salami is case hardened, it would be like stuffing meat into an iron pipe and welding it shut at both ends. Nothing can get in and nothing can get out.

It is quite easy to distinguish a case-hardened product. You will see a grey ring around some reddish meat when it is sliced. As you can see, it is important to maintain the proper humidity and correct temperatures in order to attain a properly cured product.

After the product is mixed, recipes call for various holding periods at various temperatures. Other formulas allow for the meat to be stuffed and held at various temperatures. In either case, the greatest acid production in the dry-cure process comes at temperatures of 100-110 degrees F. The length of time the product is held depends entirely on the product in question and the tang desired. It can vary from a low of four hours to beyond 24 hours.

The last part of this process is to stop the fermentation after we have reached the desired tang. This is very simply done by heating the product until the internal temperature of the product reaches anywhere from 138-150 degrees F.

SODIUM ACETATE AND RELATIVE HUMIDITY

Making a dry-cured or semi-dry cured sausage can be a difficult undertaking if you live in a desert climate or any other part of the country that has a consistently low relative humidity. Living near large bodies of water, like the oceans or lakes, is no guarantee of high humidity — it can be erratic from day to day. Obviously, it would be better if we could semi-dry cure or dry-cure sausage under controlled consistent conditions.

A great number of recipes in this book call for various percentages of humidity for good reasons. **You do not dry-cure or semi-dry cure a sausage by placing it behind a warm stove or in your attic.** A more likely spot is a damp cellar, if you have one. You have to be able to maintain a high humidity in order to produce these products properly.

Fortunately for us, Charles L. Jean of Glendale, Arizona has helped us solve the problems of dry-curing meat in low-humidity areas. A chemist by trade, Mr. Jean advised me how he overcame this problem, since he limits his sausage making to the dry-cured or semi-dry cured products. In an area (Arizona) that rarely has a relative humidity reading beyond 15%, this is quite a feat, and he has requested that I pass along this information to all other sausage makers like himself.

Mr. Jean constructed a sealed Plexiglas container and made a saturated solution with sodium acetate crystals in the bottom of the Plexiglas container. This, he advised me, will maintain a constant humidity of 75% while at room temperature or a refrigerated temperature. Seventy-five percent is an ideal humidity, simply great for dry-cured or semi-dry-cured sausage or meat.

In other words, Mr. Jean more or less constructed a sort of smoker, but to be used solely for curing sausage. It should contain some type of smokehouse sticks on which to hang the sausage. This container should be of a size that can be fit in a refrigerator, since the temperatures to be maintained are usually on the cool side (50-60 degrees F.). The possibility of using a second refrigerator and putting a pan of a sodium acetate solution in it is appealing, because with almost no work and just the expense of an extra refrigerator, you can solve the humidity problem.

331

There are other, less expensive materials one might want to try. Plain old wood that is lined with a heavy gauge plastic would also do. There are also materials like sheet metal (galvanized or stainless) that are just laying around which can be used. Even acrylic or epoxy paints that are used to make aquariums at home can be used.

Probably the most important factor in creating humidity is using a food-grade sodium acetate. There are also commercial grades of sodium acetate not recommended for use around food. The food-grade sodium acetate is more commonly used as a buffering agent with other pharmaceuticals.

AIR DRYING COOKED SAUSAGE

From time to time you may run across a recipe telling you to grind the meat and then let it dry out by being spread out on a table overnight. This is supposed to remove some of its moisture. Clearly, this is a bad practice and should be avoided, as you would be adding all types of bacteria and losing all control in the type of finished product you want to get. It is even worse from a practice of sanitation and would never be permitted in a sausage kitchen that is inspected by a health department.

I think it now is quite clear that making a semi-dry or dry-cured sausage has its limitations as to what area of the country it can be made in. The desert areas of the southwest clearly are very bad for these processes, as the humidity is dramatically low all year long. On the other hand, the Great Lakes region and other areas near large bodies of water have exceptionally high humidity all year long, along with the cooler temperatures that are required. It is obvious that these types of sausage should be made during the cooler seasons of the year like autumn, winter and spring.

It also is important to note that these types of sausages are made commercially all year long, using air-conditioned rooms. This also can be accomplished at home by using a confined area, like an extra refrigerator, in which one could control the temperature as well as the moisture.

FERMENTO

Fermento is an innovative new product recently developed. To some degree, it solves the problems of special shipping and packaging, as it does not require freezing or refrigeration. It is a dairy-based, controlled fermentation product in powdered form.

Fermento imparts a tangy flavor and may be used in the manufacture of all fermented-type sausages similar to summer sausage, thuringer, pepperoni, etc. This new product allows the production of fermented-type sausage at home as well as the smaller commercial sausage kitchens. Fermento should only be used in the production of semi-dry products.

The recommended usage levels are 1-6 percent, depending on the flavor characteristics desired. However, 3 percent generally is the accepted level to start with. If you desire more tang in the product, you may go as high as 6 percent as mentioned above. It is important that you do not go beyond 6 percent, as it can cause the sausage to break down and become mushy. Obviously, you may use less than 3 percent if you desire less tang. The uses referred to are only a guideline to start with, and the user should determine the suitability of this product for each product that is made.

DRYING SAUSAGE

The objective of drying a sausage is to gradually and constantly extract the moisture from its interior. The periods of time could range from 30 days to 6 months. Refrigeration or air conditioning plays a very important part in the drying of these sausages. This will become evident by simply reading the formulas of this book. For the most part, making this type of sausage always was limited to the colder seasons of the year.

Needless to say, these dry or semi-dry sausages came into demand at all times of the year and, therefore, prompted the introduction of mechanically controlled rooms. The dry and semi-dry sausages still can be made during the colder seasons of the year without the use of air conditioned or refrigerated rooms.

It is also noted that making this sausage in the colder seasons, rather than under controlled conditions, makes it extremely difficult to produce a uniform product, since the drying room is affected by the outside weather conditions. You can vary the temperatures and relative humidity in a sausage-drying room, depending on the product itself. Dry sausage is processed by a combination of curing and drying which assures its safety for eating without further processing or cooking.

DESTROYING TRICHINAE

I think it is important to note that of the 10 or 12 sausage-making books circulating in the U.S., a number of them have attempted to explain that trichinae in pork can simply be destroyed by freezing. Unfortunately, it really is not that simple, but then these authors know nothing about this process, or what it takes to get the job done. Needless to say, it is a case of very bad research and people writing about a subject they know nothing about. Because they have never worked on or studied this subject, it just isn't possible for them to know where to research this information. They simply omitted this very critical information on how to destroy trichinae by freezing when preparing pork. Simply freezing pork will not destroy trichinae, as these authors so loosely claim.

The following are U.S.D.A. specifications, and are very detailed as to what it really takes to destroy trichinae by freezing. You must follow these instructions to the letter to get the job done. Not doing so can cause sickness and bodily harm.

The good news on the horizon is that much research has been going on using a technique of "irradiating" pork. It seems this will be a safe and low-cost way of destroying all trichinae in pork just after the animal is slaughtered. This would mean you could eat a rare or medium rare pork steak without worry. I surmise we should see approval of this process in less than 5 years.

BEAR MEAT

As a precautionary note to hunters, it is imperative to let you know that bear meat more often than not is infected with the trichinae parasite. Bear meat must be processed the same as any pork product when it's used in sausage making or meat curing and smoking.

The following government regulations are recognized as adequate to destroy the live trichinae that are sometimes found in fresh pork by the Meat Inspection Service of the United States Department of Agriculture:

GOVERNMENT REGULATIONS
FOR CURING DRY OR SEMI-DRY SAUSAGE

Dry and semi-dry sausages usually are eaten by the consumer without further cooking, yet they are not heated during processing to an internal temperature which assures destruction of live trichinae in pork flesh, the parasite that causes trichinosis in humans.

As a safety measure to guard against trichinosis, the Meat Inspection Division (MID) of the United States Department of Agriculture has established processing regulations in the treatment of pork with regard to sausage making.

Sausage may be stuffed into animal casings, hydrocellulose casings, or cloth bags. If animal casings are used, according to government regulation, it is permissible to use potassium sorbate only to retard mold on dry sausages (salami type). Use a water solution containing 2.5% potassium sorbate; it may be applied to casings after stuffing, or casings may be dipped in the solution prior to

336

stuffing.

DRY CURING

In the preparation of sausage, one of the following methods may be used.

METHOD NO. 1. – The meat shall be ground or chopped into pieces not exceeding ¾ inches in diameter. A dry-curing mixture containing not less than 3⅓ lbs. of salt per each 100 lbs. of unstuffed sausage shall be thoroughly mixed with the ground or chopped meat.

After being stuffed, sausage having a diameter not exceeding 3½ inches, measured at the time of stuffing, shall be held in a drying room not less than 20 days at a temperature not lower than 45 degrees F., except that in sausage of the variety known as pepperoni, if in casings not exceeding 1⅜ inches in diameter at time of stuffing, the period of drying may be reduced to 15 days.

In no case, however, shall the sausage be released from the drying room in less than 25 days from the time the curing materials are added, except that sausage of the variety known as pepperoni, if in casings not exceeding the size specified, may be released at the expiration of 20 days from the time the curing materials are added.

Sausage in casing exceeding 3½ inches, but not exceeding 4 inches in diameter at time of stuffing, shall be held in a drying room not less than 35 days at a temperature not lower than 45 degrees F., and in no case shall the sausage be released from the drying room in fewer than 40 days from the time the curing materials are added to the meat.

METHOD NO. 2. – The meat shall be ground or chopped into pieces not exceeding ¾ inches in diameter. A dry-curing mixture containing not less than 3⅓ lbs. of salt per 100 lbs. of unstuffed sausage shall be thoroughly mixed with the ground or chopped meat. After being stuffed, the sausage having a diameter not exceeding 3½ inches, measured at the time of stuffing, shall be smoked not less than 40 hours at a temperature not lower than 80 degrees F., and finally held in a drying room not less than 10 days at a temperature not lower than 45 degrees F.

In no case, however, shall the sausage be released from the

drying room in less than 18 days from the time the curing materials are added to the meat. Sausage exceeding 3½ inches, but not exceeding 4 inches, in diameter at the time of stuffing, shall be held in a drying room, following smoking as above indicated, not less than 25 days at a temperature not lower than 45 degrees F., and in no case shall the sausage be released from the drying room in less than 33 days from the time the curing materials are added to the meat.

METHOD NO. 3. – The meat shall be ground or chopped into pieces not exceeding ¾ inches in diameter. A dry-curing mixture containing not less than 3⅓ lbs. of salt per each 100 lbs. of the unstuffed sausage shall be thoroughly mixed with the ground or chopped meat. After mixture with the salt and other curing materials and before stuffing, the ground or chopped meat shall be held at a temperature not lower than 34 degrees F. for not less than 36 hours.

After being stuffed, the sausage shall be held at a temperature not lower than 34 degrees F. for an additional period of time sufficient to make a total of not less than 144 hours from the time the curing materials are added to the meat, or the sausage shall be held for the time specified in a pickle-curing medium of not less than 50 degrees strength (salinometer rating) at a temperature not lower than 44 degrees F.

Finally, the sausage having a diameter not exceeding 3½ inches, measured at the time of stuffing, shall be smoked for not less than 12 hours. The temperature of the smokehouse during this period at no time shall be lower than 90 degrees F.; and for 4 consecutive hours of this period the smokehouse shall be maintained at a temperature not lower than 128 degrees F.

Sausage exceeding 3½ inches, but not exceeding 4 inches in diameter at the time of stuffing, shall be smoked, following the prescribed curing, for not less than 15 hours. The temperature of the smokehouse during the 15-hour period shall at no time be lower than 90 degrees F., and for 7 consecutive hours of this period the smokehouse shall be maintained at a temperature not lower than 128 degrees F. In regulating the temperature of the smokehouse for the treatment of sausage under this method, the temperature of 128 degrees F. shall be attained gradually during a period of not less than 4 hours.

METHOD NO. 4 – The meat shall be ground or chopped into pieces not exceeding ¼ inches in diameter. A dry-curing mixture containing not less than 2½ lbs. of salt per each 100 lbs. of the unstuffed sausage shall be thoroughly mixed with the ground or chopped meat. After mixing with the salt and other curing materials and before stuffing, the ground or chopped sausage shall be stuffed in casing or cloth bags not exceeding 3½ inches in diameter, measured at the time of stuffing.

After being stuffed, the sausage shall be held in a drying room at a temperature not lower than 45 degrees F. for the remainder of a 35-day period, measured from the time the curing materials are added to the meat. At any time after stuffing, if a concern deems it desirable, the product may be heated in a water bath for a period not to exceed 3 hours at a temperature not lower than 85 degrees F., or subjected to smoking at a temperature not lower than 85 degrees F., or subjected to smoking at a temperature not lower than 80 degrees F., or the product may be both heated and smoked as specified.

The time consumed in heating and smoking, however, shall be additional to the 35-day holding period specified.

METHOD NO. 5 – The meat shall be ground or chopped into pieces not exceeding ¾ inches in diameter. A dry-curing mixture containing not less than 3⅓ lbs. of salt per each 100 lbs. of the unstuffed sausage shall be thoroughly mixed with the ground or chopped meat. After being stuffed, the sausage shall be held for not less than 65 days at a temperature not lower than 45 degrees F. The covering for sausage prepared according to this method may be coated at any stage of the preparation before or during the holding period with paraffin or another substance approved by the Director of the Meat Inspection Division, USDA.

FREEZING – Freezing under specified conditions for times and temperatures also will destroy live trichinae in pork tissue. See the MID regulations for freezing pork on page 240.

The stuffing of the meats into the casings can be very significant; the casings should be packed as tightly as possible and the artificial fibrous casings will do the job best. To help further, be sure that you pack the stuffer tightly to eliminate all the air pockets or hollow spots. If the spaces or air pockets are allowed to develop in the interior of the sausage, mold may form and ruin the sausage.

Mold once was considered necessary and desirable in the making of a dry sausage; however, it has been proven that in a mechanically controlled dry room an excellent quality sausage can be produced while preventing or minimizing mold.

In the processing of dry sausage, the moisture can only be removed from the product at the rate at which the moisture comes to the surface of the casing. Any attempt to speed up the drying rate results in overdrying the surface of the sausage, resulting in case hardening. On the other hand, if the sausage is dried at too low a rate, excessive mold occurs on the surface of the casing, leading to an unsatisfactory appearance on the casing.

Dry sausage is made in different varieties, generally uncooked, and its keeping qualities depend on the curing ingredients, spices and removal of moisture from the sausage by drying. In general, there are two distinct types of sausage; one variety being smoked, the other not smoked.

FROZEN STARTER CULTURES

A starter culture has been developed in recent years that dramatically speeds up the process of drying or fermenting the dry and semi-dry sausages. The traditional process for a semi-dry sausage ranges from 100-140 hours; the newly developed starter cultures have reduced the process to 8-24 hours, allowing a very uniform product each time the sausage is made.

When the manufacturers produce these starter culture cells, they use a flash-freezing process and store these cells at -15 degrees F. The culture is packed in 4 oz. and 6 oz. cans and used at the rate of 2 ozs. per one hundred pounds of meat. The problem of shipping this starter culture to the sausage manufacturers was overcome by packing the culture in dry ice and flying this material to its destination.

For the most part, these particular starter cultures are not for home use. To begin with, the home-type freezers seldom attain a temperature of below -15 degrees F. The manufacturers undoutedly have a minimum quantity that must be purchased, which usually is beyond our reach. And lastly, the process is completely different, even though the manufacturer does supply the new processing scheduled.

I would imagine that if a person was interested in the use of this starter culture, the best place to inquire about it would be at a sausage company that manufactures these type sausages in your general area. You would have to be prepared to use this starter culture quickly, since it can spoil if kept too long at above -15 degrees F. The organisms must be kept frozen until 30-60 minutes before use. The shelf life of this starter culture is 6 months at -15 degrees F.

Strange as it may seem, it only has been since 1957 that we have been able to control fermentation in dry or semi-dry sausages. The American Meat Institute developed a process of producing a lactic starter culture that now is being made by the Merck Chemical Company. This product goes under the trade name of "Accel" and not only guarantees consistent flavors, but also shortens processing time dramatically.

SAUSAGE DRYING ROOMS

Air conditioning of a room has become a very important part of dry curing sausage or meat on a year-round basis. The object is to produce or remove humidity and regulate temperature as well. In general, it has been found the product is most favorably processed in a drying room at 45-55 degrees F. with a humidity of 70-72%. Dry sausage is made in many varieties and generally is uncooked. Its keeping qualities depend on the curing ingredients (Prague Powder No. 2), salt, spices, and the removal of moisture from the product being dry cured.

Under very good conditions, a moisture removal of 30-35% is considered a fully-dried product; this could take from 60-75 days. Of course, the diameter of the product is important in processing a dry cured sausage.

When curing dry and semi-dry sausages, they should be spaced apart on 6-inch centers. The length of time the sausage is dry cured depends a great deal upon the diameter of sausage being cured and the various formulas followed. The individual formulas can have a variance from 2-10 days, depending on the individual sausage maker. When in doubt, refer to "Government Regulations for Curing Dry or Semi-Dry Sausage" on previous pages.

Most varieties of dry-cured sausages are not smoked. If smoked meat is preferred, however, you may smoke salami or meat after it is cured in a cold smoker, without heat. Smoking will add to preserving quality, as acids in the smoke will discourage unwanted bacteria growth during storage. To further minimize bacteria levels prior to stuffing, the natural or fibrous casings may be soaked in vinegar or liquid smoke to prevent mold.

SUMMER SAUSAGE
(Goteborg)

INGREDIENTS FOR 25 LBS.
1 oz. Prague Powder No. 1
1½ oz. black pepper
1¼ oz. ground mustard
½ oz. ground nutmeg
¼ oz. garlic powder (optional)
10 ozs. salt
2 ozs. powdered dextrose
14 ozs. Fermento
9½ lbs. bull or cow trimmings
5 lbs. beef chuck
5 lbs. beef hearts
5½ lbs. regular pork trimmings

INGREDIENTS FOR 10 LBS.
2 level tsp. Prague Powder No. 1
1 tbsp. black pepper
3 tbsp. ground mustard
2 tbsp. ground nutmeg
1 tsp. garlic powder (optional)
8 tbsp. salt
4 tbsp. powdered dextrose
6 ozs. Fermento
3½ lbs. bull or cow trimmings
2 lbs. beef chuck
2 lbs. beef hearts
2½ lbs. regular pork trimmings

GRINDING

The bull or cow trimmings should be ground through a 3/16" grinder plate. The regular pork trimmings shall be ground through a 1" plate. Place all the ground meat into mixer and add all the ingredients. Mix thoroughly until all the ingredients are evenly distributed. After mixing, place in a tub and hold in 38-40 degree F. cooler until the next day. Do not pack the meat over 6"-7" high in the tubs. After curing overnight, regrind through 1/8" plate, pack tightly in stuffer and stuff into 2½-2¾" by 24" sewed beef middles or 3½" by 24" fibrous casings. Be sure that all air pockets are eliminated—when stuffing, stuff tightly.

SMOKING & COOKING

After stuffing, hang on smokesticks and dry at room temperature for 4-5 hours. Place in smokehouse preheated at 120-130 degrees F. and apply a heavy smudge and smoke at this temperature for 3-4 hours, or until the desired color is obtained. Raise the temperature to 165 degrees F. and cook until the internal temperature reaches 145 degrees F. After cooking, shower with cold water until the internal temperature is at least 120 degrees F. After shower, allow to hang at room temperature for 1-2 hours until the desired bloom is obtained. Keep out of drafts. Place in 45 degrees F. cooler for at least 24 hours.

DRIED SAUSAGE STICKS
(SLIM JIMS)

INGREDIENTS FOR 25 LBS.
1 oz. Prague Powder No. 1
3 ozs. paprika
2 ozs. ground mustard
¼ oz. ground black pepper
¼ oz. ground white pepper
¼ oz. ground celery
¼ oz. mace
1 tbsp. granulated garlic
14 ozs. salt
4 ozs. powdered dextrose
14 ozs. Fermento

INGREDIENTS FOR 10 LBS.
2 level tsp. Prague Powder No. 1
4 tbsp. paprika
6 tbsp. ground mustard
1 tsp. ground black pepper
1 tsp. ground white pepper
1 tsp. ground celery
1 tbsp. mace
1 tsp. granulated garlic
3½ ozs. salt
1½ ozs. powdered dextrose
6 ozs. Fermento

MEAT

Dried sausage sticks are made using a fairly lean type of meat. You may use any kind of cow, bull or steer meat. The ratio is about 80% lean and 20% fat. Beef chuck is excellent meat for this sausage.

PROCESSING PROCEDURE

Meat is chilled at 30-32 degrees F. so that it will not smear when being ground through a ⅛" grinder plate. It is then mixed very well for about 2 minutes and stuffed into 22-24mm sheep casings. Desired length is 6"-9." Meat is then placed in a smokehouse at 98-110 degrees F., with cold smoke applied for about 8 hours. If you desire more tang you may hold this temperature for 12 more hours. Smokehouse temperatures are then raised until internal temperature reaches 145 degrees F. Remove from smoker and place in dry room at 50-55 degrees F.

LEBANON BOLOGNA
10 Lb. Recipe

A good Lebanon bologna is made of 100% beef chuck or lean beef trimmings. The meat is ground through a ½" grinder plate and mixed with 5 ozs. of salt. The meat is then aged for 5-6 days at 38-40 degrees F. allowing all the juice to run off. The meat is then ground through ³⁄₁₆" plate and mixed with the following ingredients:

¾ ozs. salt
2 level tsp. Prague Powder No. 2
4 ozs. corn syrup solids
1 oz. powdered dextrose
6 ozs. Fermento
1 tbsp. ground white pepper
1 tbsp. ground nutmeg
1 tbsp. paprika
1 tsp. onion powder

All ingredients are then mixed with the meat and stuffed into 5" by 24" protein-lined casing. Bologna is then placed into smokehouse as follows:

16 hours at 90 degrees F. - 90% humidity
28 hours at 105 degrees F. - 85% humidity
6 hours at 110 degrees F. - 85% humidity

During these 50 hours, the bologna is going to develop a tang that makes it unique in flavor. Bologna then can be heavily smoked a day or two without heat. If you want a fully cooked product, raise the smokehouse temperature to 150 degrees F. after 50 hours. Then hold until internal temperature reaches 137 degrees F. Bologna is then removed from smokehouse and allowed to cool until the internal temperature is 110 degrees F. It is then placed into a cooler and allowed to age for about 4-5 days before using.

THURINGER

INGREDIENTS FOR 25 LBS.

10 ozs. salt
1 oz. Prague Powder No. 1
4 ozs. powdered dextrose
1 oz. ground black pepper
¼ oz. ground ginger
¼ oz. whole or cracked
    black pepper
14 ozs. Fermento
10 lbs. extra lean pork trimmings
    or skinned fatted shoulders
5 lbs. pork butts
5 lbs. pork hearts
5 lbs. pork fat

INGREDIENTS FOR 10 LBS.

8 tbsp. salt
2 level tsp. Prague Powder No. 1
4 tbsp. powdered dextrose
1 tbsp. ground black pepper
1 tsp. ground ginger
1 tbsp. whole or cracked
    black pepper
6 ozs. Fermento
4 lbs. extra lean pork trimmings
    or skinned fatted shoulders
2 lbs. pork butts
2 lbs. pork hearts
2 lbs. pork fat

GRINDING

Grind the lean pork, pork cheeks and pork hearts through a ³⁄₁₆" grinder plate. Cut the pork cheeks or pork fat into 1½"-2" cubes. Place all the meats into the mixer along with all the ingredients and mix until evenly distributed. Put meat in curing tubs and pack very tightly to exclude the air pockets. Place in a 38-40 degree F. cooler for 3-4 days. The thuringer is properly cured when it has a nice red color. After curing, remove from the cooler and grind through a ⅛" or ³⁄₁₆" plate.

STUFFING

Pack the meat very tightly into the stuffer, eliminating all air pockets. Use single-wall beef middles for stuffing, 2¾" by 30" long or 3½" by 24" fibrous casings.

SMOKING AND COOKING

To produce a thuringer that has a consistent sour flavor, it is of great importance that correct curing and smoking temperatures are followed very closely. Close attention also should be given to the weather conditions which will govern the variations in curing and hanging time. After stuffing, hang thuringer on smoke sticks and allow to hang at room temperature (65-70 degrees F.) for 10-12 hours or until the product is thoroughly dry. When the weather is cooler than 65 degrees F., increase the hanging time to 24 hours. Place thuringer into 100-110 degree F. smokehouse. Immediately apply a heavy smudge and smoke at this temperature for 8-10 hours; raise the smokehouse temperature to 145 degrees F. and smoke at this temperature until internal temperature of 138 degrees F. is obtained. Allow to cool at room temperature and place into cooler overnight.

NOTE:

It is very important that the thuringer be smoked at a low temper-ature; maximum temperatures should not exceed 110 degrees F.

CERVELAT SUMMER SAUSAGE

INGREDIENTS FOR 25 LBS.
1 oz. ground black pepper
10 ozs. salt
2 ozs. powdered dextrose
¼ oz. ground coriander
¼ oz. ground mustard
1 oz. Prague Powder No. 1
¼ oz. garlic powder (optional)
14 ozs. Fermento
9 lbs. lean beef or cow meat
5 lbs. beef chuck
5 lbs. beef hearts
6 lbs. fat pork butts

INGREDIENTS FOR 10 LBS.
1 tbsp. ground black pepper
8 tbsp. salt
4 tbsp. powdered dextrose
1 tbsp. ground coriander
1 tbsp. ground mustard
2 level tsp. Prague Powder No. 1
1 tsp. garlic powder (optional)
6 ozs. Fermento
3½ lbs. lean beef or cow meat
2 lbs. beef chuck
2 lbs. beef hearts
2½ lbs. fat pork butts

GRINDING

Grind bull or cow meat, beef cheeks and beef hearts through a ³⁄₁₆" grinder plate. The regular pork trimmings or fat should be ground through a 1" plate or cut up in 1" cubes. Place all the ingredients and meats into the mixer until everything is mixed thoroughly. After mixing, place all the meat into curing tubs, packing the meat down tightly. Hold in a 38-40 degree F. cooler for 2 days. After curing, regrind all the meat through a ⅛" plate.

STUFFING

Pack the meat into the stuffer very tightly to exclude all the air pockets. Meat is to be stuffed into sewed beef middles 2½"-2¾" by 24" long. You may use a 3½" by 24" fibrous casing, if the beef middles are not available.

SMOKING & COOKING

After stuffing, hang on smokehouse sticks and dry at room temperature for about 4-5 hours. Place into 120-130 degree F. smokehouse and apply a heavy smudge, smoking at this temperature for 3-4 hours or until the desired color is obtained. Raise the smokehouse temperature to 160-170 degrees F. and hold until an internal temperature of 145 degrees F. is obtained. Remove from smokehouse, place under a shower of tap water and hold until temperature is reduced to 120 degrees F. internally. Permit sausage to hang at room temperature for 1-2 hours or until a desired bloom is obtained. Be sure the room is free of drafts during this period of blooming.

SEMI-DRY KIELBASA MYSLIWSKA SUCHA

INGREDIENTS FOR 25 LBS.
20 lbs. lean pork
5 lbs. lean beef
10 ozs. salt
2 ozs. powdered dextrose
2 ozs. corn syrup solids
1 oz. prague powder #1
1½ ozs. ground black pepper
½ oz. ground juniper berries
1½ ozs. garlic

INGREDIENTS FOR 10 LBS.
8 lbs. lean pork
2 lbs. lean beef
4 ozs. salt
¾ oz. powdered dextrose
¾ oz. corn syrup solids
2 level tsp. prague powder #1
½ oz. ground black pepper
1 tsp. ground juniper berries
2 garlic cloves

Grind the pork through a ¾" grinder plate and the beef through a ½" grinder plate. Grind all fat meat through a ¼" or 3/16" grinder plate. Add the remaining ingredients to the meat and mix thoroughly until evenly distributed.

Stuff the mixture into 35-38mm hog casings and form long links (8-10"). Dry the sausage at room temperature for 3 hours before placing in a smokehouse preheated to 120 degrees F. for 1 hour, applying dense smoke. Then increase the temperature to 168 degrees F., until the internal temperature reaches 158 degrees F. Let the sausage air-cool at 50-60 degrees F. The next day, smoke the sausage for 24 hours without heat. Place the sausage in a storage room at 60-65 degrees F. for 7 days with a relative humidity of 70-80%. You will achieve a 35-40% weight loss when the sausage is ready.

SEMI-DRY CURED KIELBASA KUJAWSKA PUDSUSZANA

INGREDIENTS FOR 25 LBS.
20 lbs. ham or shoulder
2½ lbs. lean beef
2½ lbs. fresh bacon
8 ozs. salt
1 oz. prague powder #1
1½ ozs. ground black pepper
½ oz. ground paprika
½ oz. garlic
2 ozs. powdered dextrose
2 ozs. corn syrup solids

INGREDIENTS FOR 10 LBS
8 lbs. ham or shoulder
1 lb. lean beef
1 lb. fresh bacon
3½ ozs. salt
2 level tsp. prague powder #1
¾ oz. ground black pepper
1 tbsp. ground paprika
1 garlic clove
¾ oz. powdered dextrose
¾ oz. corn syrup solids

Grind fat meat and bacon through a ½" grinder plate. Grind the lean meat through a ⅜" grinder plate. Add the remaining ingredients to the meat and mix thoroughly until evenly distributed. Stuff the mixture into a 35-38mm hog casing and form into 5-6" links. Place on smokesticks and keep at room temperature for 3 hours. Place sausage in a preheated smokehouse at 120 degrees F. until it starts to get a light brown color. At this point, increase the smokehouse temperature to 170 degrees F., applying a dense smoke. Keep the sausage at this temperature until you reach 158 degrees F. internally. Place the sausage in a cooler and cool overnight. The next day, remove the sausage from the cooler and keep at room temperature for about 1 hour. Then place it in a smoker preheated to 110 degrees F., applying dense smoke for 12 hours. Air-dry the sausage for 3 days at 60-70 degrees F. with a relative humidity of 70-80%. You will achieve a 15% weight loss by the time product is ready to use.

SEMI-DRY BALTIC POLISH SAUSAGE
(Kielbasa Baltycka)

INGREDIENTS FOR 25 LBS.
15 lbs. pork
7½ lbs. beef
2½ lbs. fresh bacon
8 ozs. salt
1 oz. prague powder #1
2 ozs. powdered dextrose
2 ozs. corn syrup solids
1 oz. ground black pepper
1 oz. ground marjoram
1 oz. garlic

INGREDIENTS FOR 10 LBS.
6 lbs. pork
3 lbs. beef
1 lb. fresh bacon
3½ ozs. salt
2 level tsp. prague powder #1
¾ oz. powdered dextrose
¾ oz. corn syrup solids
1 tbsp. ground black pepper
1 tbsp. ground marjoram
1 clove garlic

Grind lean meat through a ⅜" grinder plate and the fat meat through a ⅛" or 3/16" grinder plate. The bacon should be chilled to about 28 degrees F., and ground through a ⅜" grinder plate, then returned to the cooler until ready for use.

Add the remaining ingredients (except the bacon) and mix thoroughly until evenly distributed. Then add the cold bacon and mix gently until well distributed. Stuff the mixture into a hog bung or a protein-lined, fibrous 3½" x 24" casing and keep at 45-50 degrees F. for 12 hours. Then place the sausage into a smoker preheated to 120 degrees F. and keep there for 2-2½ hours until a brown color starts to show. Increase the smokehouse temperature to 170 degrees F. and maintain until the internal temperature of the sausage reaches 158 degrees F. Then remove the sausage from the smoker and air cool at 60-70 degrees F. overnight. The next day, smoke the sausage again for 48 hours more without heat or until it has a very dark brown color.

After smoking, keep the sausage at 65 degrees F. for about 10-12 days with a relative humidity of 70-80%. When a weight loss of 18-20% is achieved, the sausage is ready. The sausage should be kept in a 40-50 degree F. cooler while obtaining the weight loss.

SEMI-DRY CURED POLISH KRAKOW SAUSAGE
(Kielbasa Krakowska Sucha)

INGREDIENTS FOR 25 LBS.

20 lbs. lean pork butts
4 lbs. fresh bacon
1 lb. lean beef
8 ozs. salt
1 oz. prague powder #1
½ oz. ground nutmeg
1 oz. garlic
3 ozs. powdered dextrose
3 ozs. corn syrup solids

INGREDIENTS FOR 10 LBS.

8 lbs. lean pork butts
1½ lbs. fresh bacon
½ lb. lean beef
3½ ozs. salt
2 level tsp. prague powder #1
1 tbsp. ground nutmeg
1 large clove garlic
1¼ ozs. powdered dextrose
1¼ ozs. corn syrup solids

The bacon should be cut into ½" cubes. Then place it in a 28 degree F. cooler until it is ready to be used. Grind the pork through a ½" grinder plate and the fat meat through a ⅛" or ³⁄₁₆" grinder plate.

Chop the garlic very fine and place in a blender with a little water. Add the remaining ingredients and mix thoroughly until evenly distributed. Add the cubes of bacon and mix until evenly distributed as well. The mixture is then stuffed into a protein-lined, fibrous 3½" x 24" casing or a sewed beef middle. Hang the sausage at room temperature for 5 hours, then place in a smokehouse preheated to 130 degrees F., applying a dense smoke. After one hour, increase the temperature to 165-170 degrees F. and maintain until an internal temperature of 158 degrees F. is reached. Remove from smoker and cool at room temperature for at least 12 hours. The next day, smoke the sausage for 24 hours without heat, preferably at a temperature below 85 degrees F. When completed, the dark brown color of the bacon will be visible through the casing.

Dry the sausage for 12-14 days at 50-60 degrees F. with a relative humidity of 70-80%. This drying period will produce a weight loss of about 33%.

SEMI-DRY KABANOSY

Kabanosy sausage has no English translation as far as I know. However, I would compare this sausage to the American-style slim jims one sees in convenience stores and bar rooms throughout the country.

INGREDIENTS FOR 25 LBS.
25 lbs. pork butts
8 ozs. salt
1 oz. prague powder #1
2 ozs. powdered dextrose
1½ ozs. ground black pepper
½ oz. ground nutmeg
½ oz. ground caraway seed
1 oz. garlic
4 ozs. corn syrup solids

INGREDIENTS FOR 10 LBS.
10 lbs. pork butts
3½ ozs. salt
2 level tsp. prague powder #1
1 oz. powdered dextrose
¾ oz. ground black pepper
1 tbsp. ground nutmeg
1 tbsp. ground caraway seed
1 clove garlic
1¾ ozs. corn syrup solids

Grind lean pork through a ¼" grinder plate and fat pork through a ⅛" or ³⁄₁₆" grinder plate. Add remaining ingredients and mix thoroughly until evenly distributed. Stuff mixture into 24-26mm sheep casings and form 5-6" links. Place on smokesticks and hang at room temperature for 2 hours. Place sausage into a smoker preheated to 140 degrees F., applying a dense smoke.

After one hour, increase temperature to 190 degrees F. for 30 minutes. Kabanosy should have a dark brown color when finished. Remove sausage from smoker and cure for 7 days at 60-65 degrees F. with a relative humidity of 70-80%. Sausage is ready when weight is reduced by 50%.

SEMI-DRY CURED UKRANIAN SUMMER SAUSAGE
(Kiebasa Ukrainska Podsuszana)

INGREDIENTS FOR 25 LBS.	INGREDIENTS FOR 10 LBS.
17½ lbs. lean beef	7½ lbs. lean beef
7½ lbs. pork butts	2½ lbs. pork butts
10 ozs. salt	4 ozs. salt
1 oz. prague powder #1	2 level tsp. prague powder #1
½ oz. paprika	1 tbsp. paprika
½ oz. whole pepper	1 tbsp. whole pepper
¼ oz. ground marjoram	1 tsp. ground marjoram
3 ozs. garlic	2 small garlic cloves
5 ozs. corn syrup solids	2 ozs. corn syrup solids
5 ozs. powdered dextrose	2 ozs. powdered dextrose
8 ozs. Fermento	3½ ozs. Fermento

Grind pork through a ¼" grinder plate and beef through a ⅜" grinder plate. Add remaining ingredients and mix until evenly distributed. Stuff mixture into either 38-40mm or 40-43mm beef rounds. The casings are usually filled to about 15-18 inches long, leaving at least 3-4 inches on each end. Then tie the casings, resulting in a round ring of sausage. Place the sausage on a smokestick and hang at room temperature (65-70 degrees F.) for about 3 hours. This will allow the sausage to dry while its temperature rises. Put the sausage in a preheated smokehouse at 165 degrees F., applying a dense smoke for 2 hours. After smoking, cook the sausage in the smoker until you reach an internal temperature of 152 degrees F. Remove the sausage from the smoker and cool overnight without refrigeration at 60-70 degrees F. Put the sausage in the smoker at 90 degrees F. for 12 more hours in a dense smoke. The result will be a reddish-brown sausage.

The sausage should then be allowed to air-dry at 50-60 degrees F. with a relative humidity of 70-75%. The sausage is ready to eat when you achieve shrinkage of about 15%.

SEMI-DRY POLISH MOUNTAIN SAUSAGE
(Kielbasa Podhalanska Podsuszana)

INGREDIENTS FOR 25 LBS.
15 lbs. lean sheep meat
2½ lbs. smoked bacon
7½ lbs. fat pork meat
8 ozs. salt
1 oz. prague powder #1
2 ozs. ground black pepper
½ oz. whole black pepper
¼ oz. ground marjoram
1¼ ozs. fresh garlic
2 ozs. powdered dextrose
8 ozs. Fermento

INGREDIENTS FOR 10 LBS.
7 lbs. lean sheep meat
1 lb. smoked bacon
2 lbs. fat pork meat
3½ ozs. salt
2 level tsp. prague powder #1
¾ oz. ground black pepper
1 tbsp. whole black pepper
½ tsp. ground marjoram
2 garlic cloves
¾ oz. powdered dextrose
3½ ozs. Fermento

Grind fat pork and bacon through a ½" grinder plate. Grind sheep meat through a ¾" grinder plate. Combine the meat with the remaining ingredients and mix until thoroughly distributed. Stuff the mixture into 32-35mm hog casings, making 8-10" long links. Then put the links on smokesticks and hang at room temperature (65-70 degrees F.) for about 3 hours. By this time, the sausage will be fully dried. Place in a smokehouse and keep at about 110 degrees F. until they show a light brown color. Then raise the smokehouse temperature to 160-165 degrees F. and cook the sausage until you reach an internal temperature of 150 degrees F. Then remove the sausage from the smoker and cool for 24 hours. After this time, a second smoking process takes place. The sausage is placed in the smokehouse again for 12 hours, applying a cold smoke (no heat). Then remove the sausage and dry in 75-80% humidity with a temperature of 50-60 degrees F. The sausage must be allowed to shrink at least 15% before it is ready to use.

SHEBOYGAN SUMMER SAUSAGE

The Sheboygan summer sausage is distinguished more by the type of meat used to make it than by the spices with which it is seasoned. However, they do work hand-in-hand to make it unique.

INGREDIENTS FOR 25 LBS.

15 lbs. beef chuck
3¾ lbs. pork hearts
6¼ lbs. pork butts
12 ozs. salt
1 oz. prague powder #1
1 oz. garlic powder
12 ozs. Fermento
4 ozs. powdered dextrose
4 ozs. corn syrup solids
1 oz. ground black pepper
1 oz. ground mustard seed
1 oz. ground nutmeg

INGREDIENTS FOR 10 LBS.

5½ lbs. beef chuck
1½ lbs. pork hearts
3 lbs. pork butts
5 ozs. salt
2 level tsp. prague powder #1
1 tsp. garlic powder
5 ozs. Fermento
2 ozs. powdered dextrose
2 ozs. corn syrup solids
1 tsp. ground black pepper
1 tsp. ground mustard seed
1 tsp. ground nutmeg

Grind beef, chuck and pork hearts through a ⅛" grinder plate. Grind pork butts through a ½" grinder plate. Add all ingredients to meat mixture and blend thoroughly until evenly distributed. Then place the mixture into a 38-40 degrees F. cooler for at least 48 hours. Pack the meat tightly in a container not more than 6" high, eliminating all air pockets.

After this period of time, remove the meat from the cooler and grind through a ¼" grinder plate. Then stuff it into a 3½" by 24" protein-lined fibrous casing. Allow the sausage to dry and cure at room temperature for 3 hours.

Sausage is then placed in a preheated smokehouse at 90 degrees F. and kept there in heavy smoke for about 24 hours, or until a dark color is reached. Then increase the smoker temperature to 130 degrees F. for 4 hours and then 4 more hours at 150 degrees F., or until the internal temperature reaches 138-140 degrees F. Be sure to check the internal temperatures of several sausages from different parts of the smokehouse to ensure these temperatures have been attained.

Shower the sausage to reduce the internal temperature to 90-95 degrees F. and store at 60-65 degrees F.

SPANISH CERVELAT SAUSAGE
(SALCHION)

INGREDIENTS FOR 25 LBS.

17½ lbs. lean pork butts
5 lbs. lean beef
2½ lbs. cured backfat
11 ozs. salt
1 oz. prague powder #1
4 ozs. corn syrup solids
4 ozs. powdered dextrose
1 oz. whole black pepper
½ oz. ground nutmeg
1 oz. ground mustard seed
14 ozs. Fermento

INGREDIENTS FOR 10 LBS.

7 lbs. lean pork butts
2 lbs. lean beef
1 lb. cured backfat
5 ozs. salt
2 level tsp. prague powder #1
1¾ ozs. corn syrup solids
1¾ ozs. powdered dextrose
1 tsp. whole black pepper
1 tsp. ground nutmeg
½ oz. ground mustard seed
6 ozs. Fermento

Grind beef through a ⅛" grinder plate and the pork butts through a ³⁄₁₆" or ¼" grinder plate. Dice the cured backfat into ½" cubes and keep in the cooler at about 28-30 degrees F. for later use.

All the meat (except backfat) should be mixed well with all the other ingredients, then packed tightly into pans not more than 6" high. Be sure meat is packed very well to eliminate the air pockets. Place meat into a cooler at 38-40 degrees F. and keep there for 48 hours.

Then remove meat and grind through a ³⁄₁₆" grinder plate. At this time, gently mix the diced backfat with the meat until distributed. Stuff meat into hog bungs or a 3½" x 24" protein-lined casing. Hang the stuffed sausage in a cooler at 45 degrees F. for 36 hours. Allow the sausage to hang overnight at room temperature (65-70 degrees F.) until it develops a nice red color on the outside. Place sausage in a preheated smokehouse at 110 degrees F., holding it there for 24 hours while applying a heavy, dense smoke. The temperature of the smokehouse should then be increased to 150 degrees F. and maintained until the sausage reaches an internal temperature of 138°F. Then hang the sausage for several days at 50-60 degrees F. before storing in cooler at 40-45 degrees F.

DANISH SUMMER SAUSAGE
(SPEGEPOELSE)

INGREDIENTS FOR 25 LBS.
6 lbs. pork hearts
12 lbs. lean beef
*7 lbs. pork snouts
1 oz. prague powder #1
4 ozs. corn syrup solids
4 ozs. powdered dextrose
14 ozs. Fermento
12 ozs. salt
1 oz. ground coriander
2 ozs. ground mustard

INGREDIENTS FOR 10 LBS.
2 lbs. pork hearts
6 lbs. lean beef
*2 lbs. pork snouts
2 level tsp. prague powder #1
1¾ ozs. corn syrup solids
1¾ ozs. powdered dextrose
6 ozs. Fermento
5 ozs. salt
½ oz. ground coriander
1 oz. ground mustard

*If you have difficulty in obtaining pork snouts, you may substitute pork butts.

All the beef and pork hearts should be ground through a ³⁄₁₆" grinder plate. Grind pork snouts through a ½" grinder plate. Then add all the ingredients to meat and mix well until evenly distributed.

Pack the meat mixture tightly into pans, removing all air pockets. Do not pack meat over 6" high in pans.

Place the meat in a 38-40 degrees F. cooler and keep there for 48 hours. Then regrind the meat through a ³⁄₁₆" grinder plate and stuff into a 3½" x 24" protein-lined casing. Allow sausage to dry at room temperature for at least 3 hours. Then place in preheated smokehouse at 90 degrees F. applying heavy smoke for 12-18 hours.

After this period of time, the temperature in the smokehouse should be raised 10 degrees every hour until you reach 150°F. Keep sausage at this temperature until you reach an internal temperature of 140 degrees F. Hang sausage at room temperature for 48 more hours, then place in a cooler at 38-40 degrees F. for storage.

TRAIL BOLOGNA

Country-style or trail bologna, as it is sometimes called, is a bologna made with coarse cuts of meat. In the early days of sausage making there were no emulsifying machines and most of the meat was cut by hand. At best, there were grinders. Country-style bologna is made by grinding the fat meat through a ⅛" or ³⁄₁₆" grinder plate. The lean meat is ground through a ¼" or ⅜" grinder plate. The coarseness of the meat greatly depends on the person making the bologna.

INGREDIENTS FOR 25 LBS.

15 lbs. lean beef
10 lbs. pork
1 oz. prague powder #1
1¼ oz. ground white pepper
1 oz. paprika
¼ oz. ground nutmeg
¼ oz. allspice
¼ oz. onion powder
8 ozs. salt
2 ozs. powdered dextrose
2 ozs. corn syrup solids
4 ozs. Fermento

INGREDIENTS FOR 10 LBS.

6 lbs. lean beef
4 lbs. pork
2 level tsp. prague powder #1
2 tbsp. ground white pepper
1 tbsp. paprika
1 tbsp. ground nutmeg
1 tbsp. allspice
1 tbsp. onion powder
3½ ozs. salt
¾ oz. powdered dextrose
¾ oz. corn syrup solids
1¾ ozs. Fermento

After the meat is ground, add the remaining ingredients and mix thoroughly until evenly distributed. Then place the meat in containers or tubs and pack tightly to eliminate air pockets. Do not pack more than 6" high. Then place the mixture in a cooler at 45-50 degrees F. for 48 hours. Regrind it through a ⅜" grinder plate and stuff it into protein-lined 3½" x 24" casings or beef middles and keep at 45-50 degrees F. for 12 hours. Place bologna into 120 degree F. preheated smoker until it starts to take on a brown color, with draft and damper ½ open. Increase the smokehouse temperature to 170 degrees F. and keep the sausage there until an internal temperature of 158 degrees F. is reached. Remove the sausage and air-cool it over night at 60-70 degrees F. Smoke the sausage again the next day for about 48 hours, or until it has a dark brown color.

After smoking, store the sausage at 65 degrees F. for 10-12 days with a relative humidity of 70-80%. Place the sausage in a cooler at 40-45 degrees F. to achieve 18-20% weight loss.

DRY CURING A COOKED SAUSAGE

Dry curing cooked sausage is a process widely practiced by the small sausage makers throughout the country. What exactly does this mean? For instance, we could simply make a smoked kielbasa that is ready to eat. We can, however, take this sausage one step further and prolong its keeping qualities by drying it out, much the same way as we would a pepperoni. These sausages would be kept about 45-50 degrees F. at 70-80% humidity. What we have here is a sausage that is ready to eat at all times. But we are removing moisture equal to about 30-35% of its original weight. This can take up to two months at the above-mentioned temperatures without spoilage. During this time the sausage may be eaten at any time, as it already has been cooked to destroy trichinae and cured to prevent botulism.

If the sausage does get some mold on it, it is simply washed off with a vinegar solution, or the mold may simply be left on and the casing with the mold peeled off before the sausage is eaten.

The 40-50 degree F. temperatures and high humidity are excellent conditions for mold to form.

Be sure that during the dry-curing process, sausages are spread from 3-4" apart to allow moisture to escape. It is doubtful that this cooked dry-cured sausage would last the two-month period, as you would most likely eat it by then.

Remember, your attic is not the place to dry-cure a sausage. The humidity and coolness of a cellar is much better. The following recipe may be made using this process.

SEMI-DRY CURING
COOKED PEPPERONI STICKS

INGREDIENTS FOR 25 LBS.
1 oz. Prague Powder No. 1
8 ozs. salt
1 oz. powdered dextrose
½ oz. ground hot pepper
½ oz. ground allspice
1¼ ozs. ground anise seed
12 ozs. soy protein concentrate
2½ lbs. water
8 ozs. Fermento
4 ozs. corn syrup solids

INGREDIENTS FOR 10 LBS.
2 level tsp. Prague Powder No. 1
6 tbsp. salt
2 tbsp. powdered dextrose
1 tbsp. ground hot pepper
1 tsp. ground allspice
5 tsp. ground anise seed
2 cups soy protein concentrate
1 pint water
3 ozs. Fermento
1½ ozs. corn syrup solids

Pepperoni can be made of 100 percent lean beef, such as chuck, or 100 percent lean pork butts. Or, you may use any combination of these two meats. The meat is ground through a ³⁄₁₆" grinder plate and placed into a mixing tub with all ingredients. Mix very well until all ingredients are properly distributed.

STUFFING

The size of casings used to make pepperoni can vary from 16-18mm lamb casings, to 38-42mm hog casings. The size and type of casings used generally is determined by what is traditional in your particular area. The pepperoni will dry out by 30% when ready, which reduces the size of the sausage.

SMOKING

Place sausage into smokehouse at 125 degrees F. with dampers wide open and no smoke until casing is dry. Close damper to ¼, raise temperature to 165 degrees F. and hold until internal temperature is 145 degrees F. Remove from smoker and chill with cold water until internal temperature is reduced to 90-100 degrees F.

Traditionally, a dry-cured pepperoni is not smoked. It simply is not part of the process. If you like the flavor of smoke, however, that is your option, and your pepperoni will have a preserved quality.

CHAPTER XIII

Dry-Cured Sausage and Meat

DRY CURING HAM

Probably the oldest method of curing ham today is the dry-cure method. Using this method, you simply rub in a mixture of sugar, salt and cure. The ham is rubbed every 2-3 days and allowed to cure at least 40 days or more, since it takes that long for the cure to penetrate to the center of the ham.

Using this method, you should cure the ham at temperatures not lower than 36 degrees F. and not higher than 38 degrees F. If the temperatures are permitted to drop below 36 degrees F., it slows the curing process. If you allow the temperatures to go above 40 degrees F., the ham may start to sour from the inside. You may use the following combination to mix your own cure:

3½ lbs. salt

12 ozs. powdered dextrose

12 ozs. Prague Powder No. 2

When curing meats, the lean parts of the ham or shoulder will cure much faster, as these parts allow the cure to penetrate with less restriction. The skin and fat definitely are a barrier and prevent the meat from curing properly.

Since this type of cured meat is usually eaten without further cooking, sufficient precautions must be taken to destroy the trichinae. The following are federal meat regulations prescribing the treatment of these meats:

METHOD NO. 1:

The ham shall be cured by a dry-salt curing process for not less than 40 days at a temperature not lower than 36 degrees F. The ham shall be laid down in salt, not less than 4 lbs. to each hundred-weight of ham, the salt being applied in a thorough manner to the lean meat of each ham. When placed in the cure, the ham may be pumped with pickle if desired. At least once during the curing process, the ham shall be overhauled and additional salt applied, if necessary, so that the lean meat of each ham is thoroughly covered.

After removal from the cure, the ham may be soaked in water at a temperature of not higher than 70 degrees F. for not more than 15 hours, during which time the water may be changed once; but they shall not be subjected to any other treatment designed to

367

remove salt from the meat, except that superficial washing may be allowed. The ham shall finally be dried or smoked not less than 10 days at a temperature not lower than 95 degrees F.

METHOD NO. 2:

The ham shall be cured by a dry-salt curing process at a temperature not lower than 36 degrees F. for a period of not less than three days for each pound of weight (green) of the individual hams. The time of cure of each lot of ham placed in cure should be calculated on a basis of the weight of the heaviest ham of the lot.

Hams cured by this method before they are placed in the cure shall be pumped with a pickle solution of not less than 100 degrees strength (salometer). About 4 ozs. of the solution is injected into the shank and a like quantity alongside of the body bone (femor). The ham shall be laid down in the salt, not less than 4 lbs. to each hundredweight of ham, the salt being applied in a thorough manner to the lean meat of each ham.

At least once during the curing process, the ham shall be overhauled and additional salt applied, if necessary, so that the lean meat of each ham is thoroughly covered. After removal from the cure, the hams may be soaked in water at a temperature of not higher than 70 degrees F., for not more than 4 hours, but shall not be subjected to any other treatment designed to remove salt from the meat, except that superficial washing may be allowed.

The ham shall then be dried or smoked, not less than 48 hours at a temperature not lower than 80 degrees F., and finally shall be held in a drying room, not less than 20 days at a temperature not lower than 45 degrees F.

DESTROYING TRICHINAE

Because many pork products are used to make smoked, dry and semi-dry sausage, and are generally eaten without further cooking, the Meat Inspection Division (M.I.D.) of the USDA has established regulations for the destruction of trichinae that are sometimes found in pork. When the meat is being inspected, the trichinae are not being searched for and the process of destroying this parasite is left up to the individuals who process the meat. To put a part of each hog that is slaughtered in this country each day under the microscope is not possible from a standpoint of economics. Therefore, this part of it simply is left to the housewife or processor, whichever the case may be.

Most of the recipes and formulas in this book will show you that the internal temperatures required will average at about 152 degrees F. This is a fully-cooked product, ready to eat. All the larger processors of lunch meats and sausage cook their products until these temperatures are attained internally. I think the 138 degrees F. margin the M.I.D. requires is a safe one. The treatments consist of heating, refrigerating, or curing as follows:

NO. 1: HEATING & COOKING

All parts of the pork musle tissue shall be heated to a temperature of not less than 138 degrees F. If you are cooking the product in water, it is important that the entire product has been submerged so that the 138 degrees F. can be attained internally. It is equally important that the largest pieces of the product be included in this test, since it will always take longer to attain 138 degrees F. internally. When using cooking cabinets or smokehouses, the products should be tested in a number of places to be sure that this temperature is attained, especially in the cooler parts of the cooker cabinet or smokehouse.

NO. 2: REFRIGERATING

At any stage of preparation and after preparatory chilling to a temperature of not above 40 degrees F., or preparatory freezing, all parts of the muscle tissue of pork or product containing such tissue shall be subjected continuously to a temperature not higher

than one of these specified in Table 1, the duration of such refrigeration at the specified temperature being dependent on the thickness
of the meat or inside dimensions of the container.

TABLE 1: Required period of freezing at temperature indicated.

Temperature	Group 1 - Days	Group 2 - Days
5 degrees F.	20	30
-10 degrees F.	10	20
-20 degrees F.	6	12

Group 1 comprises product in separate pieces not exceeding 6"
in thickness, or arranged on separate racks with the layers not
exceeding 6" in depth, or stored in crates or boxes not exceeding
6" in depth, or stored as solidly frozen blocks not exceeding 6" in
thickness.

Group 2 comprises product in pieces, layers, or within containers,
the thickness of which exceeds 6" but not 27," and product in containers including tierces, barrels, kegs and cartons having a thickness not exceeding 27." The product undergoing such refrigeration
or the containers thereof shall be spaced while in the freezer to
insure a free circulation of air between the pieces of meat, layers,
blocks, boxes, barrels, and tierces in order that the temperature of
the meat throughout will be promptly reduced to not higher than 5
degrees F., -10 degrees F., or -20 degrees F., as the case may be.

NO. 3: CURING SAUSAGE

Sausage may be stuffed in animal casings, hydrocellulose casings, or cloth bags. During any stage of treating the sausage for
the destruction of live trichinae, these coverings shall not be coated
with paraffin or like substance, nor shall any sausage be washed
during any prescribed period of drying. In preparation of sausage,
one of the following methods may be used:

METHOD NO. 1:

The meat shall be ground or chopped into pieces not exceeding
¾" in diameter. A dry-curing mixture containing not less than 3⅓
lbs. of salt to each hundredweight of the unstuffed sausage shall
be thoroughly mixed with the ground or chopped meat.

After being stuffed, sausage having a diameter not exceeding

370

3½," measured at the time of stuffing, shall be held in a drying room not less than 20 days at a temperature not lower than 45 degrees F., except that in sausage of the variety known as pepperoni; if in casings and not exceeding 1⅜" in diameter at the time of stuffing, the period of drying may be reduced to 15 days.

In no case, however, shall the sausage be released from the drying room in less than 25 days from the time the curing materials are added, except that the sausage of the variety known as pepperoni, if in casings not exceeding the size specified, may be released at the expiration of 20 days from the time the curing materials are added.

Sausage in casings exceeding 3½" but not exceeding 4" in diameter at the time of stuffing shall be held in a drying room not less than 35 days at a temperature not lower than 45 degrees F., and in no case shall the sausage be released from the drying room in less than 40 days from the time the curing materials are added to the meat.

METHOD NO. 2:

The meat shall be ground or chopped into pieces not exceeding ¾" in diameter. A dry-curing mixture containing not less than 3⅓ lbs. of salt to each hundredweight of the unstuffed sausage shall be thoroughly mixed with the ground or chopped meat.

After being stuffed, the sausage having a diameter not exceeding 3½," measured at the time of stuffing, shall be smoked not less than 40 hours at a temperature of not lower than 80 degrees F. and finally held in a drying room not less than 10 days at a temperature not lower than 45 degrees F. In no case, however, shall the sausage be released from the drying room in fewer than 18 days from the time the curing materials are added to the meat.

Sausage exceeding 3½," but not exceeding 4" in diameter at the time of stuffing, shall be held in a drying room following the smoking as above indicated, not less than 25 days at a temperature not lower than 45 degrees F., and in no case shall the sausage be released from the drying room in less than 33 days from the time the curing materials are added to the meat.

LANDJAGER SAUSAGE

Literally, Landjager means land hunter in German. A Landjager in Germany was similar to our National Guard or Army Reserve. It seems this sausage was used by the field troops, as our armed forces use K or C rations. Landjager also is referred to as a pressed sausage and is very popular sausage in the midwestern part of the U.S.A.

INGREDIENTS FOR 25 LBS.
11 ozs. salt
1 oz. Prague Powder No. 2
4 ozs. corn syrup solids
¾ oz. ground white pepper
½ oz. ground caraway seeds
1 tbsp. ground coriander
14 ozs. Fermento
3 ozs. powdered dextrose
19 lbs. lean beef
6 lbs. fat pork

INGREDIENTS FOR 10 LBS.
9 tbsp. salt
2 level tsp. Prague Powder No. 2
1½ ozs. corn syrup solids
1 tsp. ground white pepper
1 tsp. ground caraway seeds
1 tsp. ground coriander
6 ozs. Fermento
1 oz. powdered dextrose
7½ lbs. lean beef
2½ lbs. fat pork

PROCESSING PROCEDURE

All meat should be chilled at 32-34 degrees F. before grinding. Then grind through a ¼" grinder plate, add all ingredients and mix well. The mixing of the meat should be done as quickly as possible to avoid smearing the fat meat. Ingredients can be properly distributed in about 2 minutes of mixing. The meat then is stuffed loosely into a 32-35mm hog casing and made into links 7-8" long. Sausage is held at 70-75 degrees F. for 3-4 days with humidity of 70-80%. The Landjager sausage is placed into a wooden mold and pressed into a unique flat but oblong shape. The sausages are placed very tightly against each other and a weighted board placed on top of them. The sausages then are removed from molding boards and placed on smokehouse sticks. Hold in room at 52-55 degrees F. for 2 days, drying with humidity around 70%.

Sausage then is cold-smoked until desired color is obtained. Be sure your smoke never exceeds 80 degrees F.

Only certified pork trimmings should be used in processing Land-jager sausage. This processing procedure does not conform to government regulations concerning destruction of live trichinae. Since certified pork is nearly impossible to purchase, you may follow these instructions:

PRESCRIBED TREATMENT OF PORK PRODUCTS
TO DESTROY TRICHINAE

Required period of freezing at temperature indicated:

Temperature Degrees F.	Group 1 Days	Group 2 Days
5	20	30
-10	10	20
-20	6	12

Group 1 comprises product in separate pieces not exceeding 6 inches in thickness or arranged on separate racks with layers not exceeding 6 inches in depth, or stored in crates or boxes not exceeding 6 inches in (depth) thickness.

Group 2 comprises product in pieces, layers, or within containers, the thickness of which exceeds 6 inches but not 27 inches and product in containers including tierces, barrels, kegs and cartons having a thickness not exceeding 27 inches.

The product undergoing such refrigeration or the containers thereof shall be so spaced while in the freezer as will insure free circulation of air between the pieces of meat, layers, blocks, barrels or tierces in order that the temperature of the meat throughout will be promptly reduced to exceed 5 degrees F., -10 degrees F., or -20 degrees F. as the case may be.

DRY-CURED SOPRESSATA

Sopressata can be made of either fresh hams or pork butts. It sometimes is made using beef, but pork is the traditional meat used. In either case, the fat and sinews should be removed before starting.

INGREDIENTS

10 lbs. lean pork
9 tbsp. salt
1 oz. powdered dextrose
2 tbsp. whole black pepper
2 tbsp. ground black pepper
3 ozs. corn syrup solids
2 level tsp. Prague Powder No. 2
1 tbsp. hot cayenne pepper (optional)

Grind all meat through ½" or ¾" grinder plate. Add all ingredients and mix well. Remove meat to tub container, packing meat tightly (not over 6-7" high) and refrigerate for 48 hours. Remove from cooler, grind meat through ¼" plate and stuff into hog middle 8-10" long. Sausage then is held for 48 hours at about 55 degrees F. and then is placed into smokehouse. Sausage is smoked for 48 hours with cold smoke until color is obtained.

Remove from smokehouse and keep at 50-60 degrees F. with humidity around 70-80%. Hold about 8-10 weeks. Product will be ready when it loses about 30% of its green weight.

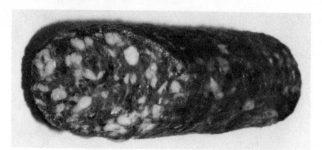

The above sopressata has been cut to show that it does contain a lot of fat. This is proper and preferred by the lovers of this sausage.

DRIED CHORIZOS

INGREDIENTS FOR 25 LBS.
15 ozs. salt
2 cups water
1 pint white vinegar
4 ozs. Spanish paprika
2½ ozs. hot cayenne pepper
3 ozs. granulated garlic
1½ ozs. oregano
1½ ozs. black coarse pepper
1 oz. Prague Powder No. 2
4 ozs. corn syrup solids
14 ozs. Fermento

INGREDIENTS FOR 10 LBS.
9 tbsp. salt
1 cup white vinegar
1 oz. Spanish paprika
3 tbsp. hot cayenne pepper
3 tbsp. granulated garlic
1 tbsp. oregano
2 tsp. black coarse pepper
2 level tsp. Prague Powder No. 2
1½ ozs. corn syrup solids
6 ozs. Fermento
1 cup water

A dried chorizo can be made using any combination of lean meats or 100% pork butts. Grind all chilled meats (32-34 degrees F.) through a ½" grinder plate. Add all ingredients to meat and mix well. Remove meat to a container and pack very well to avoid air pockets. Cure overnight at 34-36 degrees F.

Before stuffing, regrind meat through a ¼" or ⅜" plate. This will allow easier stuffing into a 35-38mm hog casing. Sausage is placed on smokesticks, spaced properly, and allowed to ripen for 3 days at 70-75 degrees F. with humidity of 70-80%. Then space sausages about 3-4 inches apart and dry for 15 days at 50-55 degrees F.– humidity at 60-70%.

Sausage may then be placed into containers and filled with lard. This is an especially popular method of storage with the Cuban people.

CAPICOLA - DRY CURED

INGREDIENTS FOR 100 LBS.
4 lbs. salt
12½ ozs. powdered dextrose
5 ozs. Prague Powder No. 2

INGREDIENTS FOR 25 LBS.
1 lbs. salt
3 ozs. powdered dextrose
1 oz. Prague Powder No. 2

MEAT

Lean boneless pork butts that are 3-4 lbs. apiece and well-trimmed should be used. The internal temperature of the butts should be chilled to 34-36 degrees F. before use.

PROCESSING

The 5 lb. total of the above cure is used to cure 100 lbs. of pork butts. Rub all the pork butts very well with this dry cure mixture. Lay down a layer of this cure mixture in the container; place the first layer of the pork butts inside. Leftover cure then is sprinkled in between each layer, and butts are placed into the cooler at 36-46 degrees F. for not less than 25 days. After 10 or 12 days, the pork butts should be overhauled; the top ones placed on the bottom, and the bottom ones placed on top.

Be sure you have additional spice-cure mixture ready to lay down in between each layer. After 25 days, the pork butts are removed from the cooler and washed lightly. Allow to drain; then rub with Spanish paprika and red ground pepper. The pepper to be rubbed in depends on individual preference. The pork butts are then stuffed into beef bungs.

After stuffing, there will be many air pockets; be sure you pin prick these air pockets to allow the entrapped air to escape. Hang on smokesticks, properly spaced.

SMOKING

Pork butts are placed in a preheated smokehouse at 90 degrees F. with the dampers wide open to dry the casings. Hold at this temperature for 10 hours. During this period, you may close dampers

376

to ¼ open after the casings are dry, applying a light smoke; continue to smoke for another 15-20 hours at 90 degrees F.

Butts then are removed from the smoker and dipped in hot boiling water momentarily to shrink the casing onto the capicola. Then place in dry room at 70-75 degrees F. with a relative humidity of 65-75%. Capicola must be held in dry room not less than 20 days before using.

PROSCUITTI (DRY CURED)

INGREDIENTS FOR 100 LBS.	INGREDIENTS FOR 25 LBS.
1 lb. ground white pepper	4 ozs. ground white pepper
5 ozs. ground black pepper	1 oz. ground black pepper
27 ozs. allspice	7 ozs. allspice
5 ozs. ground nutmeg	5 tbsp. ground nutmeg
1 oz. ground mustard	1 tbsp. ground mustard
1 oz. coriander	3 tbsp. coriander
20 ozs. powdered dextrose	5 ozs. powdered dextrose
1¾ lbs. Prague Powder No. 2	5 ozs. Prague Powder No. 2
4 lbs. salt	1 lb. salt

The hams selected for "proscuitti" should be free of bruises and in the 10-15 lb. range. The skin is left on the entire ham, but be sure that the fat is not over 1½" thick. Before using, be sure that the hams have been chilled to 34-36 degrees F.

Premix all the above ingredients except the salt and cure. Add 7 ozs. of ingredients to each 4 lbs. of salt and 1¾ lbs. of cure for each 100 lbs. of hams. The hams should be well rubbed on all sides with the spice-cure mixture. Hams then are stacked between layers of the spice mixture. The hams may be stacked as many as four high, as the "proscuitti" ham is known for its flat shape. You may flatten the hams in a single layer by covering the top with a suitable weight. STACK HAMS SKIN SIDE DOWN.

Cure hams about 10 days in cooler at 36-38 degrees F.; be sure the temperature never drops below 36 degrees F. Hams should also be kept covered during the curing time to keep out as much air as possible. After 10 days, remove hams from cooler and place in cool water for at least 15 hours to soak.

Be sure water isn't over 65 degrees F.; you must change the water after 7-8 hours. After removing from the water, scrub the skin of the ham with a soft brush to remove the salt. Hams are then tied and hung on a smokestick spaced properly.

SMOKING

Hams are placed in a smokehouse preheated to 130 degrees F.

with dampers ¼ open. Hold for 48 hours at this temperature. After 48 hours, raise the temperature to 140 degrees F. and hold for 2 hours. Raise temperature gradually, about 10 degrees for each half-hour. After 2 hours, let the smokehouse temperature drop to 120 degrees F. and hold hams at this temperature for 8-10 hours.

All the heat then is discontinued and hams are allowed to remain in the smokehouse until their internal temperature drops to 100 degrees F. Hams are removed from the smokehouse and allowed to hang at room temperature for 8-9 hours. Ham is rubbed with equal parts of white and black pepper. After rubbing, hang hams on smokesticks, properly spaced, and remove to the dry room. Hold temperature at 70-75 degrees F. with relative humidity of 65-75% for 30 days.

NOTE:

The bone is removed from the Italian-style ham before it is cured. This enables the ham to be pressed flat to a thickness of about 2 inches.

**Proscuitti
Ham**

DRY-CURED PEPPERONI - ITALIAN STYLE

INGREDIENTS FOR 25 LBS.

14 ozs. salt
3 ozs. powdered dextrose
1 oz. Prague Powder No. 2
½ oz. ground hot red pepper
½ oz. allspice
1¼ oz. ground anise seed
4 ozs. corn syrup solids
12½ lbs. lean pork butts
2½ lbs. regular pork
10 lbs. boneless beef

INGREDIENTS FOR 10 LBS.

9 tbsp. salt
1 oz. powdered dextrose
2 level tsp. Prague Powder No. 2
1 tbsp. ground hot red pepper
1 tsp. allspice
5 tsp. ground anise seed
2 ozs. corn syrup solids
5 lbs. lean pork butts
1 lbs. regular pork
4 lbs. boneless beef

GRINDING & MIXING

Grind all the meat through a ³⁄₁₆" grinder plate. Use mixer and add all the ingredients mixing evenly; regrind through ⅛" plate. The meat now is ready for stuffing.

STUFFING

It is essential that the meat be well-chilled to avoid smearing. The meat should be stuffed into 24-26mm lamb casings.

DRYING

Hold pepperoni at 70 degrees F. for about 2 days maintaining a relative humidity of about 75%. The product should be kept in a 38-40 degrees F. cooler for at least 20 days from the time the cure has been added to the pepperoni. Be sure that casings used are not more than 1⅜" in diameter, as this formula applies only to casings below this range.

DRY-CURED HARD SALAMI

INGREDIENTS FOR 25 LBS.
14 ozs. salt
4 ozs. corn syrup solids
1 oz. Prague Powder No. 2
1 oz. ground white pepper
¼ oz. ginger
¼ oz. garlic powder (optional)
3 ozs. powdered dextrose
6½ lbs. lean boneless beef
16¼ lbs. lean pork
2½ lbs. backfat

INGREDIENTS FOR 10 LBS.
9 tbsp. salt
1 oz. powdered dextrose
2 level tsp. Prague Powder No. 2
1 tbsp. ground white pepper
1 tsp. ginger
1 tsp. garlic powder (optional)
2 ozs. corn syrup solids
2½ lbs. lean boneless beef
6½ lbs. lean pork
1 lb. backfat

GRINDING & MIXING

Be sure that all the meat is chilled around 30-32 degrees F. Grind all the beef through a ⅛" grinder plate and all the pork through a ⅜" plate. Backfat should be cut or diced into ¾"-1" squares and frozen. Place all the meat into a mixer, adding all the ingredients; mix well. Grind all the meat through a ⅛" plate. Pack all the meat into tubs not over 6" high. Be sure that the meat is packed very tightly to eliminate the air pockets. Hold in a cooler at 38-40 degrees F. for 72 hours.

STUFFING

Remove the meat, place in stuffer and pack the meat very tightly to eliminate all air pockets. The meat should be stuffed into a defatted beef middle about 3" in diameter and 20" long. If available, you can use a protein-lined fibrous casing. After stuffing the casings full, tie the ends and wrap the salami with a loop about every 2 or 3 inches, to give it that stuffed look.

CURING

Salami should be allowed to cure for 3-4 days at 70-75 degrees F. with a relative humidity of 70-80%.

SMOKING

Dry salami need not be smoked; however, if you wish to smoke, be sure that the temperature of the smokehouse never reaches over 90 degrees F. It is best to smoke the salami at temperatures of 75-85 degrees F., with a relative humidity of 70%. Keep in smokehouse until the desired color is obtained.

DRYING

The smoked salami should be kept at 50-60 degrees F. with a relative humidity of 70-72%. For salami that is not smoked, keep at 40-50 degrees F. with relative humidity of 70-72%. This salami is fully dried when it loses 25% of its green weight. This takes from 85-90 days.

DRY-CURED FARMERS SAUSAGE

INGREDIENTS FOR 25 LBS.
14 ozs. salt
4 ozs. corn syrup solids
1 oz. Prague Powder No. 2
2 ozs. ground black pepper
3 ozs. powdered dextrose
20 lbs. lean boneless beef
3¾ lbs. lean pork trimmings
1¼ lbs. backfat

INGREDIENTS FOR 10 LBS.
9 tbsp. salt
8 tbsp. corn syrup solids
2 level tsp. Prague Powder No. 2
2 tbsp. ground black pepper
1 oz. powdered dextrose
8 lbs. lean boneless beef
1½ lbs. lean pork trimmings
½ lbs. backfat

GRINDING & MIXING

Be sure all the meat has been pre-chilled at 32-34 degrees F. Grind all the beef through a ⅛" grinder plate. All the pork should be ground through a ½" plate. Place into mixer and add all the ingredients and mix well so that all the spices are evenly distributed with the meat. Place all the meat into tubs or pans, not over 6" high; pack the meat tightly to eliminate all air pockets. Leave in 34-38 degree F. cooler for 3 days.

STUFFING

After three days, meat should be packed into the stuffer very tightly and stuffed into beef middles 3½" by 20" or 3½" by 24" protein-lined casings. Sausage should then be held at 75 degrees F. with a relative humidity of 75-80% for about 12 hours.

SMOKING

The smokehouse temperature should be kept at 75-80 degrees F., with a relative humidity of 75-80%. Smoke for 3 days with a very heavy smoke. This sausage is then dried at 52-56 degrees F. for at least 30 days, maintaining a relative humidity of 65%.

DRY-CURED GENOA SALAMI

INGREDIENTS FOR 25 LBS.

14 ozs. salt
1¼ ozs. corn syrup solids
¼ oz. whole black pepper
¾ oz. ground white pepper
½ oz. garlic powder
4 ozs. good Italian dry wine
1 oz. Prague Powder No. 2
3 ozs. powdered dextrose
22 lbs. very lean pork
    or boneless beef
3 lbs. backfat

INGREDIENTS FOR 10 LBS.

9 tbsp. salt
3 tbsp. corn syrup solids
1 tbsp. whole black pepper
1 tbsp. ground white pepper
1 tbsp. garlic powder
2 ozs. good Italian dry wine
2 level tsp. Prague Powder No. 2
1 oz. powdered dextrose
8½ lbs. very lean pork
    or boneless beef
1½ lbs. backfat

PROCESSING

When selecting the meat, always be sure that all the blood clots are removed and thrown away. In addition, separate all the connective tissues, sinews, or cords. Cut all the lean pork and backfat into ½ lb. pieces and freeze. All the meats are removed from the freezer and ground through a ¼" or 3/16" grinder plate.

Start the mixer and add all the ingredients; mix until the spices are evenly distributed. The meat then is placed into tubs or pans not over 6" high and packed tightly to omit all the air pockets. Place in 38 degree F. cooler for 48 hours.

STUFFING

For stuffing salami, use a hog bung, with a diameter 3½" by 20" long. After stuffing you may wrap a loop with the twine about every 2 inches. You can also use protein-lined casings as well, or some of the cloth casings that are available today.

CURING

The salami should be cured at 70-75 degrees F. with a relative humidity of 70-80% for 48 hours. Genoa salami is not smoked and after 48 hours should be placed into a cooler at 45-55 degrees F. for 70-80 days with a relative humidity of 75%.

NOTE:

GENOA SALAMI CAN BE MADE ENTIRELY OF PORK OR ENTIRELY OF BEEF. WHEN USING HOG BUNGS, YOU MAY, AFTER STUFFING THE SALAMIS, PLACE THEM IN A BRINE AT 50 DEGREES SALINOMETER READING, AT A TEMPERATURE OF 34-38 DEGREES F. OR 1 OR 2 DAYS. After removing the salami from the brine, place into a hot simmering water for 3 seconds. This process will help to remove all the excess fat and open the pores of the hog bung, which in turn promotes better drying of the salami.

DRY-CURED COUNTRY HAMS

(This ham need not be refrigerated after curing and smoking.)

INGREDIENTS FOR 100 LBS.

7 lbs. salt
1½ lbs. powdered dextrose
1¾ lbs. Prague Powder No. 2
5½ gallons ice water
    38-40 degrees F.

INGREDIENTS FOR 25 LBS.

1 lb. 12 ozs. salt
5 ozs. powdered dextrose
5 ozs. Prague Powder No. 2
5 quarts ice water
    38-40 degrees F.

PROCESSING

Artery-pump the ham 8% by weight. Be sure you weigh the pickle. Then dry-rub the ham, using the same curing mix–using 3 lbs. for each 50 lbs. of ham. The ham then is placed on a rack in the cooler at 38-40 degrees F. for 15 days. Re-rub the ham with cure mix on the 7th day. Ham is then removed and scrubbed under running water to remove the surface salt. DO NOT SOAK. Ham is then dried off and removed to the smokehouse.

SMOKING

Smoke hams as follows: preheat smokehouse to 120 degrees F. Hold for 8 hours at 120 degrees F. with draft open, no smoke; 16 hours at 125 degrees F., drafts ½ open, light smoke; 48 hours at 120-125 degrees F. until the internal temperature is not more than 122 degrees F.

SPECIAL NOTE:
Do not smoke the hams at higher temperatures and do not allow the internal temperature to reach beyond 122 degrees F. Otherwise, the keeping quality is greatly reduced. A country ham has to be of low moisture and a high salt content to preserve it.

SMITHFIELD HAM

Over the years many people throughout the country have tried to duplicate the flavor of the Smithfield ham. The following information is not a formula; rather it shows how difficult it can be to process such a ham. This is a unique product because the hams are made only from peanut-fed hogs. Regular pork will not cure as completely nor as uniformly as peanut-fed hogs due to the oiliness and softness of the pork. These hogs are continuously on a diet of peanuts.

The Smithfield ham also has a unique look because the ham is cut at the hip and the full shank is left on. Only the toes are cut off and the full skin is left on the ham. The hams then are rubbed all over with straight salt peter, as much as will adhere to the leg. The hams then are left to cure for 24 hours.

After 24 hours, the hams are placed on a bed of salt, after being rubbed with plain salt. The hams then are stacked on edge, overhauled every 7 days, and stacked on the opposite edge after each overhaul. The hams are cured this way for 30-45 days, depending on size. After the ham is cured, it is washed, hung in a very large smokehouse, and allowed to dry for 3-4 days.

It is then smoked by burning 3"-4" hickory logs and sassafrass for at least 7 days. The logs are burned in 55-gallon drums that are distributed around the smokehouse. This is a cold-smoke process. After smoking, it is left in the smokehouse for about 6 months.

The Smithfield ham or a reasonable facsimile is rather difficult to produce unless you have a steady supply of peanuts and a huge smokehouse 3-4 stories high.

Notice only the toes have been cut off and the full shank has been left on. The full skin is also left on.

387

DRY-CURED OLD-STYLE SUMMER SAUSAGE

INGREDIENTS FOR 25 LBS.
15 lbs. pork butts
8 lbs. lean beef
2 lbs. back fat
12 ozs. salt
14 ozs. Fermento
1 oz. prague powder #2
2 ozs. powdered dextrose
4 ozs. corn syrup solids
1¼ ozs. ground black pepper
1¼ ozs. ground mustard seed
¼ oz. ground ginger
½ oz. granulated garlic

INGREDIENTS FOR 10 LBS
6 lbs. pork butts
3 lbs. lean beef
1 lb. back fat
5 ozs. salt
6 ozs. Fermento
2 level tsp. prague powder #2
1 oz. powdered dextrose
1½ ozs. corn syrup solids
¼ oz. ground black pepper
¼ oz. ground mustard seed
1 tsp. ground ginger
1 tsp. granulated garlic

Before making this summer sausage, you must first dry-salt the back fat for 2 weeks in order to cure it properly. For 25 lbs. of back fat, it should be held at a temperature of 38-40 degrees F., using the following mixture:

4 ozs. prague powder #2
1¼ lbs. salt

Rub the entire piece of back fat with this mixture, coating the surface, and place in a cooler for 2 weeks. Use plenty of this mixture and rub very well.

After the back fat is cured, the excess salt should be brushed away, but not washed. Then grind the fat through a ⅛" grinder plate. The rest of the meat should be ground through a ¼" grinder plate. Add the remaining ingredients and mix thoroughly until evenly distributed. Pack the mixture tightly into tubs about 6" high, making sure there are no air pockets. Place in a cooler at 38-40 degrees F. for at least 4 days, but not more than 6. Then stuff the mixture into protein-lined casings, 3½" x 24", or 3½" beef middles.

Hang the sausage in the drying room at 45-50 degrees F. for 60-70 days with a relative humidity of 70-80%.

DRY-CURED PLOCKWURST
(Block Sausage)

INGREDIENTS FOR 25 LBS.

20 lbs. lean beef
5 lbs. frozen fresh bacon
14 ozs. salt
1 oz. prague powder #2
5 ozs. powdered dextrose
5 ozs. corn syrup solids
1½ ozs. ground white pepper

INGREDIENTS FOR 10 LBS.

7½ lbs. lean beef
2½ lbs. frozen fresh bacon
5½ ozs. salt
2 level tsp. prague powder #2
2 ozs. powdered dextrose
2 ozs. corn syrup solids
½ oz. ground white pepper

Chill the meat to 32-34 degrees F. The beef should be ground through a ¼" grinder plate; the frozen bacon (at about 26-28 degrees F.) should be sliced about ¼" thick and then ground through a ⅜" grinder plate. Add the remaining ingredients, mixing thoroughly until evenly distributed. Stuff the mixture in a beef middle or 3½" x 24" protein-lined casing.

Cure the sausage at 65-70 degrees F. for 48 hours with a relative humidity of 70-80%. Place it in a cooler at 45-50 degrees F. with a relative humidity of 70-75%. Keep sausage there for about 70-80 days before using.

DRY-CURED WESTFALIA HAM SAUSAGE

INGREDIENTS FOR 25 LBS.
7½ lbs. lean beef
10 lbs. lean pork
7½ lbs. frozen fresh bacon
14 ozs. salt
1 oz. prague powder #2
5 ozs. corn syrup solids
1 oz. ground black pepper
1 oz. good rum
5 ozs. powdered dextrose

INGREDIENTS FOR 10 LBS.
2½ lbs. lean beef
5 lbs. lean pork
2½ lbs. frozen fresh bacon
5½ ozs. salt
2 level tsp. prague powder #2
2 ozs. corn syrup solids
¼ oz. ground black pepper
½ oz. good rum
2 ozs. powdered dextrose

Remove bacon rind and then freeze the bacon at about 26-28 degrees F. Then remove the bacon from the freezer and cube it into 1" squares. Grind the lean pork and beef through a ⅜" grinder plate. Thoroughly mix the frozen bacon and meat with the remaining ingredients. Then stuff into protein-lined fibrous casings (3½" x 24") or a hog bung.

Let the ham sausage cure at 65-70 degrees F. for about 48 hours with a relative humidity of 70-80%. Put sausage in a cooler at 45-50 degrees F. with a relative humidity of 70-75%. Store sausage for 70-80 days before using.

DRY-CURED HOLSTEINER SAUSAGE

INGREDIENTS FOR 25 LBS.
18¾ lbs. lean beef
6¼ lbs. lean pork
14 ozs. salt
1 oz. prague powder #2
5 ozs. corn syrup solids
5 ozs. powdered dextrose
2 ozs. ground black pepper
4 ozs. Fermento

INGREDIENTS FOR 10 LBS.
7½ lbs. lean beef
2½ lbs. lean pork
5½ ozs. salt
2 level tsp. prague powder #2
2 ozs. corn syrup solids
2 ozs. powdered dextrose
¾ oz. ground black pepper
1½ ozs. Fermento

Be sure meat is chilled to 32-34 degrees F. before starting. Grind the pork through a ½" grinder plate and the beef through a ⅛" grinder plate. Add the remaining ingredients and mix thoroughly until evenly distributed. Pack the mixture into a container not more than 6" high, packing tightly to omit any air pockets. Place mixture in a cooler at 36-38 degrees F. and allow to cure for 72 hours.

After three days, stuff the mixture into protein-lined fibrous casings (3½" x 24") or a 3½" beef middle. Then keep sausage for 12 hours at 75 degrees F. with a relative humidity of 70-80%.

SMOKING

Unlike most dry-cured sausage, the Holsteiner sausage is smoked. Place in smokehouse using no heat but a dense smoke for 3-4 days. Place sausage in a cooler at 50-55 degrees F. and allow to cure for at least 30 days with a relative humidity of 65-60%.

DRY-CURED SMOKED POLISH SAUSAGE
(Kielbasa Polska Surowa Wedzowa)

INGREDIENTS FOR 25 LBS.

25 lbs. pork butts
1 oz. prague powder #2
12 ozs. salt
1½ ozs. coarse black pepper
3 ozs. powdered dextrose
3 ozs. corn syrup solids
½ oz. ground marjoram

INGREDIENTS FOR 10 LBS.

10 lbs. pork butts
2 level tsp. prague powder #2
5 ozs. salt
1 tbsp. coarse black pepper
1¼ ozs. powdered dextrose
1¼ ozs. corn syrup solids
1 tsp. ground marjoram

Grind meat through 1" or 3/16" grinder plate. Add remaining ingredients and mix well until evenly distributed. Stuff mixture into 35-38mm hog casings and form 5-6" links. Place sausage in cooler for 48 hours at 38-40 degrees F. After this, place in a cold smokehouse (no heat), applying very dense smoke for at least 12 hours. This will produce a dark brown sausage. Store at 50-60 degrees F. with a relative humidity of 70-80% until you achieve a weight loss of 20-30% (around 15 days).

DRY-CURED ITALIAN SAUSAGE

INGREDIENTS FOR 25 LBS.
25 lbs. pork butts
14 ozs. salt
1 oz. prague powder #2
½ oz. cracked fennel seed
4 ozs. powdered dextrose
½ oz. ground cayenne pepper
4 ozs. corn syrup solids
¼ oz. ground coriander

INGREDIENTS FOR 10 LBS
10 lbs. pork butts
6 ozs. salt
2 level tsp. prague powder #2
1 tbsp. cracked fennel seed
1¾ ozs. powdered dextrose
3 tbsp. ground cayenne pepper
1¾ ozs. corn syrup solids
1 tbsp. ground coriander

Grind pork through a ¾" grinder plate. Add remaining ingredients and mix well until evenly distributed. Pack meat mixture in pans not more than 6" high, packing tightly to omit air pockets.

Place meat in 38-40 degrees F. cooler for 48 hours. Then regrind meat through a ³⁄₁₆" grinder plate and stuff in 35-38mm hog casings. Place sausage in a drying room at about 60 degrees F. with a relative humidity of 65-70 degrees F. for 48 hours. Then put sausage in a 38-40 degrees F. cooler and allow to cure for 20 days before using. Your cooler should also have a relative humidity of 60-70 degrees F. during these 20 days.

DRY-CURED POLISH SALAMI
(Salami Polskie Sucha)

INGREDIENTS FOR 25 LBS.	INGREDIENTS FOR 10 LBS.
10 lbs. lean pork	5 lbs. lean pork
7½ lbs. lean beef	2½ lbs. lean beef
7½ lbs. fresh bacon	2½ lbs. fresh bacon
12 ozs. salt	5 ozs. salt
1 oz. prague powder #2	2 level tsp. prague powder #2
1 oz. ground black pepper	1 tbsp. ground black pepper
½ oz. ground cardamon	1 tsp. ground cardamon
3 ozs. powdered dextrose	1¼ oz. powdered dextrose
3 ozs. corn syrup solids	1¼ ozs. corn syrup solids

Mix the salt and prague powder #2 and rub into the bacon thoroughly. Then wrap the bacon in freezer wrap or butcher paper, if you are making a small amount of sausage. A plastic bag is also acceptable. Place in a cooler at 40 degrees F. and store for 12 days. Be generous with the salt-cure mix when rubbing the bacon. On the 6th day, grind the lean beef and pork through a ¾" or 1" grinder plate. Add the remaining ingredients and mix thoroughly until evenly distributed. The mixture is then tightly packed into a container or tub not more than 6" high, making sure there are no air pockets. Place in cooler and remove all meat on the 12th day. Then grind the lean meat mixture through a ³⁄₁₆" or ¼" grinder plate. Clean the excess salt from the bacon and grind through a ⅜" grinder plate. Combine the two mixtures and mix thoroughly. This mixture is again tightly packed into a container not more than 6" high, being sure to eliminate air pockets. Place mixture in a cooler at 38-40 degrees F. for another 24 hours. Then remove it and stuff into 3½" x 24" casings. You may also use other casings — beef, pork or protein-lined fibrous casings.

Place the sausage in a cooler at 40 degrees F. with a 80-90% humidity rate. After 4 days, hang the sausage at 55-60 degrees F. for 6-8 weeks with a humidity of 70-80%. You will achieve a 30% weight loss in this period of time.

Place sausage in a smokehouse with no heat but dense smoke

until it has a dark red appearance. This may take several days to achieve at 8-10 hours a day of smoking.

CHAPTER XIV

Fish and Seafood

PRESERVATION ACTION
IN CURING FISH

Food preservation is essentially the prevention of spoilage. The most important cause of spoilage is through micro-biological action. Fresh, dried, salted or smoked fishery products may be rendered unfit for use by a wide variety of causes other than ordinary forms of spoilage.

The spoilage organisms require moisture and warmth for development, and the most favorable temperatures for their development are from 70-100 degrees F. Therefore, removal of a large part of the moisture from a given product and its storage at temperatures unfavorable for bacterial development have a direct effect. Cured fishery products should be held at temperatures below 70 degrees F. if the maximum preservation is to be obtained.

For the maximum length of preservation, moisture should be reduced to about 20%. This usually requires a long curing period and some special equipment. Under ordinary home conditions, cured products with a moisture content of 40% are about all that can be expected.

The chemical cause of spoilage most common in cured fishery products is oxidation. If the surface of the flesh is exposed to the air or the sunlight, it turns yellow to brown and acquires an unpleasant, rancid flavor.

To best protect home-cured fishery products against these chemical and physical spoilages, they should be placed in a tightly-closed container and kept in a dry, cool place, preferably dark. Brine-cured products should be weighed down so that they will be kept below the surface of the brine. Smoked products should be coated with a thin coating of paraffin or dusted with a fine salt, wrapped in oiled or parchment paper, and packed in a tightly-closed box or container.

PRESERVATION OF FISH

Fish may be corned, brine cured, dry salted, smoked or pickled (vinegar cured). These methods have several advantages over canning: they are simpler, do not require much equipment, are less expensive, and permit utilization of varieties not canned successfully.

One disadvantage, however, must be kept in mind. Unlike canning, these methods do not preserve indefinitely; in fact, for certain fish and certain methods, preservation is limited to a comparatively brief period. The single disadvantage, though important, does not outweigh the many advantages of fish curing. Moreover, even when containers and canning equipment are readily available, fish curing is often preferable to canning.

CORNING
(Temporary Preservation While Fishing)

Sport fishermen and the casual angler frequently bring in catches in poor condition. Sometimes the fish must be discarded. This is especially common when the weather is warm, and the fisherman is a considerable distance from home or is unaware of a method by which fish may be properly handled when refrigeration is not available.

Such waste is avoidable if the proper procedure is followed. Bleed the fish as soon as it is caught by pulling out the gills completely, leaving no remnants. Clean the fish as soon as possible, scraping out all traces of blood and intestinal material. Wash the body cavity thoroughly.

Thorough cleaning delays spoilage; if the body cavity is not thoroughly cleaned, spoilage begins sooner than if the fish were not cleaned at all.

Rub the belly cavity well with a fine table salt containing one tablespoon of pepper per cup. Rub salt into the flesh at a ratio of about one tablespoon to a ¾-pound fish, dusting a small amount on the skin side.

Place the fish into a basket or a box. A loose packing of green leaves around the fish has been found useful in inland regions. Cover the container with several thicknesses of burlap. The burlap must not rest on the fish since there should be an air space above them. Keep the cloth well moistened with water, since evaporation of moisture lowers the temperature in the container.

Treated in this manner, fish should remain in good condition for at least 24 hours when ice is not available. When rinsed thoroughly, the fish so treated are ready at once for cooking in any way desired. If rolled in salt and packed away with as much of it as will cling to them, they will keep for about 10 days. Before using, these fish should be freshened for about 10 hours in one or two changes of water.

BRINE SALTING

Brine salting of fish requires a set of 1-5 gallon containers with a tight-fitting cover; 1-2 tubs or cut-down barrels for washing or preliminary brining; and at least 2 sharp knives, one large and one small. If storing less than 50 pounds of fish, you can get by with only one sharp knife and a 2-gallon container. It is best to use stoneware or stainless steel containers, as they may be used for other purposes since they do not absorb foreign flavors.

The salt used should be pure and clean, free from dirt and moisture. It should be a fairly small grain, preferably "dairy fine." Many commercial salters prefer the coarsely-ground salt, but a finely-ground salt is preferable in home salting as it forms into brine and penetrates the flesh more rapidly. Salt that is not pure and clean can cause delay of the brine penetration and give the product an acrid, salty flavor, whereas the pure salt imparts a much milder favor. It is usually better to allow the brine to form by packing the fish and salt in layers. Even a saturated brine may be weakened sufficiently to cause spoilage during salting. The danger is that too much or too little salt may be used. Too much salt may "burn" the fish, while too little may permit fermentation and spoilage during curing.

The number of species salted commercially is quite limited, but almost any variety may be salted at home. As a rule, the so-called "lean" species are salted more readily; salt brine does not penetrate as rapidly in "fat" fish. With the latter, oxidation and rancidity occur more readily, and they need extra care both in salting and storing. When cured successfully, they make a salt fish of the finest quality.

Fresh-water fish usually salted are lake trout, whitefish, lake herring, blue pike, yellow pike (pickerel), catfish and perch. Others that may be salted at home are sheepshead, carp, suckers, buffalofish, river herring (aslewife), eels—in fact, any fish of satisfactory size.

Salt-water fish commonly salted are cod, hake, pollock, bluefish, sea trout, channel bass, rock or striped bass, salmon, shad, sea bass, rock fish, mackerel, sea herring and Florida mullet. Others that are salted but not to such an extent are crocker, hogfish, scup, butterfish, spots, whiting, grouper, halibut, sablefish and snook.

In general, the method for pickling is the same for all varieties.

400

Smaller fish are split down the back so as to lie flat in one piece with the belly not cut through. A cut is made just under the backbone and the fish is scored with the point of the knife at intervals about one inch apart. All the traces of blood or membrane are cleared away, and the gills removed form the split head.

Large fish are split into two fillets, removing the backbone. The collarbone just below the gills is not cut away. The fish are damaged more in handling if this is removed; if you intend to smoke the brined fish, the pieces will often drop from the smokehouse hangers since the skin and the flesh cannot support the weight unless the collar-bone is present.

The flesh of the large pieces of fillets is scored longitudinally to a depth of about ½" at intervals of 1-2 inches. The cuts should not penetrate to the skin. Cut the pieces just long enough to lie flat on the bottom of the container.

Thick-skinned, spiny-finned fish with large scales, such as carp, suckers, buffalo, black bass, channel bass and catfish should be skinned and the fins removed. This is best done by making a deep cut along each side of the fin, which is then pulled away by hand. This method is much faster than the usual system of clipping, and removes the small bones in the flesh at the base of the fins.

The fish, whether large or small, are thoroughly washed in fresh water, after which they are soaked for 30 minutes to one hour in a brine made in a proportion of ½ cup salt to one gallon of water to remove the diffused blood from the flesh and to cut away slime from the skin. The fish are drained for 5-10 minutes after brining.

Make a shallow box about 2 feet square and with sides 6 inches high. Fill this with dry salt. Scatter a thin layer of salt on the bottom of the container or keg in which the fish are to be salted. Dredge each piece of fish with salt and rub into the places where the flesh is scored. Pick up the fish with as much salt as will cling to it and pack into the container, skin side down. Arrange the pieces so that an even layer will result. Pieces should overlap each other as little as possible.

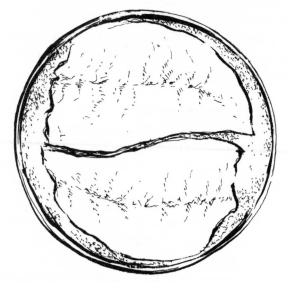

Method of packing large fish in container for brine salting.

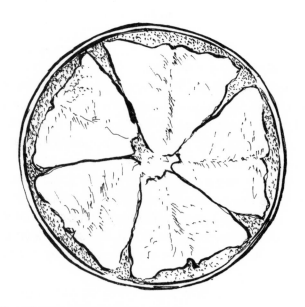

Method of packing small fish in container for brine salting.

The amount of salt used depends on the purity and grain of the salt. Less is required if the salt is of high purity and small grain. More salt is required in warm weather, and large, thick or fat fish require more salt. The proportion of salt used runs from ¼-⅓ of the total weight. A general rule is to use one part salt to three parts fish. In salting, be careful not to exceed the proper proportion—an excess will "burn" the fish, lowering the quality.

Place a loose-fitting wooden cover on the top layer of the fish, and weigh the cover down. Fair-sized rocks or bricks, thoroughly washed, make good weights. The fish will form its own brine. Small fish like spots or croakers may be "struck through," or completely brined in 48 hours; thicker, larger, fatter fish will require 7-10 days.

At the end of this time, the fish are removed, scrubbed in a fresh-saturated brine with a stiff bristle brush, then repacked with a very light scattering of salt between layers. Layers must be pressed down well. Fill the container with a fresh saturated salt brine and store the container in a cool dark place. After 3 months, or at the first sign of fermentation (especially if the weather is warm) change the brine again. Brine-cured fish should not be expected to remain in good condition for more than nine months.

HERRING

Since herring are more easily obtainable than other fish by people living at or near the seashore in the North Atlantic or Pacific regions, they are one of the most important fish for curing. Brine-curing them requires a separate discussion, however, as methods of cleaning, packing and curing differ in certain procedures.

Herring intended for brine salting must be strictly fresh and in good condition. Thin or small fish should not be used. Herring must be free of materials causing enzymic spoilage, and should not be bruised or crushed. Ice must not be used if a salted product of good quality is desired. Instead, the fish should be cured immediately on landing.

The herring may be brined whole (without cleaning), or may be gibbed—that is, cut through at the throat, removing part of the viscera without cutting the belly. In gibbing, one takes hold of the herring by the middle with the left hand, thumb on one side of the head, the fingers on the other, leaving the throat clear. A small short-bladed paring knife is stuck through the gills, just under the gill cover and with the edge of the blade toward the gibber, and given a sharp twist upward and outward.

If the herring are fresh and the operation is performed properly, the throat and pectoral fin together with the main gut and gills are taken out in a single motion. Before the knack is acquired, more than one motion may be required.

The herring are then thoroughly washed in sea water or salt brine, preferably the latter, stirring the fish about. This operation removes scales and leaches the blood from the fish. After washing, the fish are drained for about 10 minutes, or until all the excess moisture is removed, thrown into a shallow box of fine salt, and stirred about until all the salt possible clings to them.

Scatter a very thin layer of salt on the bottom of the container that you know will be free of leaks and very tight. Take up the herring with as much salt as will cling to it; place it straight against the side of the container, back down. Place two others in front of the first, their heads touching the side walls of the container, one to the right, one to the left, straight on their backs, belly up, and packed as tightly as possible. Place a fourth herring in the middle between the two; and the two others' heads to the side walls as before. The head ends of the herring should be alternated.

Continue to pack in this fashion until the layer is completed. The rows must not be irregular, and the fish must not be packed on a slant or they will not be salted evenly. The space at the sides of the container where the heads touch must be filled. Two herring are placed with their heads pointing in opposite directions. This leaves an even surface for succeeding layers. Enough salt should be scattered on top so that the layer is just covered.

Begin another layer. Pack each layer at right angles to the preceding one. The top layer should be packed with the backs up and salted a little more heavily than the other rows. Fill the container with fresh 100% brine and close tightly. Store in a cool, dry place. The brine should be changed at 2-month intervals if the fish have not been used up. Fairly fat herring will require a total of 35 pounds of salt for 100 pounds of fish.

DRY SALTING

Dry salting is the method of fish curing best adapted to warm climates, but also is widely used by non-commercial fish curers in the northern areas. Nearly all fish may be used, although fatty fish are much more difficult to cure and keep a shorter period of time. As a rule, properly dry-salted fish keep for a longer period of time than when brine salted. This depends, however, on the temperature, humidity, percentage of moisture remaining and the care used in preparation and storage.

The method generally used is the same, but there are many local modifications. The method given here is especially descriptive of the home curing of cod, haddock, hake and pollock, but is applicable to most large non-fatty fish. Variations necessitated by differences in species or by local conditions are discussed later in this book.

The fish are bled by cutting the throat and pulling out the gills as soon as caught. This results in a much lighter-colored flesh in the finished product. When the fish reach shore they must be thoroughly washed. Then the head is cut off, but the "lugs" (hard bony collar plates) must remain. If not, the fish will shred during curing or afterward in handling.

Cut down the left side of the backbone, with the knife edge at a slight downward slant, so that it scrapes the backbone. If the knife blade is held level, much flesh is left on the backbone. Continue down to the tail so that the upper side is removed in one piece. Then insert the edge of the knife blade just below the end of the backbone at a slight upward angle, and cut down to the tail. The fish now is separated into two sides of fillets. If the cutting is done correctly, the sides will be perfectly smooth with practically no flesh left on the backbone.

Another method especially adapted to smaller fish (from 2-5 lbs.) is to cut down the middle of the belly to the vent (anal opening). Lay the fish on the edge of the table so that the head overhangs. Grasp the head and give a quick downward jerk, which removes the head more quickly and easily than by cutting.

With the fish lying on its side, cut above the backbone from neck to tail holding the knife horizontally and working from the belly side. This cut must not be too deep. It must not go through the back skin.

Next, cut the backbone below the vent (leaving about one-fifth of tail section as a hinge). Cut forward just below the backbone to the head, thus removing it. Make another cut below the remaining section of the backbone in the tail section, so that salt may penetrate. The fish should now lie open in one piece.

After the fish is split, rub the inside of the belly cavity with a piece of coarse sackling to remove the black skin and to clean any blood, membrane and bits of viscera. Place the fish in a tub of water, wash, and brush thoroughly with a stiff bristle brush. Only pure, fresh drinking water should be used. Brine made in the proportion of 1 cup salt to 1 gallon of water is preferable to plain water. Afterward, drain the fish to remove surplus moisture.

Dredge the fish in a box of salt as in brine salting. Stack the fish in rows on the floor, choosing a place where the brine formed will run away to a drain. First, scatter a thin layer of salt on the spot where the fish are to be stacked, and arrange them in place by alternating heads and tails. Scatter a little salt between the layers of the fish. Fish are piled flesh side up except for the last layer, which is piled skin side up. The average amount of salt used is 1 pound to each 4 pounds of fish.

The fish are taken out of the salt in 48 hours to one week, depending upon the size of the fish and the weather. In damp or stormy weather, they are allowed to remain in the salt, as it is useless to attempt drying. Less time is required for salting in warm weather.

When the fish are ready for drying, they should be scrubbed in brine to remove all excess salt and dirt. No trace of salt should be visible on the surface. After draining 15-20 minutes, the fish are ready for the drying racks. These are frames of wood covered with chicken wire and standing on legs about 4 feet high. A slat top of thin poles or laths may be substituted for wire mesh, if a 2" space is left between the laths. The drying racks must be placed on dry ground, preferably coverd with gravel.

Oxidation or rusting of the fish occurs most readily if they are dried in direct sunlight. If the fish are kept in a breezy location, they dry well with a clear color. For this reason, drying is best done in the shade under an open-walled shed ventilated by air currents. If only a few fish are being dried, they may be hung under over-hanging eaves, or from the rafters of a shed or a barn where there is good

406

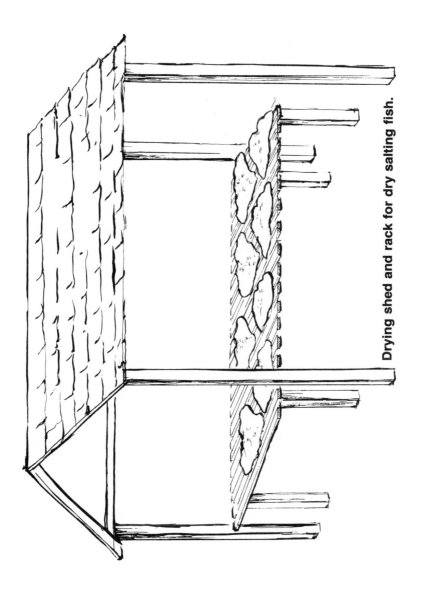

Drying shed and rack for dry salting fish.

407

cross-ventilation.

If placed on racks, the fish are laid skin side down, but should be turned 3-4 times the first day. They should be gathered up and stored each night, for they sour and mold if left spread out in the open. The fish are stacked in rows, alternating heads and tails, flesh side up except for the top layer. No stack should be more than 2 feet high, and there should be a rack at the bottom to prevent contact with the floor.

Each stack should be weighted down evenly, the weights at least equaling that of the fish in the stack. Additional moisture is pressed out of the fish. If the fish cannot be taken out to dry the next day because of unfavorable weather, they must be repiled at the close of the day, placing the top layers of the fish at the bottom. If the weather continues to be unfavorable for drying, the fish are left in the stacks, but are repiled every other day with a small amount of fine salt (about 1 lb. to 10 lbs. of fish) scattered between layers.

A smoke smudge under the drying racks may be necessary for at least the first day, to keep flies from the fish. The smudge should be made of green wood, or a wood fire smothered by green branches. Resinous woods such as pine or fir must not be used.

The time for drying depends upon the weather conditions, the size of the fish, and the length of preservation desired. Fairly large haddock, hake or pollock must receive 60 hours of air drying—about 6 good days of drying. The usual test to determine sufficiency of drying is to press the thick part of the flesh between the thumb and forefinger; if no impression can be made, the fish are sufficiently dried.

The cured fish are wrapped in wax paper, packed in a thin wooden box, tightly covered, and stored in a cool, dry place. At the first signs of rust, mold or reddening, scrub the fish in a salt brine and dry in the air for a day or two.

BARRACUDA

Remove the head, leaving the collar bones, slit down the middle of the belly to the vent and clean the body cavity thoroughly. Make a cut just above the backbone on the abdominal side, cutting along a line where the rib bones join the backbone, and continue the cut to the tail. Hold the edge of the blade at a downward angle so that no flesh is left on the backbone.

A similar cut is made just below the backbone. A sweep of the knife through the cut section of rib bones still adhering to the flesh removes the backbone, which is broken off near the tail. These cuts must not reach through to the skin. When splitting is completed, the barracuda should lie flat in a single piece. After splitting, the fish is washed thoroughly in salt brine and soaked 30 minutes to remove all the traces of blood. The flesh is scored to the skin, the cuts running longitudinally from collarbone to tail.

Fine salt should be rubbed into the flesh, the fish packed flesh side up in tubs. Scatter sufficient salt between the layers to cover any exposed surface. Place a loose-fitting cover on top of the fish with sufficient weights to keep all fish under the surface after the brine has been formed.

After 48 hours, remove the fish, scrub well in brine and dry one day as described previously. At the end of the day, the fish should be repacked in layers between thick layers of clean sacking, alternating layers of fish and sacking until the stack is completed. Weigh down the stack as heavily as possible. The next morning dry the fish for a second day. After 40 hours or 5 days of air drying, the fish should be sufficiently dry.

DRUM OR CHANNEL BASS

Split the fish in two sides, removing the backbone. Each side should be scored through the flesh longitudinally (from neck to tail), the cuts penetrating almost to the skin and about 2" apart. Wash the sides thoroughly in salt brine to remove all the traces of blood or other waste, and drain for about 20 minutes.

Dredge the sides in a box of fine salt, rubbing salt thoroughly into the flesh and especially into the cuts. Pack in even layers in tubs, flesh side up. Scatter a little more salt between each layer, and weigh down the top. Fill the tub with a saturated salt brine. The fish are allowed to remain in the tub about two weeks.

Take out and scrub the fish thoroughly to remove any blood spots, black skin, or excess salt. Stack the sides in a row like cordwood, but not more than 1 foot high. The bottom row should be laid skin-side down, but the other layers should be placed skin-side up. Cover the top with boards and weigh down with rocks.

The second day the fish are restacked, reversing the layers. The third or fourth day, depending on the weather, the sides are placed on racks in the shade for about 8 hours of air drying. The flesh during the first day's drying should not be exposed to the direct sunlight, since a crust would form that would prevent the removal of moisture from the inner flesh. At the end of the day, the fish again are stacked as before and heavily weighed down. They remain in the stack for two days, after which they are given a day of drying. Then they are repiled and given two days of pressing.

The process using one day of drying followed by two days of pressing is continued until the fish have received about 10 days of drying. The fish are cured thoroughly when the pressure of a thumb in the thick part of the back makes no impression.

MULLET

While small mullet are suitable for brine curing, only the larger fish, weighing one pound or more, make a good dry-salted product. The heads are first removed, leaving the collarbone as usual. They are split mackerel-style, along the back just above the backbone. When the knife is drawn toward the tail it must not go through the skin so that the lower half is cut in two. A cut is made under the backbone and the flesh is scored longitudinally on both sides. Intestines, black skin, and blood must be cleaned out. Scrubbing with a piece of coarse sacking canvas is the most effective means of removing black skin and blood from the fish.

The clean fish are washed thoroughly and dropped in a tub of salt brine made in the proportion of 1 lb. salt to 1 gallon of water. They should be allowed to soak in the brine for 30 minutes to remove all the traces of blood from the cut flesh. After brining, the mullet are drained for at least 20 minutes to remove surplus moisture.

Fill a shallow box about 2 feet square with salt, usually a dairy-fine grade. The drained fish are dredged in this salt, and the salt is rubbed into the slashes of the flesh. A thin layer is scattered over the bottom of a tub. The fish are then picked up with as much salt as will cling to the body and packed in even layers in the tub, flesh-side up, each layer at right angles to the preceding one. A small amount of salt is scattered between each layer.

A loose-fitting cover is placed on top and weighted sufficiently so that the fish will be covered by the brine formed. In warm weather, a saturated brine may be added immediately, instead of allowing it to form gradually by extracting moisture from the flesh. The amount of salt used should not be more than 3 lbs. per 10 lbs. of fish.

The mullet should be sufficiently salted in about 36 hours, after which they should be removed from the brine. Scrub thoroughly to remove any traces of excess salt, and place in layers, flesh side up (except for the top layer), on a low rack. The stack should be weighed down to press moisture out of the flesh, and the next morning the mullet should be hung in a shady spot where there is a good breeze or should be dried on racks as previously described.

At night they are restacked and weighed down, and set out to dry again the next morning. A small amount of salt is sometimes scattered between the layers in stacking, but any excess salt must be brushed off before the fish are taken out to dry.

In good weather the mullet will be sufficiently cured in 4 days; in unfavorable weather, and for the largest fish, more time may be required. When dried, each fish is wrapped in waxed paper, packed in a tightly covered wooden box, and stored in a cool, dry place.

SHARK

Curing must begin within the shortest possible time after catching, as spoiling occurs more rapidly with shark than in any other species. The shark is gutted and skinned, after which the carcass is split into two sides, removing the backbone. The large streak of dark meat along the middle of each side must be cut away, dividing each side into two fillets of light-colored flesh. The individual fillets may be further divided into two or more pieces if the shark is very large. The individual fillet, or piece, should not weigh more than 5 lbs.

Each piece then is scored lengthwise with a knife on both sides. The pieces are dropped into a tank of saturated salt brine to soak for about 1 hour.

The fillets are drained of excess moisture, rolled around in a box of fine salt, and the salt rubbed well into the slashes in the flesh. They are packed in layers at right angles to each other in a tub, with a scattering of salt between each layer of fish. The top is weighted to keep the flesh below the surface of the brine which is formed. They remain in salt from 5-10 days, depending on the size (larger pieces requiring more time), and weather. The fillets are kept in the salt longer during unfavorable weather.

When the meat has been sufficiently salted, the pieces are scrubbed thoroughly in fresh brine and laid in small heaps to drain for 2-3 hours. They are hung out to dry in a shady location having a good breeze, or are laid out on racks. Drying under the direct rays of the sun is apt to discolor the flesh, especially during the first days of the drying period.

At the end of the day's drying, shark fillets are piled up in small heaps with weights on top equivalent to about half the weight of the fish. The next day the fish are again dried and in the evening stacked under weights with the amount of pressure somewhat increased. The pressure is increased until it is about three times the original weight of the fillets, and curing is complete. This requires about 10 days. The fish are hung in a light smoke (the smokehouse temperature should not exceed 80 degrees F.) for one day (about 10 hours). The last step is often eliminated in good drying weather. Shark fillets are wrapped in a wax paper with a scattering of fine salt, and packed tightly in covered boxes.

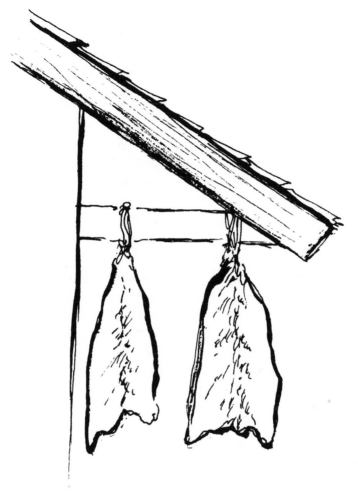

Drying a row of fish under overhanging eaves.

FISH ROE

A very good home substitute for caviar may be made from the roe of several types of fish, especially mullet, herring, chad, drum (or channel bass) and striped bass (rock). The roe must be fresh, and the skin of the roe must not be broken. The lobes of roe are first freed from blood, gall bags, and bits of intestine or black skin. After washing, the roe is allowed to drain for about 30 minutes, and rolled in fine salt. Two pounds of salt to 10 pounds of roe should be sufficient. Too much salt must not be used, as it will break the egg sacks.

The roe is taken out of the salt after 12 hours and brushed to remove any excess. The pieces are laid in direct sunlight, usually on a shed roof. During the first day of drying the roe is turned every hour. At the end of the day, it is stored indoors. Any moisture falling on the roe after drying has started will spoil or at least damage the product. Boards and weights are placed on the roe for the first night or two so as to slightly compress them.

Drying requires about one week under good drying conditions. The drying is completed if the roe feels hard when pressed between the thumb and forefinger, and when yellow to red-brown in color. The dried roe is dipped in melted beeswax. After cooling about 15 minutes, they are wrapped in waxed paper, packed in a wooden or tin box, and stored in a dry, cool place.

The roe is sliced thin, like sausage, and eaten without further preparation as an appetizer or relish.

DRYING

The curing of fish solely by drying in the open is not practiced in this country. This is because the weather is not suitable in many localities, and because the flesh of many species available to the non-commercial fisherman has a fat content of 5 percent or more, making it difficult to dry by air alone.

Another reason is that a combination of salting and drying requires much less time than air drying alone. In the North Pacific and the

Atlantic states (and for shrimp drying, in the Gulf of Mexico area) air drying offers some possibilties for those wishing to preserve fish at home.

Pressing mullet roe during drying process.

ROCKLING

This is a product introduced to this country by the Scandinavian fishermen who prepare it for home use. Large flounder, halibut, pollock, musk, hake, rock cod, or similar fish with a fat content of about 2 percent are suitable.

The fish are beheaded, leaving the collarbone, and split in two sides, removing the backbone. The sides are cut in long narrow strips, about an inch in width, and left joined together at the collarbone. They are washed thoroughly (all traces of blood must be removed) and soaked in a saturated salt brine for one hour.

They are hung out to dry, preferably in a shady place where they will not be exposed to direct sunlight. Drying requires from 1-2 weeks. When wanted for use, the rockling may be soaked for a few hours, steamed, and made into fish cakes, fish loaf, or creamed fish. It is most often eaten like jerked meat, however, without any preliminary preparation.

DRIED SHRIMP

Small shrimp not suitable for the commercial market, or large catches which cannot be used fresh, may be dried at home. The shrimp are first washed thoroughly, picking out all bits of seaweed and other waste and allowed to drain.

Prepare a salt brine in the proportion of ½ cup of salt to one quart of water. Bring to a boil. Put in whole washed shrimp. Allow them to boil for about 10 minutes, counting from the moment when the brine begins to boil after the shrimp have been added. When the meat has separated from the shell, it is cooked, which may be determined by breaking open a shrimp.

Spread the boiled shrimp in a thin layer to dry in the sun. A slanted shed roof makes an excellent drying platform. The layer of shrimp must not be more than one inch thick. Turn them at half-hour intervals the first day of drying, so that all parts of the layer will be equally dried.

The shrimp are gathered at night and stored in a dry, well-ventilated place. This must be done at the first sign of rain. Do not place a covering directly on the shrimp or they will start to heat up and sour.

Drying requires about three days if the weather is good, longer if drying conditions are unfavorable. When the shrimp are thoroughly dry and hard, place them in a sack. Beat the sack with a board. This separates the shells from the meat.

Then take a wooden frame, wire mesh screen with ¼" mesh and set it up at an angle. Shovel the mixture of meats and shells against the screen as in sifting sand. The bits of shell and waste fall through, while the meats roll down to the bottom of the screen. From 100 lbs. of green shrimp, 12-13 lbs. of dry shrimp should be obtained, together with an equal amount of shells.

The dried shrimp meat may be soaked in water for a few hours, wiped dry, rolled in butter or oil, and fried. They also are excellent in curries, gumbos, and jambalayas. When the dried meats are ground and mixed with butter and spices they make an excellent sandwich spread. The dried meats are also used with beverages as appetizers.

SMOKING

Smoking is a method which should be used much more extensively in home preservation of fishery products. When the curing is properly done, it is inexpensive and the product is of high quality, attractive in appearance and taste. Although preservation by smoking usually lasts for a shorter time than by salting, the product is much more appetizing.

If smoked fish spoils quickly and is poor in quality, it is because the smoking is improperly done. If proper attention is given to materials and methods, little difficulty should be experienced.

There are two general methods of smoking fish: hot smoking or barbecuing, and cold smoking. In hot smoking, the fish are hung near the fire usually not more than 3-4 feet distant and smoked at temperatures from 150-200 degrees F., so that they are partially or wholly cooked. Therefore, while hot smoked fish is very appetizing and requires no preparation, it will keep for only a short time.

In cold smoking, the fish are hung at some distance from a low smoldering fire and cured at temperatures of less than 90 degrees F. Degree of preservaton depends on the length of time the fish are smoked; fish smoked a few hours, for example, will keep only a short time. If an extended period of preservation is desired, fish must be cold smoked from a few days to a week or more.

HOT SMOKING

GENERAL METHOD: This process may be used with almost any species–herring, shad, trout, etc. This method is recommended if it is desired to prepare a fish that may be used immediately, without cooking. It may be kept longer without molding or souring, but even so, it will preserve for only a short time.

Split the fish along the back, just above the backbone, so that it will be open in one piece, leaving the belly solid. Scrape out all viscera, blood and membrane. Make an additional cut under the backbone for the smaller fish. For the larger fish, cut out the forward ⅗ of the backbone.

Wash thoroughly and soak in a 70 degree F. salt brine (½ cup salt to one quart water) for 30 minutes to leach out blood in the flesh. Then prepare a brine using the following ingredients, dissolved in 2½ gallons of water: 2 lbs. salt (fine grade), 1 lb. sugar, 1 oz. cure, 1 oz. crushed black peppers, 1 oz. crushed bay leaves. This is made up into a 90 degree F. brine solution.

The amounts of ingredients are increased in proportion to the amount of brine to be made. Spices may be increased or decreased according to individual taste.

The fish are held in the brine for a period of 2-4 hours, depending upon their thickness, and the desire for a lightly or heavily cured fish. Weather conditions also make a difference; the exact length of time must be determined by experiment. Rinse off the fish in cold, fresh water and hang outside in a cool, shady and breezy place to dry for about 3 hours before hanging in the smokehouse, or until a thin shiny "skin" or pellicle has formed on the surface.

For the first eight hours, keep the fire smoldering during the smoking process. The temperature should then be increased. After four hours of heavy smoking, the fire is increased until the temperature is between 130-150 degrees F. The fish are cured at this temperature for 2-3 hours, or until they have a glossy, brown surface. This partially cooks, or hot-smokes, the fish.

When smoking is finished, the fish must be cooled for 2-3 hours. They may be brushed over lightly with vegetable oil (usually cottonseed) while warm. This is sometimes done just after finishing the cold-smoking part of the process, before the temperature is increased. It gives a more attractive appearance and a light protective coating. Each fish should be wrapped in wax paper and stored in the refrigerator. Spoilage occurs more rapidly if the fish are stored in a warm place or in a cold damp place.

SMOKING EELS

Eels need not be skinned or beheaded for smoking. If you wish you may remove the head, split the abdominal cavity and remove the viscera. Eels should be cleaned thoroughly and placed in a strong brine for one full day. Remove and wash very well.

Eels are placed in a 130 degree F. smoker for about 2 hours, using gentle smoke. Increase smokehouse temperature to 165 degrees F. with a dense smoke until internal temperature of meat is 155 degrees F. at the thickest part of eel. When possible use corn cobs to smoke eels, along with regular hardwood sawdust.

FINNAN HADDIE
(Smoked Haddock)

Haddock should be cleaned and washed. The fish then is split in two from head to tail. Make a strong brine and allow the fish to season for a couple of hours. Salting depends on the size of the fish and the flavor desired. Place in smokehouse and allow to dry for 3-4 hours at a temperature of 80-85 degrees F.

After this period, allow to smoke for about 16 hours with a light smoke. Smoking then is continued for 5 more hours using a very dense smoke. Be sure you maintain 80-85 degrees F. at all times. Remove from smoker and let cool overnight.

SMOKED HALIBUT

When using a brined halibut half for smoking, be sure it is washed thoroughly in cold water. This will take at least 8 hours. Remove and permit to drain for 3-4 hours helping along by compressing excess moisture while on the rack.

Spread out on a rack used for dry salting fish and allow to remain for 2 days in dry weather. A longer time is required during damp weather. Fish then is cut up into smaller pieces, placed into a smokehouse, and kept there for about 5 days at 75-80 degrees F. using a moderate, dense smoke. When this process is completed, 100 lbs. of fish will yield 30 lbs.

421

SMOKED MACKEREL

Fresh mackerel are cured without cleaning and salted in brine for about half a day. After this period of time, they are removed from the brine and allowed to drain. The vent of each fish must be opened to allow excess brine to drain from the cavity.

Place in smoker at 75-80 degrees F. and allow to further dry and smoke for about 5 hours. After this period, increase temperature to 220 degrees F. and let cook for 2 hours using a dense smoke. Remove and let cool before using.

SMOKING CARP

Clean fish very well by removing head, fins, skin and scales. Fish then is cut up into pieces 2-3" wide. Place into 90 degree salinometer brine and remove after 12 hours. Fillets are then placed into fresh water to remove all excess salt and slime.

Place in smoker at 100 degrees F. with dampers wide open until fish has begun to dry, using a gentle smoke. Temperature then is increased to 170 degrees F. with dampers ¼ open using a dense smoke until internal temperature or thickest part of meat is 160 degrees F. Remove from smoker and let cool overnight before using.

HARD SMOKED SALMON

Split fresh salmon into 2 sides, removing the backbone. After cleaning and washing, fish is salted in a container for about 4-5 days. Remove and soak in fresh water for 3-4 hours to remove excess salt from fillets. If you are going to smoke a dry salted salmon, you must allow the salmon to soak for at least 48 hours before smoking. Fish are then allowed to drain, helped along by pressing out the excess moisture (water horsing).

Fillets are then placed into the smokehouse and allowed to dry for about 3-4 days. Be sure all dampers are open to allow good circulation and you must maintain a low temperature of around 75-80 degrees F. The fillets must be allowed to form a pellicle (a glossy brown surface).

When the fillets are properly dried, the dampers are closed to ¼ open and allowed to smoke for 5-6 more days using a medium dense smoke. Smoke salmon up to 10 days if you want a hard-dried smoked salmon that will have good keeping qualities. Be sure smoker temperature never exceeds 75-80 degrees F.

KIPPERED SALMON

To make kippered salmon you may use either the red or white meat fish. After cleaning and washing, cut into pieces 5-6" long and about 3" wide. Fillets then are placed in a strong brine to season for about 8 hours. Remove and let drain. Place fillets in the smokehouse and allow to dry for 15-20 hours maintaining a temperature of 70-80 degrees F., using a gentle smoke. Do not allow to overheat beyond these temperatures. (These temperatures are easily maintained if you are using a smoker that has a vent in the top and a damper in the bottom.)

After this period, bake the fish at about 220 degrees F. for at least a half-hour or until the thickest part of the fish has an internal temperature of 160 degrees F. When cooked, remove to cooler overnight before using.

NOTE: Freezing the fish before smoking allows you to have a much firmer product, since it helps to remove the moisture. It also is popular to dip fillets into harmless vegetable oil after brine-seasoning the fillets.

COLD SMOKING

GENERAL METHOD: Small fish, such as herring, may be cold-smoked in the round (without cleaning), but they should be gibbed. Gibbing is making a small cut just below the gills and pulling out the gills, heart and liver, leaving the belly uncut. Fish larger than 1 lb. should be spit along the back to lie flat in single piece, leaving the belly portion uncut. All traces of blood, black skin, and viscera must be removed, paying special attention to the area just under the backbone.

The head does not need to be removed. If the head is cut off, the hard bony plate just below the gills is allowed to remain, as it will be needed to carry the weight of the fish when it is hung in the smokehouse.

Wash the fish thoroughly and place them in a brine made in the proportion of 1 cup of salt to 1 gallon of water. They should be left in the brine at least 30 minutes to soak out the blood diffused through the flesh. At the end of this time, rinse in fresh cold water and drain for a few minutes.

Drop each fish singly in a shallow box of fine salt, dredged thoroughly. The fish is picked up with as much salt as will cling to the body and packed in even layers in a box or wooden tub. A small amount of salt may be scattered between each layer. The fish are left in salt from 1-12 hours depending upon weather, size of fish, fatness, length of time for which preservation is desired, and whether the fish are split or round.

Salting is an essential feature in smoking, as smoking is not a sufficient preservative in itself. Unsalted fish usually will sour or spoil under temperature and humidity conditions found in the smokehouse before they can be cured. Fish such as halibut, herring, mackerel, or salmon may be smoked after being held in salt for a year. In these cases the excess salt is removed by soaking the fish in fresh water. Fish given a heavy salt cure and held in storage for some time before smoking are not so desirable in quality as those given a light salting and smoked immediately.

When the fish are taken out of the salt, they should be rinsed thoroughly. All visible particles of salt or other waste should be scrubbed off. They are hung to dry in the shade, as direct sunlight causes rusting of the fish. If the fish are kept shaded in a breezy location, they will dry well with a clear color. If only a few fish are being dried, they may be hung in a shady undercover area where there is good cross-ventilation. An electric fan may be used if there is not much breeze. Drying racks may be made with chicken wire; the fish are placed skin-side down and turned. They will dry on both sides, but the impression of the wire detracts from the appearance.

The fish are dried until a thin skin, or pellicle, is formed on the surface. This should take about 3 hours under average conditions. If smoking is begun while the skin still is moist, the time required is longer, the color will not be as desirable, the fish will not have as good a surface, and will steam and soften in smoking. In damp weather, fish sometimes are dried by hanging in the smokehouse over a low clear fire with little smoke. But the use of electric fans or blowers is a better procedure.

A low smoldering fire is started an hour or two before the fish are hung in the smokehouse. The fire must not give off too much smoke during the first 8-12 hours, if the total cure is 24 hours, or for the first 24 hours, if the cure is longer. The temperature in the smokehouse should not be higher than 90 degrees F. in northern states and the Pacific Northwest.

If available, a thermometer should be used in controlling smokehouse temperatures; if not, a simple test is to insert your hand in the smokehouse—if the air feels distinctly warm, the temperature is too high.

When the first part of the smoking process is ended, a dense smoke may be built up and maintained for the balance of the cure. If the fish are to be kept for about 2 weeks, they should be smoked for 24 hours; if for a longer time, smoking may require 5 days or more. Hard-smoked herring may require 3-4 weeks.

A few general rules must be followed in tending the fire. It must be kept low and steady; where hardwood sawdust is not available, chips and bark do almost as well. The fire must not be allowed to die out at night, nor should it be built up before leaving, as this will create too much heat. It must be tended regularly during the night.

The general method of cold smoking may be used with most fish if the proper consideration is given to size, climate, humidity, salting, and other limiting factors.

FILLETS: Any white-fleshed "lean" fish which will produce fillets weighing more than 1 lb. may be used. Cut the fish in fillets, removing the backbone and skin. Cover with a 90 degree F. brine and hold for two hours. Remove and drain for 10-15 minutes and air-dry for 2 hours. Hang across a 3-sided smokestick. Cure over a fire with a fairly light smoke for 4 hours at a temperature not higher than 90 degrees F.

Turn the fillets so that the side resting on the smokestick is uppermost, and smoke 4 hours longer. Smother the fire so that a dense cloud of smoke is obtained, and smoke until the fillets are a deep straw yellow, turning the fillets once or twice so that both sides will be evenly colored. This operation should take about 6 hours. Cool the fillets and wrap each separately in waxed paper. Store in a cool, dry place. They will keep about 10 days.

SALMON: All species of salmon, steelhead and lake trout may be smoked. The general cold-smoking method is most commonly used, but the following method gives a more appetizing product.

The heads should be cut off and the fish gutted. Split into two sides and remove the backbone. To do this, the shoulder of the salmon is forced down on a sharp-pointed nail protruding from the cleaning table to prevent slipping. Short incisions are made under the anal fin, just above and below the backbone. With the upper lug or shoulder tip of the fish held by the left hand, begin cutting at the shoulder above the backbone, holding the blade steady, with the edge at a slight downward angle touching the bone. Take the whole side off with one sweep of the knife.

If the work has been done well, little flesh will be left on the backbone, and the side will be smooth. A thin line of backbone edge should run down the center of the side. To remove the second side, a cut is made at the shoulder just under the backbone. With the edge of the knife blade resting against the backbone at a slight upward angle, give one sweep of the knife down to the root of the tail. This separates the backbone from the flesh without removing the fish from the nail. The two sides should be similar.

Wash the sides thoroughly, and trim ragged edges and blood clots. Blood remaining in the veins along the belly cavity should be removed by pressing it toward the back either with the fingers or the blade of the knife. If the blood is not removed, it will harden and discolor the flesh.

The sides are placed in a tub of 90-degree salinometer brine (a saturated salt solution) and chilled with ice. This removes diffused blood, makes the sides a little firmer, and stops oil from oozing out of the flesh. The fish should remain in the brine for 60-90 minutes.

The sides should be drained for 15-20 minutes. A shallow box is filled with a salting mixture made in the following proportions:

2 lbs. salt
1 oz. brown sugar
1 oz. Prague Powder No. 1
1 oz. white pepper
1 oz. ground bay leaves

1 oz. ground allspice

1 oz. ground cloves

1 oz. ground mace

This amount should be enough for about 20 lbs. of fish. The salmon is placed in the box, one side at a time, and dredged in the mixture, which is rubbed lightly into the flesh. The sides are packed in a tub or other suitable container, with as much of the curing mixture as will cling to the flesh. A loose-fitting cover is placed on and weighed down.

The fish are left for 8-12 hours, then rinsed and scrubbed to remove all traces of the salting mixture. The sides are fixed on hangers and dried in the air for about 6 hours. If air drying conditions are not favorable, fans may be used. Hang the fish in the smokehouse and smoke in a gentle heat (not more than 100 degrees F.) for 8 hours. Build up a dense smoke and continue the cure for 16-24 hours at a temperature not higher than 70 degrees F. To obtain a product having the maximum of preservation, the second part of the smoking period should be 48 hours.

The fish should be allowed to cool for several hours before handling, then brushed with vegetable oil and stored in a cool, dry place.

SMOKING METHOD FOR SPORTSMEN

Fishermen who wish to preserve their catch immediately have used this method successfully. This method may be used with almost any fresh or salt-water fish.

Cut off the heads and gut the fish. A cut is made above the backbone almost to the tail. Another cut is made under the backbone, which is broken off, leaving not more than ⅕ of the tail section uncut. The fish should lie flat in one piece. The flesh is scored longitudinally from head to tail, with the cuts about ¼" deep and 1" apart. After washing thoroughly and wiping dry, the fish are rubbed inside and out with a mixture of 1 oz. pepper to 1 lb. salt.

Store the fish in a cool place overnight and rinse carefully the next morning. Two or three thin, flat wooden sticks are fastened across the back to keep the fish spread open. The roughly pointed sticks pass through the skin. Dry the fish in a breezy place until the surface mosisture has dried and a thin skin formed on the surface.

A shallow fire pit is dug, about 3 feet in diameter, and a fire is started while the fish are drying so that a good bed of red coals will be ready immediately. Hardwood should be used. When the fish have dried—about 3 hours under average conditions—each fish is fastened to the fork end of a stick, about 4-5 feet in length. The other end of the stick is thrust into the ground so that it hangs over the bed of coals at an angle. The sticks should be placed so the fish will not touch each other.

Two or three fish may be fastened across a stick and thrust into the ground, as in the first method, but must not be placed as close to the fire.

A tripod of poles is then erected above the smokesticks; on this is laid a thick thatching of green boughs and grass. A hole may be left in the thatching near the ground. Green wood is placed on the coals, building up a dense smoke, and the hole is covered. It will be necessary to place additional green wood on the fire from time to time. The fish are smoked from 6-18 hours, depending on size and degree of smoke-cure desired.

After cooling, the smoked fish are wrapped and stored in a cool, dry place. They should keep from 2-4 weeks.

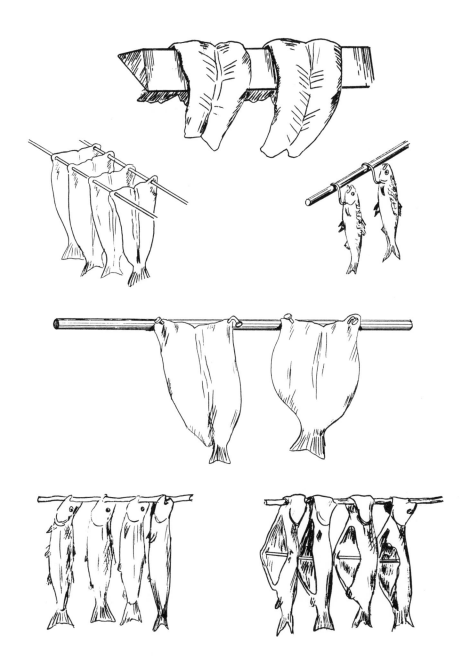

Methods of hanging fish for smoking.

PICKLED FISH

While the term pickled fish is sometimes used to include fish cured in brine, it should be applied only to those products in which vinegar is used. Only a few types of fish are preservd commercially by pickling, but almost any species may be prepared for home use.

Herring is the most important fish for pickling; both sea and river herring are used. Other popular species are haddock, mullet, catfish, salmon, carp, buffalofish, eels, lake herring, lake trout, pike, pickerel and shellfish, especially shrimp, oysters, clams and mussels. Practically all other food fish, both fresh and salt water, are pickled by non-commercial, or home methods.

Preservation by this method usually keeps for shorter periods than by salting and drying. The difference may be due to local weather conditions, but depends on the species of fish (certain fish do not remain fresh as long as others), and the method of pickling.

The acetic acid content of the vinegar is also a factor. To stop bacterial growth, an acetic acid of 15 percent is required. The ordinary commercial vinegar contains 5-6 percent, and even this may be too strong for the average palate. Pickling solutions containing as little as 3 percent acetic acid, however, will retard spoilage for a week or more, and the product may even be preserved for months if stored in a cool, dry place at a temperature of about 50 degrees F.

Distilled vinegar is preferred for pickling since it has a standardized acetic acid content. Cider or other fruit vinegars usually are considered unsuitable, since the acetic acid content is extremely variable and the fruit residues in the vinegar may give the fish an off-taste. Spices used in pickling should be fresh. Best results are secured by buying fresh whole spices and making up the mixture by recipe at the time it is to be used, rather than by the use of prepared mixtures.

HERRING

Ordinary salt herring may be pickled in vinegar, but herring not specially cured for spicing have a shorter period of preservation, are darker in color, lack flavor, are tougher and are more fibrous in texture.

430

The first step in curing herring for pickling is to cut off the head and trim off the thin fish belly to the vent. The herring are cleaned thoroughly, paying special attention to removal of the kidney which is the dark streak along the backbone. The fish are washed thoroughly in fresh water and drained.

Pack the drained fish loosely in a crock and cover with a brine testing to 80 degrees salinometer (⅝ cup salt to 1 quart water) and containing sufficient vinegar to give it an acidity of 2.5 percent. This requires about equal quantities of water and distilled vinegar.

The fish are left in this brine until the salt has "struck through," but must be removed before the skin starts to wrinkle or lose color. Length of cure depends upon the judgment of the pickler and varies with the temperature, freshness, and size of the fish. The average time is about 5 days, but may be from 3-7 days.

When the herrings are judged sufficiently cured, they are repacked more tightly. Very little dry salt is spattered around them and they are covered with a salt vinegar brine one-half the strength just stated. The crock is stored in a cool place. At this stage the fish cannot be kept for more than 2-3 weeks.

Final processes in the manufacture of spiced herring include the soaking of the herring in a tub of cold water for 8 hours. Remove the fish, drain and place in a solution of vinegar, salt and water for 48 hours. This solution is made up in the proportions of 1 gallon of 6 percent distilled vinegar, 1 gallon of water and 1 lb. of salt. Some prefer to eliminate this last step, utilizing the herring immediately after they have been freshened in cold water.

CUT SPICED HERRING

Cut the vinegar-salt cured herring across the body in pieces of 1-1½" long. Pack in layers in a crock with sliced onions, bay leaves and spices. Cover with vinegar diluted with water in which the sugar is dissolved. Allow to stand in a cool place at least 24 hours before using.

The cut spiced herring may be repacked in pint or quart jars. If packed in jars, the herring may be stored in a refrigerator where they will remain in good condition for as long as 6 months. Add to each jar a few fresh spices, a bay leaf or two, and a slice of lemon at the side of the jar to give an attractive appearance. Rubber jar rings should not be used, since the vinegar causes them to deteriorate.

The quantities given in the formula below are sufficient for 10 lbs. of cleaned herring. Whole spices are used in all recipes, unless otherwise specified.

1 qt. vinegar	1 oz. red peppers
1 pt. water	1 oz. white peppers
3 ozs. allspice	1 oz. sugar
2 ozs. bay leaves	1 oz. cloves
2 ozs. mustard seed	1 sliced onion
1 oz. black pepper	

*NOTE: for herrings in wine sauce use 1 qt. wine in place of the vinegar and use 1 pt. vinegar in place of the water.

The vinegar-salt cured herrings are cut into two fillets, and the backbone is removed. Each fillet then is rolled around a small piece of dill pickle and fastened with a wooden toothpick. The rolls are packed on end in a crock. Sliced onions, bay leaves, and the spices used in the following sauce formula are scattered on the bottom and between layers:

Slowly cook 1 quart vinegar, sliced onions, and 1 oz. sugar until the onions are soft. Add the following:

1 oz. mustard seeds	1 oz. cracked whole ginger
1 oz. black pepper	1 oz. bay leaves
1 oz. cracked cinnamon stick	½ oz. cloves

This quantity is sufficient for 10 lbs. of cut herring. The sauce is simmered, *not boiled,* for 45 minutes. The spices are strained to

432

pack with the rollmops. The sauce is cooled and poured over the fish until covered. Allow to stand for 2-3 days before using. Rollmops will remain in good condition for about 2 weeks in summer, and from 6-8 weeks in winter, at ordinary storage temperatures. This product may be kept much longer if held in a refrigerator.

RUSSIAN SARDINES

Wash and scale 10 lbs. of small herrings (from 7-10"); remove the gills and as much of the intestines as possible by pulling them out through the gill flap without tearing the throat or belly. Rinse again, drain, and pack in a crock. Cover with 3 parts of distilled vinegar and 1 part water. Allow to stand for 12 hours. Make up a mixture of the following ingredients:

2 lbs. fine salt	1 oz. bay leaves
1 lbs. powdered sugar	1 oz. cloves
1 oz. allspice	1 oz. ginger
1 oz. pepper	1 oz. hops
½ oz. Prague Powder No. 1	½ oz. nutmeg

The spices should be finely ground and thoroughly blended.

After the fish have been drained, dredge them in the mixture and pack in a crock, belly up. A small additional amount of the mixture may be scattered between each layer. The layers should be packed at right angles to each other with the top one packed backs up.

Scatter the balance of the spice-curing mixture over the top layer and weigh it down so that the fish will be entirely covered when the brine forms. Some people also scatter diced onions, ground or sliced horse radish and capers between each layer. The amount required for 10 lbs. of small herring is ½ lb. of onions, 1 lb. horse radish and a small bottle of capers (about 2½ ozs.). The fish are allowed to cure for 10-14 days before using. Under proper storage conditions they should keep from several months to a year.

HERRING IN CREAM SAUCE

INGREDIENTS
1 pint sour cream
1 pint sweet cream
1 pint white wine dry
½ pint distilled vinegar
½ oz. pickling spice (mixed spices)
2 cups thin sliced onions

The above ingredients are enough for about 1 gallon of mild cured herrings. The fillets should be soaked in cold water for 2 to 3 hours keeping the melts separate. Drain fillets of excess moisture. Milts are rubbed through a fine sieve and boiled together with fillets, mixed spices, wine and vinegar. Gently boil for 5 minutes, let cool and then remove the spices. Pack fillets into a large container placing the sliced onions along as well. Blend sour cream, sweet cream with cooled vinegar, and wine and cover fillets in the container. Marinate in cool place for 4 days before using.

PICKLED CARP OR HADDOCK

Clean the fish carefully, skin, and cut into fillets, removing the backbone. Divide the fillet into 1 to 2 inch lengths and dredge the pieces in fine salt. Pick them up with as much salt as will cling to the flesh and pack in a crock or pan. Leave in the salt 12 hours, rinse off salt and soak in fresh water for ½ hour. Cook the vinegar, water, sugar, garlic and spices for 10 minutes, add the fish and cook 10 minutes longer. Pack the cooked fish in sterilized jars, adding some chopped onions a few spices and a slice of lemon to each jar. Strain the spice-vinegar sauce and bring the sauce to a boil. Fill the jars immediately and seal tight. The mixture recommended is as follows:

1½ pints distilled vinegar	1 tsp. cloves
1½ pints water	1 tbsp. allspice
2 cups chopped onion	1 tbsp. mustard seed
1 clove chopped garlic	1 tbsp. bay leaves
	1 tsp. black peppers

This amount is enough for at least 5 lbs. of fish, cleaned and prepared.

PICKLED EELS

Clean and skin the eels and cut into pieces 5/8 inch thick. Wash, drain, dredge in fine salt, and allow to stand for 1 hour. Rinse off the salt, wipe the pieces dry, and rub with a cut clove or garlic. Brush with melted butter or salad oil, and boil until the surface is light brown. Place pieces of cooked eel on absorbent paper. When cool, pack them in layers in a crock with a scattering of sliced onion, allspice, bay leaves, mustard seed, whole cloves, peppers and mace between layers of the fish. Weigh the mixture down to keep it compressed. Store for 24 hours. Add distilled vinegar in proportions of 3 parts vinegar and 1 part water, sufficient to cover the pieces. Cover the crock tightly and allow to stand 48 hours before using. For 10 pounds of eels the ingredients are as follows:

1 qt. distilled vinegar   ½ oz. mustard seeds
1 pt. water   ½ oz. cloves
1 oz. allspice   ½ oz. black peppers
1 oz. bay leaves   ½ oz. mace

PICKLED SALMON

Cut 10 pounds of salmon into individual serving portions. Wash well in cold water, drain and dredge in fine salt. After ½ hour rinse off the salt and simmer the salmon until done. Place the warm fish in an earthenware crock and cover with a vinegar spice sauce made as follows:

1 qt. distilled vinegar   1 tbsp. mustard seed
1 qt. water   1 tbsp. cloves
1 cup olive oil*   1 tbsp. black peppers
1 cup sliced onions   1 tbsp. bay leaves
1 tbsp. white peppers

Cook the onions in olive oil slowly until they are yellow and soft. Add the rest of the ingredients and simmer slowly for 45 minutes. Allow the sauce to cool, and pour over the fish, making sure that all the pieces are covered. Allow to stand for 24 hours before using. This method may be used for mackerel, shad and other large fish.
*Peanut oil or cottonseed oil may be used in place of olive oil.

PICKLED CLAMS, OYSTER AND MUSSELS

Scrub the shells well and steam just enough to open the shells. Save the liquor or nectar. Remove the meats from the shells: cool meats and nectar separately. When cool, pack the meat in sterilized jars with a few bay leaves and whole cloves. Add a slice or two of lemon to each jar.

Strain the liquor obtained in steaming. To each quart of liquor, add one-half pint distilled vinegar, one-half teaspoon each of cloves, allspice and red peppers, with a teaspoon of cracked, whole mace. Simmer for 45 minutes. When cool, pour into the jars and seal. Store in a cool, dark place. Pickled oysters and mussels become easily "light struck" and turn dark if exposed to light.

FRIED FISHCAKES

Fried fishcakes are very simple to make and provide another possibility for doing something else with an over-abundance of fish.

INGREDIENTS FOR 5 LBS.
5 lbs. potatoes, peeled and diced
2½ lbs. fish
8-12 whole eggs, beaten
¼ lb. butter
8 ozs. chopped onions
1 tsp. ground white pepper

The fish is shredded into smaller pieces and placed in water along with the diced potatoes. The water is brought to boiling and then reduced to simmer. Cook until tender. The water is then drained and the potatoes and fish are allowed to cool. After cooling, grind through a ³⁄₁₆" grinder plate. The fish and potatoes are then placed in a mixing bowl. Mix thoroughly with remaining ingredients until evenly distributed. This mixture is then made into patties or cakes and dipped into fine bread crumbs. Deep fat fry until light brown.

LOX

Lox is a cold-smoked fish — it is not cooked, but is ready to eat after this process is finished. Lox is a great favorite of many Jewish people and can always be found at Jewish delis, restaurants or markets.

However, lox can now be found on the menus of virtually every big-city hotel in this country. It is not uncommon to pay $10-$15 per pound for good lox. An egg omelet with onions and lox has long been one of my favorite breakfasts.

The following recipe is one that was passed on to me from Mr. Gerald Cone, Box 1005, Suquamish, WA.

Chinook salmon is the best for making lox because it is the fattiest of the entire salmon family. However, you may substitute steel head or silver salmon with good results.

INGREDIENTS FOR 5 LBS. OF LOX

½ cup of kosher salt
½ cup of sugar (either white or brown)
1 teaspoon ground white pepper
1 level teaspoon of prague powder #1

Scale and fillet the salmon. Cut several slits through the skin on each fillet. Then dredge the fillets with the above mixture in a glass or plastic container. Then cover the fish with a board (preferably good hardwood), placing a weight of approximately 3 pounds on top. The fish is then left in the salt for 48 hours. The fillets should be about ¾" thick. If for some reason they are thicker, fish should then be left in the salt longer.

After two days, remove the fish from the salt and rinse with cold water. Fillets must then be dried very well, which will take from 4-6 hours. After this period the fish will become tacky. Drying is best done on racks in a cool, well-ventilated room but kept out of drafts.

Place fillets in a cool smokehouse where the temperature will not exceed 85-90 degrees F. It is important to maintain this temperature for at least 6 hours. Then remove the fillets from the smoker and brush them very lightly with vegetable oil while still warm. Fillets are then placed in a cooler or refrigerator for a day or two until they become firm.

This is one of the more difficult recipes in this book. This is because you must use some sort of control to maintain the 85-90 degrees F. temperature. If you smoke the fillets at a higher temperature you will not have the flavor of lox, but rather of cooked salmon.

The raw, smoked, seasoned lox has a very definite and unique flavor. It must be cold-smoked. The commercial producers of lox can easily maintain these low temperatures, as they have controls built into their smokers.

In addition, a smoke generator is also used. The smoke is pumped into the smoker by blowing it in through a large-diameter pipe over some distance. This allows some of the heat to dissipate or cool off before it reaches the smokehouse.

BEEF CHART

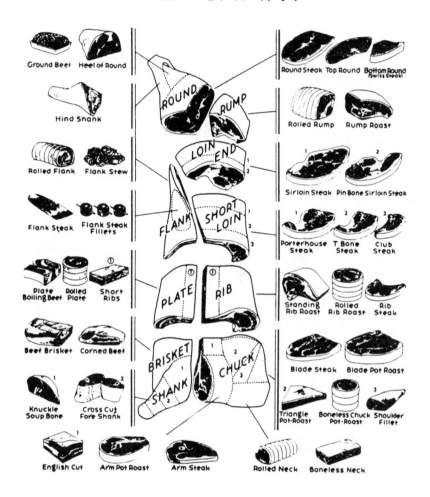

Ground Beef   Heel of Round

Round Steak   Top Round   Bottom Round (Swiss Steak)

Hind Shank

Rolled Rump   Rump Roast

Rolled Flank   Flank Stew

Sirloin Steak   Pin Bone Sirloin Steak

Flank Steak   Flank Steak Fillets

Porterhouse Steak   T Bone Steak   Club Steak

Plate Boiling Beef   Rolled Plate   Short Ribs

Standing Rib Roast   Rolled Rib Roast   Rib Steak

Beef Brisket   Corned Beef

Blade Steak   Blade Pot Roast

Knuckle Soup Bone   Cross Cut Fore Shank

Triangle Pot-Roast   Boneless Chuck Pot-Roast   Shoulder Fillet

English Cut   Arm Pot Roast   Arm Steak

Rolled Neck   Boneless Neck

ROUND   RUMP   LOIN END   FLANK   SHORT LOIN   PLATE   RIB   BRISKET   CHUCK   SHANK

439

LAMB CHART

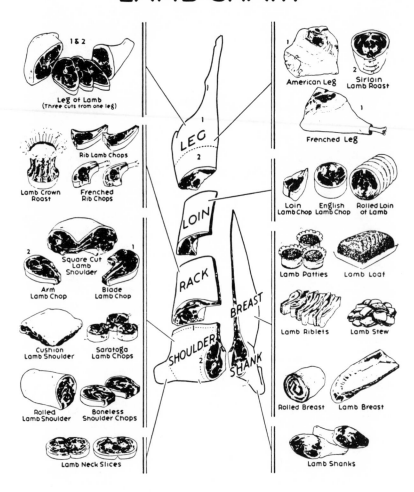

Leg of Lamb
(Three cuts from one leg)

1 & 2

Rib Lamb Chops

Lamb Crown Roast

Frenched Rib Chops

Square Cut Lamb Shoulder

2   1

Arm Lamb Chop

Blade Lamb Chop

Cushion Lamb Shoulder

Saratoga Lamb Chops

Rolled Lamb Shoulder

Boneless Shoulder Chops

Lamb Neck Slices

LEG

1

2

LOIN

RACK

SHOULDER

2

BREAST

SHANK

American Leg

1

Sirloin Lamb Roast

2

Frenched Leg

1

Loin Lamb Chop

English Lamb Chop

Rolled Loin of Lamb

Lamb Patties

Lamb Loaf

Lamb Riblets

Lamb Stew

Rolled Breast

Lamb Breast

Lamb Shanks

440

PORK CHART

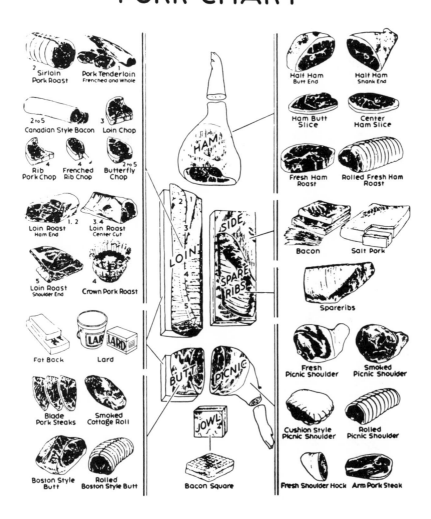

2 Sirloin Pork Roast

1 Pork Tenderloin Frenched and Whole

2 to 5 Canadian Style Bacon

3 Loin Chop

4 Rib Pork Chop

4 Frenched Rib Chop

2 to 5 Butterfly Chop

1, 2 Loin Roast Ham End

3, 4 Loin Roast Center Cut

5 Loin Roast Shoulder End

4 Crown Pork Roast

Fat Back

Lard

Blade Pork Steaks

Smoked Cottage Roll

Boston Style Butt

Rolled Boston Style Butt

HAM

LOIN

SIDE

SPARE RIBS

BUTT

PICNIC

JOWL

Bacon Square

Half Ham Butt End

Half Ham Shank End

Ham Butt Slice

Center Ham Slice

Fresh Ham Roast

Rolled Fresh Ham Roast

Bacon

Salt Pork

Spareribs

Fresh Picnic Shoulder

Smoked Picnic Shoulder

Cushion Style Picnic Shoulder

Rolled Picnic Shoulder

Fresh Shoulder Hock

Arm Pork Steak

441

VEAL CHART

Veal
Rump Roast

Rolled Veal
Rump Roast

Sirloin
Veal
Steak

Loin
Veal Chop

Kidney
Veal Chop

Veal
Crown Roast

Veal Rib Chop
(Frenched)

Veal
Rib Roast

Blade
Veal Roast

Arm
Veal Roast

Blade
Veal Steak

Arm
Veal Steak

Rolled Veal
Shoulder Roast

City Chicken

ROUND

LOIN

RIB

BREAST

SHOULDER

SHANK

Heel of
Veal Round

Veal
Hind Shank

Veal Round
Steak (cutlet)

Veal
Round Roast

Veal Scallops

Veal Rosettes

Veal Breast

Mock Chicken
Legs

Veal Loaf

Veal Riblets

Veal Stew

Veal Fore Shank

Veal Patties

442

CHAPTER XV

Wholesome Meat Act

THE WHOLESOME MEAT ACT

Through the years I have received many letters at my mail-order business asking me various questions about starting up sausage kitchens and the curing and smoking of meats. Most of these letters pertain to the "Wholesome Meat Act," even though the people who wrote me these letters did not know it at the time.

There is no question that "The Wholesome Meat Act" is one of the greatest pieces of legislation enacted in this century. Most likely, many consumers never have even heard of these new laws, which have helped to clean up the entire meat processing industry, from the smallest to the largest plants in the United States. Because of these new laws, many of the old establishments simply closed their doors and went out of business. The buildings were so old they never could meet the new requirements, and no amount of remodeling could bring them up to the new standards of "The Wholesome Meat Act."

As I go along, you will be able to compare some of these new standards against the old ones and see how important these new standards are.

To begin with, all cities have health departments that regulate the entire food industry. In any given city, a food processing plant could fall under the jurisdiction of the city, the county or the state health departments. On the surface, it would appear that it is not such a bad thing to have all these health standards of sanitation. In the past, however, the problem was that you had to deal with three different agencies and three different sets of rules and regulations. Not only were there no books or guidelines to go by, but what was right or wrong was up to the discretion of individual inspectors. I actually have experienced three different answers to a simple problem, from three different health inspectors of the same agency. In any case, "The Wholesome Meat Act" has helped to eliminate these problems.

Today, the same set of specifications applies to both the state-inspected establishments and the federally inspected plants. Many of the city and county health departments have adopted these new specifications. Thanks to "The Wholesome Meat Act," we now have a book of rules and regulations that we can refer to. Very simply, this HANDBOOK 191 should be used as the ROBERTS RULES OF ORDER for all the health departments of this country.

Needless to say, before you start constructing or remodeling a meat processing plant, there now are guidelines to work with. This handbook clearly states how the building must be constructed in order to be able to apply for a state or federal inspection program. It probably is worthy to note that if your establishment will sell 25% or more of its products wholesale, this automatically places you under the laws of "The Wholesome Meat Act." Naturally, if you do not plan to sell these amounts wholesale, the local health departments then have the jurisdiction over the inspection program in your plant. This is quite important to know, as many people just go into a retail business and then slowly start into the wholesale business as they grow. You do not need state or federal inspection if you sell fewer than 25% of your products wholesale.

Even though the new specifications are the same for the state-inspected establishments as well as the federally inspected, there is one major difference between them.

When being inspected by the USDA (United States Department of Agriculture) you are allowed to ship your products across state lines; you cannot ship across the state lines if you have a state inspection program. Since there always is more potential to do business in another state, it then is obvious why most people choose to have the USDA inspection. Why not; it doesn't cost any more.

In recent years, however, there has been considerable talk about letting the state-inspected plants ship to the adjoining states, but nothing has come of this to date.

BUILDING SPECIFICATIONS

Now that you have HANDBOOK 191, you will have a set of blueprints made up for the local building department. In addition, there is a complete set that is made up for USDA, including a floor plan of the entire building and all the equipment that will be installed in it. These blueprints usually are coordinated with the local building departments, and there is very little to overcome as far as problems go.

The specifications that have to be met to have a USDA or state inspection far exceed the local building codes, so it's quite obvious there won't be any problems with the local building department.

It is interesting to note that for many years meat processing always was done in the early hours of the morning. This was mainly because the temperatures are always cooler at this time of the day. For the most part this is true in many parts of the United States, but not so in the southwestern part of the country. In the southwest, the temperatures often will reach 90 degrees F. and beyond 100 degrees F. and stay there for days and even weeks. As you can see, processing meat in the early hours of the day means very little there.

For the most part, from the largest to the smallest plants, they were operating without refrigerated conditions. With the new specifications today, all meat processing areas must be refrigerated and must maintain 50 degrees F. or lower during working hours. This by itself was a tremendous accomplishment of the "Wholesome Meat Act."

PROCESSING

Under these new laws, there are specified times that are negotiated with the USDA for the establishments to do their processing. This usually is a simple 5-day week from Monday through Friday, consisting of 40 hours. The starting and quitting times are arrived at by mutual agreement, and it is between these hours that you are permitted to process the meat.

Keep in mind that the USDA pays the wages of these inspectors. If there is any overtime to be worked, the establishment has to pay the wages at time and one half. These overtime wages need not be expensive, since many times there is more than one establishment that wishes to work extra hours. In this case, they simply split the cost of overtime wages among themselves, which in turn reduces the individual cost. As stated earlier, this would only pertain to the smaller cities with small processing plants. When talking about the large meat processor, there generally is more than one inspector on the premises on a full-time basis.

I think it is worthy to note that you can process meat a full 8 hours of each day with clean-up time not included. There are many little shops that operate in this manner. They process meat for a full eight hours and then clean up for as long as it takes them. In the smaller cities, the inspectors generally inspect several establishments. Since the cities are small, the meat-processing plants usually are small as well. The inspector goes in and out of these plants at random to make his inspections more effective.

In each new establishment that is built according to the "Wholesome Meat Act," a private office must be provided for the USDA inspector. This may seem ridiculous to some people, but these inspectors must have some place to do their paperwork and file it as well. Even though these buildings are built to meet the requirements of the new specifications, the inspector must be there every day to see that sanitary conditions are maintained at all times and kept at the highest possible level. This includes the outside of the premises as well.

It has been my experience that these inspectors are very reasonable people. They will work along with everybody and help as many as they can. If there are any problems, it is best to get them taken care of. This makes the job easier for the inspector and the owners as well. The inspectors fill out reports each week and send them into the regional office of the USDA. These reports consist of sanitation for the past week from the particular establishments that they inspect.

Another of the inspector's duties is to check the internal temperatures of the meats that are being smoked and cooked. This generally applies to all products that are made with pork or have pork added to them. Since pork can contain trichinae from time to time, there is a USDA regulation specifying that all pork that is smoked must be cooked enough to destroy the trichinae.

Surprising as it may seem, these pork products have to be cooked only until the internal temperature reaches 138 degrees F. When this temperature is reached, the trichinae are destroyed. The industry, however, usually cooks the meat to an internal temperature of around 152 degrees F. This doesn't sound like it is much higher, but at these temperatures the meat is completely cooked. The 138 degrees F. the USDA requires would only make your meat rare or medium rare, so the 152 degrees F. makes it completely cooked.

There are times when some processors might cook the meat to an internal temperature of 160 degrees F., but this is not often the case. The higher the temperature used to cook meat, the greater the risk of shrinkage in the smokehouse. When you are in business for yourself and you have shrinkage in your smokehouse, you then have a financial problem and it's all going up in smoke. Strange as it may seem, all the hot dogs and luncheon meats you buy at your favorite market or store are only cooked until the internal temperature reaches about 152 degrees F.

In either case, the inspector actually has to see that this meat is cooked to the required specification, and make a report for each batch inspected. Random tests are taken with an accurate thermometer to be sure that the proper temperature is maintained. In addition, the inspector also takes a sample of the sausage and has a fat analysis made.

Another USDA specification is that sausage, hot dogs, luncheon meat, etc. may not contain more than 30% fat. In the smaller cities, these samples usually are mailed to the nearest regional office, where there will be a complete test to analyze their fat content. In the larger cities, they would most likely be delivered by the inspector the same day to an agency that would have a computer. The large manufacturers of sausage usually have their own computers to do this work right on the premises, if not right in the production rooms.

The monumental amount of sausage that a large manufacturer makes at one time just about necessitates this computer. The computer can make an analysis right on the spot and the inspector can make out the report right there. In addition, if a particular batch of sausage has a fat content that is too high, lean meat can be added right on the spot to bring it up to the required specifications.

I think that it should be brought out that the USDA is not completely unreasonable in their demands when it comes to the fat content of your sausages. If you own a small sausage kitchen and are a little high in the fat content on the analysis, they won't come in and close you down. They understand that without a computer it is difficult to keep up to this specification.

But if your analysis consistently shows more than 30% fat content, you will develop problems. A good sausage maker usually can tell when he is going over the 30% fat content. I have always said that a good sausage should never have over 20% fat content, so I never had this problem. The fact of the matter is that meat can be bought today from meat packers who will give you the content you specify.

If you are going to operate a sausage kitchen under the laws of "The Wholesome Meat Act" you should know that any and all materials that will be used to process the meat must be purchased from approved dealers. Be it paper, sawdust, spices, soap or chemicals, there are companies that sell this material and have a USDA number, the same as any meat processing plant would have. Generally, the dealers have the number handy, to let you know that they are on the approved list to be able to sell their products to you.

If you don't know if the product you want to buy is approved, ask your inspector. The inspectors usually have a book with this information, and if it's not in the book, they will get it for you. In addition, when the product arrives, the inspector will see if it is on the approved list. In fact, the inspector must check all the products entering a USDA establishment. It also is the job of the inspector to date all the boxes that contain meat when they first enter the building. This means that you would have to rotate your meat and use the oldest meat first, which is nothing more than good business sense. As you can see, an office for the inspector is not so far-fetched. After all, an inspector can keep busy even in a small meat processing plant.

In further designing the "Wholesome Meat Act," the electrical specifications play a very important role today. The new buildings must have enough lighting in the processing areas and coolers to have what is called "foot-candle power." There are no longer dark and dingy plants in operation. The buildings must now have adequate lighting, which helps to provide better sanitation and keeps dirt from accumulating.

PLUMBING

Tremendous improvements also have been made in the area of plumbing. To begin with, you no longer are able to operate a meat processing plant by depending on a septic tank for your sewage disposal. The sewage must now be fed into the municipal sewage system.

When the drawings are first made up, adequate floor drains must be provided for in the plans. Depending on what the rooms are to be used for, two or three floor drains are adequate in a small operation. These floor drains have a 4" opening and also a device with which to catch large particles of waste. This eliminates the grease traps, which are nothing more than breeding grounds for bacteria and odors. Floor drains also are allowed in walk-in coolers. This makes each room easy to clean and wash one at a time.

Along with these floor drains, the new specifications call for a separate system for the toilet, shower, and sink sewage. In addition, these sewer lines will have built into them a backstop on the outside of the building, just before your sewers are connected to the municipal system. What this system does is prevent a backup of sewage into your building, in case the municipal system should become overloaded. A backstop is simply a round disc that is built into your sewer line which opens up with the sewage is leaving the buiding. If the sewage started to enter the sewer lines toward your building, the backstop would close up against a ridge in the pipe and the more pressure that would be applied on the backstop, the tighter it would stay closed.

CEMENT FLOORS

To complement this plumbing system, the specifications now call for a special way to pour your cement floors. The specifications require that all floors must be poured and finished in such a manner that they have a fall of ⅛" to ¼" per foot from all outside walls towards the floor drains. The ⅛" is really a drastic fall in a 10 ft. stretch, even though it doesn't seem so. At any rate, it's a good specification and prevents water from lying in puddles, helping to breed bacteria.

After the floors are poured, the USDA has placed safety over the sanitation factor. Rather than have a smooth finish, they insist on a rough broom finish in the entire building. Since processing meat is somewhat messy and you may drop pieces of meat and fat on the floor, a smooth finish would make them dangerous to walk on. A broom finish makes the floors rough and easier to walk on, but a little harder to clean. There are good chemicals available today that help to clean the floors easily and keep them sanitized as well.

Strangely enough, a regular kitchen sink is not needed in a sausage kitchen. You can get by without one. All the utensils that are used can be washed on the sausage stuffing table, since the specifications call for a mixture of hot water and steam with which to wash all the equipment. Steam by itself will not wash anything. You need the volume of the hot water to blast off the unwanted particles.

If you can make an adjustment on the hot water tank to heat your water to 180 degrees F., you need not bother with steam. If you are going to cook sausage, however, you would be wise to have the steam installed, since steam cabinets are the best way to cook sausage and the fastest as well.

Elimination of a kitchen sink should not be confused with the wash room sinks, because a sink is required in each room and they must be of the type operated with a foot or knee-type lever. Conventional bathroom sinks are not allowed, because the handles on the faucets will breed bacteria.

Frankly, it's a good idea to confer with the USDA people before you buy equipment of any kind. It also should be noted that the USDA will approve used equipment that is in good condition, so don't get the idea that all equipment must be bought new.

I generally have covered the more expensive parts of building a structure to get USDA approval. There are a number of other items: air curtains on all outside doors, and smooth finished inside walls, for example. If you are intent upon opening a meat processing plant, these are some of the requirements you must meet today. It would be best to contact a meat inspector at one of the locally-inspected processing plants or your nearest local health department. All health departments are aware of "The Wholesome Meat Act" today.

CHAPTER XVI

Opening a
Sausage Kitchen

OPENING A SAUSAGE KITCHEN

After writing "Great Sausage Recipes and Meat Curing" and tens of thousands of copies later, I've been deluged with letters for one reason or another. A great number of these letters were from people who wanted to start a sausage-making business for the first time. These people soon found out how good home-made sausage could be, and that it really wasn't all that difficult to learn. Many of these people started to sell their products, especially when they discovered they could make a better and a much cheaper product than they would pay for in a market.

In fact, they also found out that they were making quality sausage that wasn't even available in the markets. They had no competition to speak of, so why not sell some to their friends? They also found out that their quality products commanded a far better price as well.

One thing leads to another, and the next thing you know these people are running a small business out of their homes. At a certain point these people write to me or call and ask my advice on starting a sausage kitchen in their area. In other words, they are experiencing growing pains. There are quite a number of things involved before you open a sausage kitchen in your area.

First of all, the most frequently-asked question is, "Do you think I can make a go of it in my area?" It just isn't possible for me to make such a prediction, or even encourage someone to open a business of this nature. The person or persons wanting to open such a business must do some research.

One of the first things to consider is whether anyone else in your area has the same idea as you. When I first opened a sausage kitchen in Las Vegas, we almost lost the business. We took so long in opening, by doing most of the work ourselves, that another sausage kitchen opened and almost put us out of business.

Needless to say, it would have been better if we had opened our business first and established ourselves with the quality products we were producing. You make your competition work even harder when they have to overcome you. In either case, most businesses of this type have to apply to a health department or building department to get various permits or approvals for equipment that will be purchased. It is worth your time to check this out.

If there is another sausage kitchen already in your area, what then? The big question here is can the area support more than one sausage kitchen? What kind of products does the other sausage kitchen produce? Will you produce better products? It is best not to compete; make quality sausages and stick with them. Don't make the same products the other sausage kitchen is making unless you know yours will be superior—not better but superior. That's what it takes to beat someone who has been in business for a while.

If you think the area can support another sausage kitchen, you have to know how much sausage you'll be able to sell each week. This is extremely important! You have to plan on spending some money to advertise so that people know you exist. You can only get a small amount of help from your friends by word-of-mouth. If you can't afford some advertising, it's a lost cause.

Opening a sausage kitchen may be able to get you a free plug on TV. A food editor from the local newspaper may come over, take some pictures and run an article about you.

But again, you have to continue some sort of advertising. Free plugs aren't seen by everyone in your area so don't plan on people running over to your store. They're not going to break the doors down to get to you.

The original question still hasn't been answered. How much sausage can I sell? The best way to approach this is to sit down with a pencil and paper and figure out some of the costs on a monthly basis. You'll have to consider your wages, water, gas, phone, electric, advertising and rent costs. Maybe there are some additional items not mentioned.

You have to come up with some kind of figure; and this will tell you how much sausage you must sell to pay for your obligations. I didn't say how much sausage you can sell, but how much sausage you must sell. Hypothetically, let us say you'll pay yourself $200 a week, or roughly $800 a month. Let's say the rest of the operating costs will be $1000 a month. Your total cost to operate is $1800 a month.

Now let's say it costs you $1.50 a pound for all the meat and ingredients to produce one pound of sausage. The sausage is then sold at $3 per pound. If you sold 100 lbs. a day you would gross $750 a week or about $3000 per month. Needless to say, you'd be

455

making some pretty good money after expenses. Could you sell 50 lbs. a day? This translates into $1500 a month and your wages would only drop to $500 a month since the $300 would be needed to pay the bills.

In either case, it is the latter part we just discussed which is usually the case. Very few businesses are smashing successes from the beginning. It's an exception rather than the rule, but I have seen it happen from time to time.

There is no question that you should have a reserve of money to carry you over 6 months or so. The more money you can spend on advertising, the sooner you'll be successful. The less you spend, the longer it will take.

A husband and wife team can easily produce 100-200 lbs. of sausage in a day with minimum of work and equipment. You should only make sausages of the coarsely ground variety. Emulsified sausages like wieners or bologna immediately drive up the cost of an operation, because you have to purchase a meat chopper. You are better off purchasing emulsified sausages from another sausage kitchen that makes good products, even if you have to have them shipped in from another state. Stick with coarsely ground products and you can get by with a cooler, sausage stuffer, stuffing table, meat scale, freezer, some mixing tubs and a store fixture. These items can be bought, used and approved for use by the health department. This is exactly the way I opened the first sausage kitchen in Las Vegas. We built our own smokehouse and cooler and saved a considerable sum of money.

We mixed our meat by hand and saved several thousand dollars by not purchasing a mechanical mixer. We mixed 25 lbs. of meat at a time and did a good job. The sausages were consistently good. We tried mixing 50 lbs. of meat at one time, but found ourselves working 5 times as hard with poorer results.

However, when we were able to buy our first mechanical mixer, it was like being reborn. We were then able to produce up to 1000 lbs. of sausage a day and more. But again, mixing 100-200 lbs. of meat a day is easily possible without any great strains when you're just getting started.

There isn't much more I can add to this, but I do have a few more words of advice. If you do get started in a sausage kitchen, my advice is to try and visit an existing sausage kitchen. I would even offer to work there free for a week or two. This will be of immense help and will familiarize you with things I can't easily put in print for you. I would even go to another city, if need by, to accomplish this.

Don't go into the wholesale end of selling your products unless you have grown and are equipped to handle it. I personally would never sell sausage wholesale if I opened another sausage kitchen. You wind up doing all the work and the other retailers make all the money. In addition, you'll wind up waiting for your money and getting nothing but complaints that your prices are too high or other such things. I even had a customer spoil some of our sausages by mis-handling them, and then refuse to pay me. Several customers also went bankrupt on us as well.

Stay with the retail end of sausage making; you'll do less work and make more money. If you do less work, then you're really making money. On top of all this, the retail customer pays you on the spot. I would never consider selling sausage on a wholesale basis again.

Another hint is to make a lot of fresh sausage. You grind the meat, mix it, stuff it and sell it. When you sell out what you have, you can quickly make another 25 lbs. or so in minutes. Less work simply reduces the cost of producing a sausage.

HOW I GOT INTO SAUSAGE MAKING

In the past 5 or 6 years, I've had as many people ask me how I ever got into sausage making as I've had ask how I got to write a book. This question has been answered many times, but I know it'll be asked again, so it's a good idea to write a little bit about it.

To begin with, there are many ethnic groups who make sausage as a part of their heritage or traditions around the Easter or Christmas holidays. The Christmas holidays have always been very special in our family—more so than any other holiday. The meat was ordered so that we could purchase it during Christmas and we usually picked it up about 2 days before Christmas. This process was followed because we only owned an ice box, and ice was not delivered during the winter months. Besides, we wanted the meat as fresh as we could get it.

My partner, Henry Kutiej, and I on opening day of The Hickory Shop in the summer of 1966.

458

It was only the well-to-do who could afford an electric refrigerator during the depression days of the 1930's. If we got the meat a bit early, it was usually stored in a cold room that was unheated. In colder years our little ice box was kept outside in the back yard. Since there were seven of us, we usually made 25 lbs. of sausage.

On the day before Christmas Eve, my mother would clean all the casings and peel all the garlic. The meat was cut up by hand, which was my father's job, and I was allowed to chop the garlic very fine with a sharp knife. It seems like I was the only one of 5 children who took any interest in sausage making. When I got to the third or fourth grade, I was already helping to cut the meat. We simply could not afford the price of a little hand-operated grinder until the late 1930's.

The meat was then mixed well and seasoned. It was Christmas time to me as the aromas of garlic, marjoram and black pepper permeated the entire house. The meat was then allowed to season overnight and, early the next morning, it was stuffed into a large-size hog casing. The sausage was then placed in a 55-gallon drum and smoked over a low fire until 1 or 2 p.m. in the afternoon of Christmas Eve. You really knew it was Christmas.

Somewhere in the middle of our house there was the aroma of smoked kielbasa and a freshly-cut Christmas tree. These combined smells were unmistakably Christmas.

This was the beginning of my sausage-making days as a little boy during the depression of the early 1930's. As time went on and my parents got older, I was allowed to mix the meat and stuff it in the casings. Each successive year my parents taught me another step in the art of making sausage, until they could sit back and allow me to make it from beginning to end under their supervision. I learned it all—washing casings, cutting meat, stuffing meat and smoking as well.

As time went on I grew a little older and World War II came upon us. I was only a teenager and went to work in an A&P supermarket. After a short peroid, I started working as a butcher, learning to cut meat, etc. However, I had to give it up for health reasons, but not before I learned to bone meat and distinguish the cuts of meat. This was to become very useful to me over the years—knowing how to tell a good cut of meat from a bad one.

In either case, the years progressed and I managed to escape the Second World War. I was just 17 when it ended, but I got caught up in the Korean War. Following my discharge after four years of service, I moved to Las Vegas, Nevada,. As you might expect, I moved to a city that didn't even have a sausage kitchen. In fact, there were only four supermarkets in the entire area and there just wasn't any need for a sausage kitchen.

At that particular time, the city of Las Vegas simply did not have the ethnic groups one finds in the East or Midwest. When I moved to Las Vegas, I not only gave up kielbasa, but all other Polish foods as well. I began to find out I couldn't find the good charcoal-broiled hot dogs with natural skins. On top of this, there were none of the Italian restaurants or bakeries I grew up with.

Worst of all, they never even heard of a mom-and-pop market, the type where you can phone in your order and have it delivered to your home. This type of market still exists in the Buffalo area to this day. When you unpacked your bags, everything was perfect and you never got any surprises like you do now with supermarkets and prepacked meat—nice on top with unpleasant surprises on the bottom.

However, all was not lost. I was able to have my mother (my father died while I was in the service), air-freight the sausage to me any time I wanted it. It was a little expensive to do, but it was worth it; a dollar a pound for the sausage and a dollar a pound for the air freight. However the $2 per pound went against my frugal upbringing.

I decided one day to call my mother and asked her to mail me the recipe. She not only mailed me the recipe, but, to my big surprise, also sent along the family sausage stuffer. Needless to say, I went out and bought some meat and made a 10-lb. batch of fresh Polish sausage. It was as great as ever and I never lost the touch. I was so pleased with myself that I gave some to my neighbors and personal friends, Steve and Muriel Gresh. In addition, I gave some to my other good neighbors, Wayne and Kay Puckett. They were all so pleased they couldn't wait for more.

It wasn't more than a week or so before we made another batch. As it turned out, Steve and Muriel were happy just being able to have good sausage (Steve is Slavic and their customs are similar to the Polish). But my other good friend, whom I called Puck for short, decided that I had a winner and we should spread it around Las Vegas. He figured it would be a good way to earn some extra money. He was a blackjack dealer at the Sahara Hotel and knew many people who came to Las Vegas from the Midwest and Eastern U.S. He felt sure many of these people would jump at the chance to buy this excellent sausage.

As it turned out, I had to refuse this little venture as I was working for the Atomic Energy Commission. I commuted back and forth to work each day, driving 65 miles each way. I just didn't want a part-time job on the weekend after traveling 130 miles each day. Besides, I never felt that fresh kielbasa would be as saleable as the smoked, and this was to become a big problem. I simply didn't know how to cure sausage.

Even though I helped my parents make sausage most of my life, I simply didn't pay attention to all the ingredients my father used. I knew when he made sausage it always had that nice pink color on the inside. I knew if I was to sell sausage to anyone, it would have to have that pink color in it. My mother didn't have the answer, and I didn't know anyone I could turn it. I tried smoking sausage a number of times, but never could get that nice-looking color to present itself. I simply threw the sausage in the garbage, completely disgusted because it wasn't right. All I knew was the fact that I wanted my sausage to be pink or reddish on the inside in order to be saleable.

I figured that the best thing to do was go to a library and get the information. To my dismay there wasn't a single book in the Las Vegas Library on sausage making or curing meat. Since Las Vegas was such a tiny city at the time, the logical thing to do was go to a big city that had a bigger library system. I went to the county library in Los Angeles and the public library in San Bernardino, California, and, again, there wasn't anything to be found regarding these subjects. Now what?

While in California, I decided to look through a telephone directory. When thumbing through the sausage-making ads, I inadvertently discovered that there were companies supplying all sorts of products for sausage making. Among them were some spice companies. I didn't know it at the time, but that was the best move I ever made, as I picked out the biggest producer of spices, cures and related

461

products.

Needless to say, when I contacted these people, they knew what I wanted instantly. Not only that, they loaded me up with all kinds of literature and samples and sent me on my way back to Las Vegas. They explained to me that it was a cure that I was looking for. A short time later I made a 10-lb. batch of smoked Polish sausage, and, as you can guess, it was a smashing success. The sausage was not only nice and pink on the inside, but the cure allowed the sausage to be smoked to a deeper shade of brown. I was so happy that I went next door to my buddy Puck and showed him the latest accomplishment.

We were both so happy that we immediately made plans to make 100 lbs. of sausage the following weekend. I relented, and decided to make sausage on the weekends.

After the first 100 pounds of sausage were made, Puck took it all to work at the Sahara Hotel and sold it all in one day. He not only came home with all the money, but more orders besides. As time went on, I got a few friends interested at the Nevada Test Site where I worked. In a short time I found myself taking a hundred pounds or more of sausage to work once a week. We were already up to 200 lbs. a week. We didn't know it at the time, but we were already starting to build a clientele. I had so many customers I had to limit them to 5 or 10 lbs. once a month because I just couldn't make enough.

Since we were making sausage at home, our capacity was limited. We could never make over 200 lbs. on one weekend, and even with just that amount I was creating a mess. A home is not the place to be processing 200 lbs. of meat each week, as it gets all over the floor, walls, etc. We went along for a while, and then I took another job. I would now have to travel 130 miles to work each way, or I could live in a dormitory on the job site. I made up my mind quickly, decided my job was a greater priority.

This meant I would have to work every weekend and then rest in the evening on the job site. In fact, I found even more customers, so the business grew even more. We would make our customers wait up to 6-7 weeks for a delivery of sausage. This put them in the mood a little more since they had to wait so long.

Things went along for a while and then I got bored living on the job site. One weekend while I was in town I decided to take the Las Vegas telephone directory to work. I did this because my mother had visited me a couple of years prior and only stayed 2 days. She simply didn't like Las Vegas in that short period of time because she missed her Polish-speaking neighbors. Two days and that was it; I only got to spend 48 hours with her after not seeing her for 6-7 years. When I took her to the airport, I promised her that the next time she visited Las Vegas, the Polish-American Club of Las Vegas would be there to greet her.

I combed through the phone directory and wrote down the names and addresses of people I thought would be Polish. I then arranged to rent a hall on a Saturday night and sent out 400-500 newsletters. It was a very simple letter explaining that I was starting a Polish Club in Las Vegas. On that Saturday more than 200 people showed up. Needless to say, these people wanted a Polish Club.

For the first time in my life I was going to make a public speech, something I never planned. There I was in front of 200 or more people and I thought it would be better to just jump out of the second story window and run away.

However, I was egged on by one of the crowd who kept telling me what a good job I was doing. Alongside this man was a young lady who was also encouraging me. I later learned that this man was Joe Pavlikowski, the city attorney for Las Vegas, and the young lady was his secretary, Elaine Pringle. I didn't realize who these people were because I didn't read the newspapers due to my long absences from home. In either case, my friend Joe Pavlikowski became our first president (he is currently a district court judge).

We all became friends. We soon leased a hall for our meetings, and had a pot-luck dinner to enhance our good times. The members offered some sort of food and I offered all the smoked sausage.

That did it. After our first meeting, Puckett and I were swamped with orders (Puckett was an associate member of our club). In fact, a few meetings later, the membership voted to buy the sausage from us and advertise in our monthly newsletter that there would be free Polish sausage sandwiches. At that point we decided that we would stop or get a commercial building. The mess around my home was just too much and we were getting too many orders.

Finally, Puck located a nice building in Las Vegas and we proceeded to work on it. Instead of making sausage, we were building a sausage kitchen on weekends. We had to do it all—build a smokehouse, coolers, plumbing, electrical work, etc. After almost a year of weekends, Puck got disgusted and wanted out. He had already had enough. He never bargained for this much work, and neither had I, for that matter.

As luck would have it, Henry Kutiej (no relation) of the Polish Club found out about this, negotiated an agreement with Puck and quickly bought him out. This was really a stroke of luck because at that time Henry knew more about building than Puck and I together. He was a roofer by trade and had seen and learned many things by being around new construction. On top of this, he was a very hard worker and even drove me on weekends to get the job finished. Without Henry, the Hickory Shop would never have opened.

The Hickory Shop was well on its way to opening. Being of Polish descent, Henry was already familiar with making sausage, so there wasn't much to teach him. During the first few sausage-making sessions, I taught him about curing and smoking.

After many confrontations with the county health department, we were finally allowed to open the doors of The Hickory Shop. I should point out that our confrontations with the health department were largely due to the fact that the Las Vegas area was growing rapidly. Due to this we never had the same official inspect us twice in a row.

New inspectors were always being hired, and it seemed as if we got a new inspector every time. What got approved by one inspector one time would be disapproved by another inspector the next time around. Miles of red tape were created that had to be cut through. There were no real guidelines that the inspectors had to work with; they just sort of made their own rules as they went along.

On the final day of inspection, a supervisor came in with one of the inspectors to give us an approval to open. Upon entering, the supervisor commented on what a nice job we had done building this sausage kitchen. However, when he got to our walk-in refrigerated cooler, he opened the door and decided that we wouldn't be allowed to open our new sausage kitchen. He wouldn't approve our cooler because the floor was raised and inlaid with square blocks of linoleum. He insisted we should have a metal floor.

We let him finish and then told them both to leave the premises;

464

we would see them both in court. We were just plain sick and tired of the health department's bumbling. We were totally disgusted, because we had invited the health department more than a month earlier and asked them what kind of floor they would want us to install. It was at their request that we installed the linoleum. We had not made an idle threat to sue; we were more than ready to go to court.

Fortunately, the inspector managed to talk us out of suing, and we verbally agreed that when the floor got bad, which was only a few months later, we would replace it. If any of them had had any kind of training at all, they would have been able to tell us not to build a floor and just let the cement floor do the job for us. It would be easier to clean and wouldn't rot.

There were many incidents of this nature on our way to opening our little Hickory Shop. One of the funniest incidents that will stay with me the rest of my life is the stainless-steel sink fiasco. When we first purchased this sink we called the health department in to approve it. They immediately said no. Our sink only had two tubs, and we needed a sink with three tubs. He explained that the first sink is filled with soapy water, the second with rinsing water and the third with water and disinfectant. We persuaded the inspector to return to his superior and tell him that we didn't serve the public and had no dishes to disinfect. The inspector returned and approved the sink, which we promptly installed.

Since we were dragging our feet in building our little shop, wouldn't you know it, a new inspector appeared the next month and told us to remove the sink. He told us he'd reg-tag the entire operation until we got a 3-compartment sink. So help me, my good partner Henry literally took this inspector by the collar and the seat of his pants and bodily threw him out the door.

About 30-40 feet before he reached the street, I started egging Henry on, encouraging him. After the man was thrown out, Hank looked at me, and I looked at him, and we started to laugh. We laughed so hard and so long that we couldn't work any more that day. We were so weak from laughter that we went out and drank about 20 bottles of beer while congratulating ourselves. We were fed up, and just had no intention of putting up with such nonsense. We never saw that inspector again, nor did we ever hear from the

465

health department about this incident. They simply didn't do a thing about it, probably realizing how frustrated we were.

When I think of this incident, I still have to chuckle about it to this day. It was this type of nonsense that led to our confrontation over the cooler when we tried to open our store. We no longer could accept it.

Needless to say, as Las Vegas grew, so did the health department. They became better organized, were allocated more money and printed some guidelines for people to follow. This eliminated a lot of the bumbling and red tape, and they were able to assign a health inspector to each installation for longer periods of time. Over the years we became friends with many of the inspectors as we worked together. I can honestly say, wihout reservation, that the Clark County Health Department in Las Vegas has developed one of the finest sets of standards for building and inspecting that I have ever seen in the U.S. or anywhere. I get back there frequently and am completely at ease when dining out. Many little cities having growing pains would do well to model their health department after this city's.

In either case, we got approval to open our little shop and we were on our way. We ordered about 800 pounds of fresh pork butts and were going to use it all to make Polish sausage. It was at this point that we learned even more about how bitter life can sometimes be. We felt that when our doors opened, the customers would be lined up out there, waiting to buy up all our sausage.

Well, it didn't happen. The only people who showed up were some of our personal friends. We tried contacting people by phone and thought it would get around like wildfire. Probably one of the stupidest things we did was opening the shop while making only one kind of sausage. One customer walked in and said, "What? Is this all you have?" I can hear that ringing in my ears to this day.

Opening our store in this manner was like opening a butcher shop and only selling hamburger. We made much more than we could sell. In fact, we threw out at least 400 pounds of meat.

After the first week we quickly realized by the few people who patronized us that it was our job to sell. When a customer comes into the store you have to present him with a variety or products, products not even related to sausage in many cases. We also knew that we had to spend some money advertising in order to let people know we existed.

I guess we had some luck, because more people started to show up. In fact, many of them gave us their recipes for various sausages and asked us to make some for them. We did this gladly as we got more recipes. On top of this, we made 25-pound orders for these people and they bought it all up and distributed the sausage among their own ethnic groups. Now we were moving along and could even afford a little more money for advertising and some long-over-due helpers.

We poked along and were even able to go out and solicit some restaurant business. We got into problems here, however. Before we even got to open our little shop, another sausage kitchen opened, not a half-mile from our shop. They got into the restaurants and gambling casinos very quickly and managed to corner this business. Fortunately for us the other sausage business was only interested in the wholesale end of the business, which was bigger volume.

Luckily for us we were able to poke along and get the retail business. We couldn't compete with them anyway; they had better equipment and a lot more money behind them. The man who opened this business was John Sommers of Burlingame, California. As a professional sausage maker, he was fully aware that the Las Vegas hotels were using breakfast sausage literally by the ton. These hotels were giving their breakfasts away in those days as an inducement to staying in their hotels. It was not uncommon to buy a complete breakfast for 49¢, 39¢ and 29¢—24 hours a day. Breakfast sausage was literally consumed by the tens of thousands of pounds each week.

At one time, Mr. Sommers was manufacturing 50,000 pounds of breakfast sausage per week. All he made was fresh breakfast or Italian sausages. He simply wasn't set up to sell retail and didn't even want that kind of business. This probably is the biggest reason we were able to get our smoked Polish sausage into some of the restaurants and supermarkets around town.

We started calling on the local bars around town with a creation called a "beer sausage." It was simply our good smoked Polish sausage with a little hot pepper added to the sausage. We were able to purchase some 4-quart steam cookers, which we sold to the bar owners at cost. We always went into a bar with our little cooker and some sausage. We steam-cooked some samples for the owner and the patrons at the bar.

It was like taking candy from a baby. Once they tasted it, we usually left the steam cooker behind and delivered the sausage later. It was such a smashing hit, our production rose to 5,000 lbs. a week. We couldn't have been happier.

However, our happiness was to be short-lived. Our good friend Mr. Sommers, who we never met, decided to sell his sausage business and move on. The new owners decided they wanted all the sausage business in Las Vegas and began competing directly with our little company. They started to cut prices and tried to drive us out, but we had several things in our favor.

First of all, they didn't have the formula for our good "beer sausage." On top of this, there wasn't a real sausage maker in the bunch, as Mr. Sommers only taught them how to make the products he was selling in Las Vegas. Polish sausage was not one of the varieties they could make.

The last consideration was that they were making an inferior product. We lost a number of customers, but held our ground. We knew we had a good product and could weather the storm. After a brief period, almost all our former customers returned. The beer drinkers knew the difference in the sausages and made it known to the bar owners very quickly. They simply learned you can't get a quality product at cut-rate prices.

It wasn't long after this that we got to meet the former owner, John Sommers. This happened because his relationship with the new owners deteriorated. It was probably for this reason that Mr. Sommers arrived on the scene and introduced himself. We were really happy to meet him because we knew he had to be a nice person—he had simply left us alone and stuck to his own business.

After meeting him and talking with him for a while, he just jumped in with us and started making sausage, helping us along. He taught us more in a few hours than we had learned by ourselves in over two years. He would visit us from time to time, put on an apron and work along with us. He kept teaching us as we went along and taught too many things to mention. He made me aware of the many new suppliers, as well as some bigger and better equipment.

As we developed over the years, about three-quarters of our

468

business was now wholesale. We had grown and had become a formidable sausage-making company in our own right. We grew to the point where the State of Nevada inspected us, as well as the county. It was the State of Nevada now who held power over us, because more than 25% of our business was dependent on wholesale customers. They visited us one day with an official from the United States Department of Agriculture. They advised us that a new law was passed called The Wholesale Meat Act. It was further explained to us that we had to start thinking about remodeling our little sausage kitchen or close up shop.

They gave us a year to make up our minds. Since we were only renting the building, Hank and I felt that we had already improved the building enough. We both decided we would buy our own building so that we could do whatever we wanted, whenever we wanted. In fact, we needed a lot more room, as we were really cramped. We picked one out that was at that time just outside the city limits. We told the realtor we would buy it. The realtor told us the owner was from California and that he would notify him so he could come down and close the deal. To our great surprise, the owner was none other than "The Bavarian Sausage Maker," John Sommers. We were all pleased and quickly negotiated a deal. Not only did Mr. Sommers sell us the building—he even helped draw up the plans for remodeling it.

Probably the best part of this whole deal was the fact that he would lease us about $15,000 worth of sausage-making equipment. He really wanted us to compete with the other sausage company. Best of all, Mr. Sommers agreed to work with us for a period of time until we were accomplished sausage makers. We were going to go after the big hotels, where the real money was. How could we fail?

The Hickory Shop was closed down so Henry and I could build our 3000-square foot sausage kitchen. This was going to take about another year of hard work, so I finally left my job with the Atomic Energy Commission. I devoted all my time to building this shop. We worked seven days a week and never rested until it was finished. Before we even had our new building approved, we just had to sneak out one or two thousand pounds of our now very famous beer sausage. Even though we were in the very last stages of completing this building, we just couldn't put off our good customers

469

any longer. Our coolers were already operational, so Hank and I decided to bootleg some sausage on a weekend. Our reasoning was that the health departments were all closed and we could get away with it. We ordered 2000 lbs. of meat for a particular weekend and went to work on a Friday evening, waiting until all the health officials were on their way home. It was agreed that Hank would keep up the construction work since he was better at it, and I would make the sausage. We would make the sausage and get rid of it all that weekend. The bars were open seven days a week, 24 hours a day, and our customers would take delivery at any time of the day or night.

Well, we got started and it really felt great to be making sausage again. Since the building departments were also closed for the weekend, Hank decided to do a little illegal plumbing. He rented a gasoline-powered cement cutter so that he could cut out a certain part of the floor to do some plumbing. I was happily making sausage and Hank was cutting the floor.

I don't remember how long we were working, but I began to feel very weak. A short while later I started getting what I thought was a dizzy spell, and yelled to Hank to come and help me. I got no answer after several calls of help. Somehow I managed to stagger over to where Hank was cutting the cement floor. There he was, sitting on a little box, head resting on the handle. The gasoline-powered cutter was running and Hank had passed out. Instantly I knew we were being poisoned by carbon monoxide. I'll probably never know how I did it or where the strength came from, but I started to drag Hank out of the building. I managed to get to the doors which were opened, and about that time either Hank's wife or son drove up to the building. Whoever it was saw me struggling and helped get Hank out the rest of the way. We both got out and, lucky for us, the fire station was about 100 yards from our building.

Whoever it was quickly brought over the fire department and some oxygen. It just wasn't our time to go, and it became the best-kept secret in Las Vegas. For some reason or other we never spoke of it; the incident ended that night. I guess we both felt a little stupid, even though we had all the doors open to let the carbon monoxide out.

Shortly thereafter, "The Hickory Sausage Company" opened for

470

business. We prepared ourselves a little differently this time; we went out and got some firm orders for sausage before buying any meat at all. We learned our lessons well when opening our first sausage kitchen and, besides, we now had a giant freezer. We could freeze leftover meat or sausage, rather than throw it out.

In either case, we went after the big hotels and casinos as well as the hospitals, schools and other institutions. To our dismay, we soon discovered that all of these people took 90 days to pay a bill. To explain this a little further, we would deliver 100 pounds of saus- age weekly for 12 weeks before we finally got paid for the first week's delivery. The following week we were paid for what was delivered 11 weeks ago. In other words, they would tie up a com- pany's money for 12 weeks as long as they chose to do business with them. Many of the hotels were willing to pay their bills a little ahead of schedule if you gave them a substantial discount. They not only tried to take your money away from you at the gambling tables, but tried to take it away from the local vendors as well.

The real problem that these late payments created was the fact that the large meat packers, like Swift or Morrell, had their own terms that we had to obey rigidly. All meat bills must be paid within seven days from the date of delivery of the meat—or you would not receive your next shipment of meat. In effect, we subsidized these customers if we chose to take on their business. We discussed it a little and decided to go after it. We concluded that we could go slowly and just take no more of this business than we could afford.

Besides, we had a lot of good customers who paid their bills on time as we requested. I do remember a small casino at the time that was just wonderful to us—the Lady Luck Casino in downtown Las Vegas. The other was Caesar's Palace.

In either case, we felt everything would work out for us, but it just wasn't to be. We encountered more problems than we ever did.

First of all, the hotels were only interested in the price of our products and positively not the quality. They could care less about the quality. I was stunned whenever the hospitals gave us the same treatment; I just couldn't believe it. The biggest problem this created for us was the fact that Hank and I never did learn how to make junk sausage.

However, as we were going along, Mr. Sommers even explained

471

that aspect of it to us. Our competition was using pork jowls to make their sausage and we were using pork butts; we just couldn't compete. Our only defense was to be able to get a chef to cook our product alongside the competition's. There was never any competition—we always won. The others just shrank away while ours showed a minimum of shrinkage.

The executive chef really had the last word. If you could get him to complain to the buyer about a certain product, there was some chance of getting in. Unfortunately, the chefs were very hard to get to and you had to get past the purchasing agents or buyers to see him. If you weren't prepared to pay off a purchasing agent or two, it was a waste of time to even talk to some of the people. In fact, we made a survey and actually found out beforehand what purchasing agent or chef had to be paid off. We simply avoided these people and never did call on them.

The other problem we created for ourselves was the simple fact that we overbuilt our new sausage kitchen and had a hard time paying the bills just to keep it open. We didn't bother to save money for advertising as we used it all up to build. We felt the hotel business didn't require advertising.

To further compound our problems, the Meat Cutters' Union in Las Vegas got into our little act. Just before opening our shop, they simply told us that we could sell a lot of sausage in the hotels as *all* the kitchen help, chefs, etc. were unionized. They told us in plain English that we wouldn't be able to sell a pound of sausage to a hotel until we joined their union. They did indicate if we joined their union they would help us get into the hotels as well.

Well, we discussed this a little and decided we even had to compete there, since our competitors were also unionized. Hank and I joined and started paying our dues each month. On top of this, our company had to pay an equal amount each month, and we had to go into our savings to do this. To make matters even worse, we were not allowed to hire part-time help when we started to grow a little. The union said that was taking away a full-time job from one of their members.

In the meantime, Hank and I had to kill ourselves because we only had enough money for part-time help and just couldn't afford the high union wages. It became clearer and clearer now that the

Meat Cutters' Union lied to us. They never did help us get any business as they promised and did nothing to help. They were just there to bleed us of our money, money that we took out of our savings. Needless to say, my feelings for unions today are somewhat less than charitable.

The crushing blow came to us when John Sommers was driving in from California after visiting with his family. On the way in he was involved in a serious traffic accident. We not only lost our master sausage maker, but our star salesman. We were already accomplished sausage makers at this time, but it was through him that we were making inroads into some of the hotels and casinos. We tried to hang on a while, but it was no use; our bills exceeded our profits each week.

We kept going deeper into debt. Hank and I practically cried after all our hard work, but it was very clear. We had to close or sell so we wouldn't lose all our money. We finally agreed to sell, but had to be very careful how we did it. We had thousands and thousands of dollars out there on the books, including some bad-paying hotels. If they found out your company was in trouble, it would be impossible to recoup your money. Taking all these companies to court is not only time-consuming but impractical. We would be spending all our time in court, getting enough money to pay for legal fees.

We needed the money right now, and that's all there was to it. There just had to be a way to do this. The first thing we had to do was stop the incoming shipments of meat. We had to have the confidence of my very good friend, Stuart Wilson, who sold us our meat while representing the Morrell Company in Las Vegas. A salesman of this type easily recognizes the situation when he calls on you each week, especially if you stop buying meat and you haven't placed an order with anyone else. This would get around like wildfire.

Well, we called Stuart in and gave him the bad news; he felt as badly as we did. At this time he was no longer just a salesman; he had been our personal friend for some years. He agreed to help in any way possible. My plans were simple. Hank stayed in the shop, answering the phone and taking care of the few orders that came in. My job was simply to get out there and collect all our money.

My first stop was Sunrise Hospital, and I went directly to their accounting department. I asked to see the head accountant and then told him who I was and presented three months in bills. He proceeded to tell me it was their custom to pay meat bills in 90 days. I simply told him that I wanted all my money right now. I further explained that I didn't want any of their business, either. I made him understand that I wasn't going to leave without my money and he'd better pay me right now.

It worked! I walked out smiling to myself and for the first time in months, I really felt good. I then went on to all the rest of the people who owed us money and came back with every nickel due us.

We were able to sell all the remaining sausage for a pretty decent price to the Rainbow Casino on Water Street in Henderson, Nevada, a small town adjoining Las Vegas. We chose this casino because the owner had always paid his bills promptly. In fact, we patronized his casino and restaurant more than the others because he really was our favorite customer. More than once, when we ate there, he would not allow us to pay the bill. He was a lover of good sausage and treated us like human beings. Even in the end, when he approached us, he didn't try to take advantage of our situation. He just wanted to buy up all the good sausage he could get his hands on; he knew there wouldn't be any more.

We closed "The Hickory Shop," shutting down the machinery one day. It was like burying your best friend. How could we not feel badly? Hank couldn't stand it and I told him not to bother coming back. He immediately returned to his old roofing job. It was all over now; all the bills were paid and we needed to find a buyer for our building. This proved to be easy, as many companies were about to be closed down for failing to comply with the Wholesome Meat Act. Most of them were on extensions, so my first phone call to a chicken-cutting company gave an immediate buyer. It was all over within about a month.

Regarding the equipment, we returned the leased machinery to John Sommers in Burlingame, California. The rest went to Hank; I simply had had enough and had no intention of being in the sausage business any more. I told Hank he could have it all; he took it home and put it in his garage.

We were lucky enough that all we lost was a year and half of hard work and $10,000 between us out of a $50,000 investment. When I got my money I simply laid back in the nice warm sun of

Las Vegas. It was mid-May; I didn't do anything for 3-4 months, as I needed the rest very badly. I'm sure that I worked about 3-4 years without a vacation and felt I was entitled to this good time.

Unfortunately, my good friend Hank would not be so lucky. After a month or two he went out one evening with some of his co-workers. In the process of that evening (and I was told this by his co-workers), Henry managed to bump into an old customer of ours who had bought some sausage from us but never paid the bill. This bill was over $150 and Hank wasn't going to let him get away with it, even though I told him three years before to forget it.

An argument ensued and the former customer left the bar. Hank stayed behind with his friends. A short time later he decided to leave and go home. He left the bar and proceeded to cross the street. At that very moment a giant truck ran him down and killed him instantly. It was our former customer who killed Henry and it was premeditated. He was waiting for Hank.

There were at least five witnesses to this killing, but justice did not prevail. This man was taken to jail and held there until his trial, then was found innocent and released. However, after his release, this murderer was never seen again. Over the years I did manage to run into some of Hank's old friends who were at the bar that evening, and asked whatever happened to that murderer. All I ever got was an insidious smile and I never asked again. I eliminated all these faces and names from my mind. I didn't want to believe it at the time I heard it, but while Henry's murderer was being held in jail, I was told some of his co-workers tried to break into the jail and kill him.

Some months passed and Hank's wife called me. The equipment Hank stored in his garage was now in her way. She said that if I didn't remove it she'd throw it out. I thought it over and decided to take it all. I simply rented a small warehouse for $20 a month and forgot about it. After a year or two and frequent inquiries from certain old bars, I decided to take another fling at sausage making. This time I had firm commitments and already knew how much money I was going to make. I even decided to charge a little more money for the product and make it worth my while.

Since Hank wasn't around now, I had to do it all, including the deliveries. I got to meet a lot of people I had only heard of (Hank had done all the deliveries). Among the first people I met was a Julius Bozinski, who had a mail-order business producing identification cards. I delivered some sausage at his business one day and, of course, introduced myself. We hit it off quite well, and I began showing up at his business even when he didn't want sausage.

I was absolutely fascinated by the mail-order business. He was mail-ordering these I.D. cards to every part of the world, not only the U.S.A. and Canada. The stacks of dollar bills his helpers were counting each day just drew me there like a magnet; I couldn't keep away. I was starting to show up so regularly he became concerned that I might want to duplicate his business and compete with him.

I quickly put him at ease and convinced him I wasn't interested in the identification business. I gave him a number of good reasons for this and he took me at my word and accepted my explanations. He was then relieved and we became good friends.

During this period, I found out that he also migrated to Las Vegas from Buffalo, New York. In fact, after discussing it even further, we found out we were from the same neighborhood and even worked at the same golf course as caddies during our younger years. We didn't remember each other, but we had a lot of mutual friends. At this time, Bo took to me even more and started discussing the ways or things I could do to get into the mail-order business.

After quite a few months of dropping in and out of his establishment, Bo finally said, "Why don't you write a book on sausage making; you know a lot about it." He was right; there it was right under my nose. In fact, I had been saving all kinds of recipes and information over the years. The best part of it all was that I had documented it as we were going along. I just figured it was the only thing to do; in case something ever happened to me, Hank could go on without me.

In either case, we both decided I would put together a little booklet of 30 pages or so and call it "Home Meat Curing and Sausage Making." It became a modest success, but at that time I was as foolish as most professional sausage makers—I simply didn't give enough information in that book. I gave some recipes freely and others, later on, were tied into the mail-order business that soon started. I guess because of all my hard work and frustrations, I also went about dispensing this information backwards.

However, there was a definite need for a really good book on sausage making and meat curing. It would have to be a book with no secrets of any kind, containing detailed explanations.

In my spare time I started to compile the formulas in greater detail. I honestly don't know how many years I was at it. I just kept writing and writing and writing. In fact, it was growing so big I began to doubt if I would ever be able to publish the book. I had hundreds and hundreds of hand-written formulas, which really make a big stack of paper. However, after typing, the original book only came out to be about 167 pages.

From the beginning I never considered getting a publisher for my book; I just never thought about it. Besides, Bo had a printing shop and I could already run some of his printing presses. I don't know how I ever started being a do-it-yourselfer, but I guess that's what I am. In either case, I was doing odd jobs like plumbing and electrical work and the rest of the time was devoted to the mail-order business.

I would continue to write this new book whenever I had time, and even decided that the title of this new book would be "Great Sausage Recipes and Meat Curing."

I was almost finished with my book when some old friends showed up in Las Vegas for a funeral I attended in 1976. Later, we got together and talked over old times as well as the present. I found out my friend was now a junior executive with a company that had some huge contracts in Saudi Arabia as well as all over the world. He offered me a very high-paying job and a 3-year contract. I just couldn't say no. I figured I could finish the rest of the book in Saudi Arabia, as I would have lots and lots of time. Then, after three years, I would have lots and lots of money to publish and advertise the book. After all the negotiating was completed, I was given 90 days to clean up the loose ends.

However, I was doing that anyway, so I decided I would leave for New York, which was acceptable to the company. I had some personal belongings to take to Buffalo and, furthermore, it was 1976. What better time to see the U.S.A. than on its birthday?

I arrived in Buffalo and visited old friends and relatives for about two weeks. I quickly became bored. I decided to continue work on "Great Sausage Recipes and Meat Curing" and, to my amazement, was done in about one week. I then proceeded to find out that I could get my book printed in a matter of days and at a fraction of the price it would have cost me in Las Vegas.

Why? Because Buffalo is the printingest town in the U.S.A. Some of the print shops here are the world's finest. Anytime you can find a company that can print 20,000,000 copies of the Readers' Digest each month, it has to have some really good technology.

I immediately had the printer make me 3,000 copies of "Great Sausage Recipes and Meat Curing," and sold them all in 30 days. Needless to say, I was stunned. I knew there was a great demand for a good sausage-making book, but not this great. One of my first thoughts was "Who needs Saudi Arabia?" especially since I wasn't too far from 50 years of age.

And that's the true story behind "Great Sausage Recipes and Meat Curing."

At one time or another I've had inner struggles about writing this chapter in my book. I didn't know whether it was worth the time or not. However, as I've read it over a number of times, I can now see that there is a lot to learn from my struggles as well as my successes.

Employees filling orders in the shipping and receiving department of The Sausage Maker, Inc.

478

Laying Out A Sausage Kitchen

Laying out a sausage kitchen doesn't seem important, but I can assure you it is. It really doesn't take much to do the job right and it's better to get it done correctly in the first place. If you have an idea of the type of operation you're going to establish, you will have a much better idea of how big a building you'll want to rent or build. There are many buildings that are not suitable for sausage kitchens. When the Hickory Shop first opened in Las Vegas, it was just such a building. I rented it because the rent was low but, worst of all, I didn't realize what a bad location I picked. This particular building was 50-60 feet in length but only about 12 feet in width. If you are going to set up any size kitchen, the building should be at least 20 feet in width and 20-25 feet in length. Even a square building will allow a more efficient operation. The size of the equipment needed to manufacture sausage properly demands a building this size. Otherwise, it's almost a guarantee your operation will be inefficient.

The sketch you see on page 482 will easily allow you to manufacture several thousand pounds of sausage per week. Keep in mind that you'll also be needing another room for an office and possibly a retail area as well. The building will then need additional space for these other operations.

Take special note there is a wall between the kitchen and the smokehouse room. There are some good reasons why this should be incorporated into your plans. From time to time, you'll want to look into the smokehouse during the course of processing. It is better to contain this smoke, with the associated heat, in one room (possibly installing an exhaust fan). Additionally, meat may have to be cooked to make sausage. This would produce heat and steam, which would be better kept away from the actual sausage making operation. It is best to have these heat-producing operations in one room. Whenever possible, the sausage-making room should be kept cool, even air-conditioned if necessary.

As a point of interest, you should store your spices and other ingredients away from the sausage kitchen area. This is clearly a high-humidity area. Spices should be stored in a dry area, then brought into the kitchen when you're ready to start making sausage.

479

When setting up a sausage kitchen, it is best to follow this layout and I'll explain why.

Figure 1

The meat is first brought into the building for storage. We begin by taking the meat out of the cooler for boning.

Figure 2

A sink is required nearby for a number of reasons. From time to time a piece of meat will fall on the floor during boning. If a sink is close by you can get to it quickly and rinse the meat. I have never met a sausage maker in my life who would throw out a piece of meat because it fell on the floor. It is also handy to have a sink nearby to flush casings and wash utensils as well. Additionally, you can wash down the whole kitchen with a mixture of hot and cold water using the sink with a hose.

Figures 3 and 4

A boning table serves two purposes in a small operation. It is a place to bone the meat and pile it up until it's ready to be further cut up. It is also a good place to mount a meat grinder since it is close by.

Figures 5 and 7

The meat mixer is always placed under the meat grinder and the product is then transferred to the sausage stuffer.

Figure 6

After the meat is ground and mixed, the foot pedal sink is handy to have nearby because you'll need to wash your hands after filling the stuffer (you can wash up in the large, two-compartment sink if you want to save money).

Figures 7A and 8

A sausage stuffing table is almost a must in any size operation. It is a great table because they are all made with the edge curled up about 1 inch. This prevents sausage from falling on the floor. You can easily store 25-50 lbs. of sausage on the table if you are a one-man operation. In other words, you can stuff all the sausage first and then do the linking and hanging on smoke sticks.

Figure 9

Obviously, you'd want your smokehouse truck or sausage cage close by when you are linking or hanging sausage.

Figure 10

After the sausage is made, the truck is then pushed into the smokehouse and the smoking is begun. After smoking, the sausage is usually cooled with water over a drain installed between the smokehouse and the cooler.

If it is at all possible, you should incorporate a floor drain in the sausage kitchen so you can hose down the entire area and send it down the drain. This beats mopping by a long way. Of course, the floor drain would also be great in the smokehouse room, not only to cool the sausage but also to wash out the smokehouse from time to time. Last but not least, washing a cooler is much easier if you have a floor drain installed.

One bit of advice: if you are going to install a floor drain, be sure they are large drains and the sewer pipe is 4 inches in diameter. When the Hickory Shop first opened, the plumber installed a 2" pipe. We would have been better off without a floor drain as it was always getting plugged.

Schematic Drawing of a Well-Organized Sausage Kitchen

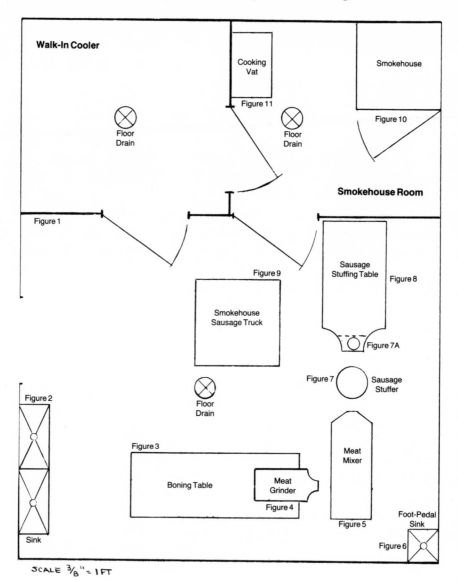

Walk-In Cooler

Cooking Vat

Figure 11

Smokehouse

Figure 10

Floor Drain

Floor Drain

Smokehouse Room

Figure 1

Sausage Stuffing Table

Figure 8

Figure 9

Smokehouse Sausage Truck

Figure 7A

Figure 2

Floor Drain

Figure 7

Sausage Stuffer

Figure 3

Meat Mixer

Boning Table

Meat Grinder

Figure 4

Foot-Pedal Sink

Figure 5

Sink

Figure 6

SCALE 3/8" = 1 FT

EQUIPMENT SUPPLIERS

Anco Chemetron
PO Box 35600
Louisville, KY   40232
(502) 491-4310   Telex 20-4283

Dickey John
PO Box 10
Auburn, IL   62615
(217) 438-3371

Enviro-Pak
15495 S.E. Formor Ct.
Clackamas, OR 97015
(503) 655-6117

Famco
421 N. Braddock Av.
Pittsburgh, Pa   15221
(412) 241-6410
Telex 86-6336   Algage-Pgh

Grant-Letchworth
46 Letchworth St.
Buffalo, NY   14213
(716) 882-3222

International Natural Sausage
    Casing Association (INSCA)
710 N. Rush St.
Chicago, IL   60611
(312) 664-7800

T.W. Kutter
91 Wales Ave., PO Box 7
Avon, MA   02322
(617) 588-2600

Koch Processing Equipment
1411 W. 29th St.
Kansas City, MO   64108
1-800-821-7787

Leland Southwest
PO Box 79400
Ft. Worth, TX   76179
(817) 232-4482

Linker Machines
38 Division St.
Newark, NJ   07102
(201) 481-3700

Chemtron, Mepaco Div.
PO Drawer 7025
Oakland, CA   94601
(415) 532-1655

The Sausage Maker, Inc.
177 Military Rd.
Buffalo, NY   14207
(716) 876-5521

Smith Equipment Co.
PO Box 4056   27 Styertowne Rd.
Clifton, NJ   07012
1-800-631-8300
(201) 473-8500

Zuber Engineering & Sales
800 W. 79th St.
Minneapolis, MN   55420
(612) 884-5311

CHAPTER XVII

100 Lb. Meat Combination Formulas

"And receive whomsoever is sent." Walking through the regal beeches and elm, we can hear the string melodies of the Mountain Folks String Band, and we keep our toes a tappin with cloggers heard in the woods. The enchanted forest bears a garden where the harmony of the Barber Shop Quartet brings a pleasing smile to many a face. Down the path, warming the hearts of all ages, are the Ascensions, who have been delighting audiences with their Gospel Music. Over in the glen, you can linger upon the miniature horses and baby sheep grazing and just waiting to be petted by the young and old. The cool woodland trail takes us upon a nostalgic scene . . . the dulcimer maker works with his hands to make an instrument that in time will carry tunes throughout the woodlands. Down the rustic trail, the footing is rustic too, so bring a stout shoe. Stepping back into history and recapturing the past are the Fiddlers and Banjo players strumming their tunes of days gone by to the delight of all!

The finest in Country Music is being performed by Darryl and Don Gatlin, they'll keep your hands a clappin'. What is this I hear, gee its the Beaver Creek Band playing great sounds of Bluegrass. As the trail crosses over watch for the Mill Creek Ramblers and the primitive old time forest ways and Indian lifestyles as The Clear Fork Valley Rangers captivate the spirit of real Mountainmen. Past the garden I see Emmett Kelly — Golly Be — he had brought all the clowns, full of devilment and excitement.

Sat., Aug. 12	Sun., August 13	Sat., Aug. 19	Sun., Aug. 20
Old Time Fiddle Banjo Contest	Beaver Creek Band	Darryl and Don Gatlin & The Southern Comfort Band	Darryl and Don Gatlin & The Southern Comfort Band
Mountain Folks String Band	Mountain Folks String Band	Mill Creek Ramblers	The Ascensions
Cloggers	Cloggers		

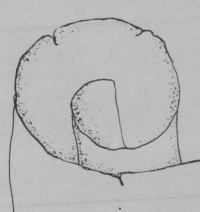

Hear Ye! Hear Ye! Hear Ye!

We make you kindly welcome for the Annual . . . .

Hands to Work, Hearts to God

SHAKER WOODS FESTIVAL

One Mile North of State Routes 7 & 14 on State Route 7 — Columbiana, Ohio

— *2 Special Weekends* —

Saturday and Sunday	Saturday and Sunday
AUGUST 12 & 13	**AUGUST 19 & 20**
10 a.m. to 6 p.m.	10 a.m. to 6 p.m.

1989

In honor of the Shaker memory Shaker Woods Festival . . . . **"Opens the doors and windows,"** gathering artisans from near and far bearing the highest quality, demonstrating and offering their wares with traditional excellence.

'Tis the gift to be simple. Simplicity over the past 200 years brings you elegance of design in hand-wrought stoneware, pottery, porcelain, hand-crafted furniture,

FARMER-STYLE LIVER SAUSAGE
MEAT

Pork livers	35
Pork snouts	35
Beef tripe	30

THURINGER
MEAT

	1	2
Extra lean pork trimmings or skinned fatted shoulders	40	80
Pork cheeks	20	20
Pork hearts	20	
Pork fat	20	
	100	100

CERVELAT SAUSAGE
MEAT

	1	2	3
Lean bull or cow meat	35	80	75
Beef cheeks	20		
Beef hearts	20		
Regular pork trimmings	25		25
Pork fat		20	
	100	100	100

LINGUISA
(LONGANIZA)

100 lbs. frozen certified pork butts

KOSHER STYLE SALAMI
MEAT

	1	2
Cow meats	60	40
Beef plates	40	40
Beef cheeks		20
	100	100

SMOKED POLISH SAUSAGE
(KIELBASA)
MEAT

100 lbs. boneless pork butts

KRAKOWSKI
MEAT

100 boneless fresh hams

BOCKWURST
MEAT

	1	2
Boneless veal	30	50
Lean pork shoulder trimmings	50	
Pork back fat	20	
Regular pork trimmings		50
	100	100

BRATWURST
MEAT

20 lbs. boneless veal
50 lbs. fresh pork shoulders
30 lbs. lean pork trimmings

KNOCKWURST
MEAT

	1	2
Boneless veal	70	
Regular pork trimmings	30	
Bull or cow meat		70
Pork back fat		30
	100	100

COOKED SALAMI
MEAT

	1	2	3	4	5
Very lean bull or cow trimmings	65	40	30	50	50
Very lean pork trimmings					40
Regular pork trimmings	35	20		50	10
Pork cheeks		20	20		
Beef cheeks		20	30		
Pork fat			20		
	100	100	100	100	100

BRAUNSCHWEIGER LIVER SAUSAGE
MEAT

	1	2
Pork livers	55	50
Pork jowls	45	50
	100	100

LIVERWURST
MEAT

35 lbs. pork livers
35 lbs. pork snouts
30 lbs. beef tripe

487

MORTADELLA
MEAT

95 lbs. lean pork
5 lbs. backfat or jowls

CHINESE STYLE SAUSAGE
MEAT

65 lbs. very lean pork
35 lbs. back fat

SMOKED PORK SAUSAGE
(BREAKFAST)
MEAT

	1	2
Regular pork trimmings	40	50
Special lean pork trimmings	60	20
Pork cheeks		30
	100	100

BLOOD & TONGUE SAUSAGE
MEAT

30 lbs. pork tongues
30 lbs. pork snouts
15 lbs. pork skins
15 lbs. beef blood
10 lbs. pork fat

BLOOD SAUSAGE
(KISZKA)
MEAT

50 lbs. pork snouts
20 lbs. pork tongues
10 lbs. pork skins
20 lbs. buckwheat groats or barley

FRESH PORK SAUSAGE
(BREAKFAST)
MEAT

	1	2
Lean pork butts	50	
Lean pork trimmings		50
Regular pork trimmings	50	50
	100	100

FRESH POLISH SAUSAGE
(KIELBASA)
MEAT

100 lbs. boneless pork butts

FRESH ITALIAN SAUSAGE—MILD HOT
MEAT

100 lbs. boneless pork butts

KOSHER STYLE BEEF SAUSAGE—FRESH
MEAT

35 lbs. beef plates
35 lbs. beef flanks
30 lbs. beef navels

LEBERKASE
MEAT

35 lbs. boneless beef, cow or bullmeat
35 lbs. regular pork trimmings
28 lbs. lean shoulder or pork butts
2 lbs. pork liver

HEAD CHEESE
MEAT

50 lbs. cured pork tongues
40 lbs. pork snouts cured
10 lbs. pork skins
Cure tongues for 3 to 5 days in a brine made with:
10 gal. water
10 lbs. salt
3 lbs. cane sugar
1 lb. of cure

CHORIZO
MEAT

100 lbs. boneless pork butts

SOUSE
MEAT

50 lbs. cured pork tongues
40 lbs. pork snouts cured
10 lbs. pork skins
Cure tongues 3 to 5 days in a brine made with:
10 gal. water
10 lbs. salt
3 lbs. cane sugar
1 lb. of cure

OLD FASHION LOAF
MEAT

75 lbs. pork butts
25 lbs. beef plates

CAPICOLA
MEAT

Lean boneless pork butts

PEPPERONI STICKS
MEAT

	1	2	3
Boneless cowmeat	50	40	
Lean pork butts			50
Beef cheeks	20	40	
Regular pork trimmings			10
Beef flanks or plates	30	20	
Boneless beef			40
	100	100	100

HARD SALAMI
MEAT

25 lbs. lean boneless beef
65 lbs. lean pork trimmings
10 lbs. backfat

DRIED FARMERS SAUSAGE
MEAT

80 lbs. lean boneless beef
15 lbs. lean pork trimmings
5 lbs. backfat

GENOA SALAMI
MEAT

85 lbs. very lean pork trimmings
   or boneless beef
15 lbs. backfat

GAME SAUSAGES

SMOKED VENSION POLISH SAUSAGE
MEAT

80 lbs. lean elk or venison
20 lbs. regular pork trimmings

VENISON THURINGER
MEAT

70 lbs. lean elk or venison
30 lbs. fat beef trimmings

SMOKED VENISON BREAKFAST SAUSAGE
MEAT

80 lbs. lean elk or venison
20 lbs. pork or beef fat

VENISON SALAMI
MEAT

80 lbs. lean elk or venison
20 lbs. pork fat (preferably back fat)

SMOKED VENISON SUMMER SAUSAGE
MEAT

80 lbs. lean elk meat or venison
20 lbs. regular pork trimmings

GOTEBORG SUMMER SAUSAGE
MEAT

	1	2	3
Bull or cow trimmings	35	80	75
Beef cheeks trimmed	20		
Beef hearts	20		
Regular pork trimmings	25		25
Pork fat		20	
	100	100	100

METTWURST
MEAT

	1	2	3
Regular pork trimmings	50		20
Boneless veal	50	20	
Bull meat		50	20
Pork back fat		30	
Boneless Boston butts			60
	100	100	100

BRAUNSCHWEIGER
MEAT

	1	2
Pork livers	55	50
Pork jowls	45	
Regular pork trimmings		50
	100	100

PASTRAMI
MEAT

Use a very good grade of beef plates or well trimmed briskets.

493

WIENERS
(FRANKFURTERS)
MEAT

Wieners can be made from many different meats, as well as a combination of meats. In some cases many people want to use the left overs when they butcher their livestock and others wish a quality wiener. It is worthy to note that wieners can be made from these various meats:

	1	2	3	4	5	6
Bull or cow trimmings, lean	60	50	30	60	40	70
Regular pork trimmings	40	50			25	10
Beef cheeks			30			
Skinned pork jowls			30			
Pork cheeks trimmed			10	20	15	
Fat pork trimmings				20		
Fat beef trimmings					20	
Pork fat						20

LARGE, LONG AND RING BOLOGNA
MEAT

	1	2	3	4	5	6	7	8	9
Bull or cow trimmings	60	50	30	60	40	70	55	60	60
Reg. pork trimmings	40	50			25				
Beef cheeks (trimmed)			30						
Pork cheeks (trimmed)			10	20	15				
Fat pork trimmings				20			25		
Fat beef trimmings					20	30			
Lean pork trimmings							20		
Beef hearts								20	
Pork snouts								20	20
Pork hearts			30						20
	100	100	100	100	100	100	100	100	100

GLOSSARY

Ascorbate — A chemical or salt that is derived from the vitamin C family.

Botulism — A deadly form of food poisoning; a deadly toxin that can be created without a sign of foul odor or contamination.

Brine Injection — The injecting of cure into the meat. A rapid form of curing meats.

Brine Soaking — A process for curing meat by submerging in water that usually contains a combination of salt, cure and spices.

Certified Pork — Pork products that have the trichinae already destroyed by the process of freezing.

Cure — This word is commonly used in place of the term sodium nitrite – sodium nitrate. The word "cure" is used throughout this book in many recipes. Cure could also mean potassium nitrite, potassium nitrate, sodium nitrite and sodium nitrate.

Dextrose — A sugar less sweet than cane sugar, a form of glucose.

Erythorbates — A chemical or salt closely related to ascorbates.

Fermentation — A process used in semi-dry and dry-cured sausages to obtain a tangy flavor.

Fermento — A dairy-based, controlled fermentation product in powdered form. It is used much the same as lactic acid starters, but needs no special handling, such as refrigeration or freezing.

Green Weight — A cut of meat in its fresh state, before curing or processing.

Humidity — Used in the process of dry curing or semi-dry curing sausages. Humidity prevents the surface of the meat from drying out too quickly, allowing the moisture to escape from the center.

Hygrometer — An instrument for measuring humidity when making semi-dry or dry-cured sausages.

Lactic Acid Starter Cultures — A form of bacteria added directly to meat to speed the fermenting of the sausages. This is a highly perishable product that must be used quickly after it is thawed.

Liquid Smoke — A liquid that is obtained by condensing the smoke of green hickory wood.

Meat Pump — A large hypodermic needle used to distribute pickle cure more evenly.

Monosodium Glutamate — Commonly known as MSG. Usually made from beets or molasses, it is only used to enhance the flavor of food.

Nitric Oxide — A by-product of sodium nitrite. It is nitric oxide that really cures the meat.

Nitrosamines — A cancer-producing substance. Sodium nitrite – sodium nitrate has been implicated as producing this substance under certain conditions when used in curing certain meats, especially bacon.

Non-Fat Dry Milk — A skim milk used in making lunchmeats and sausage products. Dried skim milk is made by drying sweet skim milk from cows' milk from which the fat has been separated. The skim milk has the ability to help retain moisture in sausages and lunchmeats. This skim milk has no effect on the flavor of the meat until its usage exceeds 12 percent. Federal laws allow 3½ percent usage per 100 pounds of meat.

Overhauling — Changing the position of meat being cured. Usually placing the meat on top to the bottom of the curing box and the bottom meats to the top. This is done at specified intervals.

Phosphate — An ingredient used commercially to increase the water-holding capability of the muscle protein found in meat. Phosphates decrease the amount of cooked juices that will escape from hams, picnics, loins, etc.

Potassium Chloride — A salt with most of the same properties of common table salt (sodium chloride). Usually, it is used in place of sodium chloride.

Prague Powder — A trade name for the word "cure." Can be either sodium nitrite or sodium nitrite in combination with sodium nitrate. Both are on a salt carrier.

Regular Trimmings — Pork trimmings that are 50 percent fat and 50 percent meat.

Salometer — An instrument or hydrometer used to test the degree of saturation of salt brines. The temperature of the water should be 38 degrees F. when taking a reading. Pure water will read 0 degrees and a salt saturated brine will read 100 degrees on the salometer. Many times the term salinometer is used in place of salometer.

Salt — Common ordinary table salt. The chemical name is sodium chloride.

Smearing — A term used to describe a sausage that has an outside appearance of looking very fat but is actually very lean. This condition is caused by letting the temperature of the meat rise by improper refrigeration. It can also be caused by a dull grinding plate and cutting blade which mash the meat rather than cut it. Smearing can also be caused by using equipment that has not been properly cooled before it's used, such as warm grinder heads or a warm stuffer cylinder.

Smokehouse Shrink — The loss of moisture in the product. Usually caused by cooking at too high a temperature in the smoker.

Sodium Acetate — A food-grade chemical used in creating an artificial humidity for semi-dry or dry-cured sausages.

Sodium Nitrate — A colorless crystal that is used to make meat cures, explosives and fertilizers. Nitrate is poisonous.

Sodium Nitrite — A salt or ester of nitric acid. Also a poison.

Soy Protein Concentrate — When mixed directly with meat this product helps to make the meat juicy. It helps to prevent shrinkage and increases the weight of the end product. Generally speaking, it does the same job that non-fat dry milk performs. Its use is also regulated. Federal laws limit its use to 3½ percent per 100 pounds of meat.

Special Trimmings — The commercial term used to purchase pork trimmings that are generally 80 percent meat and 20 percent fat.

Starter Cultures — A product developed in recent years for speeding the process of drying and fermenting dry and semi-dry sausages.

Stitch Pump — A piece of meat is generally pumped along its length using this method. Many times a gang of needles is used to employ this method.

Sugar — The flavoring of meats is generally done with white or brown sugars. Sugar is made from cane or beets. Maple sugar is also used to impart a special flavor and aroma. Dextrose and similar products are less sweet.

Trichinae — Parasites sometimes found in pork and some wild game meat, like bear meat. These parasites in meat are usually destroyed by cooking at the proper temperature or using proper cures when dry-curing meat in combination with salt.

Trichinosis — Infestation of the infective parasite worm trichina sometimes found in the muscle tissue of a swine carcass. This parasite causes no particular inconvenience as far as can be judged from the external appearance of these animals. There is no practical system to inspect the carcass of a swine for trichinae and the destruction of this parasite is left up to cooks, meat processors and anyone else preparing this meat. Fresh pork should be cooked to at least 138 degrees F. to destroy the trichinae parasite. Infestation in a human being may cause severe, excruciating pain, prolonged illness, and even death.

Vinegar — Acetic acid is commonly known as vinegar. Since early times it has been used for preserving and flavoring. Vinegar in conjunction with a salt mixture has a very pronounced effect on microorganisms. Vinegar is gauged by grain. A pickle can be made using a 100 grain vinegar, 3½ percent salt and 3½ percent vinegar (4¼ parts vinegar to 5½ parts water).

INDEX

Air Drying — 333

Ascorbic Acid — 163

Ascorbates — 163

Artery Pumping Meat — 36

Back Ribs, Smoked — 314

Back Slopping — 328

Bacon, Beef, Smoked — 310

Bacon, Canadian-Style — 308

Bacon, Dry-Box Cured — 307

Bacon, Honey-Cured — 301

Bacon, Pea Meal — 309

Bacon, Spray-Injection Cured — 304

Barracuda — 409

Bass-Drum or Channel — 409

Beef, Dried — 320-21

Beef Jerky — 275

Beef Rounds, Peppered — 316

Beef Sausage, Kosher-Style, Fresh — 186

Beef Tongues, Cured, Smoked — 315

Beer Sausage — 208

Berliner Sausage — 215

Bierwurst — 209

Block Sausage, Dry-Cured (Plockwurst) – 389

Blood and Tongue Sausage — 254

Blooming Sausage — 61

Bockwurst — 198

Boiled Ham — 295

Bologna, Lebanon — 346

Bologna, German — 230

Bologna, Ring or Large — 205

Bologna, Trail — 362

Botulism — 18

Boudin — 247

Boudin, Cajun-Style — 249

Bratwurst — 196

Brine Tester (Salometer) — 293

Braun Loaf — 261

Braunschweiger — 220

Braunschweiger Liver Sausage — 225

Breakfast Sausage, Brown and Serve — 172-73

Breakfast Sausage with Cabbage — 185

Breakfast Sausage, English — 184

Breakfast Sausage, Regular, All-Pork — 172

Breakfast Sausage, Smoked — 210

Breakfast Sausage, Tomato — 173

Brine Soaking — 42

Brine Salting Fish — 400

Butts, Pork, Boneless, Smoked — 319

Capicola, Dry-Cured — 376

Capicola, Fully Cooked — 318

Carp, Pickled—434

Carp, Smoked — 422

Casings, Beef — 81-83

Casings, Collagen — 98-101

Casings, Fibrous — 103

Casings, Flushing — 93-96

Casings, Hog — 84-86

Casings, Preflushed — 89

Casings, Salted — 90

Casings, Sheep — 87

Casings, Tough — 90

Cervelat Summer Sausage — 349

Chili Con Carne — 263

Chinese-Style Sausage — 222

Churka (Hungarian Rice-Liver Sausage) — 255

Chorizo, Dry-Cured — 375

Chorizo, Fresh — 180

Chorizo, Loaf, Cooked — 181

Clams, Pickled—436

Containers for Curing Meat — 295

Controls for Smokehouses — 66

Cooked Salami — 224

Cooking Cabinet — 57

Cooking Meat — 245

Corn Syrup Solids — 157

Corned Beef Hash — 260

Corned Beef, Kosher Style — 312

Corning Fish — 399

Country Hams, Dry-Cured — 386

Cultures, Starter — 341

499

Cures — 43

Curing Fresh Meat — 45

Damper — 69

Danish Summer Sausage (Spegepoelse) 361

Dextrose — 157

Diet Sausage — 171

Draft — 65

Dry-Cured Sausage and Meat — 335
    Capicola — 376
    Chorizo — 375
    Country Ham — 386
    Farmers Sausage — 383
    Genoa Salami — 384
    Hard Salami — 381
    Holsteiner Sausage — 391
    Italian Sausage — 393
    Landjager — 372
    Old-Style Summmer Sausage — 388
    Pepperoni — 380
    Plockwurst (Block Sausage) — 389
    Polish Salami — 394
    Polish Sausage — 392
    Proscuitti — 378
    Smithfield Ham — 387
    Sopressata — 374

Dry Salting Fish — 405

Dutchloaf — 273

Eels, Pickled—435

Eels, Smoked — 421

English Bangers — 184

Erythorbates — 163

Farmers Sausage, Dry-Cured — 383

Farmer's Style Liver Sausage — 251

Fermentation — 328

Fermento — 334

Finnan Haddie — 421

Fish Cakes, Fried – 436

Fish Sausage — 229

Fleischwurst, Rheinische (Rhineland Ham Sausage — 236

Frankfurters (Wieners) — 199

Fresh Sausage
    Bangers, English — 184

Bratwurst — 196

Breakfast Sausage — 172

Cabbage Breakfast Sausage — 185

Chorizo — 180

Hot Whole Hog Sausage — 188

Italian, Mild-Hot — 183

Italian, Sicilian with Wine and Cheese — 187

Italian, Sweet — 182

Kielbasa — 174

Onion Sausage — 179

Potato Sausage — 190

Garlic — 153

Genoa Salami, Dry-Cure — 384

German Bologna — 230

Goetborg Summer Sausage — 343

Goose Liver Sausage — 245

Grinding Meat — 145

Halibut, Smoked — 421

Haddock, Pickled—434

Ham, Boiled — 295

Ham, Curing — 290

Ham, Country-Style, Dry-Cured – 386

Ham, Dry Curing — 367

Ham, Italian-Style — 299

Ham, Smithfield, Dry-Cured — 387

Ham, Smoked — 297

Ham, Westfalia, Dry-Cured — 390

Hard Salami, Dry-Cured — 381

Hash — 260

Head Cheese — 264

Herring, Cut, Spiced — 432

Herring, Cream Sauce—434

Herring, Pickled — 430

Herring, Salted — 403

Holsteiner Sausage, Dry-Cured — 391

Honey Loaf — 271

Hot Whole Hog Sausage — 187

Humidity — 330

Hungarian Rice-Liver Sausage (Churka) — 255

Hungarian Paprika Sausage, Smoked—242

Hygrometer — 329

Internal Temperature in Sausage Making — 59
500

International Natural Sausage Casings Association (INSCA) — 80
Italian Sausage, Dry-Cured — 393
Italian Sausage, Mild-Hot — 183
Italian Sausage, Sweet — 182
Italian Sausage, Sicilian-Style — 187
Italian-Style Ham — 299
Jagdwurst (German Hunters Sausage) — 238
Jerky, Venison or Beef — 275
Kielbasa
    Baltycka — 353
    Fresh — 174
    Krabonsky, Semi-Dry — 355
    Krakowska, Semi-Dry — 354
    Kujawska Pudsuszana — 352
    Myslieska — 351
    Podhalanska — 357
    Serdelowia (Serdelki) — 233
    Smoked — 207
    Surowa Wedzowa — 392
    Ukrainska — 356
Kiszka, Polish Watrobiana (Liver) — 250
Kiszka with Buckwheat Groats — 253
Knockwurst — 199
Kosher-Style Beef Sausage — 186
Kosher-Style Corned Beef — 312
Kosher-Style Salami — 216
Krakow Polish Sausage, Semi-Dry — 354
Krakowska — 218
Landjager — 372
Linguisa (Longaniza) — 211
Liquid Smoke — 62
Liver and Onion Sausage — 231
Liverwurst — 256
Low Cholesterol Sausage — 245
Liver Sausage, Goose — 245
Liver Sausage, Farmer-Style — 251
Lox — 437
Mackerel Smoked — 422
Meat, Frozen — 149
Mettwurst — 227
M.I.D. Regulations (Meat Inspection Division of U.S.D.A.) — 369
Monosodium Glutamate (MSG) — 165

Mortadella — 213
Mullet — 410
Nitrite Use — 24
Nitric Oxide — 32
Non-Fat Dry Milk — 158
Old-Fashioned Loaf — 269
Onions, Dehydrated — 154
Onion Sausage — 177
Opening a Sausage Kitchen — 453
Oysters, Pickled—436
Pastrami — 311
Pea Meal Bacon — 309
Pennsylvania Scrapple — 266
Peppered Beef Rounds — 316
Pepperoni, Cooked, Semi-Dry Cured—365
Pepperoni, Dry-Cured — 380
Permissible Ingredients — 163
Phosphates, Use in Curing — 167
Pickle and Pimento Loaf — 270
Pickled Fish — 430
Picnics, Smoked — 298
Plockwurst (Block Sausage) — 389
Polish Blood Sausage with Buckwheat Groats — 253
Polish Ham Sausage (Kielbasa Szynkowa) — 232
Polish Hard Salami — 394
Polish Lemon Sausage — 234
Polish Mountain Sausage (Kielbasa Podhalanska) — 357
Polish Sausage, Fresh — 174
Polish Sausage, Smoked — 207
Polish Sausage, Smoked, Dry-Cured—392
Polish Sausage, Smoked in Vinegar Pickle — 267
Pork Butts, Boning — 116-18
Pork Butts, Smoked, Cured — 319
Pork Hocks or Pigs Feet, Vinegar-Pickled — 268
Pork Shoulders, Cured, Smoked — 299
Potato Sausage, Swedish — 190
Potassium Chloride — 166
Potassium Nitrate — 34
Poultry, Smoked and Cured — 323-26
Prague Powder #1 — 43

Prague Powder #2 — 43

Protein-Coated Casings — 103

Proscuitti — 378

Refrigeration — 119

Relative Humidity — 330

Reusing Brines — 45

Rice Liver Pudding — 252

Rice Liver Sausage (Hungarian Churka) — 255

Rheinische Fleischwurst (Rhineland Ham Sausage — 236

Rocking — 416

Roe, Fish — 414

Russian Sardines — 433

Salami, Cooked — 224

Salami, Genoa — 384

Salami, Hard — 381

Salami, Kosher-Style — 216

Salami, Polish, Dry-Cured — 394

Salami, Venison — 287

Salmon, Cold-Smoked — 426

Salmon, Hard-Smoked — 422

Salmon, Kippered — 423

Salmon, Pickled—435

Salometer (Brine Tester) — 293

Salt (Sodium Chloride) — 155

Salting Fish — 400, 405

Saltpeter — 34

Salt Pork — 317

Sanitation — 120

Sawdust — 54

Schinkenspeck (Ham Bacon) — 305

Shark — 412

Shoulders, Smoked Pork — 298

Showering Meat — 61

Shrimp, Dried — 416

Slim Jims — 345

Slownina Papkrykowa (Salt Pork, Polish-Style with Paprika — 317

Smithfield Ham — 387

Smoke Generators — 51

Smokehouses — 64

Smokehouse Controls — 66

Smoked Meat — 47

Smokers, Barrel-Type — 76

Smoking Procedures — 55

Sodium Acetate — 331

Sodium Chloride — 155

Sodium Erthorbate — 163

Sodium Nitrate — 43

Sodium Nitrite — 43

Sodium-Nitrite-Sodium Nitrate — 43

Sodium Phosphate — 167

Souse — 265

Sopressata — 374

Soy Protein Concentrate — 158

Spegepoelse (Danish Summer Sausage) —361

Spices — 153

Spices, Premixed — 160

Spray-Injected Bacon — 304

Spray Pump or Stitch Pump — 38

Stuffers, Sausage — 138-142

Stuffing Sausage — 122

Sulzwurst Einfach — 237

Summer Sausage

    Cervelat — 349

    Danish (Spegpoelse) — 361

    Goetborg — 343

    Lebanon Bologna — 346

    Sheboygan – 358

    Spanish Cervelat (Salchion) — 360

    Thuringer — 347

    Ukrainian — 356

    Venison — 285

Summer Sausage, Dry-Cured, Old-Style — 388

Sweeteners — 157

Teewurst — 239

Thuringer — 347

Tomato Sausage — 173

Tough Casings — 90

Trail Bologna — 362

Trichinae — 369-71

Turkey

    Loaf, Jellied — 259

    Roll — 244

    Sausage — 243

    Smoked — 325

    Wieners — 203

502

Ukrainska Kielbasa — 356
Veal Loaf — 270
Vienna Sausage — 204
Venison
    Breakfast Sausage, Smoked — 284
    Country Sausage Smokies — 283
    Jerky — 275
    Polish Sausage — 280

Salami, Smoked — 287
Summer Sausage — 285
Thuringer — 281
Water — 166
Weisswurst — 241
Wieners (Frankfurters) — 201
Wieners, Turkey or Chicken — 203
Westphalia Ham Sausage — 390

NOTES

NOTES

NOTES

NOTES

NOTES